The Microsoft®

VISUAL BASIC™ for MS-DOS® WORKSHOP

The Microsoft®

VISUAL BASIC™ for MS-DOS® WORKSHOP

John Clark Craig

PUBLISHED BY
Microsoft Press
A Division of Microsoft Corporation
One Microsoft Way
Redmond, Washington 98052-6399

Library of Congress Cataloging-in-Publication Data
Craig, John Clark.
The microsoft visual Basic for MS-DOS workshop / John Clark Craig.
p. cm.
Includes index.
ISBN 1-55615-504-2
1. BASIC (Computer program language) 2. Microsoft Visual BASIC.
3. MS-DOS (Computer file) I. Title.
QA76.73.B3C715 1992
005.26'2--dc20 92-24010
CIP

Printed and bound in the United States of America.

1 2 3 4 5 6 7 8 9 MLML 7 6 5 4 3 2

Distributed to the book trade in Canada by Macmillan of Canada, a division of Canada Publishing Corporation.

Distributed to the book trade outside the United States and Canada by Penguin Books Ltd.

Penguin Books Ltd., Harmondsworth, Middlesex, England
Penguin Books Australia Ltd., Ringwood, Victoria, Australia
Penguin Books N.Z. Ltd., 182-190 Wairau Road, Auckland 10, New Zealand

British Cataloging-in-Publication Data available.

Acquisitions Editor: Michael Halvorson
Project Editor: Casey D. Doyle
Technical Editor: Jim Fuchs

CONTENTS

Part III: Advanced Programming Concepts

ACKNOWLEDGMENTS

This book has been a joy to create, thanks to the help of many fine people at Microsoft Press. Casey Doyle and Jim Fuchs provided excellent editing and technical guidance. Michael Halvorson's expert suggestions and guidance also added much to the book. Many others also contributed, behind the scenes, and I appreciate their efforts.

I also want to thank Microsoft for once again empowering us with another great programming language. I hope you enjoy working with Visual Basic for MS-DOS as much as I have.

INTRODUCTION

As you'll soon discover, Visual Basic for MS-DOS is an exciting computer programming language. This book provides information and ideas that quickly enable you to begin working with this revolutionary new way of creating MS-DOS–based applications.

I hope you have as much fun working with Visual Basic for MS-DOS as I have had. You'll find that the built-in menu and window capabilities as well as the event-driven programming technology make this one of the most advanced high-level languages for the MS-DOS environment.

With other languages, a programmer might need months to get up to speed creating menus, windows, and other state-of-the-art user-interface features for MS-DOS–based applications. With Visual Basic for MS-DOS, however, you can develop applications for MS-DOS that use these features after only a few hours of familiarizing yourself with the language. You'll be excited to see your first attempts at creating advanced applications come to life more easily and quickly than you thought possible!

This book takes a "learn by example" approach, inviting you to review and modify useful, real-world programs to build your programming skills with Visual Basic for MS-DOS as you step through the examples. The text explains various concepts, techniques, and tricks as it develops and demonstrates the example programs. Visual Basic for MS-DOS is a highly interactive, hands-on programming language, which makes learning by example both enjoyable and productive.

The selection of program examples covers subject areas that should be of interest to a wide range of users. Some of the example programs demonstrate the features and capabilities of Visual Basic for MS-DOS, and others provide useful utilities and applications that make your computer time more productive. You might enjoy expanding the capabilities of some of the programs as you gain experience with Visual Basic for MS-DOS.

Another goal of this book is to provide a source of useful and timesaving forms for you to use in your own applications. (In Visual Basic for MS-DOS terminology, a *form* is a window and its associated controls and code.) For example, the GETFILE form presented in Chapter 5 lets the user select a file from any directory on any drive connected to the user's computer. This form closely mimics the Open dialog box found in many of today's advanced applications (including the Open Project dialog box for the Visual Basic for MS-DOS development environment itself).

A companion disk is included with the book for your convenience. The disk contains all the forms and source code discussed in Chapters 4–17. (See "Using the Companion Disk" at the end of this Introduction.)

Part I gets you started with Visual Basic for MS-DOS. Chapter 1 presents a short history of the Basic programming language to demonstrate how Visual Basic for MS-DOS represents an evolutionary leap for Basic in the MS-DOS environment. Chapter 2 lists some important features and advantages of the Visual Basic for MS-DOS Standard Edition and the Visual Basic for MS-DOS Professional Edition, explaining why these products are essential tools for MS-DOS–based software development. Chapter 3 presents a comparison of a simple program written in three Basic languages: The first example is written in GW-BASIC, the second example is written in QuickBasic, and the third example is written in Visual Basic for MS-DOS. Chapter 4 walks through the steps required to create your first complete Visual Basic for MS-DOS application.

Part II offers a wide variety of Visual Basic for MS-DOS forms and applications, so feel free to skip directly to the subjects that interest you most. Chapter 5 presents some useful forms that perform common programming tasks. Many of these forms appear again in other applications that you'll see in later chapters. Chapters 6 and 7 provide programs designed to help you learn more about the inner workings of Visual Basic for MS-DOS. For example, one program displays all the standard mouse pointers; another program displays messages that describe each of the various mouse events generated by moving the mouse and clicking mouse buttons. Chapters 8 through 11 present a variety of Visual Basic for MS-DOS applications: calendar functions, random-number generators, sorting routines, screen savers, and graphics examples, to name only a few.

In Part III, you learn about some advanced programming features of Visual Basic for MS-DOS. Chapter 12 presents several useful techniques for managing large programming projects. The chapter includes a working example of using Quick Libraries to incrementally build a programming project, followed by a discussion of the use of huge dynamic arrays and overlays. Chapter 13 presents a useful application that demonstrates an MDI (Multiple Document Interface) form for editing a file of "notecards." Chapter 14 covers working examples of calling BIOS and MS-DOS interrupts, allowing you access to a wealth of technical information directly from the operating system. Chapter 15 presents sample functions written in macro assembler and

C that are called from a Visual Basic for MS-DOS application to show you working examples of mixed-language programming.

Part IV covers the Visual Basic for MS-DOS Professional Edition. If you have the Professional Edition or are thinking about purchasing it, this section will be of particular interest to you. Chapter 16 provides a working example of a custom control, a handy way to extend the Visual Basic for MS-DOS language. Chapter 17 explores professional toolkits included with the Professional Edition: Indexed Sequential Access Method (ISAM), Presentation Graphics, and Matrix Math.

Much of this book is patterned after my previous book, *The Microsoft Visual Basic Workshop*, which covers Visual Basic for Windows. Where possible, I have updated and improved the applications and have added many of the features unique to Visual Basic for MS-DOS. During the conversion of applications from the first book, I was struck by the fact that Visual Basic provides a programming language common to developing applications in both MS-DOS and Microsoft Windows, two very different environments.

Using the Companion Disk

Bound into the back of this book is a companion disk that contains all the Visual Basic for MS-DOS programming projects and applications described throughout the chapters. Whether you're a newcomer to Visual Basic for MS-DOS programming or an experienced developer, these programming projects and applications will help you make the most of this exciting language. For specific information about how these programs are created, executed, and reused in the programming projects, see the relevant sections of the book.

Installing the Disk Files

To install *The Microsoft Visual Basic for MS-DOS Workshop* companion disk files on your system:

1. Insert the companion disk in drive A.
2. Type *a:\install* at the MS-DOS prompt.
3. Follow the installation instructions on the screen. In a few minutes, the contents of the companion disk will be expanded and copied to the \VBDWSHOP directory on drive C.

(continued)

continued

Exploring the Disk

The following items are included on the companion disk:

- All the program code files, forms, message files, and make files described in the book. In all, the disk contains 54 sample programming projects, exploring topics such as password protection, file-access dialog boxes, and custom controls.
- Ready-to-run executable files for each programming project. Simply run the EXE files directly, as you would any MS-DOS executable program, to try them out.
- VBDRT10E.EXE, the Visual Basic for MS-DOS runtime module. This file allows a user to run the executable versions of the Visual Basic for MS-DOS applications without having the Visual Basic for MS-DOS product.

The Microsoft Visual Basic for MS-DOS Workshop book-disk package has been designed to encourage fun and experimentation. As you read through the chapters, you'll learn how the special effects—which you can observe by running the disk's executable files—were achieved. Soon you'll be creating innovative programs of your own!

PART I

GETTING STARTED WITH VISUAL BASIC FOR MS-DOS

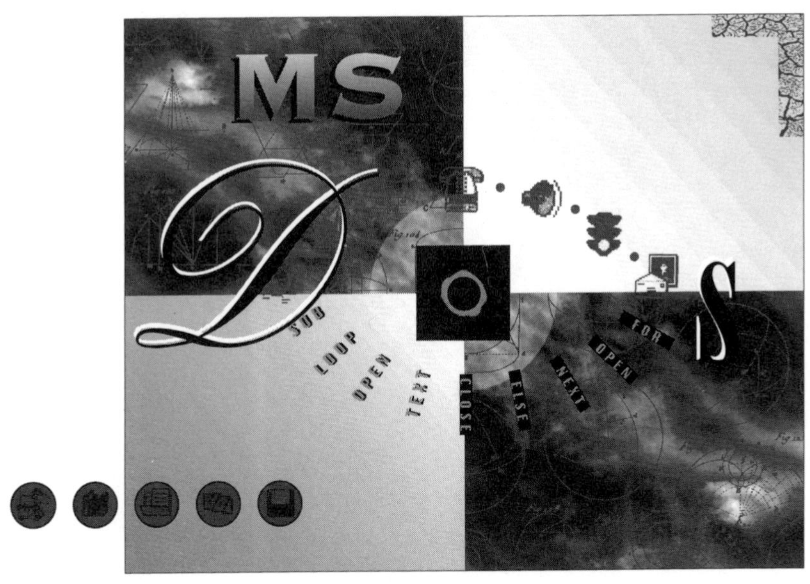

CHAPTER ONE

A SHORT HISTORY OF BASIC

The Basic programming language was created in 1963 by John Kemeny and Thomas Kurtz at Dartmouth College. They designed Basic to teach programming concepts, emphasizing program clarity at the expense of speed and efficiency. They accomplished this by doing away with the job control language and the compile/link steps required for creating programs in other programming languages such as FORTRAN and assembly language. (Actually, the Basic system itself was a complete, compiled program, designed simply to interpret lines of text input. The system read, decoded, and executed one line of program code at a time. This is why Basic was considered an "interpreted" language.) As a result, Basic was the first easy-to-use language that allowed the user to concentrate on methods and algorithms for solving programming tasks rather than on the methods and algorithms the computer hardware required simply to build and debug programs.

Several characteristics of the earliest versions of Basic are notable. Each line of a program began with a line number, and statements were generally not indented (as is often done today to enhance readability and to clarify structure). All characters were entered and displayed in uppercase letters. All *GOTO* and *GOSUB* statements, which transfer program control to another part of the program, used line numbers as their destinations.

These characteristics tended to encourage the creation of hard-to-follow "spaghetti code"—so called because the logical flow of the program often wound and branched around, as do strands of limp spaghetti on a plate. Figure 1-1 on the following page shows a typical example of spaghetti code. Even in this short program, you can easily get lost trying to follow the code. Fortunately, Basic has come a long way since those days.

Early Basic gained the reputation of being a toy language that was not suitable for real-world programming tasks. Over the years, however, Basic evolved from a slow, unstructured, interpreted language into a fast, structured, compiled language suitable for creating a wide variety of applications. Hewlett-Packard, Microsoft, and several other companies have created enhanced versions of Basic with highly advanced features. If you haven't used Basic for a while, it's time for you to take another look at the language.

```
10 REM - PRIME NUMBERS LESS THAN 500
20 N=N+1
30 IF N=500 THEN GOTO 120
40 I=1
50 I=I+1
60 J=N/I
70 IF INT(J)=J THEN GOTO 20
80 IF I>=SQR(N) THEN GOTO 100
90 GOTO 50
100 PRINT N,
110 GOTO 20
120 END
```

Figure 1-1.
An early Basic program that typifies spaghetti code.

Basic Marches On

The progress of Basic has closely followed the personal computer revolution. In the mid-1970s, Microsoft got its start with the introduction of interpreted, ROM-based Basic for the early personal computers. The Radio Shack TRS-80, for example, introduced Basic (and the concept of personal computing) to many of us. This original version of Microsoft Basic is still with us today, without too many modifications, in the form of GW-BASIC, the interpreted Basic that shipped with versions 4.01 and earlier of MS-DOS.

Although GW-BASIC is a great tool for whipping up quick calculations and performing simple tasks, it does pretty much fit the description of a toy language. No serious software developer today would consider marketing software written in GW-BASIC, for the same reasons that MS-DOS–based utilities are not written and marketed in the form of batch files. In both cases the programs are too slow, the source code must be provided to the user, and much better ways now exist to create such programs.

In 1982, Microsoft QuickBasic revolutionized Basic and legitimized it as a serious development language for the MS-DOS environment. QuickBasic effectively combined the interactive, productive nature of GW-BASIC with the power and speed of a compiled language. Line numbers became unnecessary, and modern language features (such as subprograms and user-defined structured data types) were added. Graphics and sound capabilities provided QuickBasic programmers with power beyond that commonly available with C, Pascal, and FORTRAN. QuickBasic programs had another advantage: They could run interactively, in interpreted mode, or be compiled into stand-alone, executable programs suitable for the marketplace.

Visual Basic for Windows

Today the Windows revolution is well under way, providing a powerful and standardized environment to match the capabilities of the newest microprocessors. Visual Basic for Windows, the next great advance for the Basic language, was introduced in 1991 and has already earned the reputation of being the best high-productivity programming environment currently available for Windows. Learning how to create full-featured Windows-based applications has become quick and easy, at last making programming for Windows interactive, productive, and fun!

Visual Basic for MS-DOS

Visual Basic has now come full circle back to the MS-DOS world. The advantages are numerous. Menus and other advanced user-interface features are now part of the language, rather than awkward and bulky add-ons. Visual Basic for MS-DOS provides a powerful and natural way to create highly structured programs using modern, event-driven code. And, for the first time, programs can be easily developed to run in both the MS-DOS and Windows environments. Visual Basic for MS-DOS is even completely compatible with previous versions of QuickBasic, QBasic, and GW-BASIC. It's an extremely versatile and powerful development language.

The Basic language has undergone many changes over the last three decades, and Visual Basic for MS-DOS continues this trend. You'll soon be seeing on store shelves a host of full-featured applications developed using this language. In the next chapter, we'll look at some of the unique features of Visual Basic for MS-DOS, and you'll begin to see what all the excitement is about.

CHAPTER TWO

FEATURES AND ADVANTAGES OF VISUAL BASIC FOR MS-DOS

Visual Basic has several features that make it an ideal development language for both MS-DOS and Microsoft Windows. These features not only increase productivity, they also provide all the tools and hooks you need to develop some very sophisticated applications. This chapter highlights several of these features.

Visual Basic for MS-DOS retains most of the advanced features of QuickBasic and has many new enhancements to make it compatible with Visual Basic for Windows. For example, you can load and run previously developed QuickBasic programs with virtually no modifications. And with only minor restrictions, you can easily port programs and forms developed using Visual Basic for Windows to the Visual Basic for MS-DOS environment. You can easily develop new applications to run in both environments, greatly increasing your productivity and the marketability of your software.

One of the great advantages of Visual Basic for MS-DOS is the short time required for you to become a productive programmer. If you're already familiar with QuickBasic or with Visual Basic for Windows, you'll quickly feel right at home with Visual Basic for MS-DOS. In contrast, if you look at the amount of information you would have to digest and comprehend while learning to create MS-DOS–based applications and Windows-based applications in other programming languages such as C, you'll greatly appreciate the interactive and intuitive nature of both versions of Visual Basic. Learning to program in Visual Basic is by far the quickest way to get up to speed developing full-featured applications for MS-DOS and Windows.

Even if you're a seasoned programmer, you'll appreciate the interactive interface-development cycle that Visual Basic for MS-DOS provides. The Basic language has usually been superior to other programming languages in allowing users to interactively try out programming ideas. For example, it was often faster and easier to run a line or two of GW-BASIC code to see how a statement worked than it was to look up the statement in the documentation. This interactive development concept now applies to creating a sophisticated user interface for your application using Visual Basic for MS-DOS. Nothing compares to being able to get quick visual feedback as the interface design progresses. Unless you have the uncommon ability to hold in your mind all the details of an application's user-interface design, you'll find the interactive nature of Visual Basic for MS-DOS to be a real time-saver!

Extendibility of Visual Basic for MS-DOS

Visual Basic for MS-DOS applications run quickly, although optimized C and macro assembler functions can run faster. You can capitalize on the exceptional speed that C and macro assembler functions offer while programming with Visual Basic for MS-DOS by making use of Visual Basic's extendibility. In Part III, you'll find examples of Visual Basic for MS-DOS applications that call C and macro assembler functions. You'll also find applications that enhance and extend the Visual Basic for MS-DOS language even further with BIOS and MS-DOS interrupt calls and Quick Libraries. In addition, if you have the Visual Basic for MS-DOS Professional Edition, Part IV will show you how to extend the Visual Basic for MS-DOS language with custom controls and professional toolkits.

The Future

The Visual Basic for MS-DOS applications you develop today will be around for a long time. Even if the MS-DOS environment were to be completely replaced by Windows, you could easily port the applications you develop using Visual Basic for MS-DOS to Visual Basic for Windows. Most experts, however, believe that MS-DOS will still be with us for many more years. In any event, you can't go wrong using Visual Basic for MS-DOS as your primary application development tool!

CHAPTER THREE

EVENT-DRIVEN PROGRAMMING

Visual Basic for MS-DOS programs are *event driven*, a concept that's at the heart of today's modern programming languages. After you do this type of programming, you'll never want to go back to the old ways. You'll discover a whole new level of creative, effective techniques for developing your applications.

Fortunately, the conceptual difference between event-driven code and procedural code isn't as drastic a leap as you might initially think. Much of the code you write for Visual Basic for MS-DOS programs will be very familiar to you. To demonstrate, I've prepared three versions of a short program to show the progression from GW-BASIC code to QuickBasic code and finally to Visual Basic for MS-DOS code. You'll see that the Visual Basic for MS-DOS example requires very little additional explanation yet provides a good example of an event-driven routine.

All three programs display *Testing...1 2 3* at the top of the display (or at the top of a window in the Visual Basic for MS-DOS version). Let's take a look at the GW-BASIC version first, good old line numbers and all:

```
10 REM - GW-BASIC Test Program
20 CLS
30 PRINT "Testing...";
40 FOR I = 1 TO 3
50 PRINT I;
60 NEXT I
70 PRINT
80 END
```

The QuickBasic program, on the following page, displays exactly the same output. The program demonstrates some of the improvements of QuickBasic over interpreted Basic, such as not needing line numbers.

```
'QuickBasic Test Program
CLS
PRINT "Testing...";
FOR i = 1 TO 3
     PRINT i;
NEXT i
PRINT
END
```

And now, here's what you've been waiting for...your first look at an event-driven application, written entirely in Visual Basic for MS-DOS:

```
'Visual Basic for MS-DOS Test Program
SUB Form_Click ()
     PRINT "Testing...";
     FOR i = 1 TO 3
          PRINT i;
     NEXT i
     PRINT
END SUB
```

Notice how much of the Visual Basic for MS-DOS code looks the same as the QuickBasic code; the syntax remains basically unchanged. The major difference between this version of the program and its predecessors is that the code in the Visual Basic for MS-DOS version has been placed in an event-driven subprogram called *Form_Click.*

Why not put the code in the main part of the program? The answer to this question is very important, striking at the heart of the Visual Basic for MS-DOS programming philosophy. Yes, you can put the code in the main module, if you want to be compatible with previous versions of QuickBasic. However, to use the new forms, event-driven coding, and other advanced features of the language, as well as for compatibility with Visual Basic for Windows, you should place all the executable code of a Visual Basic for MS-DOS program in either a subprogram or a function; no executable statements should exist at the module level. These subprograms and functions are activated by events (such as a mouse click, a command-button activation, or an entry in a text box) or by calls from other routines (which can be traced back to some routine that was event activated).

Compatibility with QuickBasic and Visual Basic for Windows

It's useful to think of Visual Basic for MS-DOS as having two unique modes: QuickBasic compatibility mode and Visual Basic for Windows compatibility mode. This distinction is necessary because of subtle conflicts that arise between "old style" user interaction (as in QuickBasic) and "new style" user interaction (as in Visual Basic for Windows). For example, the *PRINT statement* sends characters to the screen (as in QuickBasic), but the *PRINT method* sends output to a specific form or to a specific control on a form (as in Visual Basic for Windows). Visual Basic for MS-DOS determines whether the *PRINT* keyword is a statement or a method, based on the keyword's context. In a form, the *PRINT* keyword is always interpreted as a method. In a source-code module (and only if no forms are showing), the *PRINT* keyword is considered a statement. The same context-sensitive interpretation occurs with the *CLS* keyword. As a method, *CLS* clears only the form when the keyword is located in form code or in a BAS module when forms are showing. As a statement, *CLS* clears the entire screen when the keyword is located in a BAS module and no forms are showing.

Some other statements have no method counterpart, but their behavior can be at odds with the way forms work. Most of the graphics commands fall into this category. For example, the *SCREEN* statement results in the error notification "Invalid when forms are showing" if you use the statement in a program when forms are displayed. You can use the *SCREEN* statement after using the *SCREEN.HIDE* method, which temporarily removes all forms from the display. In general, graphics commands can be located in either FRM or BAS modules, but they can be called only when no forms are showing.

These context-sensitive rules for using some I/O-related keywords are necessary for Visual Basic for MS-DOS to be compatible with both QuickBasic and Visual Basic for Windows.

Names of Subprograms

Visual Basic for MS-DOS names event-driven subprograms for you. In our simple test program, *Form_Click* indicates that this subprogram runs when the user clicks the mouse in the form's window. It's all really quite simple: When you run the program, a blank window appears; click the mouse anywhere in the window, and *Testing...1 2 3* appears in the window.

In this example, the Click event activates a subprogram that displays the text. We could just as easily place the code in a *Form_DblClick* subprogram, in which case *Testing...1 2 3* would appear only after the user double-clicked the mouse anywhere in the form's window. Or we could place the code in a *Form_Paint* subprogram so that the message would appear immediately when the program ran.

By now you've probably guessed that you can use many other events to activate subprograms in Visual Basic for MS-DOS. As you'll see in the sample programs throughout the book, this event-driven design is extremely versatile and greatly facilitates the development of powerful, responsive applications.

CHAPTER FOUR

YOUR FIRST VISUAL BASIC FOR MS-DOS APPLICATION

When people encounter Visual Basic for MS-DOS for the first time, they often think, "Okay, now just where do I start?" This chapter will help you get acclimated and will build your confidence by walking you through the steps of developing a simple but complete application.

The WINDCHIL Application

The WINDCHIL application displays the windchill index for a given wind speed and air temperature. The windchill index is a measure of how fast heat is drawn from your skin. As wind speed increases and you lose heat more quickly, the windchill index decreases. The index is based on the air temperature that would produce the equivalent rate of heat loss from your skin if no wind were blowing.

Single-Form Application Development Checklist

1. Begin with a new project.
2. Design the form:
   - Change the size, shape, and location of the form's window.
   - Draw controls with the size, shape, and location you want.
   - Change other form and control properties as you like.
3. Add subprograms to the form for the events you want the program to handle.
4. Test the application, repeating the above steps as necessary.
5. Save the project on disk.
6. (Optional) Create an executable (EXE) file.

This application isn't large, yet it handily demonstrates several controls on a single form in a simple, easy-to-understand way. For example, one pair of option buttons lets the user select the type of temperature units to be used, either degrees Fahrenheit or degrees Celsius, and a scroll bar enables the efficient selection of wind speed.

We'll use the checklist at the bottom of the previous page to build the WINDCHIL application. While you're becoming familiar with the Visual Basic for MS-DOS environment, you might find it useful to refer to this checklist to develop other single-form applications.

Beginning a New Project

Let's begin creating the WINDCHIL application in Visual Basic for MS-DOS. To start with a clean slate, choose New Project from the File menu. Figure 4-1 shows the opening screen.

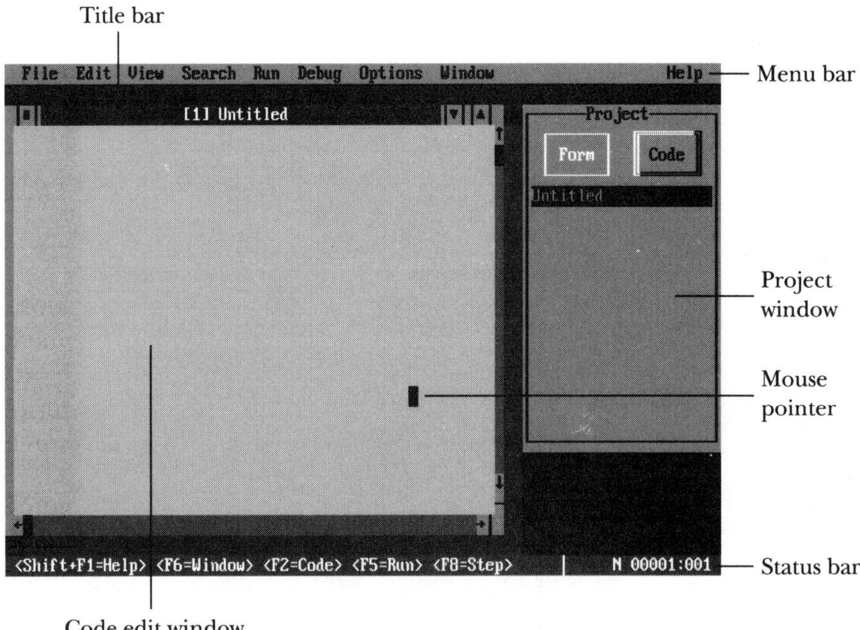

Figure 4-1.
The opening screen of Visual Basic for MS-DOS.

Changing the Form's Properties

This project consists of a single form. A *form* is an application window that has associated code and controls that are necessary to perform one or more specific tasks. Choose New Form from the File menu. A dialog box appears and asks you for a name for the new form. Type *WINDCHIL* and click OK. Visual Basic for MS-DOS then starts the development-environment program named FD.EXE, which lets you develop the appearance and general layout of forms.

Changing the form's Caption property

The default Caption property (title) of the new form's window is the same as the form's name (in this case, Windchil), although capitalization might differ. You can change the Caption property, and hence the form's title, easily. By default, the Caption property is selected in the Property list box when you create a new form. When you type *Windchill Index* in the Value list box, the Caption property changes from the name of the form to the new title you key in. Figure 4-2 shows the form window after the change.

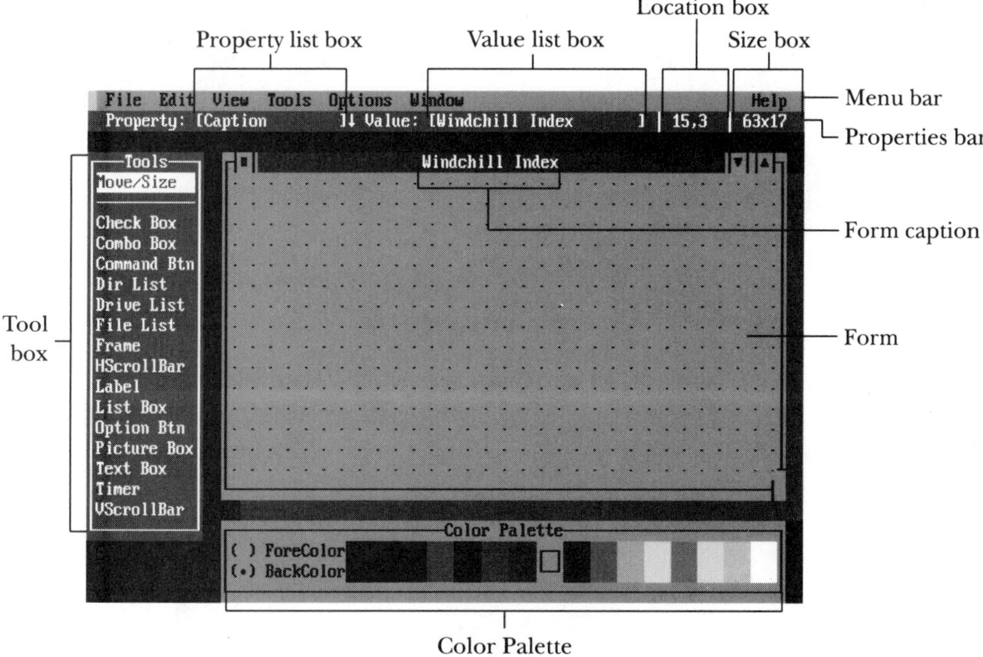

Figure 4-2.
The form window after you change the Caption property to Windchill Index.

Changing the form's size

The default form is a little too short for the set of controls we'll be placing on it. Drag the sides of the form to change the form's shape. (You can change the form's width and height simultaneously by dragging a corner of the form.)

You can move a form by dragging its title bar. Move and size the form so that it resembles the form shown in Figure 4-3. You needn't worry about being precise because you can easily change the form's shape as we go on.

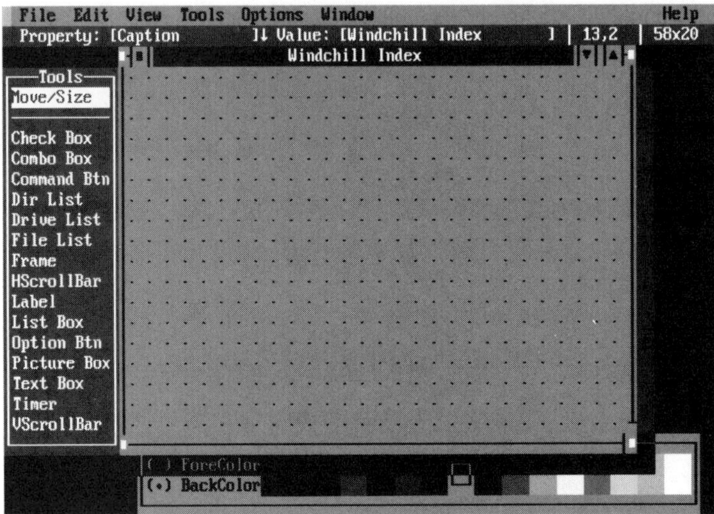

Figure 4-3.
The appearance of the WINDCHIL form after you change the form's size.

Adding a menu to the form

It's usually best to create the form's menus before adding controls. That way you can situate the controls closer to their final positions. If you place the controls first and then create the menus, the form's menu bar pushes down everything on the form but the form's overall size remains unchanged, obscuring the controls at the bottom of the form. Although you can easily adjust the visual appearance of the form, if you create the form's menus first the steps are a little more straightforward.

The menu title To create the form's menus, choose Menu Design Window from the Window menu. The Menu Design Window dialog box appears, similar to the one shown in Figure 4-4. Click in the Caption text box and type *&Help.* This is the title of the WINDCHIL form's only menu. The ampersand (*&*) lets the user open the Help menu by pressing Alt-H. Press Tab to move to the CtlName text box and type *menTop.* Each menu title and menu item has a control name, which is used in the code portion of the form to name a subprogram that activates when the user chooses a menu title or a menu item. I've developed the habit of prefixing these menu control names with *men*, which lets me immediately identify the parts of a program's code that are directly associated with menus.

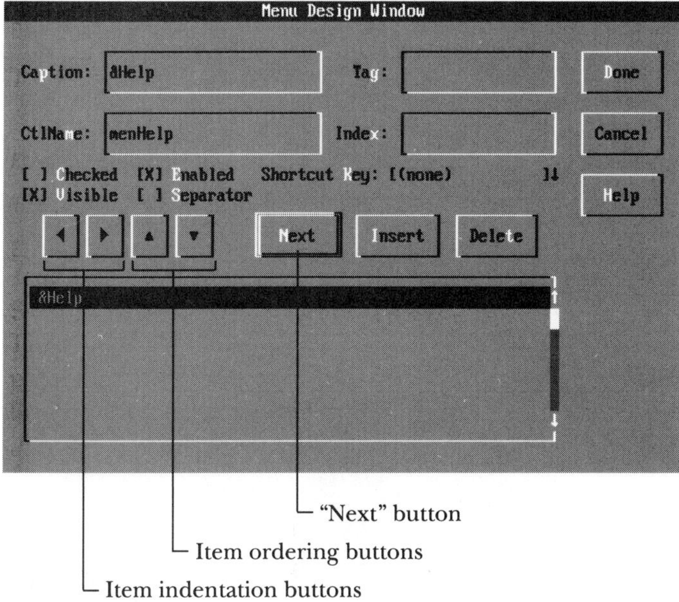

Figure 4-4.
Appearance of the Menu Design Window after you enter the menu information.

Menu items To add menu items to the Help menu, click the Next button. Indent the Caption name you're about to enter by clicking the right arrow indentation button located in the middle row of the Menu Design Window. Two dots appear in the highlighted line in the list box below. Indenting an entry once in the Menu Design Window causes it to drop down as a menu item when the user clicks on a menu title in the finished application. Indenting an entry twice in the Menu Design Window causes the entry to appear as a cascading menu on the drop-down menu.

After you click the indentation button, enter *&Help* in the Caption text box and *menHelp* in the CtlName text box for the first menu item. For the second menu item enter *E&xit* in the Caption text box and *menExit* in the CtlName text box. Notice that the second menu item retains the indentation of the item above; you do not have to click the right arrow indentation button again. The table on the following page illustrates how menu titles and menu items similar to the ones described above are listed throughout the book.

WINDCHIL.FRM Menu Design Window Entries

Caption	CtlName	Indentation
&Help	menTop	0
&Help	menHelp	1
E&xit	menExit	1

The menu for WINDCHIL is now complete. Click Done to exit the Menu Design Window. Immediately you'll see the Help menu on the menu bar of the form. Click on the form's new Help menu to see the Help menu items. Figure 4-5 shows the form with its Help menu open.

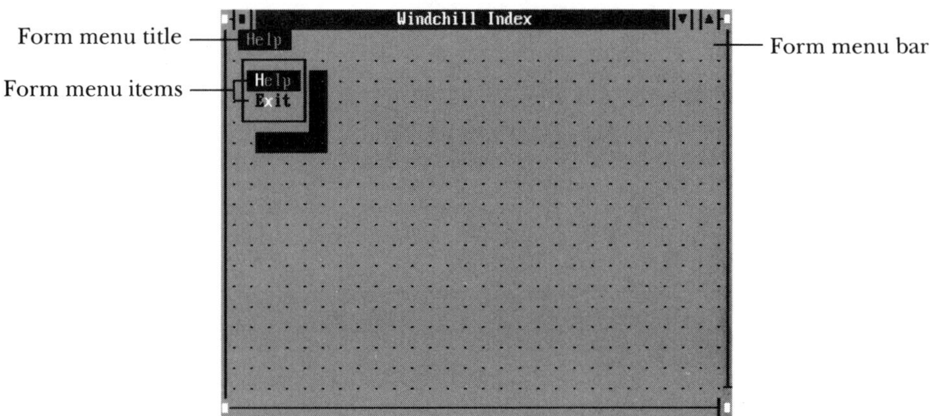

Figure 4-5.
The WINDCHIL form with its Help menu open.

Adding controls to the form

The next step is to add and modify the form's controls, which you can select from the Toolbox. See Figure 4-2. *Controls* are the buttons, labels, text boxes, and other items that make up the user interface on the form. The selection and placement of controls on a form's window determines much of the functionality of the form. You can use controls to display text, provide user-alterable text-input fields, define a rectangular graphics-output region, display lists, provide toggle selections, and so on. Each type of control is described in detail in your Visual Basic for MS-DOS manual.

Figure 4-6 shows the WINDCHIL form with the controls in place. The following sections describe the controls and the process of placing them on the form.

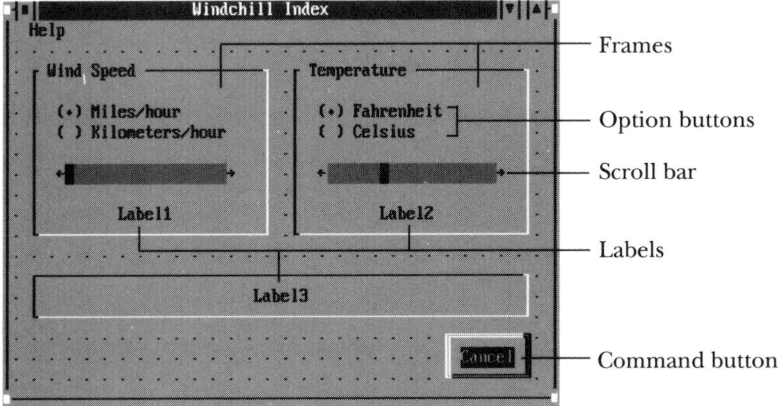

Figure 4-6.
The WINDCHIL form with controls in place.

Frames In the Toolbox, click on Frame to select the Frame control. On the form, click near the upper left corner (under the Help menu) and drag to about the middle of the form to draw the first frame. This will be the Wind Speed frame on the left side of the finished form. You can go back and resize or move this frame at any time to get the placement on the form exactly right, so don't worry about being too precise as you start. In the Properties bar at the top of the screen, select Caption from the Property list box (if Caption is not already selected), and then type *Wind Speed* in the Value list box. The frame's caption changes to *Wind Speed.* Follow the same steps to create the second frame, placing the new frame to the right of the first frame (using the same height and vertical position), and enter *Temperature* in the Value list box of the new frame's Caption property.

Option buttons Click on Option Btn in the Toolbox to draw each of the four option buttons on the form. Drag to draw the first two option buttons inside the Wind Speed frame, and then draw the next two option buttons inside the Temperature frame. (It's important that you create the option buttons in this order.) Click on Option Btn again after each time you drag to create each new option button. Set each option button's Caption property to match Figure 4-6.

When you group option buttons inside frames in this way, Visual Basic for MS-DOS allows only one option button in each group to be selected at any given time. See the FRAMOPT application in Chapter 6 for another example of how frame-grouped option buttons work. Click the Miles/hour and Fahrenheit option buttons to make them active when the application runs.

Scroll bars You can now add the two scroll bar controls in a similar way. Click on HScrollBar in the Toolbox, and then drag to draw the scroll bars inside each frame. Draw the scroll bar in the Wind Speed frame first. Refer to Figure 4-6 for placement. Now it's time to change five properties of these scroll bars. Click on the scroll bar inside the Wind Speed frame, select LargeChange from the Property list box, and enter *10* in the Value list box. In the same manner, change the values for the SmallChange, Max, Min, and Value properties to reflect the values shown in the table below. Throughout the rest of the book, form and control properties are listed in this format.

WINDCHIL.FRM Form and Control Properties

Property	Value
HScroll1:	
LargeChange	10
Max	50
Min	5
SmallChange	1
Value	8
HScroll2:	
LargeChange	10
Max	90
Min	–50
SmallChange	1
Value	10

Labels Click on Label in the Toolbox to draw the two labels inside the frames. (Remember to click on Label in the Toolbox again after drawing each label.) Also draw a third label on the form below the frames, as shown in Figure 4-6. For this third label only, change the BorderStyle property to *1 - SingleLine.* For all three labels, change the Alignment property to *2 - Center.*

Command button The last control to add is a command button. Click on Command Btn in the Toolbox, and draw the button at the bottom right corner of the form, as shown in Figure 4-6. Change the button's Caption property to *Cancel,* and change the Cancel and Default properties to *True.* The Cancel property tells Visual Basic for MS-DOS to choose this command button if the user presses the Esc key, and the Default property makes the button the active command button when the form loads. (The active command button is chosen when the user presses the Enter key.)

Adding Code to Create Subprograms

The only task remaining in order to complete this application is to add some event-driven code that calculates and displays the windchill index. Exit from the form development environment by choosing Exit from the File menu. Click Yes in the dialog box that appears asking whether you want to save your work. This returns you to the code development environment.

Adding event-driven procedures

Choose the Event Procedures command from the Edit menu to select an event-driven subprogram to edit. The list of procedures to edit is shown in Figure 4-7.

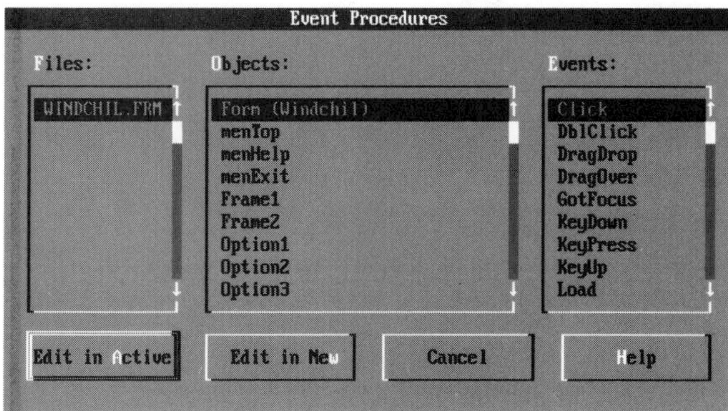

Figure 4-7.
The Event Procedures dialog box.

Select Form (Windchil) from the Objects list and Load from the Events list. Click the Edit In Active button to edit the *Form_Load* subprogram. Visual Basic for MS-DOS creates the following two lines in a code edit window:

```
SUB Form_Load ()

END SUB
```

You type code lines to build the subprogram between the beginning and ending lines that Visual Basic for MS-DOS provides.

Notice that Visual Basic for MS-DOS inserts the name of the *Form_Load* subprogram. All event-driven subprogram names have the same syntax: *Object_Event*. The *Object* portion is the name of the form or control associated with the event in the *Event* portion. An underscore always separates the two parts of event-driven subprogram names. In this example, the subprogram is activated when the form first loads—hence the name *Form_Load*.

Add the following lines of code to the *Form_Load* subprogram:

```
'Force scroll bars to update
HScroll1_Change
HScroll2_Change
```

Figure 4-8 shows what your code edit window looks like after you enter the *Form_Load* code:

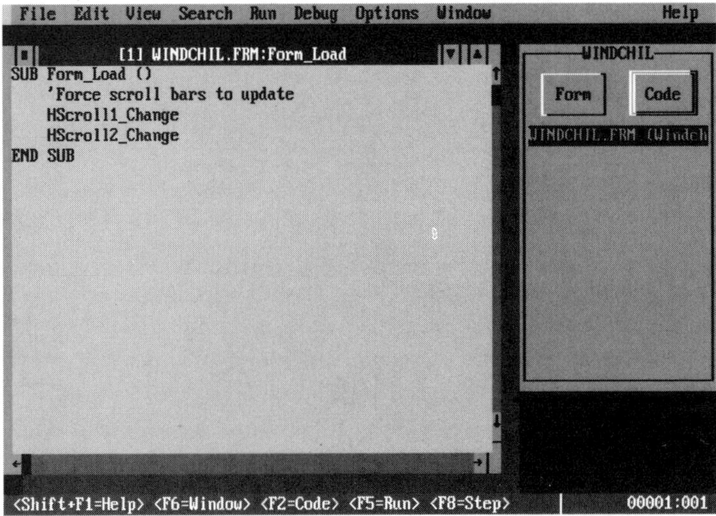

Figure 4-8.
The Form_Load *subprogram.*

Now create the *Command1_Click* subprogram, for which you supply a single line of code. Choose the Event Procedures command from the Edit menu, choose Command1 from the Objects list, choose Click from the Events list, and then click the Edit In Active button to edit the routine.

```
SUB Command1_Click
    UNLOAD Windchil
END SUB
```

You can jump directly to an existing subprogram or function at any time by choosing the Code command from the View menu, which displays a list of all available subprograms and functions. Select a subprogram, a function, or the form name, and click Edit In Active to edit the code associated with the subprogram, function, or form.

Adding functions

The WINDCHIL application needs a function that converts temperature from degrees Celsius to degrees Fahrenheit. To create this function, choose the New Function command from the Edit menu, type *Fahrenheit* in the Name text box of the New Function dialog box, and click the Edit In Active button. Visual Basic for MS-DOS creates these two lines in the code edit window:

```
FUNCTION Fahrenheit ()

END FUNCTION
```

This function takes one parameter—the temperature in degrees Celsius—and returns the temperature in degrees Fahrenheit. Edit the function as shown:

```
FUNCTION Fahrenheit (C)
  'Convert Celsius to Fahrenheit
  Fahrenheit = (C + 40) * 9 / 5 - 40
END FUNCTION
```

Source code for WINDCHIL.FRM

Throughout the rest of the book, the source-code listings for each form are presented in the following format. This format provides all the source-code listings for the entire form, including comments and other lines appearing at the form level. Remember that you have already entered the necessary code for the *Form_Load* and *Command1_Click* subprograms and for the *FAHRENHEIT* function. Enter the program lines as shown to finish development of the WINDCHIL application.

TIP

A quick way to create a new subprogram is to move the cursor below the last line of the current subprogram or function, type *SUB subprogram_name*, (where *subprogram_name* is the name of the subprogram), and press Enter. This method also works for creating new functions—simply substitute the *FUNCTION* keyword for the *SUB* keyword.

```
'================================================
' WINDCHIL
' Calculates windchill index
'================================================

'$INCLUDE: 'CONSTANT.BI'

DECLARE SUB HScroll1_Change ()
DECLARE SUB HScroll2_Change ()
DECLARE SUB ChillOut ()
DECLARE SUB Command1_Click ()

DECLARE FUNCTION Mph! (K!)
DECLARE FUNCTION Celsius! (F!)
DECLARE FUNCTION Fahrenheit! (C!)
DECLARE FUNCTION Kph! (M!)

FUNCTION Celsius (F)
   'Convert Fahrenheit to Celsius
    Celsius = (F + 40) * 5 / 9 - 40
END FUNCTION

SUB ChillOut ()
    Wind = HScroll1.Value
    Temp = HScroll2.Value

    'Convert to MPH if KPH selected
    IF Option2.Value = TRUE THEN
        Wind = Mph(Wind)
    END IF

    'Convert to Fahrenheit if Celsius selected
    IF Option4.Value = TRUE THEN
        Temp = Fahrenheit(Temp)
    END IF

    'Calculate the windchill index
    x = .303439 * SQR(Wind) - .0202886 * Wind
    Chill = INT(91.9 - (91.4 - Temp) * (x + .474266))

    'Convert back to Celsius if selected
    IF Option4.Value = TRUE THEN
        Chill = Celsius(Chill)
    END IF

    x$ = "Windchill Index is " + STR$(CINT(Chill))
    x$ = x$ + SPACE$(1) + CHR$(248)
```

(continued)

WINDCHIL.FRM *continued*

```
    IF Option3.Value = TRUE THEN
        Label3.Caption = x$ + "F"
    ELSE
        Label3.Caption = x$ + "C"
    END IF
END SUB

SUB Command1_Click ()
    UNLOAD Windchil
END SUB

FUNCTION Fahrenheit (C)
   'Convert Celsius to Fahrenheit
   Fahrenheit = (C + 40) * 9 / 5 - 40
END FUNCTION

SUB Form_Load ()
    'Force scroll bars to update
    HScroll1_Change
    HScroll2_Change
END SUB

SUB HScroll1_Change ()
    Tmp$ = STR$(HScroll1.Value)
    IF Option2.Value = TRUE THEN
        Tmp$ = Tmp$ + " KPH"
    ELSE
        Tmp$ = Tmp$ + " MPH"
    END IF
    Label1.Caption = Tmp$
    ChillOut
END SUB

SUB HScroll2_Change ()
    Tmp$ = STR$(HScroll2.Value) + " " + CHR$(248)
    IF Option4.Value = TRUE THEN
        Tmp$ = Tmp$ + "C"
    ELSE
        Tmp$ = Tmp$ + "F"
    END IF
    Label2.Caption = Tmp$
    ChillOut
END SUB
```

(continued)

WINDCHIL.FRM *continued*

```
FUNCTION Kph (M)
    'Convert MPH to KPH
    Kph = M * 1.609344
END FUNCTION

SUB menExit_Click ()
    'Activate the Cancel button
    Command1_Click
END SUB

SUB menHelp_Click ()
    'Create newline characters
    NL$ = CHR$(13) + CHR$(10)

    'Build the Help message
    Msg$ = "Use the scroll bars to select wind speed and" + NL$
    Msg$ = Msg$ + "air temperature.  The calculated Windchill" + NL$
    Msg$ = Msg$ + "Index is displayed below.  You may select" + NL$
    Msg$ = Msg$ + "metric units if desired." + NL$

    'Display the Help message
    MSGBOX Msg$
END SUB

FUNCTION Mph (K)
    'Convert KPH to MPH
    Mph = K / 1.609344
END FUNCTION

SUB Option1_Click ()
    'Convert current wind speed to MPH
    x% = Mph(CSNG(HScroll1.Value))

    'Reset scroll bar for MPH
    HScroll1.Min = 5
    HScroll1.Max = 50
    HScroll1.Value = x%
END SUB

SUB Option2_Click ()
    'Convert current wind speed to KPH
    x% = Kph(CSNG(HScroll1.Value))

    'Reset scroll bar for KPH
    HScroll1.Min = 8
    HScroll1.Max = 80
    HScroll1.Value = x%
END SUB
```

(continued)

WINDCHIL.FRM *continued*

```
SUB Option3_Click ()
    'Convert current temperature to Fahrenheit
    x% = Fahrenheit(CSNG(HScroll2.Value))

    'Reset scroll bar for Fahrenheit
    HScroll2.Min = -50
    HScroll2.Max = 90
    HScroll2.Value = x%
END SUB

SUB Option4_Click ()
    'Convert current temperature to Celsius
    x% = Celsius(CSNG(HScroll2.Value))

    'Reset scroll bar for Celsius
    HScroll2.Min = -45
    HScroll2.Max = 32
    HScroll2.Value = x%
END SUB
```

Testing the Application

The WINDCHIL application is now ready to run! Choose the Start command from the Run menu to start the application. The Windchill Index window appears, displaying a default wind speed, air temperature, and calculated windchill index, similar to Figure 4-9.

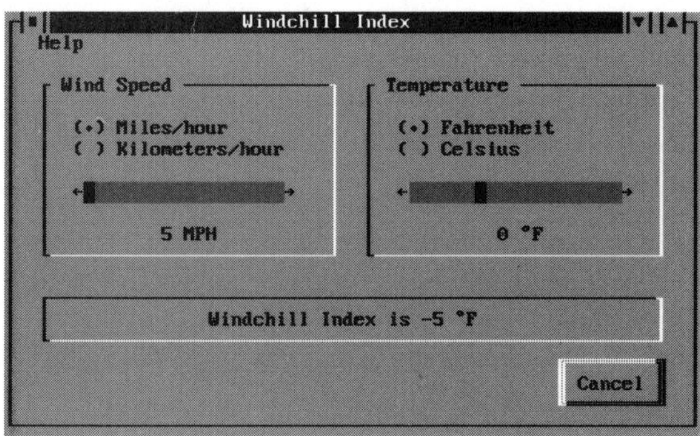

Figure 4-9.
The WINDCHIL application in action.

Use the scroll bars to change the wind speed and air temperature settings. Click to the left or right of the scroll box to move the scroll box in large increments; click on the scroll arrows to move the scroll box in small increments. You can also drag the scroll box to the position you want. The application's calculation of the windchill index is valid over a prescribed range of wind speeds and air temperatures. Your setting of the *Max* and *Min* values of the scroll bars to these range limits in the program code serves as a convenient way to guarantee that the user can't enter data outside the range limits for these quantities.

If you prefer to use metric units, click the appropriate option buttons. The scroll bar ranges and current values all change to reflect the new units.

Arranging Application Help

In this application, the Help message text is embedded directly in the *menHelp_Click* subprogram. This is an effective technique only when short Help messages are displayed. Most of the programs in this book use a more flexible approach to displaying Help messages, storing them in separate text files that are loaded and displayed when the user asks for Help. See the FMSGDEMO application in Chapter 5 for more information.

Saving a Project on Disk

Now that you've created your first Visual Basic for MS-DOS application, you should save the application on disk. To do so, choose the Save Project command from the File menu. Each Visual Basic for MS-DOS project has two main files associated with it: a *form (FRM) file*, which contains the form and its associated source-code modules, and a *make (MAK) file*, which contains the list that defines the overall project. (Any subprograms that are not event driven are saved in a third type of file, called a *BAS file*.) You already saved WINDCHIL.FRM, between the time you finished creating the user interface and before you supplied the event-driven code.

In addition to form and make files, *include files* are often associated with a given project. These files, which usually have the extension *BI*, are not listed in the make file but are instead included in the source code through the *$INCLUDE* metacommand. Larger applications often have multiple FRM, BAS, and BI files for all their parts.

Creating an EXE File

The last step (which is optional) in the development checklist is to create an executable (EXE) file for the application. You can reload an application at any time into the Visual Basic for MS-DOS environment and run it from there. If you want to run the application from outside the Visual Basic for MS-DOS environment, however, choose the Make EXE File command from the Run menu to generate an executable file that can run directly from the MS-DOS prompt.

The executable file is the final form of the application that you would provide for a customer. The code is compiled and cannot be easily tampered with, and all the various parts of the application are combined in one EXE file for convenience. (The customer does not need Visual Basic for MS-DOS to run the application.)

You can choose to compile your program for stand-alone operation, or you can compile it to work with the runtime module VBDRT10E.EXE. If compiled into a stand-alone EXE file, the application is self-contained and ready to ship, although it might be rather large. If compiled to require the runtime module, however, the resulting EXE file will be much smaller. This can be a great advantage if you plan to ship several programs together on one disk. Microsoft allows you to ship the runtime module—along with your application—to your customers. See your Visual Basic for MS-DOS manual for more information.

PART II

VISUAL BASIC FOR MS-DOS FORMS AND APPLICATIONS

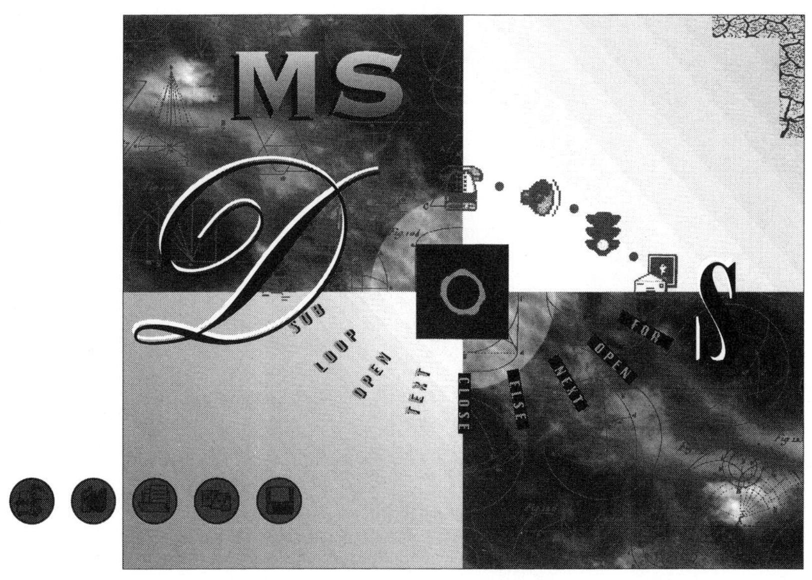

CHAPTER FIVE

SOME OFTEN-USED FORMS

This chapter presents some common forms you might want to incorporate in the applications you write in Visual Basic for MS-DOS, including an About dialog box, a Help information form, a File Open dialog box, a Save As dialog box, and many others.

The ABOUTDEM Application

The ABOUTDEM application demonstrates the ABOUT form, which is used by most of the applications in this book to display a standard About dialog box.

The ABOUTDEM project is composed of four files: ABOUTDEM.MAK, ABOUT.BI, ABOUTDEM.FRM, and ABOUT.FRM. The companion disk at the back of the book contains the files. To load them into Visual Basic for MS-DOS, install the files on your hard drive using the disk's INSTALL program, choose the Open Project command from Visual Basic for MS-DOS's File menu, and type *C:\VBDWSHOP\ABOUTDEM.MAK.* (Note: Throughout the rest of the book, when I discuss menu commands, I'll often use a shorthand statement, such as "Choose the File Open Project command," instead of the longer version, "Choose the Open Project command from the File menu.")

The following sections describe each of the project's files and provide instructions for creating them so that when you want to create a similar form, you'll know the steps to follow.

The ABOUTDEM.MAK File

ABOUTDEM.MAK is the project file for the ABOUTDEM application. Only two text lines are in this file, and they list the files that make up the project. As you create or add new files to the project, Visual Basic for MS-DOS updates the ABOUTDEM.MAK file for you. *You don't need to create or edit this file directly.* Figure 5-1 on the following page shows the contents of ABOUTDEM.MAK.

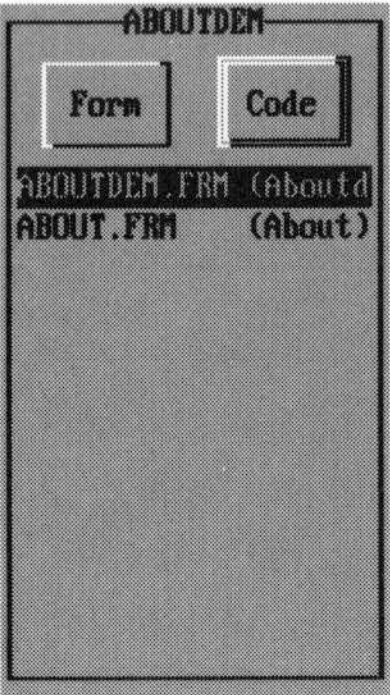

Figure 5-1.
ABOUTDEM project list.

The ABOUT.BI File

One of the first lines in ABOUTDEM.FRM is an *$INCLUDE* metacommand:

```
'$INCLUDE: 'ABOUT.BI'
```

Visual Basic for MS-DOS inserts the contents of the ABOUT.BI file (the BI extension stands for Basic Include) at this location in the ABOUTDEM.FRM file whenever you run or compile the application. ABOUT.BI is the third file in the ABOUTDEM project and contains the metacommand *$FORM*, which enables the ABOUTDEM.FRM module (or any other module in which the *$FORM* metacommand is included) to have global access to the ABOUT.FRM module's controls and properties. The subprogram *menAboutDem_Click* in the ABOUTDEM.FRM listing shows why the *$FORM* metacommand is used:

```
About.Label1.Caption = "ABOUTDEM"
```

The program places the name of the application, in this case *ABOUTDEM*, directly into the label control on the ABOUT form. Without the *$FORM* metacommand, properties of one form are not available or accessible from another form or module.

Source code for ABOUT.BI

```
'================================================
' ABOUT.BI
' Include file for accessing ABOUT.FRM
'================================================

'$FORM About
```

The ABOUTDEM.FRM File

ABOUTDEM.FRM is the main start-up form for this application. If you want to create this form yourself instead of using the form available on the companion disk, use the following guidelines. First, to add this new form to the project, choose the File New Form command. A dialog box appears, prompting you for the name of the new form. After you enter *ABOUTDEM* as the form's name, a blank form appears, ready for you to edit. Add menu commands to the form as listed in the following Menu Design Window Entries table, and add controls to the form as listed in the Form and Control Properties table. After you have finished, choose the File Save Form command, and then choose the Code command from the View menu. Finally, add the source code for ABOUTDEM.FRM, as shown on the following page.

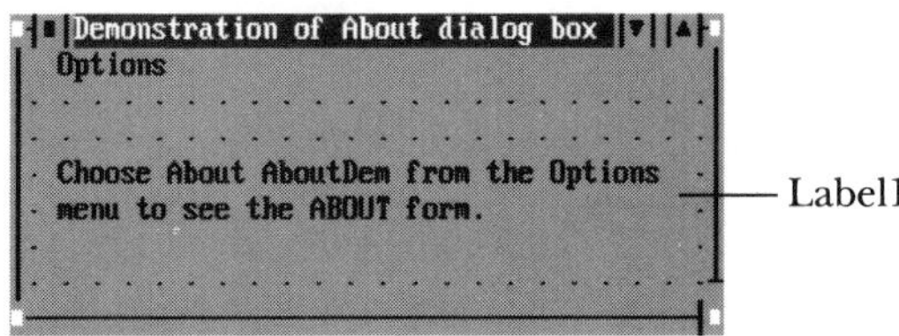

Figure 5-2.
ABOUTDEM.FRM during development.

ABOUTDEM.FRM Menu Design Window Entries

Caption	CtlName	Indentation
&Options	menOptions	0
&About AboutDem...	menAboutDem	1
E&xit	menExitAboutDem	1

ABOUTDEM.FRM Form and Control Properties

Property	Value
Form:	
Caption	Demonstration of About dialog box
FormName	Aboutdem

(continued)

ABOUTDEM.FRM Form and Control Properties *continued*

Property	Value
Label1:	
Caption	Choose About AboutDem from the Options menu to see the ABOUT form.
CtlName	Label1

Source code for ABOUTDEM.FRM

```
'==================================================
' ABOUTDEM
' Demonstrates the ABOUT form
'==================================================

'$INCLUDE: 'ABOUT.BI'
'$INCLUDE: 'CONSTANT.BI'

SUB Form_Load ()
    'Center the form on the screen
    AboutDem.Left = (Screen.Width - AboutDem.Width) \ 2
    AboutDem.Top = (Screen.Height - AboutDem.Height) \ 2
END SUB

SUB menAboutDem_Click ()
    About.Label1.Caption = "ABOUTDEM"
    About.SHOW MODAL
END SUB

SUB menExitAboutDem_Click ()
    UNLOAD AboutDem
END SUB

SUB menExit_Click ()
    UNLOAD AboutDem
END SUB
```

The ABOUT.FRM File

Finally we come to ABOUT.FRM, the form that this application is designed to demonstrate. This form has one command button and several label controls. Feel free to modify the text of these labels to suit your needs. Notice that the program replaces the second label with the name of the calling application immediately before the program displays ABOUT.FRM. I have placed default text in this label simply to document the label's purpose.

Set the BorderStyle property of the ABOUT form to *1 - Fixed Single*. With this setting, the border around the form has a slightly different appearance from the border with the default setting of *2 - Sizable Single*. In particular, the sizing marks disappear, and the user cannot alter the form's size while the program is running. There's no reason to let the user adjust the size of the About dialog box (which might degrade the appearance of the dialog box), and the program's only interaction with the user is the OK command button that unloads the form.

You can adjust the color of the characters in a label by setting the ForeColor property of the label. You might want to experiment with the colors to suit your preferences. A good way to experiment with the colors is to select one of the labels and then select alternative colors from the Color Palette. The displayed text changes immediately to reflect the new settings.

Set the Values associated with the labels' Alignment property to *2 - Center*. This setting centers any text strings that you place in the Caption property of the labels. The default setting (*1 - Left Justify*) causes the text to align along the left edge of (also described as flush left with) the label area. Or you might want to align the text along the right edge (flush right). In those cases, set the Alignment property to *3 - Right Justify*.

Set the Default property of Command1 to *True* so that the Enter key functions as a shortcut for clicking the OK command button (thereby closing the form). If you leave the Default property of Command1 set to *False*, the user must click the OK command button with the mouse in order to close the form. The Default property comes in handy when a form has multiple command buttons. You can designate any one of the command buttons as the default command button, causing that button to be "clicked" when the user presses the Enter key (assuming the user hasn't pressed the Tab key to select a different command button).

The following figure, table, and code give the details of the application's creation.

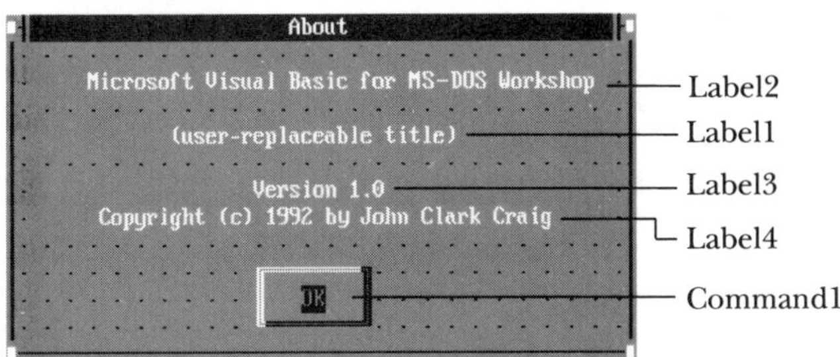

Figure 5-3.
ABOUT.FRM during development.

ABOUT.FRM Form and Control Properties

Property	Value
Form:	
BorderStyle	1 - Fixed Single
Caption	About
ControlBox	False
FormName	About
MaxButton	False
MinButton	False
Label1:	
Alignment	2 - Center
Caption	(user-replaceable title)
CtlName	Label1
ForeColor	10 - Bright Green
Label2:	
Alignment	2 - Center
Caption	Microsoft Visual Basic for MS-DOS Workshop
CtlName	Label2
ForeColor	14 - Yellow
Label3:	
Alignment	2 - Center
Caption	Version 1.0
CtlName	Label3
ForeColor	11 - Bright Cyan
Label4:	
Alignment	2 - Center
Caption	Copyright (c) 1992 by John Clark Craig
CtlName	Label4
ForeColor	11 - Bright Cyan
Command1:	
Caption	OK
CtlName	Command1
Default	True

Source code for ABOUT.FRM

```
'================================================
' ABOUT
' Standard About dialog box
'================================================

' Notes:
' Add $INCLUDE: 'ABOUT.BI' to the calling module.
' Load ABOUT.FRM into your project.
'
' Example of use:
'    About.Label1.Caption = "TITLE"
'    About.SHOW MODAL

SUB Command1_Click ()
    UNLOAD About
END SUB

SUB Form_Load ()
    'Center the form on the screen
    About.Left = (Screen.Width - About.Width) \ 2
    About.Top = (Screen.Height - About.Height) \ 2
END SUB
```

Running the ABOUTDEM Application

After you have built the forms that make up the ABOUTDEM application, choose the Run Start command to begin the demonstration. Figure 5-4 shows the ABOUTDEM application in action, and Figure 5-5 on the following page shows the About dialog box that the application displays when the user chooses the Options About AboutDem command.

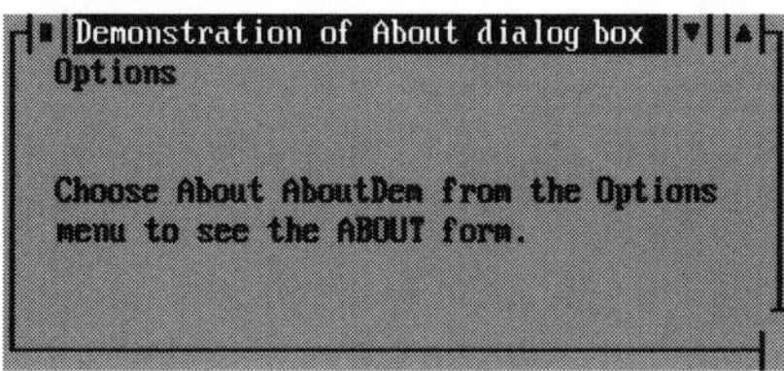

Figure 5-4.
ABOUTDEM.FRM in action.

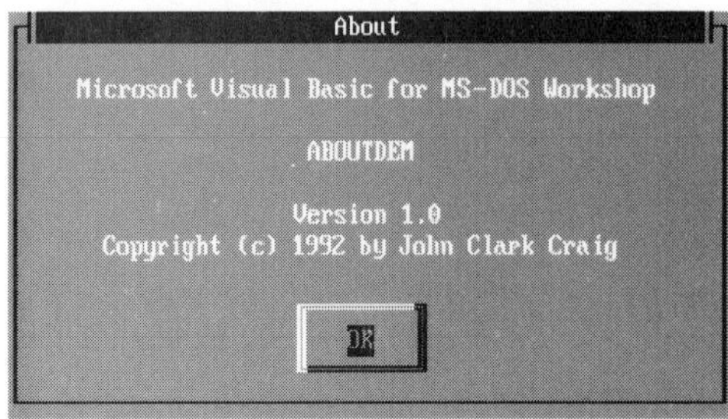

Figure 5-5.
ABOUT.FRM in action.

Many of the applications in this book use the ABOUT.FRM module. Adding the ABOUT.FRM module to a project requires only a few steps, which you can easily review in the first few comment lines of ABOUT.FRM. The Visual Basic for MS-DOS File menu contains the Add File command, which you use to add a file to a project. Use the File Add File command to add ABOUT.FRM to your current project list. Also add a declaration for the constant MODAL to your application so that your application can properly display the ABOUT form. (MODAL, along with many other useful constants, is predefined in CONSTANT.BI, an include file shipped with Visual Basic for MS-DOS.) The *menAboutDem_Click* subprogram uses the *SHOW* method to load the ABOUT form. The parameter *MODAL* specifies that the user can switch to a different window in the application only after clicking the OK command button or after choosing Close from the application's Control-Box menu. You'll also need to add an *$INCLUDE* metacommand to include ABOUT.BI in your calling modules.

The FMSGDEMO Application

The FMSGDEMO application demonstrates the FILEMSG.BAS module, which most of the applications in this book use to display Help information. The *FileMsg* subprogram in FILEMSG.BAS uses the *MSGBOX* statement to display lines (in a dialog box) from a specially formatted text file. FILEMSG.BAS can be used to display Help information or other blocks of informational text.

You can embed Help text directly in a form's code, but the *FileMsg* subprogram technique works better. Perhaps the greatest advantage of this technique is that you can edit the lines of Help text using the MS-DOS Editor (or any ASCII text editor) with much greater ease than you could if you merely enclosed the text in quotation marks and assigned the text to variables in the form's code. You can edit the Help information independently of the application, even after you compile the application.

The files for the FMSGDEMO application are included on the companion disk. To load the files into Visual Basic for MS-DOS, choose the File Open Project command and type *C:\VBDWSHOP\FMSGDEMO.MAK.* This opens the files and enables you to modify the forms and code. The following figures, tables, and code give the details of the application's creation.

Figure 5-6.
FMSGDEMO project list.

First on the list is FMSGDEMO.FRM, the startup module. FMSGDEMO.FRM contains three *$INCLUDE* metacommands for the ABOUT.BI, CONSTANT.BI, and FILEMSG.BI include files. You will find that ABOUT.BI and FILEMSG.BI are included in the startup module for most of the applications in this book. Include these two BI files (and add the associated form files) in any of your application modules that use the ABOUT form or the FILEMSG module. The contents of ABOUT.BI are described in the section "The ABOUT.BI File" near the beginning of this chapter. The contents of FILEMSG.BI are described below.

Source code for FILEMSG.BI

```
'================================================
' FILEMSG.BI
' Include file for accessing FILEMSG.BAS
'================================================

DECLARE SUB FileMsg (FileName$, Section%)
```

Next on the FMSGDEMO project list is the ABOUT.FRM file. This is the same module described in the section "The ABOUTDEM Application" at the beginning of the chapter. No change to this form or its code is required for the FMSGDEMO application to use the ABOUT.FRM module.

Last on the FMSGDEMO project list, the FILEMSG.BAS module provides online Help. This module is explained later, in the section "The FILEMSG.BAS File."

The FMSGDEMO.FRM File

FMSGDEMO.FRM, the main form for this project, is designed to demonstrate the FILEMSG.BAS module. Figure 5-7 shows the message that appears when FMSGDEMO runs, and Figure 5-8 shows the File Message Demonstration dialog box. (You can select other demonstration messages from the Help menu.) Figure 5-9 shows the Help menu options.

Use the following Menu Design Window Entries table to build the Help Menu. Notice that a hyphen serves as the caption in the fourth and sixth menu items. These hyphens cause separator lines to appear in the menu, as shown in Figure 5-9. Because all menu captions must have an associated control name, *menSep1* and *menSep2* serve as dummy control names that aren't associated with subprograms. This technique makes it easy to add separator lines to a menu.

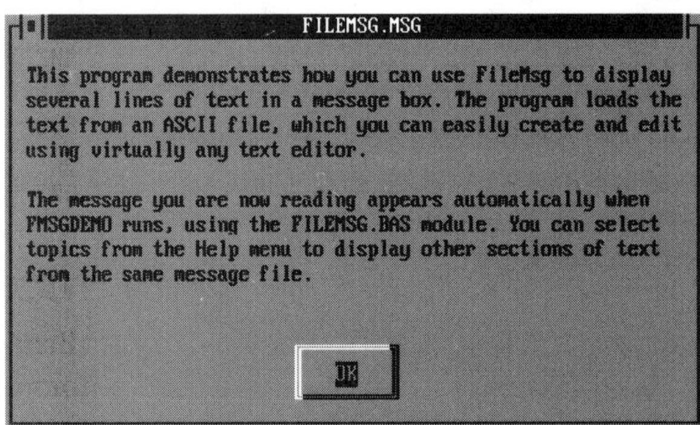

Figure 5-7.
Startup message for the FMSGDEMO program.

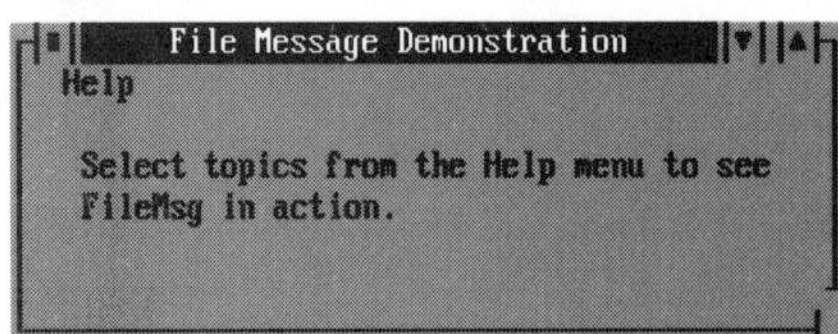

Figure 5-8.
File Message Demonstration dialog box.

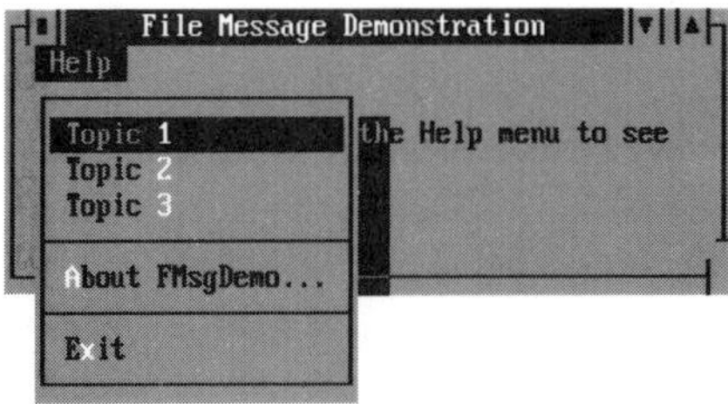

Figure 5-9.
FMSGDEMO Help menu options.

FMSGDEMO.FRM Menu Design Window Entries

Caption	CtlName	Indentation
&Help	menHelp	0
Topic &1	menTopic1	1
Topic &2	menTopic2	1
Topic &3	menTopic3	1
-	menSep1	1
&About FMsgDemo...	menAboutFMsgDemo	1
-	menSep2	1
E&xit	menExit	1

The FMSGDEMO form has only one control, a label that displays a prompt to the user. Figure 5-10 shows the FMSGDEMO form during development. The table on the following page lists the form and control properties.

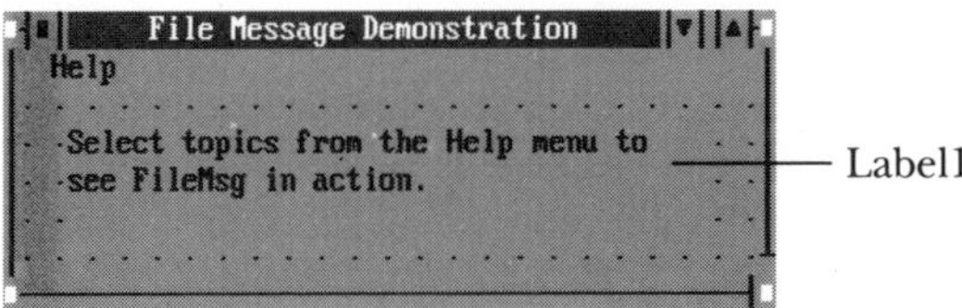

Figure 5-10.
FMSGDEMO.FRM during development.

FMSGDEMO.FRM Form and Control Properties

Property	Value
Form:	
Caption	File Message Demonstration
FormName	FMsgDemo
Label1:	
Caption	Select topics from the Help menu to see FileMsg in action.
CtlName	Label1

Add the following code to complete FMSGDEMO.FRM. The CONSTANT.BI include file comes with Visual Basic for MS-DOS. If you haven't explored the contents of this file, take a look now and become familiar with it. Most of the applications in this book include this file, often simply to make use of the constants TRUE and FALSE. CONSTANT.BI also declares many other useful constants, such as names of colors and lists of Property settings for several controls. I highly recommend that you use these constants whenever possible.

Source code for FMSGDEMO.FRM

```
'================================================
' FMSGDEMO
' Demonstrates the FILEMSG module
'================================================

'$INCLUDE: 'CONSTANT.BI'
'$INCLUDE: 'FILEMSG.BI'
'$INCLUDE: 'ABOUT.BI'

SUB Form_Load ()
    'Center the form on the screen
    FMsgDemo.Left = (Screen.Width - FMsgDemo.Width) \ 2
    FMsgDemo.Top = (Screen.Height - FMsgDemo.Height) \ 2

    SHOW
    FileMsg "FILEMSG.MSG", 1
END SUB
```

(continued)

FMSGDEMO.FRM *continued*

```
SUB menAboutFMsgDemo_Click ()
    About.Label1.Caption = "FMSGDEMO"
    About.SHOW MODAL
END SUB

SUB menExit_Click ()
    UNLOAD FMsgDemo
END SUB

SUB menTopic1_Click ()
   FileMsg "FILEMSG.MSG", 2
END SUB

SUB menTopic2_Click ()
    FileMsg "FILEMSG.MSG", 3
END SUB

SUB menTopic3_Click ()
    FileMsg "FILEMSG.MSG", 4
END SUB
```

Most of the subprograms in the FMSGDEMO.FRM source code call the *FileMsg* subprogram to open and display a particular section of text from the FILEMSG.MSG text file. One dialog box created by the *MSGBOX* statement in the *FileMsg* subprogram appears when the form first loads, and other sections of text appear in dialog boxes as the user chooses each of the Help menu topic items.

The FILEMSG.MSG File

You must now create the text file FILEMSG.MSG (or use the file on the companion disk) to enable this program to run correctly. Use the MS-DOS Editor, or any other text editor, to create this file, and be sure to save the file in unformatted ASCII text mode only. The following text and code presents the contents of FILEMSG.MSG.

Contents of FILEMSG.MSG

The first few lines of the text file are not displayed by the *FileMsg* subprogram because they lack the special line that marks the beginning of each displayed message section. Such comment lines are handy for documenting (adding comments to) the message file.

The line beginning each displayed message block starts with the greater than (>) character, followed by the block number and the *MSGBOX* title string. Commas must separate these parameters; the program ignores spaces. The program considers message blocks to end when it finds either another line that starts with > or the end of the file.

```
This is a comment line. The first message block begins where a >
character appears as the first character of a line.

> 1, FILEMSG.MSG
This program demonstrates how you can use FileMsg to display
several lines of text in a message box. The program loads the
text from an ASCII file, which you can easily create and edit
using virtually any text editor.

The message you are now reading appears automatically when
FMSGDEMO runs, using the FILEMSG.BAS module. You can select
topics from the Help menu to display other sections of text
from the same message file.

> 2, FILEMSG.MSG - Topic 1
This is the second section of text from the FILEMSG.MSG file,
representing the Help Topic 1 menu selection.

A program can display many different message blocks, all
loading from the same file.

> 3,    FILEMSG.MSG - Topic 2
This is the third message block from FILEMSG.MSG. This message
appears when the user selects Help Topic 2.

Look at FILEMSG.MSG to see how it indicates the MSGBOX type, title,
and lines of text.

Take a look at FMSGDEMO.FRM and FILEMSG.BAS to see how they display
message file contents.

> 4, Sequential messages - Topic 3

This demonstrates how sequential message blocks are displayed.
Click OK to proceed to the next message block.
>
This is the second message for Help Topic 3.  A >
character separates sections of a single message block.

One more section follows this one...
>
This is the last section of text for the Help Topic 3 message
block.
```

The rules for creating your own message files are simple and easy to remember. Lines that begin with the > character provide formatting information to the *FileMsg* subprogram. After the > character is the block number for the group of text lines that follows. Following the block number is the title string that appears in the title bar of the dialog box. The end of the block of lines occurs at the start of another block or at the end of the file, whichever occurs first.

If a > character appears on a line by itself, the text lines that follow are continuation lines for the current block of text. This means that the lines preceding the > character appear in a dialog box; when the user clicks OK, the lines that follow appear in a new dialog box. Text block 4, on the facing page, is broken into three sequentially displayed dialog boxes using this technique. Figure 5-11 shows how FMSGDEMO displays Help Topic 1.

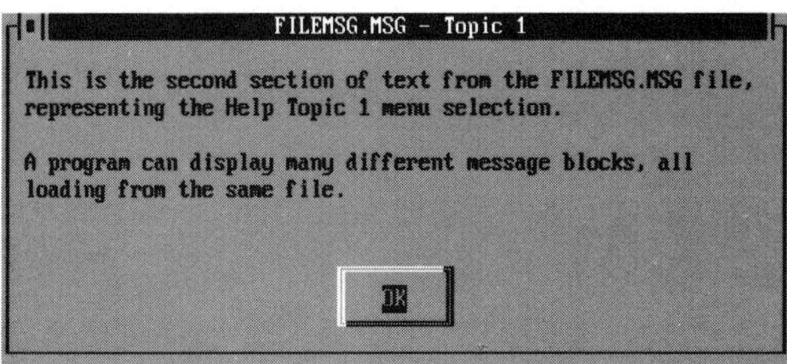

Figure 5-11.
FMSGDEMO display of Help Topic 1.

The FILEMSG.BAS File

The last module named in the project list is FILEMSG.BAS, which is the heart of this application. This module is included in most of the applications in this book. Notice that this module is not a form; it contains only Visual Basic for MS-DOS code. In particular, the *FileMsg* subprogram is contained in this module. *FileMsg* interacts with the user not through a form (or forms) but by creating standard dialog boxes using the *MSGBOX* statement.

Source code for FILEMSG.BAS

```
'================================================
' FILEMSG.BAS
' Displays message blocks from a given file
'================================================
```

(continued)

FILEMSG.BAS *continued*

```
' Notes:
' Add $INCLUDE: 'FILEMSG.BI' to the calling module.
' Load FILEMSG.BAS into your project.
'
' Example of use:
'     FileMsg "FILENAME.MSG", Section%

SUB FileMsg (FileName$, Section%)
    'Be sure file exists
    Fil$ = DIR$(FileName$)
    IF Fil$ = "" THEN
        Msg$ = "File " + FileName$ + " not found"
        MSGBOX Msg$, 0, "-FileMsg-"
        EXIT SUB
    END IF

    'Create the newline string
    NL$ = CHR$(13) + CHR$(10)

    'Open the message file for reading
    NumFile% = FREEFILE
    OPEN FileName$ FOR INPUT AS #NumFile%

    'Find the specified section
    DO UNTIL EOF(NumFile%)
        LINE INPUT #NumFile%, FileTxt$
        IF LEFT$(FileTxt$, 1) = ">" THEN
            IF VAL(MID$(FileTxt$, 2)) = Section% THEN
                EXIT DO
            END IF
        END IF
    LOOP

    'Did we reach the end of the file during the search?
    IF EOF(NumFile%) THEN
        Msg$ = "Message section" + STR$(Section%) + " not found"
        MSGBOX Msg$
        EXIT SUB
    END IF

    'Extract the message box type and title
    FileTxt$ = RTRIM$(LTRIM$(MID$(FileTxt$, 2)))
    Title$ = LTRIM$(MID$(FileTxt$, INSTR(FileTxt$, ",") + 1))

    'Loop through all sections of the block
    DO
```

(continued)

FILEMSG.BAS *continued*

```
        'Clear the message string
        Msg$ = ""

        'Read the message section
        DO UNTIL EOF(NumFile%)
            LINE INPUT #NumFile%, FileTxt$
            IF LEFT$(FileTxt$, 1) = ">" THEN
                EXIT DO
            END IF
            Msg$ = Msg$ + FileTxt$ + NL$
        LOOP

        'Chop off any ending blank lines
        DO WHILE RIGHT$(Msg$, 4) = NL$ + NL$
            Msg$ = LEFT$(Msg$, LEN(Msg$) - 2)
        LOOP

        'Display the message block
        IF Msg$ <> "" THEN
            MSGBOX Msg$, 0, Title$
        END IF

    'Continue the block if ">" was by itself
    LOOP WHILE LTRIM$(RTRIM$(FileTxt$)) = ">"

    'We're finished with the file
    CLOSE NumFile%
END SUB
```

Using FileMsg in Your Own Programs

To use the *FileMsg* subprogram in your own programs, add the FILEMSG.BAS file to your application and add an *$INCLUDE* metacommand to include FILEMSG.BI in modules that contain calls to *FileMsg*. Create an MSG text file for the program, and call *FileMsg* from your program, as shown in the source code for FMSGDEMO.FRM.

The GETDEMO Application

The dialog box that appears after a user chooses the File Open command is one of the most common standard forms. For example, consider the Open Project dialog box that is part of the Visual Basic for MS-DOS development environment and is used to select a project from any subdirectory on any drive. The GETFILE.FRM module is designed to provide this feature for any program you build.

The GETFILE form also provides a good working example of three important controls provided by Visual Basic for MS-DOS:

- The Files list box, which displays a list of files for a given directory
- The Directories list box, which displays a list of available directories
- The Drives list box, which displays a list of available disk drives

When you combine these list boxes on one form, with code to correctly connect their interactive properties, a complete file-selection dialog box results.

The GETDEMO application, which demonstrates the GETFILE form, is included on the companion disk. To load the files for the application into Visual Basic for MS-DOS, choose the File Project Open command and type *C:\VBDWSHOP\GETDEMO.MAK.*

Figure 5-12 shows the project list for the GETDEMO application. Two of these modules, ABOUT.FRM and FILEMSG.BAS, are described earlier in this chapter. If you are building this application yourself, simply choose the File Add File command to add the ABOUT.FRM and FILEMSG.BAS modules to the project list.

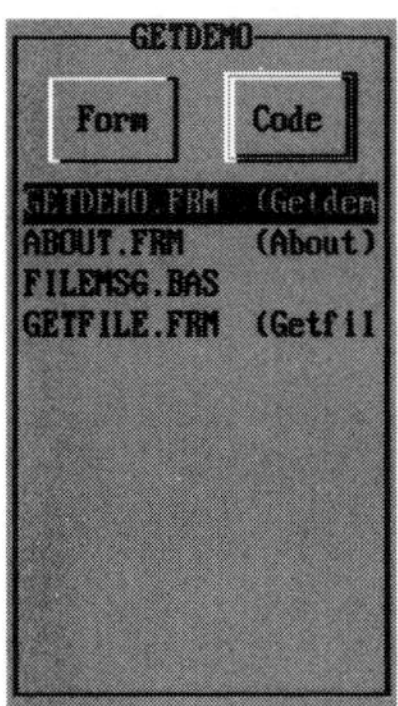

Figure 5-12.
GETDEMO project list.

The GETFILE.BI File

The GETFILE.BI include file, included in both GETDEMO.FRM and GETFILE.FRM, contains declarations for variables that the program modules share in *COMMON* blocks. Include this file in any module that uses the GETFILE form.

Source code for GETFILE.BI

```
'==================================================
' GETFILE.BI
' Include file for accessing GETFILE.FRM
'==================================================

'$FORM GetFile

COMMON SHARED /comGetFile/ WildCard AS STRING
COMMON SHARED /comGetFile/ FullPath AS STRING
COMMON SHARED /comGetFile/ PathFlag AS INTEGER
```

The contents of the *WildCard* variable determine the default file types to list when the GETFILE form first loads. If you want to use GETFILE in an application that expects filenames to have a given extension, change the value of *WildCard* to match. For example, if your application commonly works with TXT files, as the MS-DOS Editor does, assign the value **.TXT* to *WildCard* before using GETFILE.FRM.

FullPath and *PathFlag* are variables that pass critical information to and from the GETFILE form. The application assigns to the string *FullPath* the complete drive, pathname, and filename for the file that the user selects in the Select A File dialog box. This variable also keeps track of the last drive, directory, and file the user selected so that GETFILE is able to restore these selections when the user activates the Select A File dialog box multiple times. *PathFlag* contains either TRUE or FALSE (constants used in most of the forms in this book) to indicate whether the user selected a file or whether the user clicked the Cancel button.

The GETDEMO.FRM File

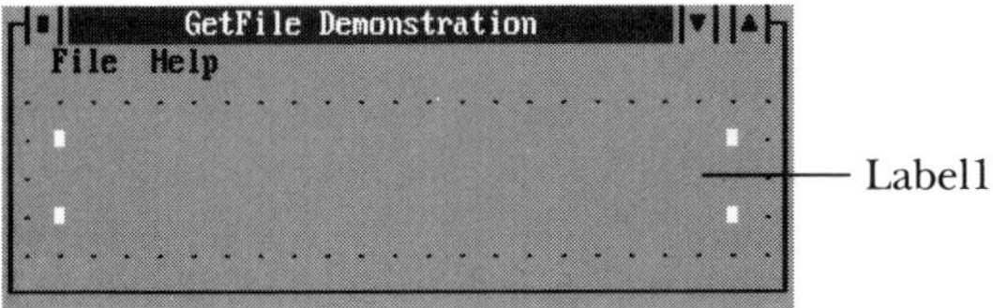

Figure 5-13.
GETDEMO.FRM during development.

GETDEMO.FRM Menu Design Window Entries

Caption	CtlName	Indentation
&File	menFile	0
&File Select...	menFileSelect	1
-	menSep	1
E&xit	menExit	1
&Help	menHelp	0
&Help on GetFile	menHelpGetFile	1
&About GetFile...	menAboutGetFile	1

The GETDEMO form contains only one control, a label field that covers most of the form. This label control displays the full pathname and filename of the file selected when GETFILE.FRM appears. The following table lists the label's control name and the nondefault settings for the form and control properties.

GETDEMO.FRM Form and Control Properties

Property	Value
Form:	
BorderStyle	1 - Fixed Single
Caption	GetFile Demonstration
FormName	Getdemo
Label1:	
Caption	*(blank)*
CtlName	Label1

The following code completes GETDEMO.FRM:

Source code for GETDEMO.FRM

```
'====================================================
' GETDEMO
' Demonstrates the GETFILE form
'====================================================

'$INCLUDE: 'CONSTANT.BI'
'$INCLUDE: 'GETFILE.BI'
'$INCLUDE: 'ABOUT.BI'
'$INCLUDE: 'FILEMSG.BI'

SUB menAboutGetFile_Click ()
    About.Label1.Caption = "GETDEMO"
    About.SHOW MODAL
END SUB

SUB menExit_Click ()
    UNLOAD GetDemo
END SUB

SUB menFileSelect_Click ()
    FullPath = ""
    WildCard = "*.*"
    GetFile.SHOW MODAL
    IF PathFlag = TRUE THEN
        Label1.Caption = FullPath
    ELSE
        Label1.Caption = "(File not selected)"
    END IF
END SUB

SUB menHelpGetFile_Click ()
    FileMsg "GETDEMO.MSG", 1
END SUB
```

The GETFILE.FRM File

The GETFILE.FRM module is used in many of the projects in this book and is demonstrated by GETDEMO. Figure 5-14 on the following page shows the GETFILE form during development. This form contains quite a few controls. The table that follows lists the controls, in approximate upper-left-to-lower-right order as they appear on the form, and lists the control names and the nondefault settings for their properties.

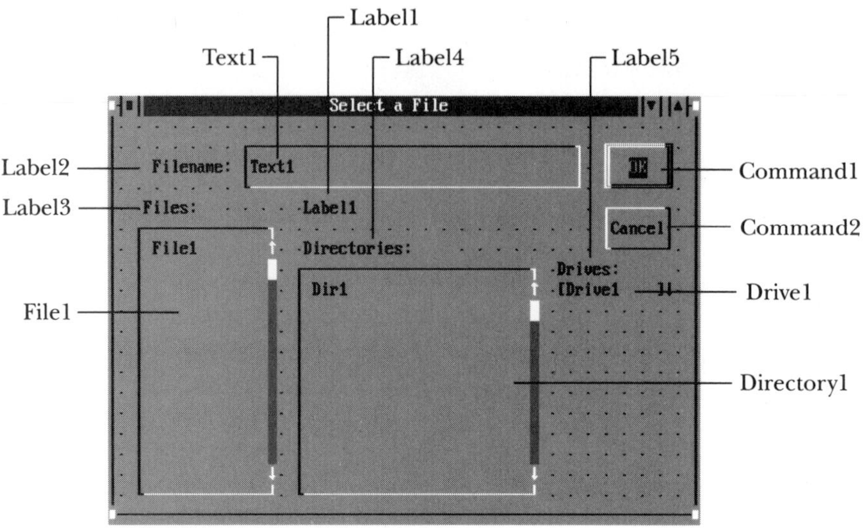

Figure 5-14.
GETFILE.FRM during development.

GETFILE.FRM Form and Control Properties

Property	Value
Form:	
BorderStyle	1 - Fixed Single
Caption	Select a File
FormName	Getfile
Text1:	
Caption	Text1
CtlName	Text1
Label1:	
Caption	Label1
CtlName	Label1
Label2:	
Caption	Filename:
CtlName	Label2

(continued)

GETFILE.FRM Form and Control Properties *continued*

Property	Value
Label3:	
Caption	Files:
CtlName	Label3
Label4:	
Caption	Directories:
CtlName	Label4
Directory1:	
CtlName	Dir1
Label5:	
Caption	Drives:
CtlName	Label5
File1:	
CtlName	File1
Drive1:	
CtlName	Drive1
Command1:	
Caption	OK
CtlName	Command1
Default	True
Command2:	
Cancel	True
Caption	Cancel
CtlName	Command2

The following code completes GETFILE.FRM:

Source code for GETFILE.FRM

```
'=================================================
' GETFILE.FRM
' Standard dialog box for accessing a file in
' any directory on any drive
'=================================================

' Notes:
' Add $INCLUDE: 'GETFILE.BI' to the calling module.
' Load GETFILE.FRM into your project.
'
' Example of use:
'    FullPath = ""
'    WildCard = "*.*"
'    GetFile.SHOW MODAL
'    IF PathFlag = TRUE THEN
'        Label1.Caption = FullPath
'    ELSE
'        Label1.Caption = "(File not selected)"
'    END IF

'$INCLUDE: 'CONSTANT.BI'
'$INCLUDE: 'GETFILE.BI'

CONST TEXTFLAG = 0
CONST FILEFLAG = 1
CONST DIRFLAG = 2

DECLARE SUB Dir1_Change ()
DECLARE SUB FillLabel1 ()

DIM SHARED SelectFlag AS INTEGER

SUB Command1_Click ()
    ON LOCAL ERROR GOTO ErrorTrap

    IF SelectFlag = TEXTFLAG THEN
        File1.FileName = Text1.Text
        IF PathFlag = TRUE THEN
            ON LOCAL ERROR GOTO 0
            UNLOAD GetFile
            EXIT SUB
        END IF
        Dir1.Path = File1.Path
    ELSEIF SelectFlag = DIRFLAG THEN
        Dir1.Path = Dir1.List(Dir1.ListIndex)
        Dir1_Change
```

(continued)

GETFILE.FRM *continued*

```
    ELSE
        IF RIGHT$(Dir1.Path, 1) = "\" THEN
            FullPath = Dir1.Path + Text1.Text
        ELSE
            FullPath = Dir1.Path + "\" + Text1.Text
        END IF
        PathFlag = TRUE
        UNLOAD GetFile
    END IF
    EXIT SUB

ErrorTrap:
    BEEP
    RESUME NEXT
END SUB

SUB Command2_Click ()
    UNLOAD GetFile
END SUB

SUB Dir1_Change ()
    FillLabel1
    File1.FileName = Dir1.Path + "\" + File1.Pattern
    Drive1.Drive = Dir1.Path
    Text1.Text = File1.Pattern
    SelectFlag = DIRFLAG
END SUB

SUB Dir1_Click ()
    SelectFlag = DIRFLAG
END SUB

SUB Drive1_Change ()
    Dir1.Path = Drive1.Drive
    Text1.Text = File1.Pattern
    SelectFlag = DIRFLAG
END SUB

SUB File1_Click ()
    Text1.Text = File1.FileName
    SelectFlag = FILEFLAG
END SUB

SUB File1_DblClick ()
    IF SelectFlag = TEXTFLAG THEN
        FullPath = File1.Path + "\" + File1.FileName
    ELSE
```

(continued)

GETFILE.FRM *continued*

```
        IF RIGHT$(Dir1.Path, 1) = "\" THEN
            FullPath = Dir1.Path + Text1.Text
        ELSE
            FullPath = Dir1.Path + "\" + Text1.Text
        END IF
    END IF

    PathFlag = TRUE
    UNLOAD GetFile
END SUB

SUB FillLabel1 ()
    'Display pathname string
    Label1.Caption = Dir1.Path

    'If too long then shrink it
    IF LEN(Label1.Caption) > 30 THEN
        a$ = LEFT$(Dir1.Path, 3)
        b$ = MID$(Dir1.Path, 4)
        DO WHILE INSTR(b$, "\")
            b$ = MID$(b$, INSTR(b$, "\") + 1)
        LOOP
        Label1.Caption = a$ + "...\" + b$
    END IF
END SUB

SUB Form_Load ()
    'Center the form on the screen
    GetFile.Left = (Screen.Width - GetFile.Width) \ 2
    GetFile.Top = (Screen.Height - GetFile.Height) \ 2

    'Parse any previous pathname
    IF FullPath <> "" THEN
        Tmp$ = FullPath
        DO UNTIL RIGHT$(Tmp$, 1) = "\"
            Tmp$ = LEFT$(Tmp$, LEN(Tmp$) - 1)
        LOOP
        Tmp$ = Tmp$ + WildCard
        File1.FileName = Tmp$
        Dir1.Path = File1.Path
    END IF

    'Set up starting parameters
    File1.Pattern = WildCard
    FillLabel1
```

(continued)

GETFILE.FRM *continued*

```
    Text1.Text = File1.Pattern
    SelectFlag = DIRFLAG
    PathFlag = FALSE
END SUB

SUB Text1_Change ()
    SelectFlag = TEXTFLAG
END SUB

SUB Text1_KeyPress (KeyAscii AS INTEGER)
    'Convert to uppercase
    KeyAscii = ASC(UCASE$(CHR$(KeyAscii)))
END SUB
```

Toward the end of the GETFILE.FRM code listing is a subprogram named *FillLabel1*. This routine is not activated by an event; rather, it is called by one or more of the other subprograms. In this case, both the *Form_Load* and *Dir1_Change* subprograms call *FillLabel1*. *FillLabel1* shortens pathname strings by replacing the middle of the pathname with an ellipsis (...) if the pathname is too long to fit in Label1's text field.

The last subprogram in GETFILE.FRM, *Text1_KeyPress*, intercepts all key presses while the Text1 control has the focus. This subprogram converts lowercase characters to uppercase; you can use the same basic technique to preprocess key presses in any way an application requires.

To use the Select A File dialog box in your own projects, add the GETFILE.FRM module to the project list and add the *$INCLUDE* metacommand to the calling module to include GETFILE.BI. Make the call to *GetFile* in the subprogram *menFileSelect_Click* as shown.

Figure 5-15 shows the GETDEMO form in action. Figure 5-16 on the following page shows the GETFILE form during the selection of a file.

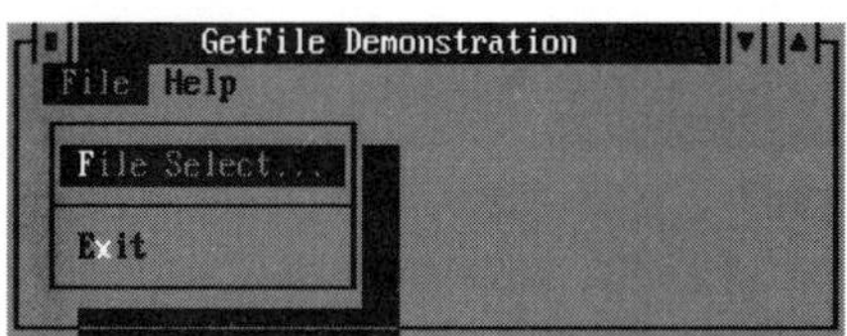

Figure 5-15.
GETDEMO.FRM in action.

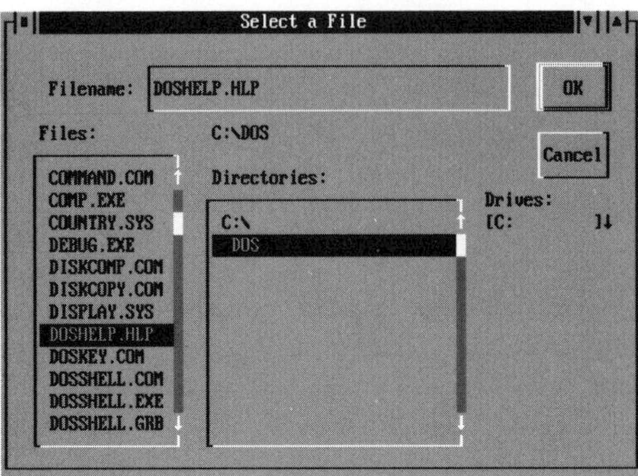

Figure 5-16.
GETFILE.FRM in action.

The SAVEDEMO Application

The SAVEDEMO application demonstrates the SAVEFILE form, which provides the user with a Save As dialog box similar to the Save As dialog box included in many Windows-based applications. This form is similar in design and appearance to GETFILE.FRM, the greatest difference being that SAVEFILE lacks a Files list box.

The files for the SAVEDEMO application are included on the companion disk. To load the files into Visual Basic for MS-DOS, choose the File Project Open command and type *C:\VBDWSHOP\SAVEDEMO.MAK*. The following figures, tables, and code give the details of the application's creation.

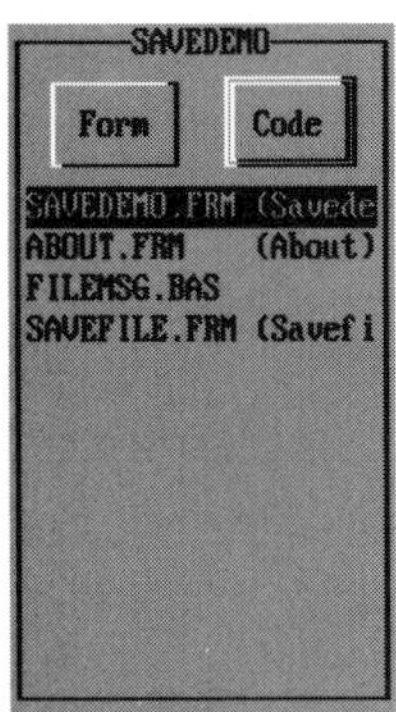

Figure 5-17.
SAVEDEMO project list.

The SAVEFILE.BI Form

Include SAVEFILE.BI in any application that loads and uses the SAVEFILE form. This include file declares two important variables in *COMMON SHARED* statements. (The *COMMON SHARED* statement allows a variable to be shared by two or more modules.) *FullPath* and *PathFlag* pass the entered filename back to the calling module so that the application can access these variables within any subprogram or function of any module that includes SAVEFILE.BI.

Source code for SAVEFILE.BI

```
'===============================================
' SAVEFILE.BI
' Include file for accessing SAVEFILE.FRM
'===============================================

'$FORM SaveFile

COMMON SHARED /comSaveFile/ FullPath AS STRING
COMMON SHARED /comSaveFile/ PathFlag AS INTEGER
```

The SAVEDEMO.FRM File

The SAVEDEMO.FRM module is the startup form that demonstrates the SAVEFILE.FRM form. Figure 5-18 shows the SAVEDEMO form during development.

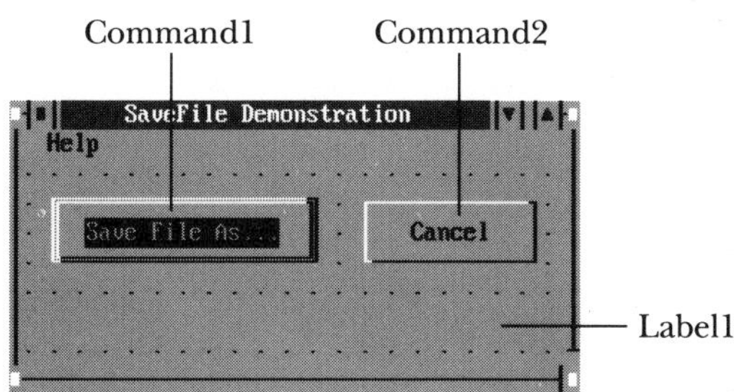

Figure 5-18.
SAVEDEMO.FRM during development.

Create the SAVEDEMO.FRM menu using the table on the following page.

SAVEDEMO.FRM Menu Design Window Entries

Caption	CtlName	Indentation
&Help	menHelp	0
&Help on SaveDemo	menHelpSaveDemo	1
&About SaveDemo...	menAboutSaveDemo	1
-	menSep	1
E&xit	menExit	1

The SAVEDEMO form contains three controls: two command buttons and a label field. The following table lists the nondefault settings for the form and control properties.

SAVEDEMO.FRM Form and Control Properties

Property	Value
Form:	
Caption	SaveFile Demonstration
FormName	Savedemo
Command1:	
Caption	Save File As...
CtlName	Command1
Default	True
Command2:	
Cancel	True
Caption	Cancel
CtlName	Command2
Label1:	
Caption	*(blank)*
CtlName	Label1

The following code completes SAVEDEMO.FRM:

Source code for SAVEDEMO.FRM

```
'================================================
' SAVEDEMO
' Demonstrates the SAVEFILE form
'================================================

'$INCLUDE: 'CONSTANT.BI'
'$INCLUDE: 'SAVEFILE.BI'
'$INCLUDE: 'ABOUT.BI'
'$INCLUDE: 'FILEMSG.BI'

SUB Command1_Click ()
    SaveFile.SHOW MODAL
    Label1.Caption = FullPath
END SUB

SUB Command2_Click ()
    UNLOAD SaveDemo
END SUB

SUB menAboutSaveDemo_Click ()
    About.Label1.Caption = "SAVEDEMO"
    About.SHOW MODAL
END SUB

SUB menExit_Click ()
    UNLOAD SaveDemo
END SUB

SUB menHelpSaveDemo_Click ()
    FileMsg "SAVEDEMO.MSG", 1
END SUB
```

The SAVEFILE.FRM FILE

SAVEFILE.FRM is the dialog box form that the SAVEDEMO application demonstrates. To use this form in another application, add the form to the application's project list and add an *$INCLUDE* metacommand to include the SAVEFILE.BI file.

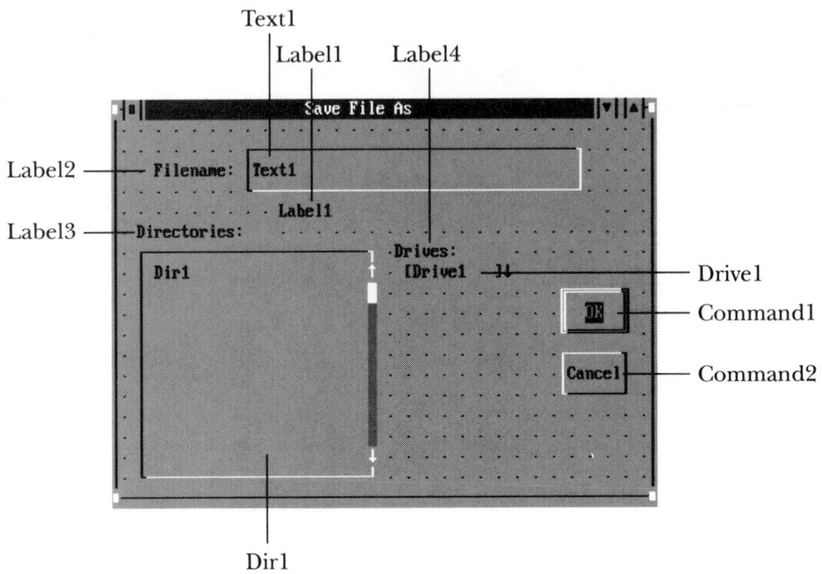

Figure 5-19.
SAVEFILE.FRM during development.

Change the settings of SAVEFILE.FRM's form and control properties to match those listed in the following table.

SAVEFILE.FRM Form and Control Properties

Property	Value
Form:	
BorderStyle	1 - Fixed Single
Caption	Save File As
FormName	Savefile
Label1:	
Caption	Label1
CtlName	Label1
Label2:	
Caption	Filename:
CtlName	Label2

(continued)

SAVEFILE.FRM Form and Control Properties *continued*

Property	Value
Label3:	
Caption	Directories:
CtlName	Label3
Label4:	
Caption	Drives:
CtlName	Label4
Text1:	
CtlName	Text1
Text	Text1
Dir1:	
CtlName	Dir1
Drive1:	
CtlName	Drive1
Command1:	
Caption	OK
CtlName	Command1
Default	True
Command2:	
Cancel	True
Caption	Cancel
CtlName	Command2

The following code completes the form. The module-level comments make it easy for you to use the SAVEFILE form in your applications.

Source code for SAVEFILE.FRM

```
'==============================================
' SAVEFILE.FRM
' Standard Save As dialog box
'==============================================
```

(continued)

SAVEFILE.FRM *continued*

```
' Notes:
' Add $INCLUDE: 'SAVEFILE.BI' to the calling module.
' Load SAVEFILE.FRM into your project.
'
' Example of use:
'     SaveFile.SHOW MODAL
'     Label1.Caption = FullPath

'$INCLUDE: 'CONSTANT.BI'
'$INCLUDE: 'SAVEFILE.BI'

CONST TEXTFLAG = 0
CONST DIRFLAG = 2

DECLARE SUB Dir1_Change ()
DECLARE SUB FillLabel1 ()

DIM SHARED SelectFlag AS INTEGER

SUB Command1_Click ()
    ON LOCAL ERROR GOTO ErrorTrap

    IF SelectFlag = DIRFLAG THEN
        Dir1.Path = Dir1.List(Dir1.ListIndex)
        Dir1_Change
        SelectFlag = TEXTFLAG
    ELSEIF INSTR(Text1.Text, "\") THEN
        Tmp$ = Text1.Text
        DO UNTIL RIGHT$(Tmp$, 1) = "\"
            Tmp$ = LEFT$(Tmp$, LEN(Tmp$) - 1)
        LOOP
        IF LEN(Tmp$) > 3 THEN
            Tmp$ = LEFT$(Tmp$, LEN(Tmp$) - 1)
        END IF
        Dir1.Path = Tmp$
        DO
            Text1.Text = MID$(Text1.Text, INSTR(Text1.Text, "\") + 1)
        LOOP WHILE INSTR(Text1.Text, "\")
    ELSE
        Tmp$ = LTRIM$(RTRIM$(Text1.Text))
        IF Tmp$ <> "" THEN
            IF RIGHT$(Dir1.Path, 1) = "\" THEN
                FullPath = Dir1.Path + Tmp$
            ELSE
                FullPath = Dir1.Path + "\" + Tmp$
            END IF
```

(continued)

SAVEFILE.FRM *continued*

```
            UNLOAD SaveFile
        ELSE
            BEEP
            Text1.SETFOCUS
        END IF
    END IF

    'All done
    EXIT SUB

ErrorTrap:
    BEEP
    RESUME NEXT
END SUB

SUB Command2_Click ()
    UNLOAD SaveFile
END SUB

SUB Dir1_Change ()
    FillLabel1
    Drive1.Drive = Dir1.Path
    SelectFlag = DIRFLAG
END SUB

SUB Dir1_Click ()
    SelectFlag = DIRFLAG
END SUB

SUB Drive1_Change ()
    ON LOCAL ERROR GOTO BadDrive

    Dir1.Path = Drive1.Drive
    SelectFlag = DIRFLAG

    EXIT SUB

BadDrive:
    BEEP
    MSGBOX "Drive not ready"
    RESUME NEXT
END SUB

SUB FillLabel1 ()
    'Display the full pathname (minus filename)
    Label1.Caption = Dir1.Path
```

(continued)

SAVEFILE.FRM *continued*

```
    'If too long, shrink the pathname string
    IF LEN(Label1.Caption) > 35 THEN

        'Extract the drive and root portion
        a$ = LEFT$(Dir1.Path, 3)

        'Extract the rest of the pathname
        b$ = MID$(Dir1.Path, 4)

        'Lop off all but the last directory
        DO WHILE INSTR(b$, "\")
            b$ = MID$(b$, INSTR(b$, "\") + 1)
        LOOP

        'Display shrunken pathname string
        Label1.Caption = a$ + "...\" + b$

    END IF
END SUB

SUB Form_Load ()
    'Center the form on the screen
    SaveFile.Left = (Screen.Width - SaveFile.Width) \ 2
    SaveFile.Top = (Screen.Height - SaveFile.Height) \ 2

    'Parse any previous pathname
    IF FullPath <> "" THEN
        Tmp$ = FullPath
        DO UNTIL RIGHT$(Tmp$, 1) = "\"
            Tmp$ = LEFT$(Tmp$, LEN(Tmp$) - 1)
        LOOP
        Dir1.Path = Tmp$
    END IF

    'Set up for text entry
    FillLabel1
    Text1.Text = ""
    SelectFlag = TEXTFLAG
END SUB

SUB Text1_Change ()
    'Detect keyboard entry of filename
    SelectFlag = TEXTFLAG
END SUB

SUB Text1_KeyPress (KeyAscii AS INTEGER)
    'Convert to uppercase
    KeyAscii = ASC(UCASE$(CHR$(KeyAscii)))
END SUB
```

Figure 5-20 shows the SAVEFILE form as executed by the SAVEDEMO program. After the user selects a valid pathname and enters a filename, the full pathname appears in the SAVEDEMO form, as shown in Figure 5-21.

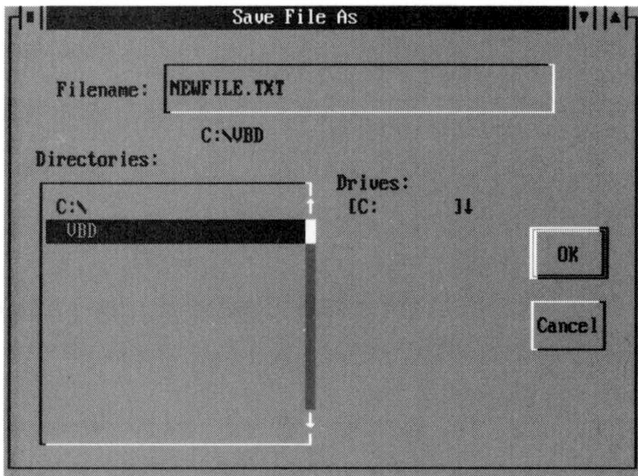

Figure 5-20.
SAVEFILE.FRM in action.

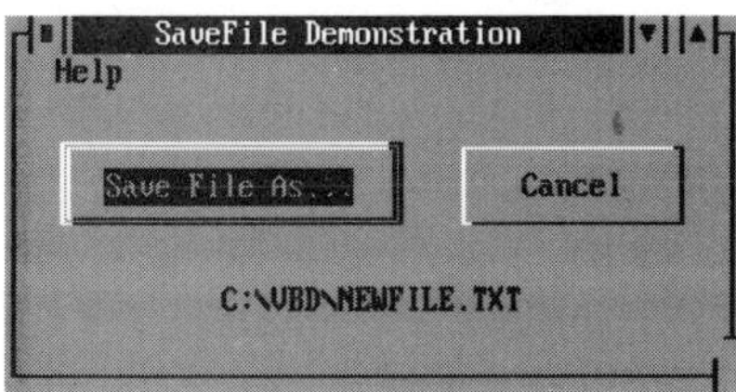

Figure 5-21.
SAVEDEMO.FRM in action.

The FILEVIEW Application

The FILEVIEW application demonstrates a useful form, FILEVIEW.FRM, that displays the contents of a text file in a scrollable window.

The application uses the GETFILE form to select a file; the pathname and filename of the file are returned in the global variable *FullPath.* FILEVIEW assigns the string contents of *FullPath* to *FullFilePath,* a string variable globally defined in FILEVIEW.BI. The application uses this string during FILEVIEW's *Form_Load* event to open the indicated file.

Notice that there are two other ways to select a file for viewing with FILEVIEW.FRM. If FILEVIEW receives a filename as a command-line argument

(*COMMAND$*), the application skips the initial display of GETFILE.FRM and immediately opens the named file for display. Also, if the global string variable *FullFilePath* contains the name of a file when FILEVIEW.FRM loads, that file displays immediately. With this feature, you can load and use the FILEVIEW form in your own projects. Simply load FILEVIEW.FRM and GETFILE.FRM into your project, add an *$INCLUDE* metacommand to include FILEVIEW.BI in the calling module, set *FullFilePath* to the name of the file to display, and use the *SHOW* method to display the FILEVIEW form.

Notice that the application is designed to display ASCII text files only. You might want to modify the application to display a warning dialog box if the user loads a file containing non-ASCII characters.

FILEVIEW reads the lines of text from the chosen file and concatenates the lines to form a single string. The application inserts carriage-return and linefeed characters at the end of each line, which causes the resulting string to display all the lines correctly. Because Visual Basic for MS-DOS string space is limited, only about the first 32 KB of large files load into the string.

You can display such a multiline string in Visual Basic for MS-DOS in several ways. After some experimentation, I found that a text box control is well suited to this task. Text boxes have the ScrollBar property, which can be used to add a horizontal or vertical scroll bar to the text box. A scroll bar lets all the interaction with the text take place automatically—that is, the text box automatically scrolls the text when the user clicks on the scroll bar. As a side benefit, the text scrolling is considerably faster than if you use the *PRINT* method to update the text yourself.

The text box in the FILEVIEW form is smaller than the form before the application runs. The *Form_Resize* subprogram, activated whenever the user resizes the FILEVIEW form, contains statements that resize the text box control. The control resizes to match the internal dimensions of the form, filling the entire window. The user can change the size of the form at any time while viewing a file, and the text box instantly resizes with the form.

FILEVIEW's *Form_Load* subprogram contains a comment that you can optionally make into a statement that sets the FILEVIEW form to cover the entire screen. To activate this statement, simply remove the single quotation mark at the start of the line. The statement sets FILEVIEW.FRM's WindowState property to *2*, or maximized.

```
'FileView.WindowState = 2
```

The files for the FILEVIEW application are included on the companion disk. To load the files into Visual Basic for MS-DOS, choose the File Open Project command and type *C:\VBDWSHOP\FILEVIEW.MAK*. This opens the project and enables you to view and modify the forms and code. The following figures, tables, and code give the details of the application's creation.

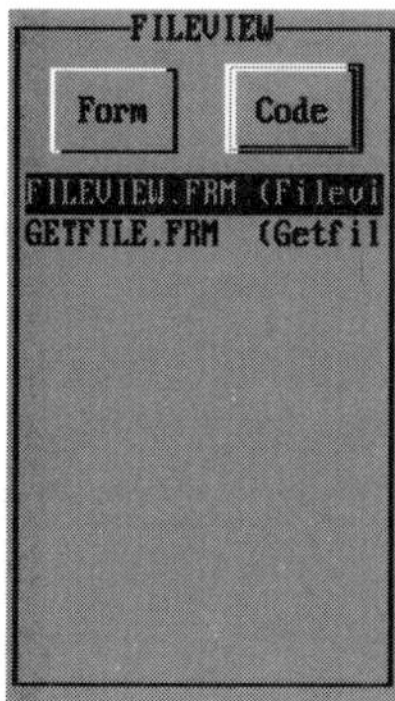

Figure 5-22.
FILEVIEW project list.

Source code for FILEVIEW.BI

```
'==================================================
' FILEVIEW.BI
' Include file for accessing FILEVIEW
'==================================================

'$FORM GetFile
'$FORM FileView

'$INCLUDE: 'GETFILE.BI'

COMMON SHARED /comFileView/ FullFilePath AS STRING
```

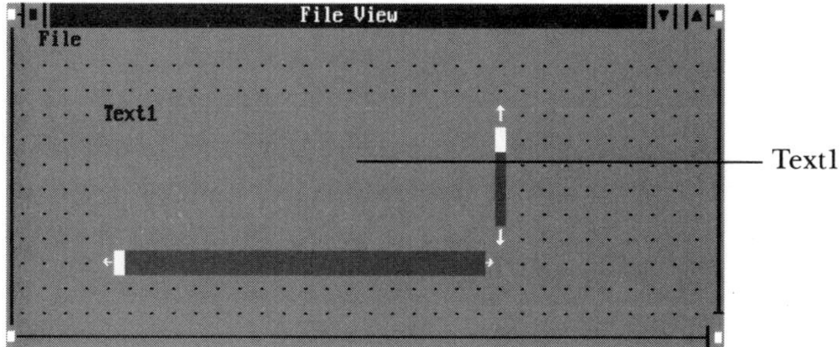

Figure 5-23.
FILEVIEW.FRM during development.

FILEVIEW.FRM Menu Design Window Entries

Caption	CtlName	Indentation
&File	menFile	0
&Select a File...	menFileSelect	1
-	menSep	1
E&xit	menExit	1

FILEVIEW.FRM Form and Control Properties

Property	Value
Form:	
Caption	File View
FormName	Fileview
Text1:	
BorderStyle	0 - None
Caption	Text1
CtlName	Text1
MultiLine	True
ScrollBars	3 - Both

Source code for FILEVIEW.FRM

```
'================================================
' FILEVIEW
' Displays a file in a scrollable window
'================================================

' Notes:
' Add $INCLUDE: 'FILEVIEW.BI' to the calling module.
' Load FILEVIEW.FRM and GETFILE.FRM into your
' project.
'
' Example of use:
'    FullFilePath = "C:\TEXT\EXAMP.TXT"
'    FileView.SHOW MODAL
```

(continued)

FILEVIEW.FRM *continued*

```
'$INCLUDE: 'CONSTANT.BI'
'$INCLUDE: 'FILEVIEW.BI'

DECLARE SUB Form_Resize ()
DECLARE SUB menSelectFile_Click ()
DECLARE SUB LoadTheFile ()

SUB Form_Load ()
    'Center the form on the screen
    FileView.Left = (Screen.Width - FileView.Width) \ 2
    FileView.Top = (Screen.Height - FileView.Height) \ 2

    'Maximize the window to start
    'FileView.WindowState = 2

    'Get the file named and view it
    IF FullFilePath <> "" THEN
        LoadTheFile
    ELSEIF COMMAND$ <> "" THEN
        FullFilePath = COMMAND$
        LoadTheFile
    ELSE
        menSelectFile_Click
    END IF
END SUB

SUB Form_Resize ()
    'Size the text box in the form window
    Text1.Top = 0
    Text1.Left = 0
    Text1.Width = ScaleWidth
    Text1.Height = ScaleHeight
END SUB

SUB Form_Unload (CANCEL AS INTEGER)
    Text1.Text = ""
    FullFilePath = ""
END SUB

SUB LoadTheFile ()
    'Prepare to load the file to be displayed
    NL$ = CHR$(13) + CHR$(10)
    T$ = SPACE$(32000)
    Ndx& = 1
```

(continued)

FILEVIEW.FRM *continued*

```
    'Try to open the file
    ON LOCAL ERROR GOTO BadFileName
    OPEN FullFilePath FOR INPUT AS #1
    ON LOCAL ERROR GOTO 0

    'Read up to 32 KB of the file
    DO UNTIL EOF(1)
       LINE INPUT #1, A$
       A$ = A$ + NL$
       IF Ndx& + LEN(A$) >= 32000 THEN
          EXIT DO
       ELSE
          MID$(T$, Ndx&, LEN(A$)) = A$
          Ndx& = Ndx& + LEN(A$)
       END IF
    LOOP

    CLOSE #1

    FileView.Caption = FullFilePath
    Text1.Text = RTRIM$(T$)

AllDone:
    IF QuitFlag = TRUE THEN
        UNLOAD FileView
    END IF
    EXIT SUB

BadFileName:
    MSGBOX "File not found"
    QuitFlag = TRUE
    RESUME AllDone
END SUB

SUB menExit_Click ()
    UNLOAD FileView
END SUB

SUB menSelectFile_Click ()
    FullPath = ""
    WildCard = "*.*"
    GetFile.SHOW MODAL
    IF PathFlag = TRUE THEN
        FullFilePath = FullPath
    END IF
    LoadTheFile
END SUB
```

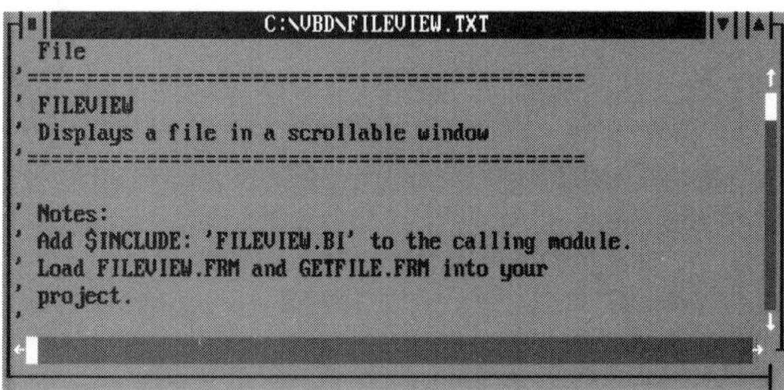

Figure 5-24.
FILEVIEW.FRM in action.

The PASSDEMO Application

The PASSDEMO application demonstrates the PASSWORD form, which prompts the user for a password. An asterisk appears as the user enters each character, preventing a casual observer from reading the password. The program communicates the entered password to the calling routine through the global string variable *Pass$*, which PASSWORD.BI declares in a *COMMON SHARED* statement.

When PASSWORD.FRM loads, the program's focus is at Command1, a button that the program moves to a position far out of view. The subprogram *Command1_KeyPress* intercepts key presses and updates two strings: *Pass$*, which saves the actual characters that the user types, and *Label1.Caption*, which displays a string of asterisks. There is one asterisk in *Label1.Caption* for each character in *Pass$*.

A timer control creates a flashing cursor in Label1. At 300-millisecond intervals, the application adds or removes a special character (ASCII value 254) from the end of *Label1.Caption*. This helps visually prompt the user to enter the password.

The files for the PASSDEMO application are included on the companion disk. To load the files into Visual Basic for MS-DOS, choose the File Open Project command and type *C:\VBDWSHOP\PASSDEMO.MAK*. This opens the project and allows you to view and modify the forms and code. The following figures, tables, and code give the details of the application's creation.

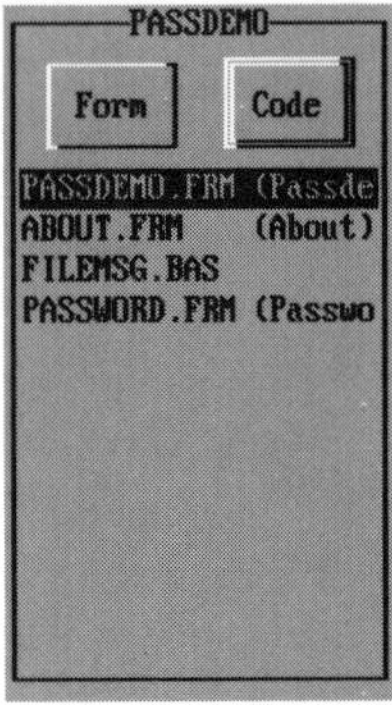

Figure 5-25.
PASSDEMO project list.

Source code for PASSWORD.BI

```
'===================================================
' PASSWORD.BI
' Include file for accessing PASSWORD.FRM
'===================================================

'$FORM Password

COMMON SHARED /comPassword/ Pass$
```

The PASSDEMO.FRM File

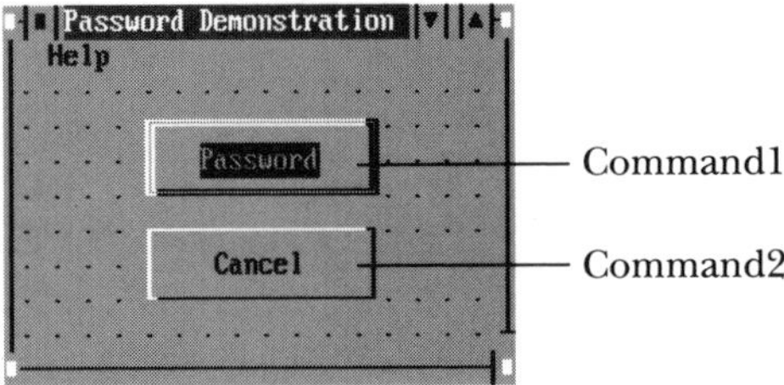

Figure 5-26.
PASSDEMO.FRM during development.

PASSDEMO.FRM Menu Design Window Entries

Caption	CtlName	Indentation
&Help	menHelp	0
&Help on PassDemo	menHelpPassDemo	1
&About PassDemo...	menAboutPassDemo	1
-	menSep	1
E&xit	menExit	1

PASSDEMO.FRM Form and Control Properties

Property	Value
Form:	
Caption	Password Demonstration
FormName	Passdemo
Command1:	
Caption	Password
CtlName	Command1
Default	True
Command2:	
Cancel	True
Caption	Cancel
CtlName	Command2

Source code for PASSDEMO.FRM

```
'================================================
' PASSDEMO
' Demonstrates the PASSWORD form
'================================================

'$INCLUDE: 'CONSTANT.BI'
'$INCLUDE: 'PASSWORD.BI'
'$INCLUDE: 'FILEMSG.BI'
'$INCLUDE: 'ABOUT.BI'
```

(continued)

PASSDEMO.FRM *continued*

```
SUB Command1_Click ()
    'Build newline character string
    NL$ = CHR$(13) + CHR$(10)

    'Get password from user
    Password.SHOW MODAL

    'Display the entered password
    MSGBOX "Password entered..." + NL$ + Pass$

    'Start over
    Pass$ = ""
END SUB

SUB Command2_Click ()
    UNLOAD PassDemo
END SUB

SUB Form_Load ()
   'Center the form on the screen
   PassDemo.Left = (Screen.Width - PassDemo.Width) \ 2
   PassDemo.Top = (Screen.Height - PassDemo.Height) \ 2
END SUB

SUB menAboutPassDemo_Click ()
    About.Label1.Caption = "PassDemo"
    About.SHOW MODAL
END SUB

SUB menExit_Click ()
    UNLOAD PassDemo
END SUB

SUB menHelpPassDemo_Click ()
    FileMsg "PASSWORD.MSG", 1
END SUB
```

The PASSWORD.FRM File

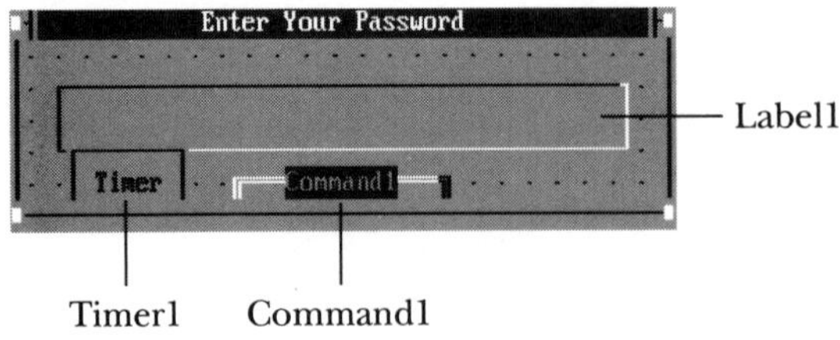

Figure 5-27.
PASSWORD.FRM during development.

PASSWORD.FRM Form and Control Properties

Property	Value
Form:	
BorderStyle	1 - Fixed Single
Caption	Enter Your Password
ControlBox	False
FormName	Password
MaxButton	False
MinButton	False
Label1:	
BorderStyle	1 - Single Line
Caption	*(blank)*
CtlName	Label1
Timer1:	
CtlName	Timer1
Interval	300
Command1:	
Caption	Command1
CtlName	Command1
Default	True

Source code for PASSWORD.FRM

```
'================================================
' PASSWORD
' Password entry dialog box
'================================================

' Notes:
' Add $INCLUDE: 'PASSWORD.BI' to the calling module.
' Load PASSWORD.FRM into your project.
'
' Example of use:
'    Password.SHOW MODAL
'    MSGBOX "Password entered..." + Pass$
```

(continued)

PASSWORD.FRM *continued*

```
'$INCLUDE: 'PASSWORD.BI'

DIM SHARED Curs$

SUB Command1_Click ()
    'Enter key pressed
    UNLOAD Password
END SUB

SUB Command1_KeyPress (KeyAscii AS INTEGER)
    STATIC Count AS INTEGER

    'Check for Backspace key press
    IF KeyAscii = 8 THEN
       IF LEN(Pass$) THEN
          Pass$ = LEFT$(Pass$, LEN(Pass$) - 1)
       END IF
    ELSE
       IF LEN(Pass$) = 0 THEN
          Pass$ = CHR$(KeyAscii)
       ELSE
          Pass$ = Pass$ + CHR$(KeyAscii)
       END IF
    END IF

    'Update the displayed asterisks
    Label1.Caption = SPACE$(7) + STRING$(LEN(Pass$), "*") + Curs$

    'Check for Spacebar press to prevent Click event
    IF KeyAscii = 32 THEN
        KeyAscii = 0
    END IF
END SUB

SUB Form_Load ()
   'Center the form on the screen
   Password.Left = (Screen.Width - Password.Width) \ 2
   Password.Top = (Screen.Height - Password.Height) \ 2

   'Move the command button out of sight
   Command1.Top = 99
END SUB

SUB Timer1_Timer ()
   'Toggle the cursor character
   IF Curs$ <> SPACE$(1) THEN
      Curs$ = SPACE$(1)
```

(continued)

PASSWORD.FRM *continued*

```
    ELSE
        Curs$ = CHR$(254)
    END IF

    'Redisplay asterisks and the cursor
    Label1.Caption = SPACE$(7) + STRING$(LEN(Pass$), "*") + Curs$
END SUB
```

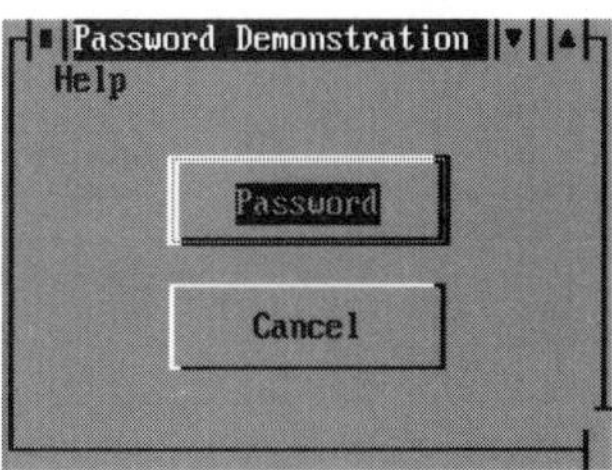

Figure 5-28.
PASSDEMO.FRM in action.

Figure 5-29.
PASSWORD.FRM in action.

The PCTBRDEM Application

The PCTBRDEM application demonstrates a useful form, PCTBAR.FRM, which informs the user of the progress of a task. You can use the PCTBAR form in any application that performs a time-consuming task in order to keep the user informed of the progress of the task. The form displays a horizontal bar that fills from left to right with solid blue, representing the percentage of the task completed.

The application continuously updates a global variable named *Percent* using a number from 0 through 100, indicating the percent-completed value. A timer event in PCTBAR.FRM reads *Percent* several times each second and updates the amount of blue displayed in the picture box on the form. When the application reaches 100 percent completion, PCTBAR unloads itself.

The PCTBRDEM application demonstrates the PCTBAR form by loading PCTBAR.FRM when the user clicks the Go button. Notice that the *SHOW* method for activating PCTBAR uses the MODELESS constant (declared by the application in CONSTANT.BI and defined at the module level), whereas most applications in this book use MODAL with the *SHOW* method. When you use MODELESS, the calling form's code continues to run while the called form is running. In this example application, if you used MODAL instead of MODELESS, the PCTBRDEM program would not update the value of *Percent*, and the blue bar would remain at the 0 percent completion point.

The numeric value of *Percent* appears at the left end of the expanding blue bar. The application truncates the value of *Percent* to an integer value and updates the blue bar only if the resulting value has changed since the last timer event.

I've used a special nongraphical technique to increase the resolution of the blue bar. The bar itself is a string of solid-blue characters (ASCII value 219) displayed as a text string in *Label1.Caption.* To effectively double the resolution of the bar, the application adds another special character (ASCII value 221) to the end of the displayed string about half of the time. This character is solid blue in only the left half of the character cell. Study the *Timer1_Timer* subprogram in PCTBAR.FRM to see how this works.

To add PCTBAR.FRM to your own applications, load PCTBAR.FRM into the application's project list, and add an *$INCLUDE* metacommand to include PCTBAR.BI in your calling program. Be sure that your calling program uses MODELESS with the *SHOW* method and that your program updates the common variable *Percent* on a regular basis.

The files for the PCTBRDEM application are included on the companion disk. To load the files into Visual Basic for MS-DOS, choose the File Open Project command and type *C:\VBDWSHOP\PCTBRDEM.MAK.* This opens the project and enables you to view and modify the forms and code. The following figures, tables, and code give the details of the application's creation.

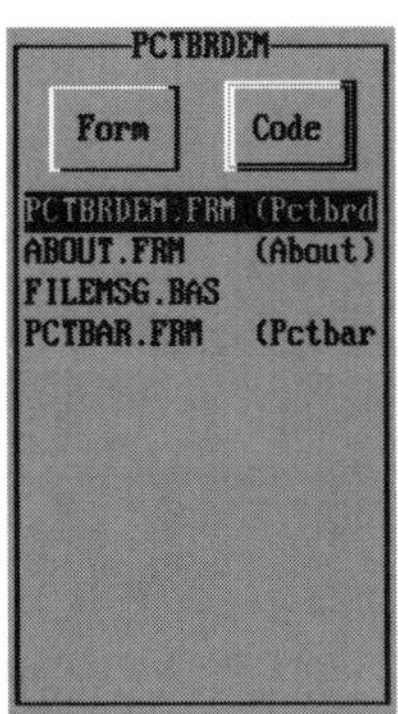

Figure 5-30.
PCTBRDEM project list.

Source code for PCTBAR.BI

```
'================================================
' PCTBAR.BI
' Include file for accessing PCTBAR.FRM
'================================================

'$FORM PctBar

COMMON SHARED /comPctBar/ Percent
```

The PCTBRDEM.FRM File

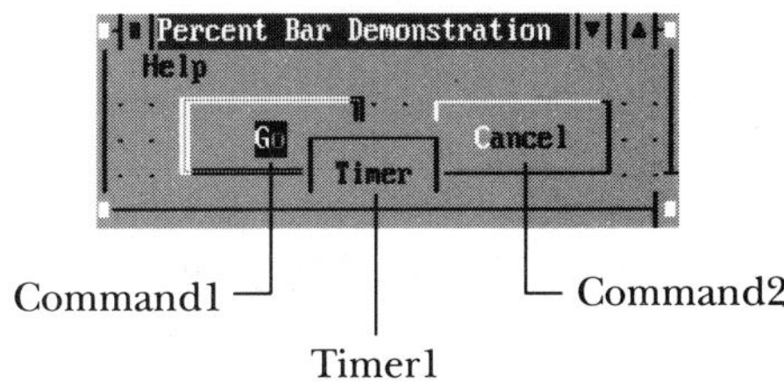

Figure 5-31.
PCTBRDEM.FRM during development.

PCTBRDEM.FRM Menu Design Window Entries

Caption	CtlName	Indentation
&Help	menHelp	0
&Help on PctBrDem	menHelpPctBrDem	1
&About PctBrDem...	menAboutPctBrDem	1
-	menSep	1
E&xit	menExit	1

PCTBRDEM.FRM Form and Control Properties

Property	Value
Form:	
Caption	Percent Bar Demonstration
FormName	Pctbrdem

(continued)

PCTBRDEM.FRM Form and Control Properties *continued*

Property	Value
Command1:	
Caption	&Go
CtlName	Command1
Default	True
Command2:	
Cancel	True
Caption	&Cancel
CtlName	Command2
Timer1:	
CtlName	Timer1

TIP

Notice that the ampersand character (&) is added to the Go and Cancel command-button captions on PCTBRDEM.FRM. I do not treat most of the command buttons in the book this way, but this seemed like a convenient place to demonstrate a useful technique. The letter following the ampersand is highlighted on the command button when the application runs. This provides a keyboard method (Alt-*X*, where *X* is the key to press) of clicking the buttons, similar to the highlighted characters in drop-down menus. Keep this technique in mind if one of your forms has many command buttons or if your users might not have a mouse.

Source code for PCTBRDEM.FRM

```
'================================================
' PCTBRDEM
' Demonstrates the PCTBAR form
'================================================

'$INCLUDE: 'CONSTANT.BI'
'$INCLUDE: 'PCTBAR.BI'
'$INCLUDE: 'FILEMSG.BI'
'$INCLUDE: 'ABOUT.BI'
```

(continued)

PCTBRDEM.FRM *continued*

```
SUB Command1_Click ()
    'Start up the PCTBAR form and come right back
    Pctbar.SHOW MODELESS

    'Simulate some process via local timer
    Timer1.Interval = 100
    Timer1.Enabled = TRUE
END SUB

SUB Command2_Click ()
    UNLOAD PctBrDem
END SUB

SUB Form_Load ()
    'Put the form in the upper left part of the screen
    PctBrDem.Left = 3
    PctBrDem.Top = 1
END SUB

SUB Form_Unload (CANCEL AS INTEGER)
    'Unload PCTBAR in case it's currently active
    UNLOAD PctBar
END SUB

SUB menAboutPctBrDem_Click ()
    About.Label1.Caption = "PCTBRDEMO"
    About.SHOW MODAL
END SUB

SUB menExit_Click ()
    UNLOAD PctBrDem
END SUB

SUB menHelpPctBrDem_Click ()
    FileMsg "PCTBAR.MSG", 1
END SUB

SUB Timer1_Timer ()
    'Pseudo time-consuming process
    IF Percent < 100 THEN
        Percent = Percent + 1
    END IF

    'Quit process when 100 percent complete
    IF Percent = 100 THEN
        Timer1.Enabled = FALSE
    END IF
END SUB
```

(continued)

The PCTBAR.FRM File

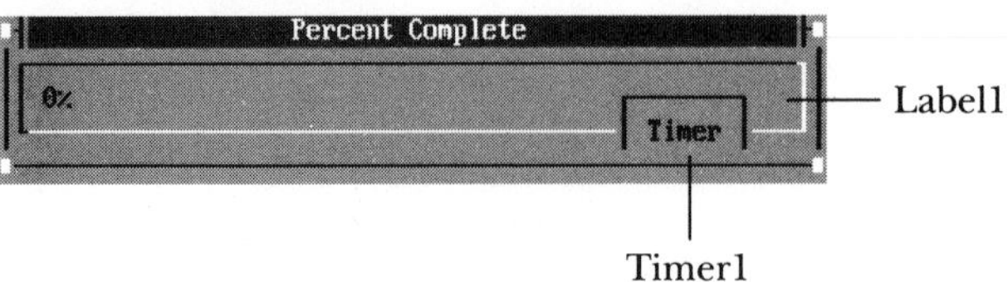

Figure 5-32.
PCTBAR.FRM during development.

PCTBAR.FRM Form and Control Properties

Property	Value
Form:	
BorderStyle	1 - Fixed Single
Caption	Percent Complete
ControlBox	False
FormName	Pctbar
MaxButton	False
MinButton	False
Label1:	
BorderStyle	1 - Single Line
Caption	0%
CtlName	Label1
ForeColor	1 - Blue
Timer1:	
CtlName	Timer1

Source code for PCTBAR.FRM

```
'================================================
' PCTBAR
' Standard Percent Finished dialog box
'================================================

' Notes:
' Add $INCLUDE: 'PCTBAR.BI' to the calling module.
' Load PCTBAR.FRM into your project.
' SHOW PctBar using MODELESS, and update common
' variable Percent on a regular basis.
' PCTBAR automatically unloads when Percent is
' greater than or equal to 100.
'
' Example of use:
'    PctBar.SHOW MODELESS
'    Percent = PctDone (progressively updated)

'$INCLUDE: 'CONSTANT.BI'
'$INCLUDE: 'PCTBAR.BI'

SUB Form_Load ()
    'Center the form on the screen
    PctBar.Left = (Screen.Width - PctBar.Width) \ 2
    PctBar.Top = (Screen.Height - PctBar.Height) \ 2

    'Start the timer
    Timer1.Interval = 100
    Timer1.Enabled = TRUE

    'Restart the percent calculation
    Percent = 0
END SUB

SUB Timer1_Timer ()
    'This value depends on the size of the label
    CONST MAXBAR = 44

    STATIC BarCount%

    'Quit when 100% is reached
    IF Percent >= 100 THEN
        UNLOAD PctBar
    END IF

    'Calculate bar size
    n% = INT(Percent / 50! * MAXBAR)
```

(continued)

PCTBAR.FRM *continued*

```
    'Redraw bar only if it's now longer
    IF n% <> BarCount% THEN

        'Percentage finished displaying
        t1$ = RIGHT$(SPACE$(2) + STR$(Percent), 3)

        'Separator characters
        t2$ = "%" + SPACE$(2)

        'Main bar
        t3$ = STRING$(n% \ 2, 219)

        'Half-character bar extension
        t4$ = STRING$(n% MOD 2, 221)

        'Display percent and bar
        Label1.Caption = t1$ + t2$ + t3$ + t4$

        'Keep track of current bar length
        BarCount% = n%

    END IF
END SUB
```

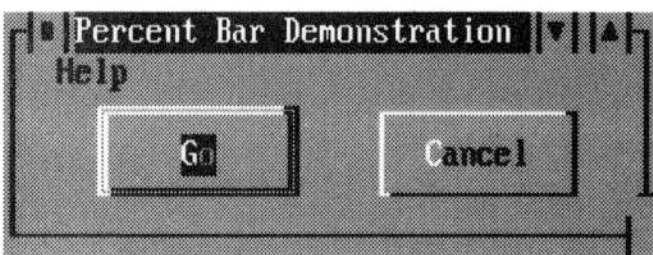

Figure 5-33.
PCTBRDEM.FRM in action.

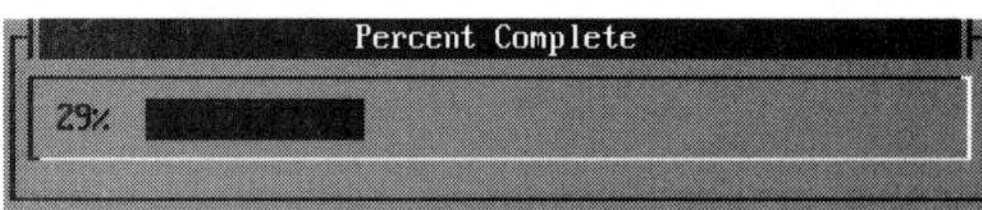

Figure 5-34.
PCTBAR.FRM in action.

The NUMDEMO Application

The NUMPAD.FRM form allows the user to enter a numeric value by using the mouse to click numbered buttons. This form also provides a good starting point for you to create your own calculator program.

Twelve of the command buttons on NUMPAD.FRM are configured as an array. The 10 digit buttons, the decimal-point button, and the change-sign buttons belong to this array; each command has an Index property that uniquely identifies that button. A click on any of these buttons activates the same subprogram, *Button_Click*, and a *SELECT CASE* statement then determines which of the 12 buttons was actually clicked. This method results in much less code than would result if each button had a unique CtlName property.

The global variable *NumPadValue* returns to the calling form the number that the user enters. After NUMPAD loads, the current value of *NumPadValue* appears. This is handy for situations in which the user is to alter or replace a given number. To always start with *0* showing, be sure to assign *0* to *NumPadValue* before NUMPAD loads.

The NUMDEMO form demonstrates the use of NUMPAD.FRM. Clicking the NumPad button activates the NUMPAD form. When the user clicks Enter, the number returned appears in a label on NUMDEMO.FRM.

The files for the NUMDEMO application are included on the companion disk. To load the files into Visual Basic for MS-DOS, choose the File Open Project command and type *C:\VBDWSHOP\NUMDEMO.MAK*. This opens the project and enables you to view and modify the forms and code. The following figures, tables, and code give the details of the application's creation.

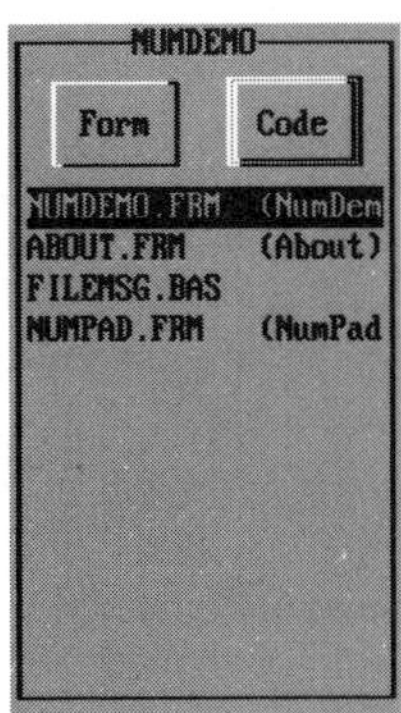

Figure 5-35.
NUMDEMO project list.

Source code for NUMPAD.BI

```
'================================================
' NUMPAD.BI
' Include file for accessing NUMPAD.FRM
'================================================

'$FORM NumPad

COMMON SHARED /comNumPad/ NumPadValue AS DOUBLE
```

The NUMDEMO.FRM File

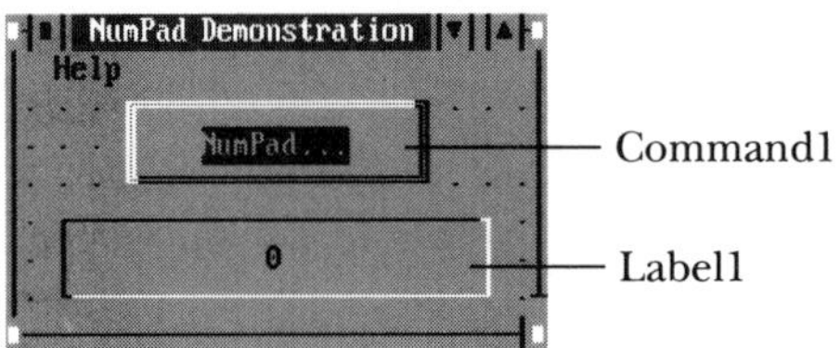

Figure 5-36.
NUMDEMO.FRM during development.

NUMDEMO.FRM Menu Design Window Entries

Caption	CtlName	Indentation
&Help	menHelpTop	0
&Help on NumPad	menHelpNumPad	1
&About NumPad...	menAboutNumPad	1
-	menSep	1
E&xit	menExit	1

NUMDEMO.FRM Form and Control Properties

Property	Value
Form:	
Caption	NumPad Demonstration
FormName	NumDemo

(continued)

NUMDEMO.FRM Form and Control Properties *continued*

Property	Value
Command1:	
Caption	NumPad...
CtlName	Command1
Default	True
Label1:	
BorderStyle	1 - Single Line
Caption	0
CtlName	Label1

Source code for NUMDEMO.FRM

```
'===============================================
' NUMDEMO
' Demonstrates the NUMPAD form
'===============================================

'$INCLUDE: 'CONSTANT.BI'
'$INCLUDE: 'NUMPAD.BI'
'$INCLUDE: 'ABOUT.BI'
'$INCLUDE: 'FILEMSG.BI'

SUB Command1_Click ()
   NumPad.SHOW MODAL
   Label1.Caption = STR$(NumPadValue)
END SUB

SUB Form_Load ()
    'Move this form to the upper left
    NumDemo.Left = 1
    NumDemo.Top = 2
END SUB

SUB menAboutNumPad_Click ()
    About.Label1.Caption = "NUMPAD"
    About.SHOW MODAL
END SUB

SUB menExit_Click ()
    UNLOAD NumDemo
END SUB
```

(continued)

NUMDEMO.FRM *continued*

```
SUB menHelpNumPad_Click ()
   FileMsg "NUMPAD.MSG", 1
END SUB
```

The NUMPAD.FRM File

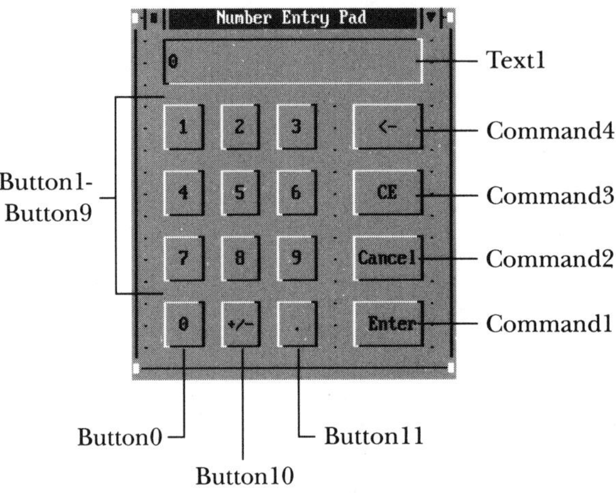

Figure 5-37.
NUMPAD.FRM during development.

NUMPAD.FRM Form and Control Properties

Property	Value
Form:	
BorderStyle	1 - Fixed Single
Caption	Number Entry Pad
FormName	NumPad
Text1:	
CtlName	Text1
Text	0

(continued)

NUMPAD.FRM Form and Control Properties *continued*

Property	Value
Command (array):	
Caption	0 *(also 1 through 9, +/–, and .)*
CtlName	Button
Index	0 *(also 1 through 11)*
Command1:	
Caption	Enter
CtlName	Command1
Command2:	
Caption	Cancel
CtlName	Command2
Command3:	
Caption	CE
CtlName	Command3
Command4:	
Caption	<–
CtlName	Command4

Source code for NUMPAD.FRM

```
'================================================
' NUMPAD
' Keypad form for number entry
'================================================

' Notes:
' Add $INCLUDE: 'NUMPAD.BI' to the calling module.
' Load NUMPAD.FRM into your project.
'
' Example of use:
'   NumPad.SHOW MODAL
'   EnteredValue = NumPadValue

'$INCLUDE: 'CONSTANT.BI'
```

(continued)

NUMPAD.FRM *continued*

```
'$INCLUDE: 'NUMPAD.BI'

DIM SHARED StartFlag%

SUB Button_Click (Index AS INTEGER)
    IF StartFlag% = TRUE THEN
        StartFlag% = FALSE
        Text1.Text = ""
    END IF

    SELECT CASE Index
    CASE 0
        T$ = Text1.Text + "0"
    CASE 1 TO 9
        T$ = STR$(VAL(Text1.Text + CHR$(48 + Index)))
    CASE 10
        IF LEFT$(Text1.Text, 1) = "-" THEN
            T$ = MID$(Text1.Text, 2)
        ELSE
            T$ = "-" + Text1.Text
        END IF
    CASE 11
        IF INSTR(Text1.Text, ".") = 0 THEN
            T$ = Text1.Text + "."
        ELSE
            T$ = Text1.Text
        END IF
    END SELECT

    Text1.Text = LTRIM$(T$)
END SUB

SUB Command1_Click ()
    NumPadValue = VAL(Text1.Text)
    UNLOAD NumPad
END SUB

SUB Command2_Click ()
    Text1.Text = LTRIM$(STR$(NumPadValue))
    StartFlag% = TRUE
END SUB

SUB Command3_Click ()
    Text1.Text = "0"
END SUB
```

(continued)

NUMPAD.FRM *continued*

```
SUB Command4_Click ()
    IF LEN(Text1.Text) > 2 THEN
        Text1.Text = LEFT$(Text1.Text, LEN(Text1.Text) - 1)
    ELSE
        Text1.Text = "0"
    END IF
END SUB

SUB Form_Load ()
    Text1.Text = LTRIM$(STR$(NumPadValue))
    StartFlag% = TRUE

    'Locate this form as desired
    NumPad.Left = 37
    NumPad.Top = 5
END SUB
```

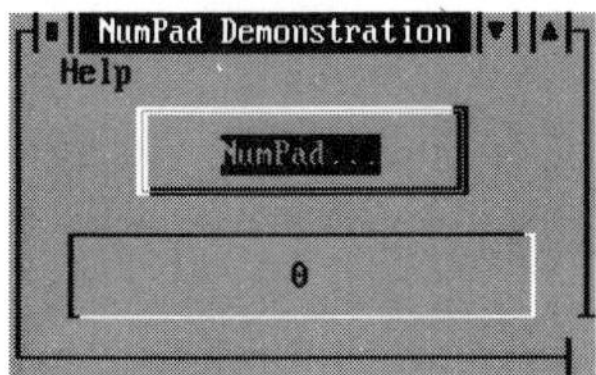

Figure 5-38.
NUMDEMO.FRM in action.

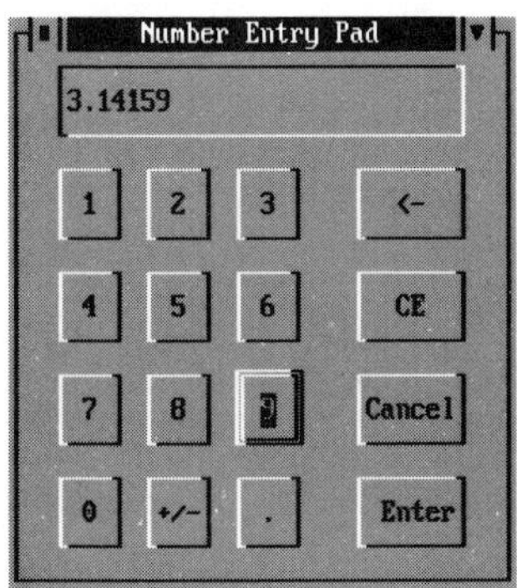

Figure 5-39.
NUMPAD.FRM in action.

The EDITDEMO Application

Although the *INPUTBOX$* function is handy for single-line user input, users often need multiline text input and editing capability. The EDITBOX form enables the user to edit text lines using techniques similar to the ones the MS-DOS Editor uses. Scroll bars allow the user to edit a lot of text, and the standard Cut, Copy, and Paste Clipboard functions are available. In fact, the EDITBOX form provides a good working example of the Clipboard.

Editing is performed using a single text box control. The ScrollBars property is set to *3 - Both* to allow horizontal and vertical scrolling through lines of text. The SelStart, SelLength, and SelText properties of the text box (to which you have access only in a form's code) provide the needed information for the application to determine where and how much to cut and copy when text is marked.

This form demonstrates a method of creating a toolbar using a row of command buttons. Although you can easily provide the same functions in a standard menu, the toolbar technique has some advantages worth exploring. With this technique, a single click on a button initiates an edit action, rather than the multiple clicks required to open a drop-down menu and select an edit action. Also, because the button captions include & characters to highlight key letters, a user without a mouse can use Alt-*X* key combinations to initiate these actions. Notice that when the user clicks the command buttons, the application immediately sets the focus on the text box control, which also cuts down on extra keystrokes.

Notice that all the lines of text actually exist in a single string variable in the Text property of the text box. The application inserts the standard newline characters *(Chr$(13) + Chr$(10))* into the string where it wants line breaks, giving the appearance of multiple strings.

To use the EDITBOX form in your own program, add the EDITBOX.FRM file to your application's project list, and add an *$INCLUDE* metacommand to include EDITBOX.BI in your calling modules. When the EDITBOX form loads, the contents of the *EditString* variables appear for editing; when the user exits the form, *EditString* contains the results of the edit.

The files for the EDITDEMO application are included on the companion disk. To load the files into Visual Basic for MS-DOS, choose the File Open Project command and type *C:\VBDWSHOP\EDITDEMO.MAK*. This opens the project and enables you to view and modify the forms and code. The following figures, tables, and code give the details of the application's creation.

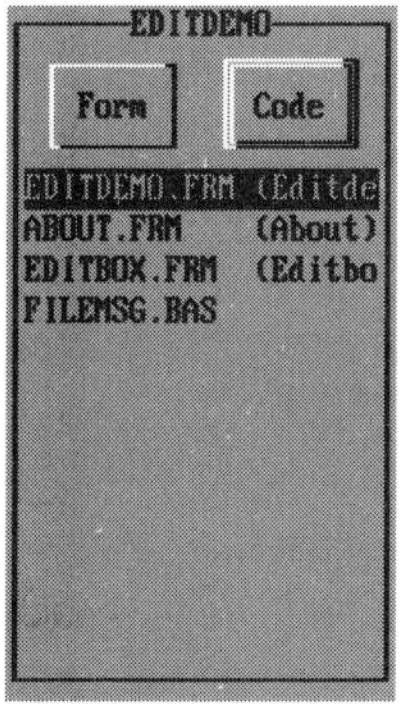

Figure 5-40.
EDITDEMO project list.

Source code for EDITBOX.BI

```
'================================================
' EDITBOX.BI
' Include file for accessing EDITBOX
'================================================

'$FORM EditBox

COMMON SHARED /comEditBox/ EditString AS STRING
```

The EDITDEMO.FRM File

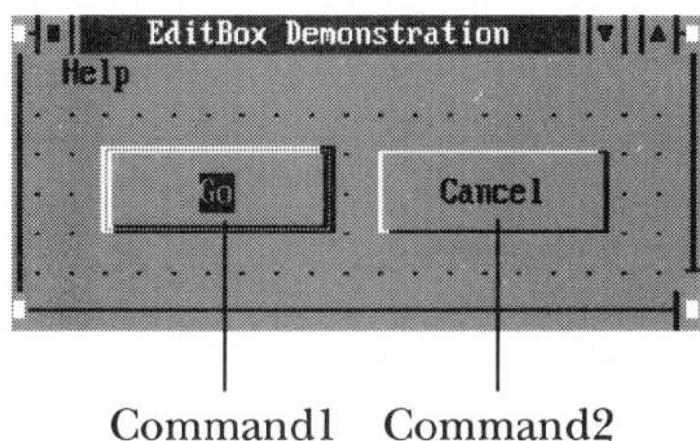

Figure 5-41.
EDITDEMO.FRM during development.

EDITDEMO.FRM Menu Design Window Entries

Caption	CtlName	Indentation
&Help	menHelp	0
&Help on EditDemo	menHelpEditDemo	1
&About EditDemo...	menAboutEditDemo	1
-	menSep	1
E&xit	menExit	1

EDITDEMO.FRM Form and Control Properties

Property	Value
Form:	
Caption	EditBox Demonstration
FormName	Editdemo
Command1:	
Caption	Go
CtlName	Command1
Default	True
Command2:	
Cancel	True
Caption	Cancel
CtlName	Command2

Source code for EDITDEMO.FRM

```
'================================================
' EDITDEMO
' Demonstrates EDITBOX.FRM
'================================================

'$INCLUDE: 'CONSTANT.BI'
'$INCLUDE: 'EDITBOX.BI'
'$INCLUDE: 'ABOUT.BI'
'$INCLUDE: 'FILEMSG.BI'
```

(continued)

EDITDEMO.FRM *continued*

```
SUB Command1_Click ()
    NL$ = CHR$(13) + CHR$(10)

    'Build the string for editing
    A$ = "This EditBox form lets you edit text" + NL$
    A$ = A$ + "using a toolbar of command buttons." + NL$
    A$ = A$ + "For this example, edit these text lines." + NL$
    A$ = A$ + NL$
    A$ = A$ + "The resulting character count will" + NL$
    A$ = A$ + "be displayed after you have finished."
    EditString = A$

    EditBox.SHOW MODAL

    IF EditString = A$ THEN
        MSGBOX "String was not changed"
    ELSE
        MSGBOX "Length of edited string: " + STR$(LEN(EditString))
    END IF
END SUB

SUB Command2_Click ()
    UNLOAD EditDemo
END SUB

SUB Form_Load ()
    'Center the form on the screen
    EditDemo.Left = (Screen.Width - EditDemo.Width) \ 2
    EditDemo.Top = (Screen.Height - EditDemo.Height) \ 2
END SUB

SUB menAboutEditDemo_Click ()
    About.Label1.Caption = "EDITDEMO"
    About.SHOW MODAL
END SUB

SUB menExit_Click ()
    UNLOAD EditDemo
END SUB

SUB menHelpEditDemo_Click ()
    FileMsg "EDITBOX.MSG", 1
END SUB
```

The EDITBOX.FRM File

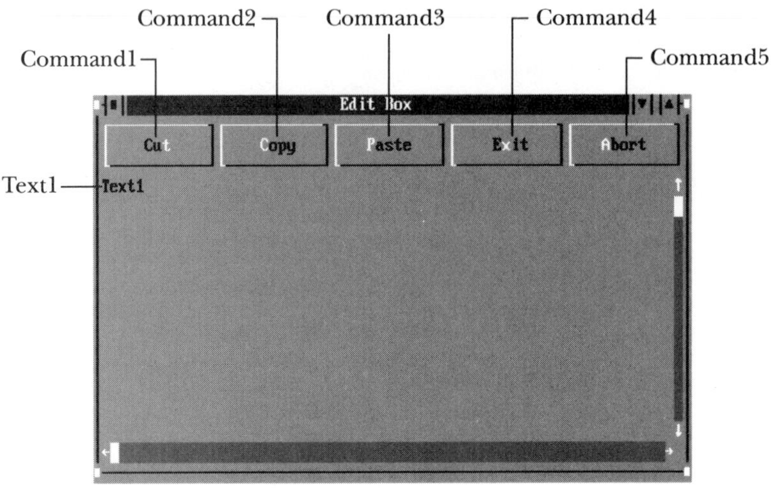

Figure 5-42.
EDITBOX.FRM during development.

EDITBOX.FRM Form and Control Properties

Property	Value
Form:	
BorderStyle	1 - Fixed Single
Caption	Edit Box
FormName	Editbox
Text1:	
BorderStyle	0 - None
CtlName	Text1
MultiLine	True
ScrollBars	3 - Both
Command1:	
Caption	Cu&t
CtlName	Command1

(continued)

EDITBOX.FRM Form and Control Properties *continued*

Property	Value
Command2:	
Caption	&Copy
CtlName	Command2
Command3:	
Caption	&Paste
CtlName	Command3
Command4:	
Caption	E&xit
CtlName	Command4
Command5:	
Caption	&Abort
CtlName	Command5

Source code for EDITBOX.FRM

```
'================================================
' EDITBOX
' Multiline text edit form
'================================================

' Notes:
' Add $INCLUDE: 'EDITBOX.BI' to the calling module.
' Load EDITBOX.FRM into your project.
'
' Example of use:
'    NL$ = CHR$(13) + CHR$(10)
'    EditString = "Text to be" + NL$ + "edited"
'    EditBox.SHOW MODAL

'$INCLUDE: 'CONSTANT.BI'
'$INCLUDE: 'EDITBOX.BI'

SUB Command1_Click ()
    'Get the working parameters
    Work$ = Text1.Text
    Wstart% = Text1.SelStart
    Wlength% = Text1.SelLength
```

(continued)

EDITBOX.FRM *continued*

```
    'Copy the cut text to the Clipboard
    Clipboard.SETTEXT MID$(Work$, Wstart% + 1, Wlength%)

    'Cut out the text
    Work$ = LEFT$(Work$, Wstart%) + MID$(Work$, Wstart% + Wlength% + 1)
    Text1.Text = Work$

    'Position edit cursor
    Text1.SelStart = Wstart%

    'Restore focus to the text
    Text1.SETFOCUS
END SUB

SUB Command2_Click ()
    'Copy the cut text to the Clipboard
    Clipboard.SETTEXT Text1.SelText

    'Restore focus to the text
    Text1.SETFOCUS
END SUB

SUB Command3_Click ()
    'Get the working parameters
    Work$ = Text1.Text
    Wstart% = Text1.SelStart
    Wlength% = Text1.SelLength

    'Cut out the text, if any, and insert Clipboard text
    Work$ = LEFT$(Work$, Wstart%) + Clipboard.GETTEXT() +
 MID$(Work$, Wstart% + Wlength% + 1)
    Text1.Text = Work$

    'Position edit cursor
    Text1.SelStart = Wstart%

    'Restore focus to the text
    Text1.SETFOCUS
END SUB

SUB Command4_Click ()
    EditString = Text1.Text
    UNLOAD EditBox
END SUB

SUB Command5_Click ()
    UNLOAD EditBox
END SUB
```

(continued)

EDITBOX.FRM *continued*

```
SUB Form_Load ()
    'Center the form on the screen
    EditBox.Left = (Screen.Width - EditBox.Width) \ 2
    EditBox.Top = (Screen.Height - EditBox.Height) \ 2

    'Display the string to be edited
    Text1.Text = EditString
END SUB
```

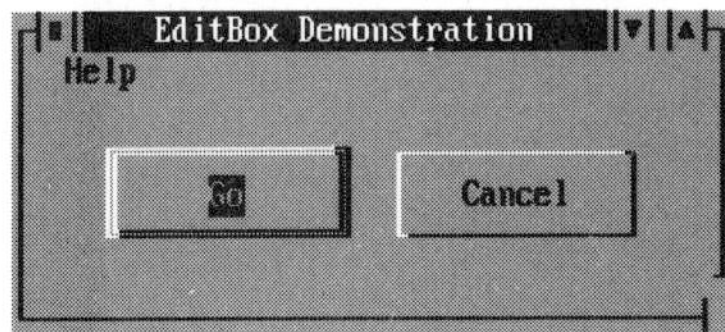

Figure 5-43.
EDITDEMO.FRM in action.

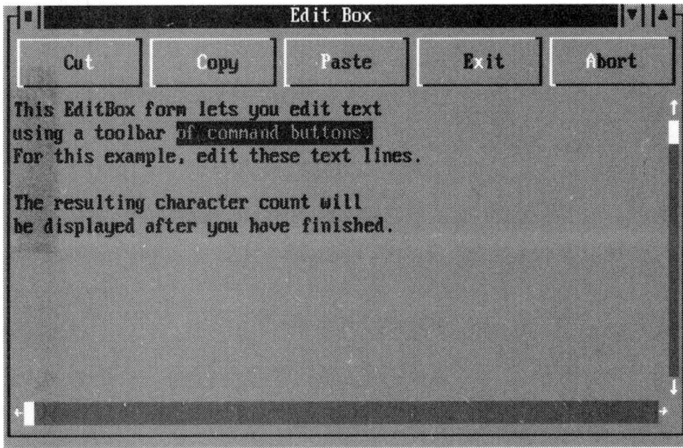

Figure 5-44.
EDITBOX.FRM in action.

The PROFDEM Application

The PROFDEM application demonstrates how to write and read private profile strings. *Profile strings* are lines of text, stored in an initialization file, that an application uses to save information about the application's state and configuration from run to run. Profile strings are an important part of Windows-based programming, but the concept is very useful for MS-DOS–based applications as well. For example, Windows saves its "changes" in WIN.INI, and Visual Basic for MS-DOS saves its information in VBDOS.INI.

The routines used by the PROFDEM application to read and write profile strings are included in the BAS module named PROFILE.BAS. See the SIDEREAL application in Chapter 8 for another example of how to use the PROFILE.BAS module.

Each profile string begins with a keyword followed by an equal sign and ends with a string associated with the keyword. The string can contain any alphanumeric information. The application groups profile strings in sections, making it easy to use the same INI file for an associated group of programs. Section names are enclosed in square brackets ([]) in the INI file.

The application passes four string parameters to the *ProfileWrite* subprogram. *IniFile$* contains the name of the INI file in which the information is to be written. *IniSection$* contains the section name, or block of profile strings, for the application to locate in the file. *IniKey$* contains the identifying name of the profile string, the part to the left of the equal sign in the file. *ProfileStr$* contains the data portion of the profile string, which is the part to the right of the equal sign.

When the application calls *ProfileWrite,* the INI file is created if the file doesn't already exist. Likewise, the application adds the section and key strings to the file if they don't already exist. This makes it easy to create or update INI files.

The application passes the *ProfileRead$* function the same first three parameters as are passed to the *ProfileWrite* subprogram, but *ProfileRead$* returns the *ProfileStr$* that the function reads from the INI file. If *ProfileRead$* does not find *ProfileStr$,* the function returns a null string.

Applications can use the profile-string technique that this program demonstrates to store user-selected settings for properties, such as colors, sizes, locations, and so on. Other possible uses include the storing of passwords, the logging of elapsed time, or the logging of the number of times that an application runs.

To use these routines in your own program, load PROFILE.BAS into your project list, and be sure to add an *$INCLUDE* metacommand to the calling modules to include the PROFILE.BI file. For convenience, at the module level, PROFILE.BAS includes notes to remind you of these steps.

The files for the PROFDEM application are included on the companion disk. To load these files into Visual Basic for MS-DOS, choose the File Open Project command and type *C:\VBDWSHOP\PROFDEM.MAK.* This opens the project and enables you to view and modify the forms and code. The following figures, tables, and code give the details of the application's creation.

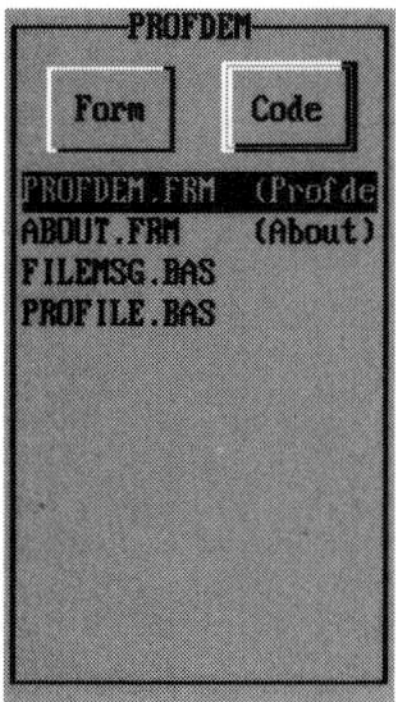

Figure 5-45.
PROFDEM project list.

Source code for PROFILE.BI

```
'=====================================================
' PROFILE.BI
' Include file for accessing PROFILE.BAS
'=====================================================

DECLARE FUNCTION ProfileRead$ (IniFile$, IniSection$, IniKey$)
DECLARE SUB ProfileWrite (IniFile$, IniSection$, IniKey$,
 ProfileStr$)
```

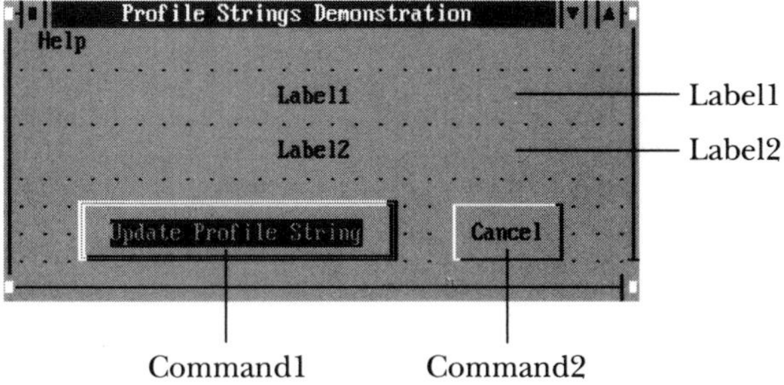

Figure 5-46.
PROFDEM.FRM during development.

PROFDEM.FRM Menu Design Window Entries

Caption	CtlName	Indentation
&Help	menHelp	0
&Help on ProfDem	menHelpProfDem	1
&About ProfDem...	menAboutProfDem	1
-	menSep	1
E&xit	menExit	1

PROFDEM.FRM Form and Control Properties

Property	Value
Form:	
Caption	Profile Strings Demonstration
FormName	Profdem
Label1:	
Alignment	2 - Center
Caption	Label1
CtlName	Label1
Label2:	
Alignment	2 - Center
Caption	Label2
CtlName	Label2
Command1:	
Caption	Update Profile String
CtlName	Command1
Default	True
Command2:	
Cancel	True
Caption	Cancel
CtlName	Command2

Source code for PROFDEM.FRM

```
'================================================
' PROFDEM
' Demonstrates PROFILE.BAS to write and read
' profile strings
'================================================

'$INCLUDE: 'CONSTANT.BI'
'$INCLUDE: 'ABOUT.BI'
'$INCLUDE: 'FILEMSG.BI'
'$INCLUDE: 'PROFILE.BI'

SUB Command1_Click ()
    IniFile$ = "PROFILE.INI"
    IniSection$ = "profile"
    IniKey$ = "Lastrun"

    Last$ = ProfileRead(IniFile$, IniSection$, IniKey$)

    ProfileStr$ = DATE$ + SPACE$(1) + TIME$
    ProfileWrite IniFile$, IniSection$, IniKey$, ProfileStr$

    Label1.Caption = "Date and time last run: " + Last$
    Label2.Caption = "Current date and time:  " + ProfileStr$
END SUB

SUB Command2_Click ()
    UNLOAD ProfDem
END SUB

SUB Form_Load ()
    'Center the form on the screen
    ProfDem.Left = (Screen.Width - ProfDem.Width) \ 2
    ProfDem.Top = (Screen.Height - ProfDem.Height) \ 2

    'Erase the two labels
    Label1.Caption = ""
    Label2.Caption = ""
END SUB

SUB menAboutProfile_Click ()
    About.Label1.Caption = "PROFDEM"
    About.SHOW MODAL
END SUB
```

(continued)

PROFDEM.FRM *continued*

```
SUB menExit_Click ()
    UNLOAD ProfDem
END SUB

SUB menHelpProfile_Click ()
    FileMsg "PROFILE.MSG", 1
END SUB
```

Source code for PROFILE.BAS

```
'=====================================================
' PROFILE.BAS
' Routines to write and read profile strings
'=====================================================

' Notes:
' Add $INCLUDE: 'PROFILE.BI' to the calling module.
' Load PROFILE.BAS into your project list.
'
' Example of use:
'    Last$ = ProfileRead(IniFile$, IniSection$, IniKey$)
'    ProfileWrite IniFile$, IniSection$, IniKey$, ProfileStr$

'$INCLUDE: 'CONSTANT.BI'
'$INCLUDE: 'PROFILE.BI'

FUNCTION ProfileRead$ (IniFile$, IniSection$, IniKey$)
    TmpSection$ = "[" + IniSection$ + "]"
    ON LOCAL ERROR GOTO BadIniReadFile
    FileNum% = FREEFILE
    OPEN IniFile$ FOR INPUT AS #FileNum%
    DO UNTIL EOF(FileNum%)
        LINE INPUT #FileNum%, A$
        IF LEFT$(A$, 1) = "[" THEN
            IF INSTR(A$, TmpSection$) = 1 THEN
                SectionFlag% = TRUE
            ELSE
                SectionFlag% = FALSE
            END IF
        END IF
        IF SectionFlag% = TRUE THEN
            IF INSTR(A$, IniKey$) = 1 THEN
                A$ = MID$(A$, INSTR(A$, "=") + 1)
                ProfileRead$ = LTRIM$(RTRIM$(A$))
```

(continued)

PROFILE.BAS *continued*

```
                EXIT DO
            END IF
        END IF
    LOOP

AllDoneRead:
    CLOSE #FileNum%
    EXIT FUNCTION

BadIniReadFile:
    RESUME AllDoneRead
END FUNCTION

SUB ProfileWrite (IniFile$, IniSection$, IniKey$, ProfileStr$)
    REDIM P$(1)

    TmpSection$ = "[" + IniSection$ + "]"
    FileNum% = FREEFILE

    ON LOCAL ERROR GOTO NoIniWriteFile
    OPEN IniFile$ FOR INPUT AS #FileNum%
    DO UNTIL EOF(FileNum%)
        n% = n% + 1
        REDIM PRESERVE P$(n%)
        LINE INPUT #FileNum%, P$(n%)
    LOOP
    CLOSE #FileNum%

AddToIniFile:
    ON LOCAL ERROR GOTO BadIniWriteFile
    FOR i% = 1 TO n%
        IF LEFT$(P$(i%), 1) = "[" THEN
            IF INSTR(P$(i%), TmpSection$) = 1 THEN
                SectionFlag% = TRUE
                SectionFound% = i%
            ELSE
                SectionFlag% = FALSE
            END IF
        END IF
        IF SectionFlag% = TRUE THEN
            IF INSTR(P$(i%), IniKey$) = 1 THEN
                P$(i%) = IniKey$ + "=" + ProfileStr$
                KeyFound% = TRUE%
                EXIT FOR
            END IF
        END IF
    NEXT i%
```

(continued)

PROFILE.BAS *continued*

```
    IF SectionFound% = FALSE THEN
        REDIM PRESERVE P$(n% + 3)
        P$(n% + 2) = "[" + IniSection$ + "]"
        P$(n% + 3) = IniKey$ + "=" + ProfileStr$
        n% = n% + 3
    ELSEIF KeyFound% = FALSE THEN
        NewLine% = SectionFound% + 1
        REDIM PRESERVE P$(n% + 1)
        FOR i% = n% TO NewLine% STEP -1
            P$(i% + 1) = P$(i%)
        NEXT i%
        P$(NewLine%) = IniKey$ + "=" + ProfileStr$
        n% = n% + 1
    END IF

    OPEN IniFile$ FOR OUTPUT AS #FileNum%
    FOR i% = 1 TO n%
        PRINT #FileNum%, P$(i%)
    NEXT i%
    CLOSE #FileNum%

AllDoneWrite:
    CLOSE #FileNum%
    EXIT SUB

NoIniWriteFile:
    OPEN IniFile$ FOR OUTPUT AS #FileNum%
    PRINT #FileNum%, SPACE$(1)
    CLOSE #FileNum%
    RESUME AddToIniFile

BadIniWriteFile:
    RESUME AllDoneWrite
END SUB
```

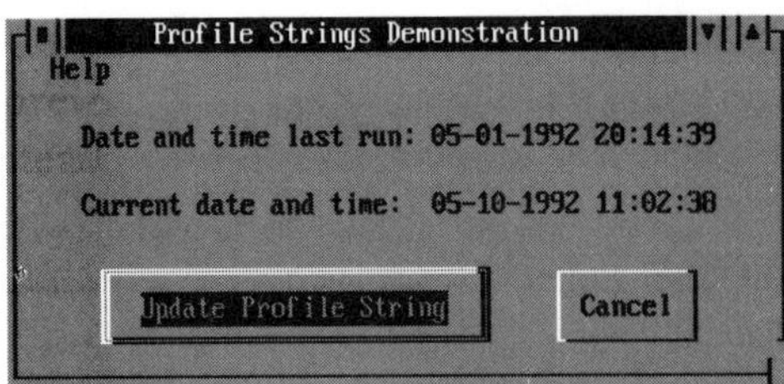

Figure 5-47.
PROFDEM.FRM in action.

CHAPTER SIX

APPLICATIONS FOR EXPLORING CONTROLS

The applications in this chapter demonstrate a variety of controls that you can create on forms. My goal is to provide you with interactive applications for each type of control with which you can experiment. These applications provide a solid means for you to develop an understanding of the behavior and use of these controls.

Each of the applications in this chapter includes the FILEMSG.BAS and ABOUT.FRM modules as part of the project file. The FILEMSG.BAS module displays online Help, and the ABOUT module displays an About dialog box when you select About from the Help menu. See Chapter 5 for the details of these modules.

The CHECKDEM Application

The CHECKDEM application demonstrates check box controls. At the bottom of the form is a check box labeled *TEST CHECK BOX*. The properties of this check box change as you click on the various check box selections above it. For example, click on Visible, and the Test check box disappears. (Click again on Visible to toggle the Test check box back to Visible.)

The application demonstrates two typical MousePointer settings, although several more settings are possible. See "The MOUSEPNT Application" in Chapter 7 for a demonstration of all the available mouse pointers. To see the mouse pointer you've selected, move the mouse pointer over the Test check box. The mouse pointer changes to the type you've selected, but only while it's over the Test check box.

The files for the CHECKDEM application are included on the companion disk. To load the files into Visual Basic for MS-DOS, choose the File Open Project command and type *C:\VBDWSHOP\CHECKDEM.MAK*. This opens the project and enables you to view and modify the forms and code. The following figures, tables, and code give the details of the application's creation.

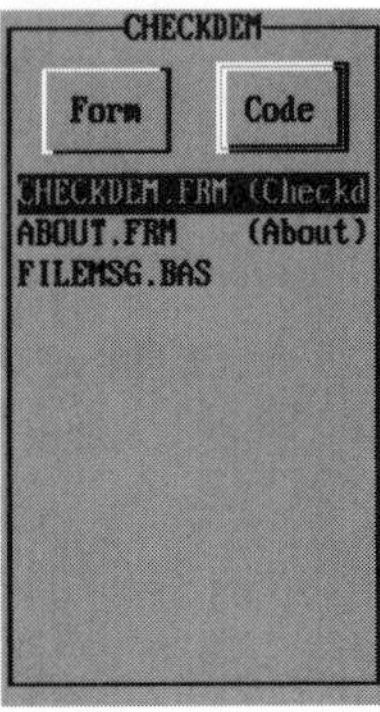

Figure 6-1.
CHECKDEM project list.

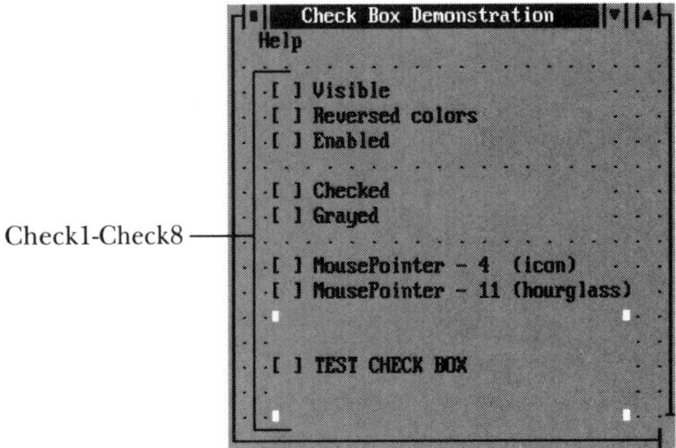

Figure 6-2.
CHECKDEM.FRM during development.

CHECKDEM.FRM Menu Design Window Entries

Caption	CtlName	Indentation
&Help	menHelp	0
&Help on CheckDem	menHelpCheckDem	1
&About CheckDem...	menAboutCheckDem	1
-	menSep	1
E&xit	menExit	1

CHECKDEM.FRM Form and Control Properties

Property	Value
Form:	
Caption	Check Box Demonstration
FormName	Checkdem
Check1:	
Caption	Visible
CtlName	Check1
Check2:	
Caption	Reversed colors
CtlName	Check2
Check3:	
Caption	Enabled
CtlName	Check3
Check4:	
Caption	Checked
CtlName	Check4
Check5:	
Caption	Grayed
CtlName	Check5
Check6:	
Caption	MousePointer - 4 (icon)
CtlName	Check6
Check7:	
Caption	MousePointer - 11 (hourglass)
CtlName	Check7
Check8:	
Caption	TEST CHECK BOX
CtlName	Check8
Height	5

Source code for CHECKDEM.FRM

```
'==================================================
' CHECKDEM
' Demonstrates check box controls
'==================================================

'$INCLUDE: 'CONSTANT.BI'
'$INCLUDE: 'FILEMSG.BI'
'$INCLUDE: 'ABOUT.BI'

SUB Check1_Click ()
    IF Check1.Value = CHECKED THEN
        Check8.Visible = TRUE
    ELSE
        Check8.Visible = FALSE
    END IF
END SUB

SUB Check2_Click ()
    IF Check2.Value = CHECKED THEN
        Check8.ForeColor = WHITE
        Check8.BackColor = BLACK
    ELSE
        Check8.ForeColor = BLACK
        Check8.BackColor = WHITE
    END IF
END SUB

SUB Check3_Click ()
    IF Check3.Value = CHECKED THEN
        Check8.Enabled = TRUE
    ELSE
        Check8.Enabled = FALSE
    END IF
END SUB

SUB Check4_Click ()
    IF Check4.Value = CHECKED THEN
        Check5.Value = UNCHECKED
        Check8.Value = CHECKED
    ELSE
        Check8.Value = UNCHECKED
    END IF
END SUB
```

(continued)

CHECKDEM.FRM *continued*

```
SUB Check5_Click ()
    IF Check5.Value = CHECKED THEN
        Check4.Value = UNCHECKED
        Check8.Value = GRAYED
    ELSE
        Check8.Value = UNCHECKED
    END IF
END SUB

SUB Check6_Click ()
    IF Check6.Value = CHECKED THEN
        Check7.Value = UNCHECKED
        Check8.MousePointer = ICON
    ELSE
        Check8.MousePointer = DEFAULT
    END IF
END SUB

SUB Check7_Click ()
    IF Check7.Value = CHECKED THEN
        Check6.Value = UNCHECKED
        Check8.MousePointer = HOURGLASS
    ELSE
        Check8.MousePointer = DEFAULT
    END IF
END SUB

SUB Check8_Click ()
    IF Check8.Value = CHECKED THEN
        Check4.Value = CHECKED
    ELSE
        Check4.Value = UNCHECKED
    END IF
END SUB

SUB Form_Load ()
    Check1.Value = CHECKED
    Check3.Value = CHECKED
END SUB

SUB menAboutCheckDem_Click ()
    About.Label1.Caption = "CHECKDEM"
    About.SHOW MODAL
END SUB
```

(continued)

CHECKDEM.FRM *continued*

```
SUB menExit_Click ()
    UNLOAD CheckDem
END SUB

SUB menHelpCheckDem_Click ()
    FileMsg "CHECKDEM.MSG", 1
END SUB
```

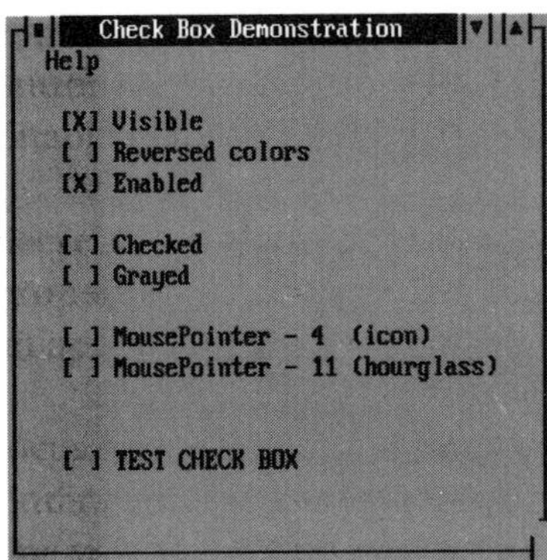

Figure 6-3.
CHECKDEM.FRM in action.

The COMBODEM Application

The COMBODEM application demonstrates combo box controls. COMBODEM presents three combo boxes, each of which has a different Style property. As a result, you can easily discover the differences among the different styles of combo boxes.

The first combo box is Style 0, or Dropdown Combo. This combo box has a downward-pointing arrow to the right of the combo box. The user clicks on this arrow to drop down a list of selectable items. The user can also type any string directly into the entry field at the top of the list next to the arrow, even if the string is not on the drop-down list.

The second combo box is Style 1, or Simple Combo. With this style, the drop-down list is always visible, and no downward-pointing arrow is shown to the right of the control. As with the Style 0 combo box, the user can select any item from the list or type a new string in the entry field at the top of the combo box.

The third combo box is Combo3, or Dropdown List. This combo box prevents the user from typing a new string at the top of the combo box; instead, the user must select a string from the drop-down list.

I have used the same list of numbers to initialize each of the three combo boxes. See Figure 6-6. The Sorted property of the third combo box is set to *True*, whereas the other two combo boxes remain set to *False* (so that the application does not sort them). Notice that the list of items in the third drop-down list is sorted into alphabetic order.

At the bottom of the window are two check boxes. These check boxes let you toggle the Enabled and Visible properties of all three combo boxes so that you can see how these properties affect the behavior of the combo boxes.

The files for the COMBODEM application are included on the companion disk. To load the files into Visual Basic for MS-DOS, choose the File Open Project command and type *C:\VBDWSHOP\COMBODEM.MAK*. This opens the project and enables you to view and modify the forms and code. The following figures, tables, and code give the details of the application's creation.

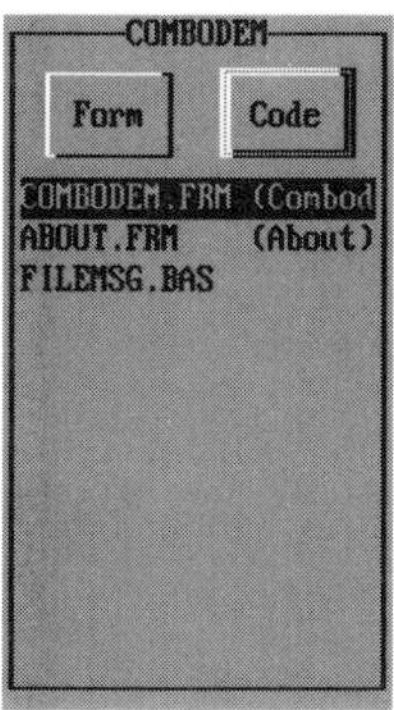

Figure 6-4.
COMBODEM project list.

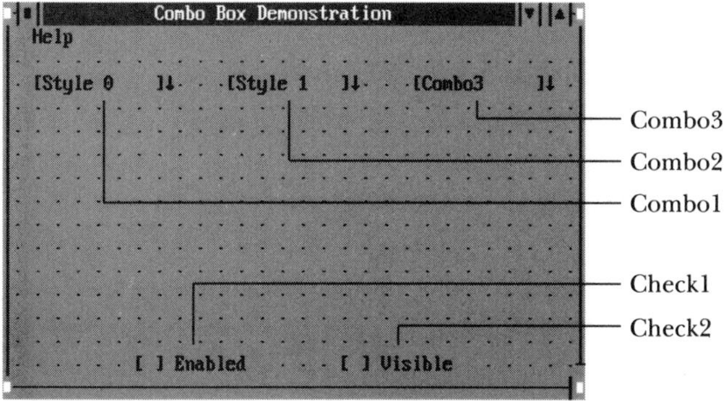

Figure 6-5.
COMBODEM.FRM during development.

COMBODEM.FRM Menu Design Window Entries

Caption	CtlName	Indentation
&Help	menHelp	0
&Help on ComboDem	menHelpComboDem	1
&About ComboDem...	menAboutComboDem	1
-	menSep	1
E&xit	menExit	1

COMBODEM.FRM Form and Control Properties

Property	Value
Form:	
Caption	Combo Box Demonstration
FormName	Combodem
Combo1:	
CtlName	Combo1
Style	0 - Dropdown Combo
Text	Style 0
Combo2:	
CtlName	Combo2
Style	1 - Simple Combo
Text	Style 1
Combo3:	
CtlName	Combo3
Style	2 - Dropdown List
Text	Combo3
Sorted	True
Check1:	
CtlName	Check1
Text	Enabled

(continued)

COMBODEM.FRM Form and Control Properties *continued*

Property	Value
Check2:	
CtlName	Check2
Text	Visible

Source code for COMBODEM.FRM

```
'===================================================
' COMBODEM
' Demonstrates combo box controls
'===================================================

'$INCLUDE: 'CONSTANT.BI'
'$INCLUDE: 'FILEMSG.BI'
'$INCLUDE: 'ABOUT.BI'

SUB Check1_Click ()
    'Enabled check box was clicked
    IF Check1.Value = CHECKED THEN
        Combo1.Enabled = TRUE
        Combo2.Enabled = TRUE
        Combo3.Enabled = TRUE
    ELSE
        Combo1.Enabled = FALSE
        Combo2.Enabled = FALSE
        Combo3.Enabled = FALSE
    END IF
END SUB

SUB Check2_Click ()
    'Visible check box was clicked
    IF Check2.Value = CHECKED THEN
        Combo1.Visible = TRUE
        Combo2.Visible = TRUE
        Combo3.Visible = TRUE

    ELSE
        Combo1.Visible = FALSE
        Combo2.Visible = FALSE
        Combo3.Visible = FALSE
    END IF
END SUB
```

(continued)

COMBODEM.FRM *continued*

```
SUB Form_Load ()
    'Fill all three combo boxes
    FOR i% = 1 TO 10
        SELECT CASE i%
        CASE 1
            a$ = "One"
        CASE 2
            a$ = "Two"
        CASE 3
            a$ = "Three"
        CASE 4
            a$ = "Four"
        CASE 5
            a$ = "Five"
        CASE 6
            a$ = "Six"
        CASE 7
            a$ = "Seven"
        CASE 8
            a$ = "Eight"
        CASE 9
            a$ = "Nine"
        CASE 10
            a$ = "Ten"
        END SELECT
        Combo1.ADDITEM a$
        Combo2.ADDITEM a$
        Combo3.ADDITEM a$
    NEXT i%

    'Set the check boxes to checked
    Check1.Value = CHECKED
    Check2.Value = CHECKED
END SUB

SUB menAboutComboDem_Click ()
    About.Label1.Caption = "COMBODEM"
    About.SHOW MODAL
END SUB

SUB menExit_Click ()
    UNLOAD ComboDem
END SUB

SUB menHelpComboDem_Click ()
    FileMsg "COMBODEM.MSG", 1
END SUB
```

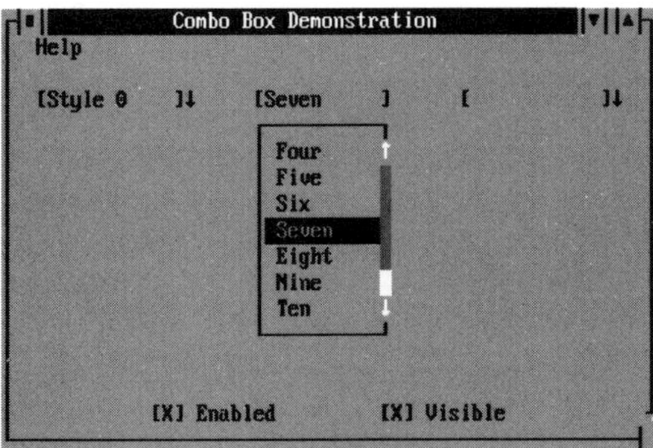

Figure 6-6.
COMBODEM.FRM in action.

The COMMAND Application

The COMMAND application lets you experiment with command buttons. The application presents 16 command buttons, each of which demonstrates one or more of the properties that you can control. As the user experiments by clicking the various command buttons, informative messages appear at the top of the form.

The first three buttons demonstrate how each button's appearance depends on the button's Height property. Button 1's Height is *1*, button 2's Height is *2*, and button 3's Height is *3*. Most of the command buttons you create will have a Height of *3* or greater, as do most of the buttons in this application. In certain circumstances, such as when many buttons must appear within a limited amount of space, you can set the command buttons' Height properties to *1* or *2*.

The large MousePointer command button demonstrates how the MousePointer property of a command button allows you to change the appearance of the mouse pointer as the user moves the pointer across the face of the button. The user can click this button to cycle through the various types of mouse pointers available.

The BackColor and ForeColor buttons cycle through the available color settings. You can set the BackColor property individually for each command button. ForeColor is not a property of each button; rather, you must set ForeColor globally in the Screen.ControlPanel object. As the user cycles through the ForeColor settings, all the buttons are affected. See "The CTRLPANL Application" in Chapter 7 for more information about the available Screen.ControlPanel properties.

The Drag button demonstrates the drag-and-drop operation. The DragMode property of this command button is set to *1 - Automatic.* The user drags this button across the face of either of the Drag Target buttons at the bottom of the form. As the user drags over each of the Drag Target buttons, the associated *DragOver* subprogram starts for that target button. With each DragOver event, these subprograms update the message at the top of the form to let the user know where on the Drag Target button the dragging is currently taking place. When the user releases the mouse button (while the Drag button is over a Drag Target button), a DragDrop event occurs, and the associated *DragDrop* event-driven subprogram starts. A message describing this event appears at the top of the form too. Several other types of controls have drag-and-drop capabilities similar to those demonstrated here.

When the user clicks the Visible command button, the button disappears. To recover the button, the user clicks the Reset button immediately to the right of the Visible button. Similarly, when the user clicks the Enabled command button, it becomes disabled, and the user must click its Reset button, immediately to the right of the Enabled button, to re-enable the Enabled button.

Each time the user clicks the Moveable button, its Left property is decremented, causing the button to slide to the left. Using the Left and Top properties in this way, you can rearrange command buttons on a form while an application runs.

The Default button has its Default property set to *True.* The application's focus sets to this button when the program starts, and the user's pressing the Enter key will, by default, click this button. This technique, incidentally, is the one you will use to set the OK command buttons in many dialog boxes.

The Cancel button is similar to the Default button. The Cancel button's Cancel property is set to *True,* which causes this button to be clicked when the user presses the Esc key. In this case, the application's focus doesn't have to be on the Cancel button when the user presses Esc.

The files for the COMMAND application are included on the companion disk. To load the files into Visual Basic for MS-DOS, choose the File Open Project command and type *C:\VBDWSHOP\COMMAND.MAK.* This opens the project and enables you to view and modify the forms and code. The following figures, tables, and code give the details of the application's creation.

Figure 6-7.
COMMAND project list.

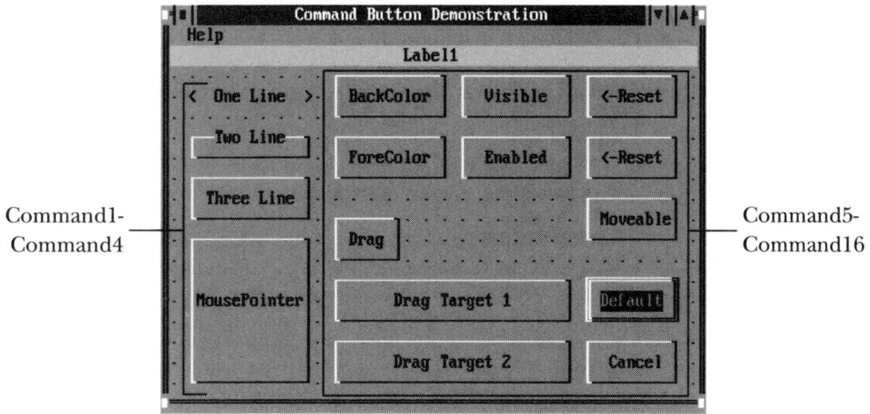

Figure 6-8.
COMMAND.FRM during development.

COMMAND.FRM Menu Design Window Entries

Caption	CtlName	Indentation
&Help	menHelp	0
&Help on Command	menHelpCommand	1
&About Command...	menAboutCommand	1
-	menSep	1
E&xit	menExit	1

COMMAND.FRM Form and Control Properties

Property	Value
Form:	
BorderStyle	3 - Fixed Double
Caption	Command Button Demonstration
FormName	Command
Label1:	
Alignment	2 - Center
BackColor	14 - Yellow
CtlName	Label1
Command1:	
Caption	One Line
CtlName	Command1
Command2:	
Caption	Two Line
CtlName	Command2
Command3:	
Caption	Three Line
CtlName	Command3
Command4:	
Caption	MousePointer
CtlName	Command4
Command5:	
Caption	BackColor
CtlName	Command5
Command6:	
Caption	ForeColor
CtlName	Command6

(continued)

COMMAND.FRM Form and Control Properties *continued*

Property	Value
Command7:	
Caption	Drag
CtlName	Command7
DragMode	1 - Automatic
Command8:	
Caption	Drag Target 1
CtlName	Command8
Command9:	
Caption	Drag Target 2
CtlName	Command9
Command10:	
Caption	Visible
CtlName	Command10
Command11:	
Caption	Enabled
CtlName	Command11
Command12:	
Caption	<–Reset
CtlName	Command12
Command13:	
Caption	<–Reset
CtlName	Command13
Command14:	
Caption	Moveable
CtlName	Command14

(continued)

COMMAND.FRM Form and Control Properties *continued*

Property	Value
Command15:	
Caption	Default
CtlName	Command15
Default	True
Command16:	
Cancel	True
Caption	Cancel
CtlName	Command16

Source code for COMMAND.FRM

```
'================================================
' COMMAND
' Demonstrates command-button controls
'================================================

'$INCLUDE: 'CONSTANT.BI'
'$INCLUDE: 'FILEMSG.BI'
'$INCLUDE: 'ABOUT.BI'

SUB Command10_Click ()
    Command10.Visible = FALSE
    Command12.Enabled = TRUE
    Label1.Caption = "Visible set to FALSE"
END SUB

SUB Command11_Click ()
    Command11.Enabled = FALSE
    Command13.Enabled = TRUE
    Label1.Caption = "Enabled set to FALSE"
END SUB

SUB Command12_Click ()
    Command10.Visible = TRUE
    Command12.Enabled = FALSE
    Label1.Caption = "Visible reset to TRUE"
END SUB
```

(continued)

COMMAND.FRM *continued*

```
SUB Command13_Click ()
    Command11.Enabled = TRUE
    Command13.Enabled = FALSE
    Label1.Caption = "Enabled reset to TRUE"
END SUB

SUB Command14_Click ()
    Command14.Left = Command14.Left - 1
    Label1.Caption = "Moved left by 1"
END SUB

SUB Command15_Click ()
    Label1.Caption = "Default button clicked"
END SUB

SUB Command16_Click ()
    Label1.Caption = "Cancel button clicked"
    UNLOAD Command
END SUB

SUB Command1_Click ()
    Label1.Caption = "One-line command button clicked"
END SUB

SUB Command2_Click ()
    Label1.Caption = "Two-line command button clicked"
END SUB

SUB Command3_Click ()
    Label1.Caption = "Three-line command button clicked"
END SUB

SUB Command4_Click ()
    n% = Command4.MousePointer
     n% = (n% + 1) MOD 13
    Command4.MousePointer = n%

    Label1.Caption = "MousePointer =" + STR$(n%)
END SUB

SUB Command5_Click ()
    n% = Command5.BackColor
    n% = (n% + 1) MOD 16
    Command5.BackColor = n%
```

(continued)

COMMAND.FRM *continued*

```
    Label1.Caption = "BackColor =" + STR$(n%)
END SUB

SUB Command6_Click ()
    n% = Screen.ControlPanel(COMBUTTON_FORECOLOR)
    n% = (n% + 1) MOD 16
    Screen.ControlPanel(COMBUTTON_FORECOLOR) = n%

    Label1.Caption = "ForeColor =" + STR$(n%)
END SUB

SUB Command8_Click ()
    Label1.Caption = "Drag Target 1 clicked"
END SUB

SUB Command8_DragDrop (Source AS CONTROL, X AS SINGLE, Y AS
 SINGLE)
    Label1.Caption = "DragDrop on Drag Target 1"
END SUB

SUB Command8_DragOver (Source AS CONTROL, X AS SINGLE, Y AS
 SINGLE, State AS INTEGER)
    Label1.Caption = "DragOver on Drag Target 1 at " + STR$(X) +
 STR$(Y)
END SUB

SUB Command9_Click ()
    Label1.Caption = "Drag Target 2 clicked"
END SUB

SUB Command9_DragDrop (Source AS CONTROL, X AS SINGLE, Y AS
 SINGLE)
    Label1.Caption = "DragDrop on Drag Target 2"
END SUB

SUB Command9_DragOver (Source AS CONTROL, X AS SINGLE, Y AS
 SINGLE, State AS INTEGER)
    Label1.Caption = "DragOver on Drag Target 2 at " + STR$(X) + STR$(Y)
END SUB

SUB Form_Load ()
    'Center the form on the screen
    Command.Left = (Screen.Width - Command.Width) \ 2
    Command.Top = (Screen.Height - Command.Height) \ 2

    Label1.Caption = "Try the various command buttons..."
END SUB
```

(continued)

COMMAND.FRM *continued*

```
SUB menAboutCommand_Click ()
    About.Label1.Caption = "COMMAND"
    About.SHOW MODAL
END SUB

SUB menExit_Click ()
    UNLOAD Command
END SUB

SUB menHelpCommand_Click ()
    FileMsg "COMMAND.MSG", 1
END SUB
```

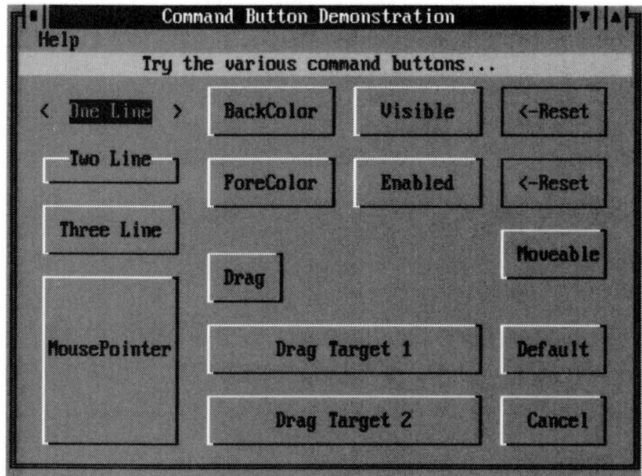

Figure 6-9.
COMMAND.FRM in action.

The FRAMOPT Application

The FRAMOPT application demonstrates how to group option buttons in frames and how the grouping affects the behavior of the option buttons.

Option buttons differ from check boxes in that the user can select only one option button (in a group) at a time. Visual Basic for MS-DOS deselects all other option buttons in the group when the user selects any one option button. You can group option buttons inside frames to tell Visual Basic for MS-DOS to allow the user to select any one option from each group, rather than one option from all the option buttons on the form.

Six option buttons appear in frames on the form (three grouped in each of two frames). The rest of the option buttons appear directly on the face of the form. Another way to look at this is to consider the option buttons outside the frames as one group and the option buttons inside the frames as additional groups. The user can select only one option button from each group at any time.

When you click an option button, an informative message appears at the top of the form. Notice how the option buttons you've previously selected in the other groups are affected. When you select and deselect option buttons in the groups, the event-driven subprograms associated with the buttons control the appearance of messages in the label control at the top of the form.

The files for the FRAMOPT application are included on the companion disk. To load the files into Visual Basic for MS-DOS, choose the File Open Project command and type *C:\VBDWSHOP\FRAMOPT.MAK*. This opens the project and enables you to view and modify the forms and code. The following figures, tables, and code give the details of the application's creation.

Figure 6-10.
FRAMOPT project list.

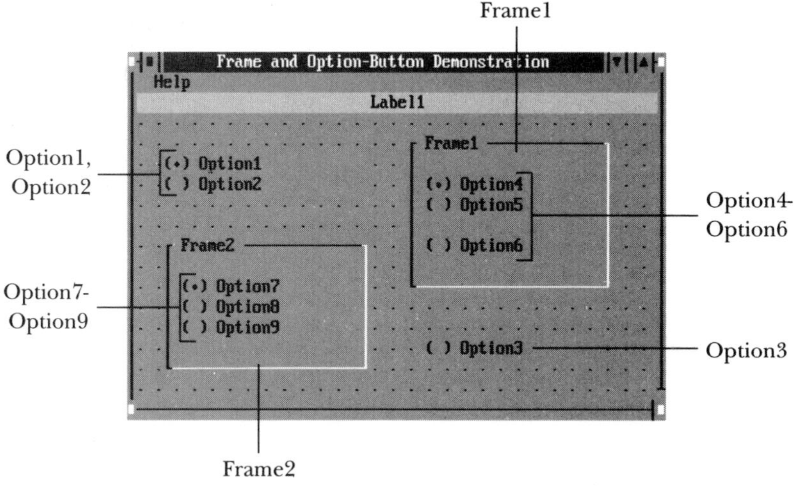

Figure 6-11.
FRAMOPT.FRM during development.

FRAMOPT.FRM Menu Design Window Entries

Caption	CtlName	Indentation
&Help	menHelp	0
&Help on FramOpt	menHelpFramOpt	1
&About FramOpt...	menAboutFramOpt	1
-	menSep	1
E&xit	menExit	1

FRAMOPT.FRM Form and Control Properties

Property	Value
Form:	
Caption	Frame and Option-Button Demonstration
FormName	Framopt
Label1:	
Alignment	2 - Center
BackColor	11 - Bright Cyan
CtlName	Label1

(continued)

FRAMOPT.FRM Form and Control Properties *continued*

Property	Value
Frame1:	
CtlName	Frame1
Frame2:	
CtlName	Frame2
Option1:	
CtlName	Option1
Option2:	
CtlName	Option2
Option3:	
CtlName	Option3
Option4:	
CtlName	Option4
Option5:	
CtlName	Option5
Option6:	
CtlName	Option6
Option7:	
CtlName	Option7
Option8:	
CtlName	Option8
Option9:	
CtlName	Option9

Source code for FRAMOPT.FRM

```
'====================================================
' FRAMOPT
' Demonstrates frames and option buttons
'====================================================

'$INCLUDE: 'CONSTANT.BI'
'$INCLUDE: 'FILEMSG.BI'
'$INCLUDE: 'ABOUT.BI'

SUB Form_Load ()
    'Center the form on the screen
    FramOpt.Left = (Screen.Width - FramOpt.Width) \ 2
    FramOpt.Top = (Screen.Height - FramOpt.Height) \ 2

    Label1.Caption = "Select the various options"
END SUB

SUB menAboutFramOpt_Click ()
    About.Label1.Caption = "FRAMOPT"
    About.SHOW MODAL
END SUB

SUB menExit_Click ()
    UNLOAD FramOpt
END SUB

SUB menHelpFramOpt_Click ()
    FileMsg "FRAMOPT.MSG", 1
END SUB

SUB Option1_Click ()
    Label1.Caption = "Form-level Option1 selected"
END SUB

SUB Option2_Click ()
    Label1.Caption = "Form-level Option2 selected"
END SUB

SUB Option3_Click ()
    Label1.Caption = "Form-level Option3 selected"
END SUB

SUB Option4_Click ()
    Label1.Caption = "Frame1 group, Option4 selected"
END SUB
```

(continued)

FRAMOPT.FRM *continued*

```
SUB Option5_Click ()
    Label1.Caption = "Frame1 group, Option5 selected"
END SUB

SUB Option6_Click ()
    Label1.Caption = "Frame1 group, Option6 selected"
END SUB

SUB Option7_Click ()
    Label1.Caption = "Frame2 group, Option7 selected"
END SUB

SUB Option8_Click ()
    Label1.Caption = "Frame2 group, Option8 selected"
END SUB

SUB Option9_Click ()
    Label1.Caption = "Frame2 group, Option9 selected"
END SUB
```

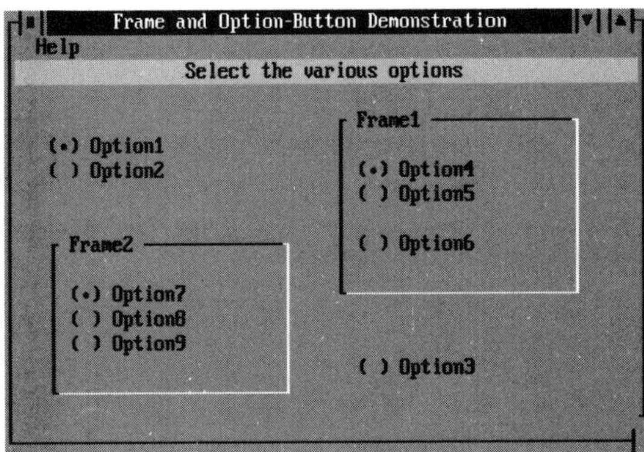

Figure 6-12.
FRAMOPT.FRM in action.

The LABELS Application

The LABELS application demonstrates some of the properties of label controls. A test label at the top of the form provides visual feedback and informative messages about the changes that occur in the label as the user clicks the command buttons.

Each of the command buttons cycles through the settings for the indicated property of the label. For instance, the BackColor command button cycles the label's background color through the 16 possible settings. The label itself displays the current BackColor value as the user cycles through the settings.

Notice how the text in the label shifts its position as the label's BorderStyle changes. A label must have a Height property of *3* or greater whenever its BorderStyle is not set to *0*; otherwise, the label's caption can't appear on the form. Unlike for command buttons, the ForeColor property can be set independently for each label control. You can see these conditions most easily by displaying the About dialog box from this or any other application in the book.

The files for the LABELS application are included on the companion disk. To load the files into Visual Basic for MS-DOS, choose the File Open Project command and type *C:\VBDWSHOP\LABELS.MAK*. This opens the project and enables you to view and modify the forms and code. The following figures, tables, and code give the details of the application's creation.

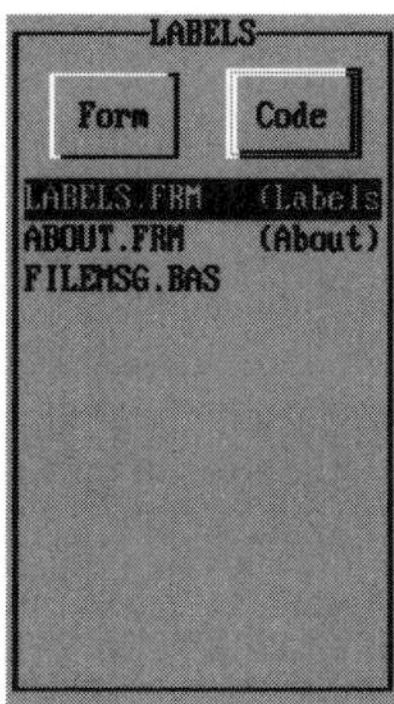

Figure 6-13.
LABELS project list.

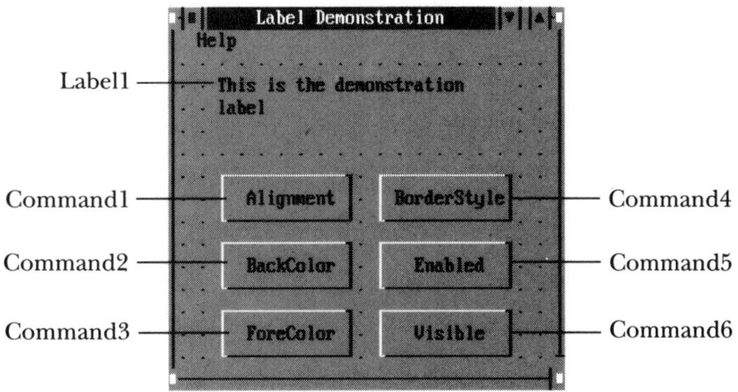

Figure 6-14.
LABELS.FRM during development.

LABELS.FRM Menu Design Window Entries

Caption	CtlName	Indentation
&Help	menHelp	0
&Help on Labels	menHelpLabels	1
&About Labels...	menAboutLabels	1
-	menSep	1
E&xit	menExit	1

LABELS.FRM Form and Control Properties

Property	Value
Form:	
Caption	Label Demonstration
FormName	Labels
Label1:	
Caption	This is the demonstration label
CtlName	Label1
Command1:	
Caption	Alignment
CtlName	Command1
Command2:	
Caption	BackColor
CtlName	Command2
Command3:	
Caption	ForeColor
CtlName	Command3
Command4:	
Caption	BorderStyle
CtlName	Command4

(continued)

LABELS.FRM Form and Control Properties *continued*

Property	Value
Command5:	
Caption	Enabled
CtlName	Command5
Command6:	
Caption	Visible
CtlName	Command6

Source code for LABELS.FRM

```
'=================================================
' LABELS
' Demonstrates label control properties
'=================================================

'$INCLUDE: 'CONSTANT.BI'
'$INCLUDE: 'FILEMSG.BI'
'$INCLUDE: 'ABOUT.BI'

SUB Command1_Click ()
    n% = (Label1.Alignment + 1) MOD 3
    Label1.Alignment = n%
    Label1.Caption = "Alignment =" + STR$(n%)
END SUB

SUB Command2_Click ()
    n% = (Label1.BackColor + 1) MOD 16
    Label1.BackColor = n%
    Label1.Caption = "BackColor =" + STR$(n%)
END SUB

SUB Command3_Click ()
    n% = (Label1.ForeColor + 1) MOD 16
    Label1.ForeColor = n%
    Label1.Caption = "ForeColor =" + STR$(n%)
END SUB
```

(continued)

LABELS.FRM *continued*

```
SUB Command4_Click ()
    n% = (Label1.BorderStyle + 1) MOD 3
    Label1.BorderStyle = n%
    Label1.Caption = "BorderStyle =" + STR$(n%)
END SUB

SUB Command5_Click ()
    IF Label1.Enabled = TRUE THEN
        Label1.Enabled = FALSE
        Label1.Caption = "Enabled = FALSE"
    ELSE
        Label1.Enabled = TRUE
        Label1.Caption = "Enabled = TRUE"
    END IF
END SUB

SUB Command6_Click ()
    IF Label1.Visible = TRUE THEN
        Label1.Visible = FALSE
        Label1.Caption = "Visible = FALSE"
    ELSE
        Label1.Visible = TRUE
        Label1.Caption = "Visible = TRUE"
    END IF
END SUB

SUB Form_Load ()
    'Center the form on the screen
    Labels.Left = (Screen.Width - Labels.Width) \ 2
    Labels.Top = (Screen.Height - Labels.Height) \ 2
END SUB

SUB menAboutLabels_Click ()
    About.Label1.Caption = "LABELS"
    About.SHOW MODAL
END SUB

SUB menExit_Click ()
    UNLOAD Labels
END SUB

SUB menHelpLabels_Click ()
    FileMsg "LABELS.MSG", 1
END SUB
```

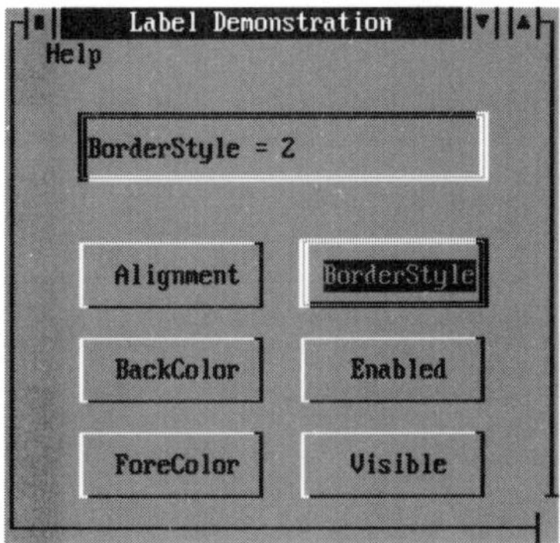

Figure 6-15.
LABELS.FRM in action.

The LISTDEM Application

The LISTDEM application allows you to explore list box controls in an interactive way. Two list boxes appear on the form: one with its Sorted property set to *True*, the other with its Sorted property set to *False* (unsorted). Both list boxes initialize using the same data in the same order. The different Sorted properties of the list boxes, however, cause the lists to appear in different orders.

The application updates the Text property of a list box when the user clicks on an item (or if the user moves the highlight bar by pressing the Up or Down direction key). If the user clicks or double-clicks on any item with the mouse, independent event-driven subprograms come to life. These subprograms control how a mouse click or double click updates the information appearing on the form. In both cases, the application reads the Text property of the item the user has selected and then displays the text.

Notice that the user's scrolling the lists also generates a Click event. The rule to remember is that a Click event is generated whenever the user moves the highlight bar to a different list item.

The files for the LISTDEM application are included on the companion disk. To load the files into Visual Basic for MS-DOS, choose the File Open Project command and type *C:\VBDWSHOP\LISTDEM.MAK*. This opens the project and enables you to view and modify the forms and code. The following figures, tables, and code give the details of the application's creation.

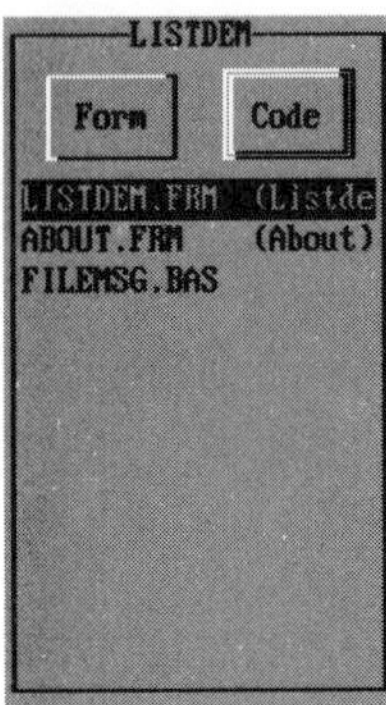

Figure 6-16.
LISTDEM project list.

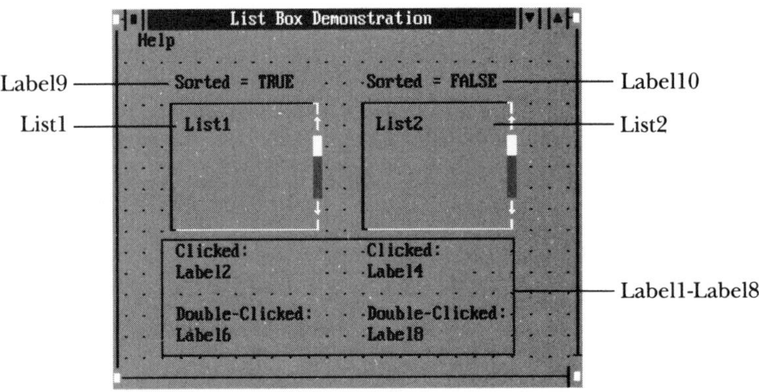

Figure 6-17.
LISTDEM.FRM during development.

LISTDEM.FRM Menu Design Window Entries

Caption	CtlName	Indentation
&Help	menHelp	0
&Help on ListDem	menHelpListDem	1
&About ListDem...	menAboutListDem	1
-	menSep	1
E&xit	menExit	1

LISTDEM.FRM Form and Control Properties

Property	Value
Form:	
Caption	List Box Demonstration
FormName	Listdem
Label1:	
Caption	Clicked:
CtlName	Label1
Label2:	
Caption	Label2
CtlName	Label2
Label3:	
Caption	Clicked:
CtlName	Label3
Label4:	
Caption	Label4
CtlName	Label4
Label5:	
Caption	Double-Clicked:
CtlName	Label5
Label6:	
Caption	Label6
CtlName	Label6
Label7:	
Caption	Double-Clicked:
CtlName	Label7
Label8:	
Caption	Label8
CtlName	Label8

(continued)

LISTDEM.FRM Form and Control Properties *continued*

Property	Value
Label9:	
Caption	Sorted = TRUE
CtlName	Label9
Label10:	
Caption	Sorted = FALSE
CtlName	Label10
List1:	
CtlName	List1
Sorted	True
List2:	
CtlName	List2
Sorted	False

Source code for LISTDEM.FRM

```
'================================================
' LISTDEM
' Demonstrates list box controls
'================================================

'$INCLUDE: 'CONSTANT.BI'
'$INCLUDE: 'FILEMSG.BI'
'$INCLUDE: 'ABOUT.BI'

SUB Form_Load ()
    'Center the form on the screen
    ListDem.Left = (Screen.Width - ListDem.Width) \ 2
    ListDem.Top = (Screen.Height - ListDem.Height) \ 2

    'Fill the two list boxes
    FOR i% = 1 TO 10
        SELECT CASE i%
        CASE 1
            a$ = "One"
        CASE 2
            a$ = "Two"
```

(continued)

LISTDEM.FRM *continued*

```
        CASE 3
            a$ = "Three"
        CASE 4
            a$ = "Four"
        CASE 5
            a$ = "Five"
        CASE 6
            a$ = "Six"
        CASE 7
            a$ = "Seven"
        CASE 8
            a$ = "Eight"
        CASE 9
            a$ = "Nine"
        CASE 10
            a$ = "Ten"
        END SELECT
        List1.ADDITEM a$
        List2.ADDITEM a$
    NEXT i%

    'Initialize some labels
    Label2.Caption = "(none)"
    Label4.Caption = "(none)"
    Label6.Caption = "(none)"
    Label8.Caption = "(none)"
END SUB

SUB List1_Click ()
    Label2.Caption = List1.Text
END SUB

SUB List1_DblClick ()
    Label6.Caption = List1.Text
END SUB

SUB List2_Click ()
    Label4.Caption = List2.List(List2.ListIndex)
END SUB

SUB List2_DblClick ()
    Label8.Caption = List2.Text
END SUB

SUB menAboutListDem_Click ()
    About.Label1.Caption = "LISTDEM"
    About.SHOW MODAL
END SUB
```

(continued)

LISTDEM.FRM *continued*

```
SUB menExit_Click ()
    UNLOAD ListDem
END SUB

SUB menHelpListDem_Click ()
    FileMsg "LISTDEM.MSG", 1
END SUB
```

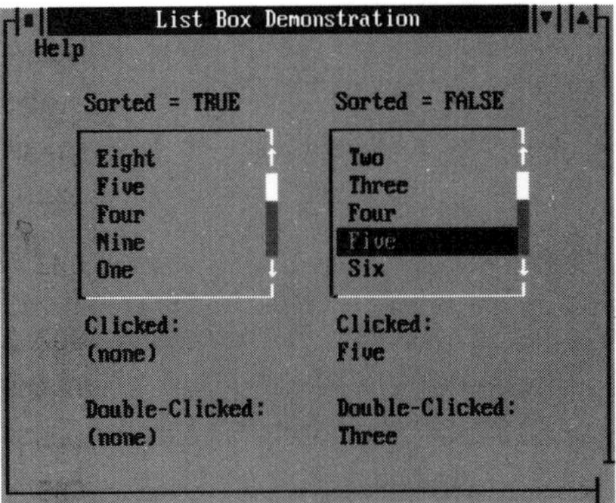

Figure 6-18.
LISTDEM.FRM in action.

The PICDEMO Application

The PICDEMO application demonstrates the properties of a picture box control. The user can click the command buttons to cause an immediate effect on the picture box at the top of the form. Informational messages appear in this picture box to inform the user about the picture box's current settings.

The command buttons cycle through the available settings for each indicated picture box property. For example, the BorderStyle command button cycles through the property values *0*, *1*, and *2*, and the border in the sample picture box changes.

Some settings obscure the results. The user must click Visible twice, for instance, to see the picture box again for further experimentation. And if the user leaves the ForeColor and BackColor properties set to the same color, the messages appearing in the picture box become invisible. (This can actually be a handy technique to remember, however, if you want to hide some text or flash a message on and off!)

The files for the PICDEMO application are included on the companion disk. To load the files into Visual Basic for MS-DOS, choose the File Open Project command and type *C:\VBDWSHOP\PICDEMO.MAK*. This opens the project and enables you to view and modify the forms and code. The following figures, tables, and code give the details of the application's creation.

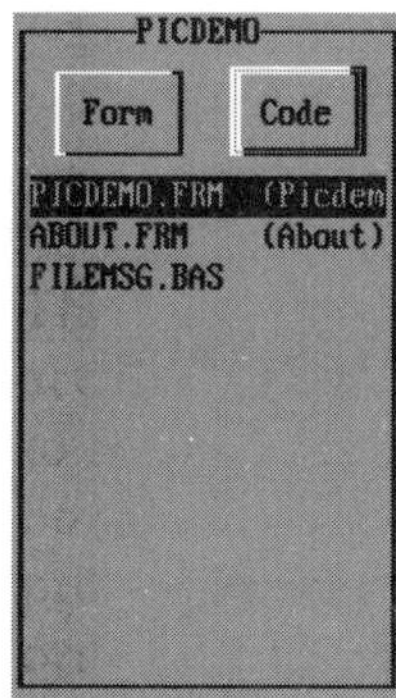

Figure 6-19.
PICDEMO project list.

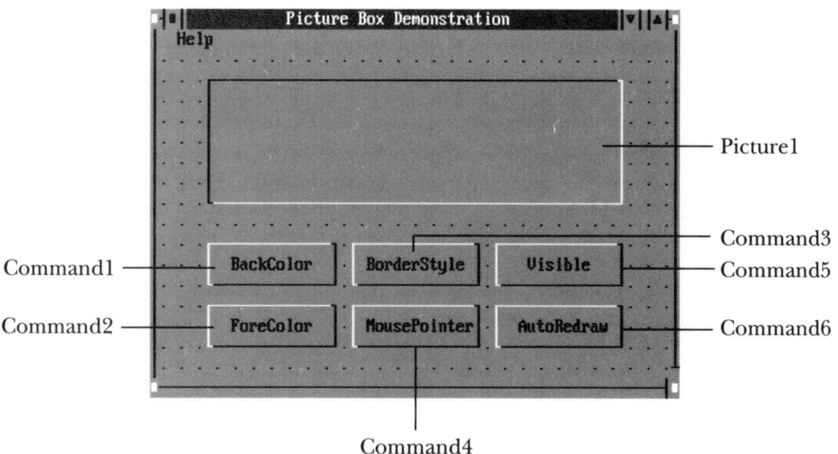

Figure 6-20.
PICDEMO.FRM during development.

PICDEMO.FRM Menu Design Window Entries

Caption	CtlName	Indentation
&Help	menHelp	0
&Help on PicDemo	menHelpPicDemo	1
&About PicDemo...	menAboutPicDemo	1
-	menSep	1
E&xit	menExit	1

PICDEMO.FRM Form and Control Properties

Property	Value
Form:	
Caption	Picture Box Demonstration
FormName	Picdemo
Picture1:	
CtlName	Picture1
Command1:	
Caption	BackColor
CtlName	Command1
Command2:	
Caption	ForeColor
CtlName	Command2
Command3:	
Caption	BorderStyle
CtlName	Command3
Command4:	
Caption	MousePointer
CtlName	Command4

(continued)

PICDEMO.FRM Form and Control Properties *continued*

Property	Value
Command5:	
Caption	Visible
CtlName	Command5
Command6:	
Caption	AutoRedraw
CtlName	Command6

Source code for PICDEMO.FRM

```
'==================================================
' PICDEMO
' Demonstrates picture box controls
'==================================================

'$INCLUDE: 'CONSTANT.BI'
'$INCLUDE: 'FILEMSG.BI'
'$INCLUDE: 'ABOUT.BI'

SUB Command1_Click ()
    n% = (Picture1.BackColor + 1) MOD 16
    Picture1.BackColor = n%

    IF Picture1.CurrentY >= Picture1.ScaleHeight THEN
        Picture1.CLS
    END IF
    Picture1.PRINT "BackColor ="; n%
END SUB

SUB Command2_Click ()
    n% = (Picture1.ForeColor + 1) MOD 16
    Picture1.ForeColor = n%

    IF Picture1.CurrentY >= Picture1.ScaleHeight THEN
        Picture1.CLS
    END IF
    Picture1.PRINT "ForeColor ="; n%
END SUB
```

(continued)

PICDEMO.FRM *continued*

```
SUB Command3_Click ()
    n% = (Picture1.BorderStyle + 1) MOD 3
    Picture1.BorderStyle = n%

    IF Picture1.CurrentY >= Picture1.ScaleHeight THEN
        Picture1.CLS
    END IF
    Picture1.PRINT "BorderStyle ="; n%
END SUB

SUB Command4_Click ()
    n% = (Picture1.MousePointer + 1) MOD 13
    Picture1.MousePointer = n%

    IF Picture1.CurrentY >= Picture1.ScaleHeight THEN
        Picture1.CLS
    END IF
    Picture1.PRINT "MousePointer ="; n%
END SUB

SUB Command5_Click ()
    IF Picture1.Visible = TRUE THEN
        Picture1.Visible = FALSE
    ELSE
        Picture1.Visible = TRUE
    END IF
END SUB

SUB Command6_Click ()
    IF Picture1.CurrentY >= Picture1.ScaleHeight THEN
        Picture1.CLS
    END IF

    IF Picture1.AutoRedraw = TRUE THEN
        Picture1.AutoRedraw = FALSE
        Picture1.PRINT "AutoRedraw = FALSE"
    ELSE
        Picture1.AutoRedraw = TRUE
        Picture1.PRINT "AutoRedraw = TRUE"
    END IF
END SUB

SUB Form_Load ()
    'Center the form on the screen
    PicDemo.Left = (Screen.Width - PicDemo.Width) \ 2
    PicDemo.Top = (Screen.Height - PicDemo.Height) \ 2
END SUB
```

(continued)

PICDEMO.FRM *continued*

```
SUB menAboutPicDemo_Click ()
    About.Label1.Caption = "PICDEMO"
    About.SHOW MODAL
END SUB

SUB menExit_Click ()
    UNLOAD PicDemo
END SUB

SUB menHelpPicDemo_Click ()
    FileMsg "PICDEMO.MSG", 1
END SUB

SUB Picture1_KeyDown (KeyCode AS INTEGER, Shift AS INTEGER)
    Picture1.CurrentX = 0
    Picture1.CurrentY = 0
    Picture1.PRINT "KeyDown, KeyCode ="; KeyCode
END SUB

SUB Picture1_KeyPress (KeyAscii AS INTEGER)
    Picture1.PRINT "KeyPress ="; KeyAscii
END SUB

SUB Picture1_KeyUp (KeyCode AS INTEGER, Shift AS INTEGER)
    Picture1.PRINT "KeyUp, KeyCode ="; KeyCode
END SUB
```

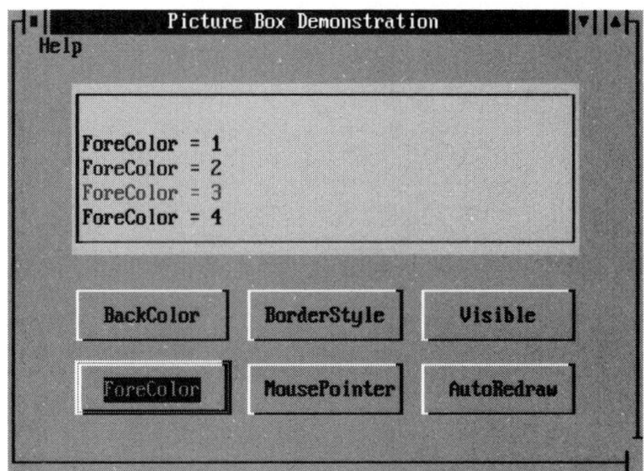

Figure 6-21.
PICDEMO.FRM in action.

The SCROLL Application

The SCROLL application lets you experiment with scroll bars to see how their properties work. The application presents four scroll bars, two vertical and two horizontal, two of which are wider than the others. As the user manipulates the scroll bars, the application displays information concerning the scroll bars' relevant property settings in a picture box.

Scroll bars have several important properties. The Min and Max properties determine the values at each end of the scroll bars. The SmallChange setting determines how much change takes place when the user clicks the arrow button at either end of a scroll bar, and the LargeChange setting determines the amount of change that occurs when the user clicks the scroll bar anywhere between the scroll box and an arrow button. For instance, suppose you were setting up an application to scroll through a display of text. You would set SmallChange to *1* to scroll through one line of text when the user clicks the arrow button at either end of a scroll bar, and you would set LargeChange to the number of displayed text lines on the form to cause the application to scroll through a screenful of text at a time when the user clicks the scroll bar anywhere between the scroll box and an arrow button.

When a scroll bar value changes as a result of any of the various user manipulations, an associated event-driven subprogram (such as *VScroll1_Change*) starts. The current value of the scroll bar is available in the scroll bar's Value property. You can use this value to define the action you want the application to perform when the user manipulates the scroll bar.

You can set the range of values for the scroll bar depending on what you require for your finished application. The Min property is always at the left side of a horizontal scroll bar and at the top of a vertical scroll bar. Often, however, you'll want the application to return the largest value when the user moves the scroll box to the top of a vertical scroll bar. In this case, simply set the Min property to be greater than the Max property. Doing so reverses the "natural" order and causes the scroll bar to behave the way you want it to. The wider vertical scroll bar in this demonstration program shows this technique.

The files for the SCROLL application are included on the companion disk. To load the files into Visual Basic for MS-DOS, choose the File Open Project command and type *C:\VBDWSHOP\SCROLL.MAK*. This opens the project and enables you to view and modify the forms and code. The following figures, tables, and code give the details of the application's creation.

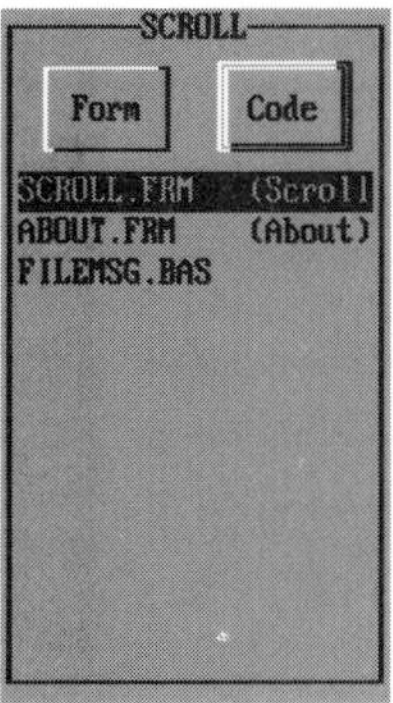

Figure 6-22.
SCROLL project list.

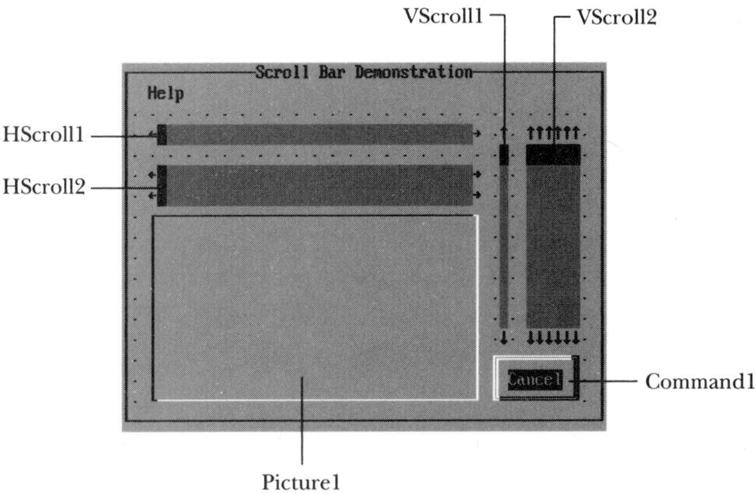

Figure 6-23.
SCROLL.FRM during development.

SCROLL.FRM Menu Design Window Entries

Caption	CtlName	Indentation
&Help	menHelp	0
&Help on Scroll	menHelpScroll	1
&About Scroll...	menAboutScroll	1
-	menSep	1
E&xit	menExit	1

SCROLL.FRM Form and Control Properties

Property	Value
Form:	
Caption	Scroll Bar Demonstration
FormName	Scroll
HScroll1:	
CtlName	HScroll1
Height	1
LargeChange	10
Max	100
Min	0
SmallChange	1
Value	0
HScroll2:	
CtlName	HScroll2
Height	2
LargeChange	100
Max	500
Min	–500
SmallChange	10
Value	–500
VScroll1:	
CtlName	VScroll1
LargeChange	20
Max	100
Min	0
SmallChange	5
Value	0
Width	1

(continued)

SCROLL.FRM Form and Control Properties *continued*

Property	Value
VScroll2:	
CtlName	VScroll2
LargeChange	7
Max	0
Min	100
SmallChange	1
Value	100
Width	6
Picture1:	
CtlName	Picture1
Command1:	
Cancel	True
Caption	Cancel
CtlName	Command1
Default	True

Source code for SCROLL.FRM

```
'================================================
' SCROLL
' Demonstrates scroll bar controls
'================================================

'$INCLUDE: 'CONSTANT.BI'
'$INCLUDE: 'FILEMSG.BI'
'$INCLUDE: 'ABOUT.BI'

SUB Command1_Click ()
    UNLOAD Scroll
END SUB

SUB Form_Load ()
    'Center the form on the screen
    Scroll.Left = (Screen.Width - Scroll.Width) \ 2
    Scroll.Top = (Screen.Height - Scroll.Height) \ 2
```

(continued)

SCROLL.FRM *continued*

```
    'Initialize the picture box control
    Picture1.AutoRedraw = TRUE
    Picture1.PRINT "Exercise the four scroll bars."
    Picture1.PRINT "The various parameters will be"
    Picture1.PRINT "displayed in this picture box."
END SUB

SUB HScroll1_Change ()
    Picture1.CLS
    Picture1.PRINT "HScroll1"
    Picture1.PRINT
    Picture1.PRINT TAB(5); "LargeChange:"; TAB(20);
 HScroll1.LargeChange
    Picture1.PRINT TAB(5); "Min:"; TAB(20); HScroll1.Min
    Picture1.PRINT TAB(5); "Max:"; TAB(20); HScroll1.Max
    Picture1.PRINT TAB(5); "SmallChange:"; TAB(20);
 HScroll1.SmallChange
    Picture1.PRINT TAB(5); "Value:"; TAB(20); HScroll1.Value
END SUB

SUB HScroll2_Change ()
    Picture1.CLS
    Picture1.PRINT "HScroll2"
    Picture1.PRINT
    Picture1.PRINT TAB(5); "LargeChange:"; TAB(20);
 HScroll2.LargeChange
    Picture1.PRINT TAB(5); "Min:"; TAB(20); HScroll2.Min
    Picture1.PRINT TAB(5); "Max:"; TAB(20); HScroll2.Max
    Picture1.PRINT TAB(5); "SmallChange:"; TAB(20);
 HScroll2.SmallChange
    Picture1.PRINT TAB(5); "Value:"; TAB(20); HScroll2.Value
END SUB

SUB menAboutScroll_Click ()
    About.Label1.Caption = "SCROLL"
    About.SHOW MODAL
END SUB

SUB menExit_Click ()
    UNLOAD Scroll
END SUB

SUB menHelpScroll_Click ()
    FileMsg "SCROLL.MSG", 1
END SUB
```

(continued)

SCROLL.FRM *continued*

```
SUB VScroll1_Change ()
    Picture1.CLS
    Picture1.PRINT "VScroll1"
    Picture1.PRINT
    Picture1.PRINT TAB(5); "LargeChange:"; TAB(20);
 VScroll1.LargeChange
    Picture1.PRINT TAB(5); "Min:"; TAB(20); VScroll1.Min
    Picture1.PRINT TAB(5); "Max:"; TAB(20); VScroll1.Max
    Picture1.PRINT TAB(5); "SmallChange:"; TAB(20);
 VScroll1.SmallChange
    Picture1.PRINT TAB(5); "Value:"; TAB(20); VScroll1.Value
END SUB

SUB VScroll2_Change ()
    Picture1.CLS
    Picture1.PRINT "VScroll2"
    Picture1.PRINT
    Picture1.PRINT TAB(5); "LargeChange:"; TAB(20);
 VScroll2.LargeChange
    Picture1.PRINT TAB(5); "Min:"; TAB(20); VScroll2.Min
    Picture1.PRINT TAB(5); "Max:"; TAB(20); VScroll2.Max
    Picture1.PRINT TAB(5); "SmallChange:"; TAB(20);
 VScroll2.SmallChange
    Picture1.PRINT TAB(5); "Value:"; TAB(20); VScroll2.Value
END SUB
```

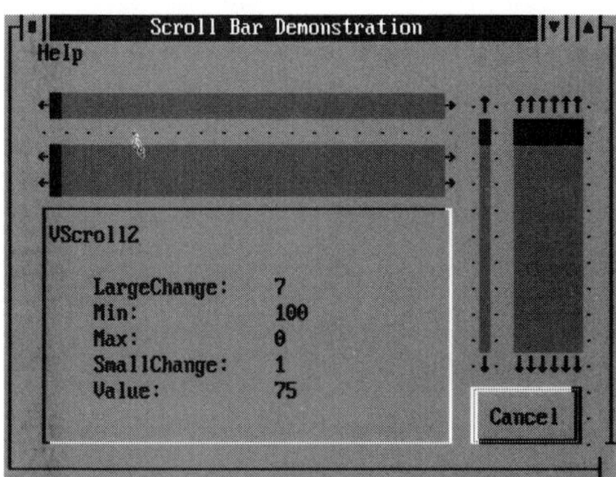

Figure 6-24.
SCROLL.FRM in action.

The TEXTDEMO Application

The TEXTDEMO application demonstrates several properties of text box controls. The user can click the command buttons to immediately affect the text box at the top of the form. Informational messages describing the current settings of the text box properties appear in this text box.

The command buttons cycle through the available settings for the indicated property. For example, the BackColor button cycles through the values *0* through *15* as the background color changes in the sample text box.

You can set several properties of text boxes only during development (and not at runtime). BorderStyle, for example, is one such property. When you click the BorderStyle button, a message appears to remind you that the BorderStyle property is read-only at runtime. You can easily experiment with these properties, however, by giving them trial settings while you're in the form development environment. When you run the program, the new settings will be in effect.

If the ForeColor command button has no effect in the finished application, you probably clicked the Enabled button only once (which disables the text box). Click Enabled again to re-enable the text box.

The files for the TEXTDEMO application are included on the companion disk. To load the files into Visual Basic for MS-DOS, choose the File Open Project command and type *C:\VBDWSHOP\TEXTDEMO.MAK*. This opens the project and enables you to view and modify the forms and code. The following figures, tables, and code give the details of the application's creation.

Figure 6-25.
TEXTDEMO project list.

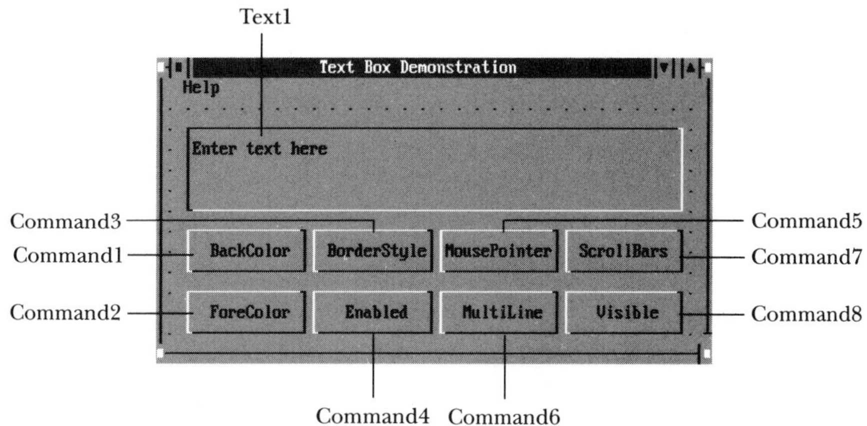

Figure 6-26.
TEXTDEMO.FRM during development.

TEXTDEMO.FRM Menu Design Window Entries

Caption	CtlName	Indentation
&Help	menHelp	0
&Help on TextDemo	menHelpTextDemo	1
&About TextDemo...	menAboutTextDemo	1
-	menSep	1
E&xit	menExit	1

TEXTDEMO.FRM Form and Control Properties

Property	Value
Form:	
Caption	Text Box Demonstration
FormName	Textdemo
Text1:	
CtlName	Text1
Text	Enter text here

(continued)

TEXTDEMO.FRM Form and Control Properties *continued*

Property	Value
Command1:	
Caption	BackColor
CtlName	Command1
Command2:	
Caption	ForeColor
CtlName	Command2
Command3:	
Caption	BorderStyle
CtlName	Command3
Command4:	
Caption	Enabled
CtlName	Command4
Command5:	
Caption	MousePointer
CtlName	Command5
Command6:	
Caption	MultiLine
CtlName	Command6
Command7:	
Caption	ScrollBars
CtlName	Command7
Command8:	
Caption	Visible
CtlName	Command8

Source code for TEXTDEMO.FRM

```
'=================================================
' TEXTDEMO
' Demonstrates text box controls
'=================================================

'$INCLUDE: 'CONSTANT.BI'
'$INCLUDE: 'FILEMSG.BI'
'$INCLUDE: 'ABOUT.BI'

SUB Command1_Click ()
    n% = (Text1.BackColor + 1) MOD 16
    Text1.BackColor = n%
    Text1.Text = "BackColor =" + STR$(n%)
END SUB

SUB Command2_Click ()
    n% = (Text1.ForeColor + 1) MOD 16
    Text1.ForeColor = n%
    Text1.Text = "ForeColor =" + STR$(n%)
END SUB

SUB Command3_Click ()
    Text1.Text = "NOTE: BorderStyle can't be set at runtime"
END SUB

SUB Command4_Click ()
    IF Text1.Enabled = TRUE THEN
        Text1.Enabled = FALSE
        Text1.Text = "Enabled = FALSE"
    ELSE
        Text1.Enabled = TRUE
        Text1.Text = "Enabled = TRUE"
    END IF
END SUB

SUB Command5_Click ()
    n% = (Text1.MousePointer + 1) MOD 13
    Text1.MousePointer = n%
    Text1.Text = "MousePointer =" + STR$(n%)
END SUB

SUB Command6_Click ()
    Text1.Text = "NOTE: MultiLine can't be set at runtime"
END SUB
```

(continued)

TEXTDEMO.FRM *continued*

```
SUB Command7_Click ()
    Text1.Text = "NOTE: ScrollBars can't be set at runtime"
END SUB

SUB Command8_Click ()
    IF Text1.Visible = TRUE THEN
        Text1.Visible = FALSE
        Text1.Text = "Visible = FALSE"
    ELSE
        Text1.Visible = TRUE
        Text1.Text = "Visible = TRUE"
    END IF
END SUB

SUB menAboutTextDemo_Click ()
    About.Label1.Caption = "TEXTDEMO"
    About.SHOW MODAL
END SUB

SUB menExit_Click ()
    UNLOAD TextDemo
END SUB

SUB menHelpTextDemo_Click ()
    FileMsg "TEXTDEMO.MSG", 1
END SUB
```

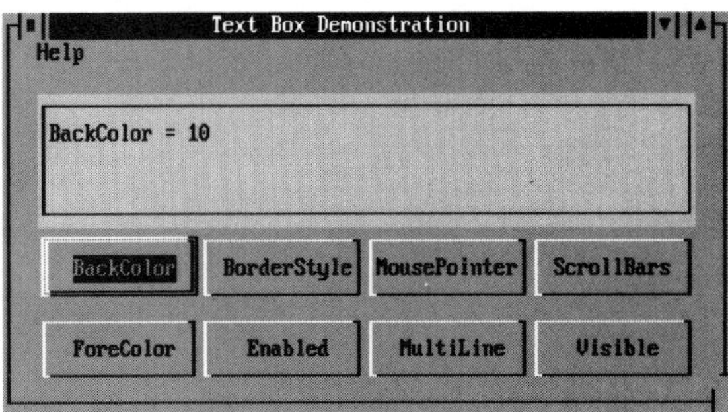

Figure 6-27.
TEXTDEMO.FRM in action.

The TIMERDEM Application

The TIMERDEM application visually demonstrates how you can use timer controls to activate subprograms at regular, timed intervals. When this program starts, it enables three timers, each of which is set to a different time interval. The interval is the amount of time the timer waits before generating a timer event. Take a look at the *Form_Load* subprogram in TIMERDEM.FRM to see how to set these properties. When an interval setting triggers a timer event, the associated *Timer1_Timer*, *Timer2_Timer*, or *Timer3_Timer* subprogram starts. Each of these subprograms changes the Left property of one of the three small picture boxes to cause the boxes to slide back and forth across the form.

The first timer is set to *100*, which means that the top picture box slides over by one position every 100 milliseconds (10 times per second). The second timer interval is set to 1000 milliseconds (once per second), and the third timer is set to 3000 milliseconds (once every three seconds). As you run the program, the differences in these time intervals become apparent as the picture boxes slide at different speeds across the display.

Feel free to experiment with other interval settings. Depending on the speed of your computer, you'll reach a threshold setting beyond which a smaller interval value doesn't speed the sliding of its associated picture box. Although you can set the timer intervals to as small as 1 millisecond, your computer might not necessarily be able to respond that quickly. Internally, Visual Basic for MS-DOS checks to see whether the indicated time interval, or a longer one, has elapsed before activating the appropriate *Timer* subprogram. Most computers aren't fast enough to keep up with the minimum 1-millisecond timer interval while they are also making substantial changes to the display or performing other actions.

The files for the TIMERDEM application are included on the companion disk. To load the files into Visual Basic for MS-DOS, choose the File Open Project command and type *C:\VBDWSHOP\TIMERDEM.MAK*. This opens the project and enables you to view and modify the forms and code. The following figures, tables, and code give the details of the application's creation.

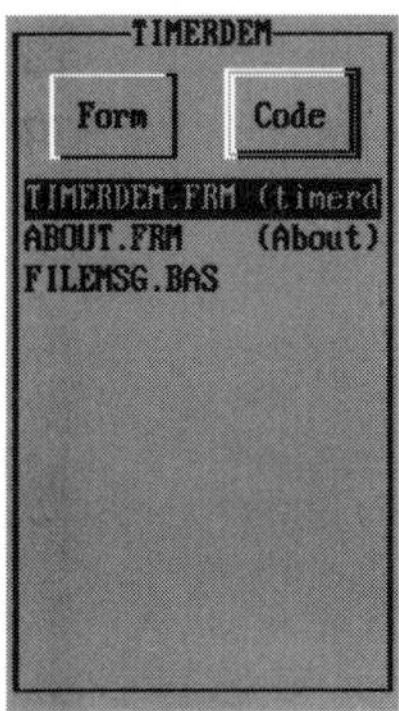

Figure 6-28.
TIMERDEM project list.

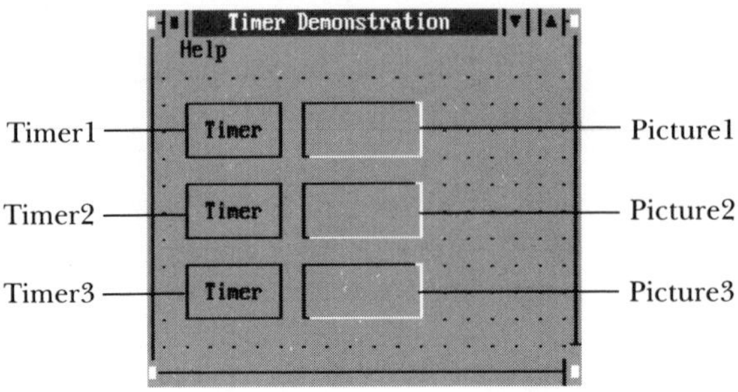

Figure 6-29.
TIMERDEM.FRM during development.

TIMERDEM.FRM Menu Design Window Entries

Caption	CtlName	Indentation
&Help	menHelp	0
&Help on TimerDem	menHelpTimerDem	1
&About TimerDem...	menAboutTimerDem	1
-	menSep	1
E&xit	menExit	1

TIMERDEM.FRM Form and Control Properties

Property	Value
Form:	
Caption	Timer Demonstration
FormName	timerdem
Timer1:	
CtlName	Timer1
Timer2:	
CtlName	Timer2
Timer3:	
CtlName	Timer3

(continued)

TIMERDEM.FRM Form and Control Properties *continued*

Property	Value
Picture1:	
CtlName	Picture1
Picture2:	
CtlName	Picture2
Picture3:	
CtlName	Picture3

Source code for TIMERDEM.FRM

```
'================================================
' TIMERDEM
' Demonstrates timer controls
'================================================

'$INCLUDE: 'CONSTANT.BI'
'$INCLUDE: 'FILEMSG.BI'
'$INCLUDE: 'ABOUT.BI'

SUB Form_Load ()
    'Center the form on the screen
    TimerDem.Left = (Screen.Width - TimerDem.Width) \ 2
    TimerDem.Top = (Screen.Height - TimerDem.Height) \ 2

    'Set the three timers to millisecond intervals
    Timer1.Interval = 100
    Timer2.Interval = 1000
    Timer3.Interval = 3000

    'Enable the timers
    Timer1.Enabled = TRUE
    Timer2.Enabled = TRUE
    Timer3.Enabled = TRUE

    'Set up the picture boxes
    Picture1.AutoRedraw = TRUE
    Picture2.AutoRedraw = TRUE
    Picture3.AutoRedraw = TRUE
```

(continued)

TIMERDEM.FRM *continued*

```
    'Display timer intervals in the picture boxes
    Picture1.PRINT Timer1.Interval; "ms"
    Picture2.PRINT Timer2.Interval; "ms"
    Picture3.PRINT Timer3.Interval; "ms"
END SUB

SUB menAboutTimerDem_Click ()
    About.Label1.Caption = "TIMERDEM"
    About.SHOW MODAL
END SUB

SUB menExit_Click ()
    UNLOAD TimerDem
END SUB

SUB menHelpTimerDem_Click ()
    FileMsg "TIMERDEM.MSG", 1
END SUB

SUB Timer1_Timer ()
    STATIC Direction%

    'Reverse direction if at right edge
    RightEdge% = Picture1.Left + Picture1.Width
    IF RightEdge% >= TimerDem.ScaleWidth THEN
        Direction% = -1
    END IF

    'Reverse direction if at left edge
    IF Picture1.Left = 0 OR Direction% = 0 THEN
        Direction% = 1
    END IF

    'Move the picture box
    Picture1.Left = Picture1.Left + Direction%
END SUB

SUB Timer2_Timer ()
    STATIC Direction%

    'Reverse direction if at right edge
    RightEdge% = Picture2.Left + Picture2.Width
    IF RightEdge% >= TimerDem.ScaleWidth THEN
        Direction% = -1
    END IF
```

(continued)

TIMERDEM.FRM *continued*

```
    'Reverse direction if at left edge
    IF Picture2.Left = 0 OR Direction% = 0 THEN
        Direction% = 1
    END IF

    'Move the picture box
    Picture2.Left = Picture2.Left + Direction%
END SUB

SUB Timer3_Timer ()
    STATIC Direction%

    'Reverse direction if at right edge
    RightEdge% = Picture3.Left + Picture3.Width
    IF RightEdge% >= TimerDem.ScaleWidth THEN
        Direction% = -1
    END IF

    'Reverse direction if at left edge
    IF Picture3.Left = 0 OR Direction% = 0 THEN
        Direction% = 1
    END IF

    'Move the picture box
    Picture3.Left = Picture3.Left + Direction%
END SUB
```

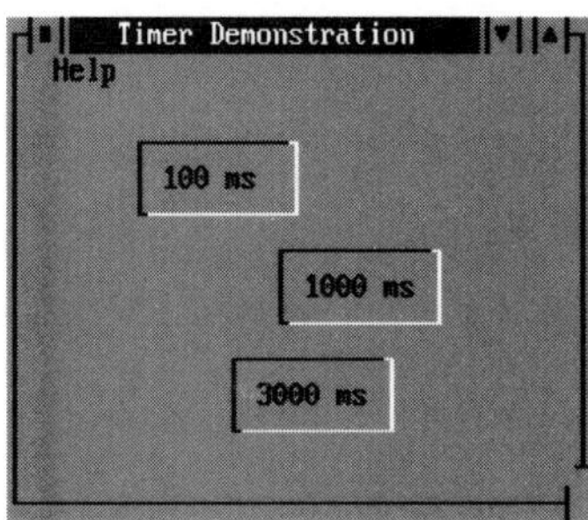

Figure 6-30.
TIMERDEM.FRM in action.

CHAPTER SEVEN

APPLICATIONS FOR EXPLORING VISUAL BASIC FOR MS-DOS

The applications in this chapter provide interactive demonstrations of forms, graphics, sound, and a variety of other features of Visual Basic for MS-DOS.

The FORMDEM Application

The FORMDEM application lets you experiment with several different form properties. As the user clicks the command buttons, the associated form properties change immediately.

Some of the form's properties cycle through all possible settings as the user clicks a command button. For instance, as the user clicks the BackColor button, the form's background color cycles through the 16 colors to which this property can be set.

Several of the form's properties are read-only at runtime, and when you click the button for these properties a message appears to remind you. You can easily change the properties, however, in the form development environment. Change and experiment with the properties and then rerun the program to see the effect.

Several of the properties report the current dimensions and location of the form. The user can resize or move the form and click on the appropriate buttons to see new values appear for these properties.

The Caption button toggles the form's caption to an alternate caption and back again. Watch the title bar at the top of the form to see the results.

The files for the FORMDEM application are included on the companion disk. To load the files into Visual Basic for MS-DOS, choose the File Open Project command and type *C:\VBDWSHOP\FORMDEM.MAK*. This opens the project and enables you to view and modify the forms and code. The following figures, tables, and code give the details of the application's creation.

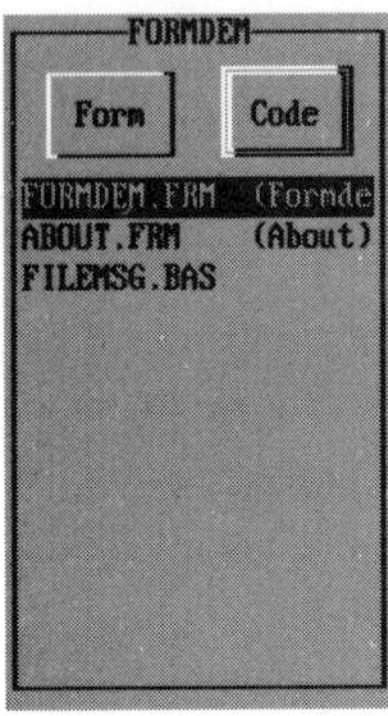

Figure 7-1.
FORMDEM project list.

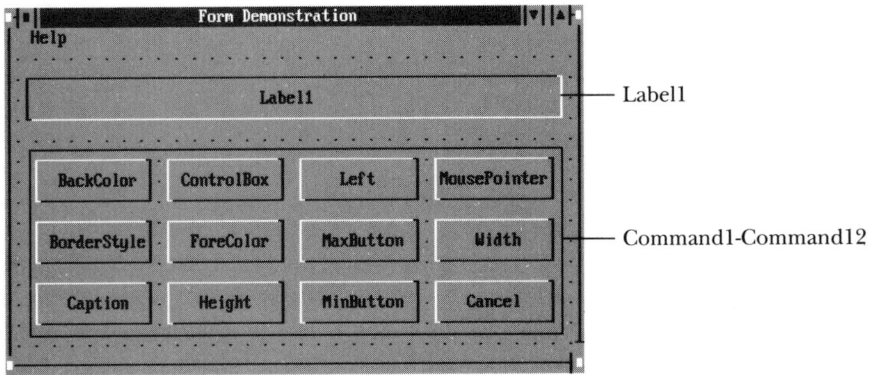

Figure 7-2.
FORMDEM.FRM during development.

FORMDEM.FRM Menu Design Window Entries

Caption	CtlName	Indentation
&Help	menHelp	0
&Help on FormDem	menHelpFormDem	1
&About FormDem...	menAboutFormDem	1
-	menSep	1
E&xit	menExit	1

FORMDEM.FRM Form and Control Properties

Property	Value
Form:	
Caption	Form Demonstration
FormName	Formdem
Label1:	
Alignment	2 - Center
BorderStyle	1 - Single Line
Caption	Label1
CtlName	Label1
Command1:	
Caption	BackColor
CtlName	Command1
Command2:	
Caption	BorderStyle
CtlName	Command2
Command3:	
Caption	Caption
CtlName	Command3
Command4:	
Caption	ControlBox
CtlName	Command4
Command5:	
Caption	ForeColor
CtlName	Command5
Command6:	
Caption	Height
CtlName	Command6

(continued)

FORMDEM.FRM Form and Control Properties *continued*

Property	Value
Command7:	
Caption	Left
CtlName	Command7
Command8:	
Caption	MaxButton
CtlName	Command8
Command9:	
Caption	MinButton
CtlName	Command9
Command10:	
Caption	MousePointer
CtlName	Command10
Command11:	
Caption	Width
CtlName	Command11
Command12:	
Cancel	True
Caption	Cancel
CtlName	Command12

Source code for FORMDEM.FRM

```
'================================================
' FORMDEM
' Demonstrates form properties
'================================================

'$INCLUDE: 'CONSTANT.BI'
'$INCLUDE: 'FILEMSG.BI'
'$INCLUDE: 'ABOUT.BI'

SUB Command10_Click ()
    n% = (FormDem.MousePointer + 1) MOD 13
    MousePointer = n%
```

(continued)

FORMDEM.FRM *continued*

```
    Label1.Caption = "FormDem.MousePointer =" + STR$(n%)

    Label1.Top = 1
    Label1.Height = 3
END SUB

SUB Command11_Click ()
    t$ = "  ...try changing the form's size"
    t$ = STR$(FormDem.Width) + t$
    Label1.Caption = "FormDem.Width =" + t$

    Label1.Top = 1
    Label1.Height = 3
END SUB

SUB Command12_Click ()
    UNLOAD FormDem
END SUB

SUB Command1_Click ()
    n% = (FormDem.BackColor + 1) MOD 16
    BackColor = n%
    Label1.Caption = "FormDem.BackColor =" + STR$(n%)

    Label1.Top = 1
    Label1.Height = 3
END SUB

SUB Command2_Click ()
    NL$ = CHR$(13) + CHR$(10)
    t$ = "BorderStyle is read-only at runtime" + NL$
    t$ = t$ + "The current setting is" + STR$(FormDem.BorderStyle) +
 NL$
    t$ = t$ + "Experiment by setting this property in the" + NL$
    t$ = t$ + "Visual Basic for MS-DOS environment"
    Label1.Caption = t$

    Label1.Top = 0
    Label1.Height = 6
END SUB

SUB Command3_Click ()
    t$ = FormDem.Caption
    IF LEFT$(t$, 1) = "F" THEN
        FormDem.Caption = "This is an alternate caption"
    ELSE
```

(continued)

FORMDEM.FRM *continued*

```
        FormDem.Caption = "Form Demonstration"
    END IF

    Label1.Caption = "See the caption at the top of this form"

    Label1.Top = 1
    Label1.Height = 3
END SUB

SUB Command4_Click ()
    NL$ = CHR$(13) + CHR$(10)
    t$ = "ControlBox is read-only at runtime" + NL$
    t$ = t$ + "The current setting is "
    IF FormDem.ControlBox = TRUE THEN
        t$ = t$ + "TRUE" + NL$
    ELSE
        t$ = t$ + "FALSE" + NL$
    END IF
    t$ = t$ + "Experiment by setting this property in the" + NL$
    t$ = t$ + "Visual Basic for MS-DOS environment"
    Label1.Caption = t$

    Label1.Top = 0
    Label1.Height = 6
END SUB

SUB Command5_Click ()
    n% = (FormDem.ForeColor + 1) MOD 16
    ForeColor = n%
    Label1.Caption = "FormDem.ForeColor =" + STR$(n%)

    Label1.Top = 0
    Label1.Height = 3

    FormDem.CurrentX = 9
    FormDem.CurrentY = 3
    FormDem.PRINT "Sample form text for ForeColor demonstration"
END SUB

SUB Command6_Click ()
    t$ = "  ...try changing the form's size"
    t$ = STR$(FormDem.Height) + t$
    Label1.Caption = "FormDem.Height =" + t$

    Label1.Top = 1
    Label1.Height = 3
END SUB
```

(continued)

FORMDEM.FRM *continued*

```
SUB Command7_Click ()
    t$ = STR$(FormDem.Left)
    Label1.Caption = "FormDem.Left =" + t$

    Label1.Top = 1
    Label1.Height = 3
END SUB

SUB Command8_Click ()
    NL$ = CHR$(13) + CHR$(10)
    t$ = "MaxButton is read-only at runtime" + NL$
    t$ = t$ + "The current setting is "
    IF FormDem.MaxButton = TRUE THEN
        t$ = t$ + "TRUE" + NL$
    ELSE
        t$ = t$ + "FALSE" + NL$
    END IF
    t$ = t$ + "Experiment by setting this property in the" + NL$
    t$ = t$ + "Visual Basic for MS-DOS environment"
    Label1.Caption = t$

    Label1.Top = 0
    Label1.Height = 6
END SUB

SUB Command9_Click ()
    NL$ = CHR$(13) + CHR$(10)
    t$ = "MinButton is read-only at runtime" + NL$
    t$ = t$ + "The current setting is "
    IF FormDem.MinButton = TRUE THEN
        t$ = t$ + "TRUE" + NL$
    ELSE
        t$ = t$ + "FALSE" + NL$
    END IF
    t$ = t$ + "Experiment by setting this property in the" + NL$
    t$ = t$ + "Visual Basic for MS-DOS environment"
    Label1.Caption = t$

    Label1.Top = 0
    Label1.Height = 6
END SUB

SUB Form_Load ()
    'Center the form on the screen
    FormDem.Left = (Screen.Width - FormDem.Width) \ 2
    FormDem.Top = (Screen.Height - FormDem.Height) \ 2
END SUB
```

(continued)

FORMDEM.FRM *continued*

```
SUB Form_Resize ()
    Label1.Caption = "Form resized"

    Label1.Top = 1
    Label1.Height = 3
END SUB

SUB menAboutFormDem_Click ()
    About.Label1.Caption = "FORMDEM"
    About.SHOW MODAL
END SUB

SUB menExit_Click ()
    UNLOAD FormDem
END SUB

SUB menHelpFormDem_Click ()
    FileMsg "FORMDEM.MSG", 1
END SUB
```

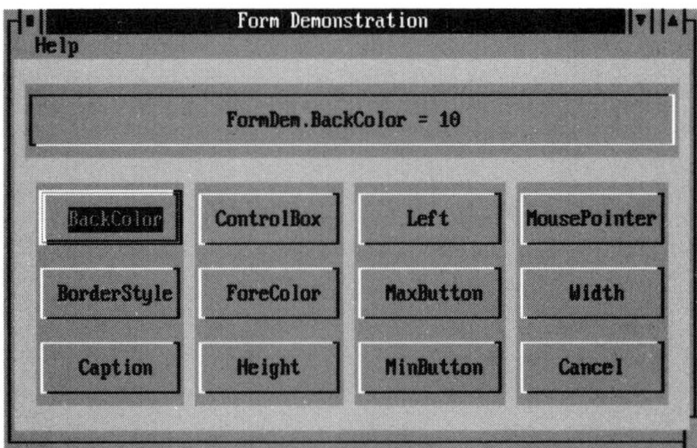

Figure 7-3.
FORMDEM.FRM in action.

The DRAWDEM Application

The *DRAW* statement is almost a graphics language unto itself. In a concise string format, you can efficiently give commands to draw complex graphic objects. This application lets you experiment interactively with *DRAW* strings until you are happy with them.

Edit a string of *DRAW* commands in the text field, and then click the DRAW button to try out the commands. DRAWDEM draws the graphics image at the center of the screen and then waits for you to press any key before returning to the DRAW Demonstration dialog box.

I have provided a command button so that you can save your *DRAW* strings in a file named DRAW.STR. When you click Save, the application prompts you for a comment line and then appends the comment line and the *DRAW* string to DRAW.STR for convenient reference. You can easily use the *DRAW* strings stored in this file in other Visual Basic for MS-DOS graphics programs that you create.

A picture box on the form displays a list of the *DRAW* commands for quick and easy reference. For more details and information about these commands, see Visual Basic for MS-DOS's online Help or your Visual Basic for MS-DOS manual.

The files for the DRAWDEM application are included on the companion disk. To load the files into Visual Basic for MS-DOS, choose the File Open Project command and type *C:\VBDWSHOP\DRAWDEM.MAK.* This opens the project and enables you to view and modify the forms and code. The following figures, tables, and code give the details of the application's creation.

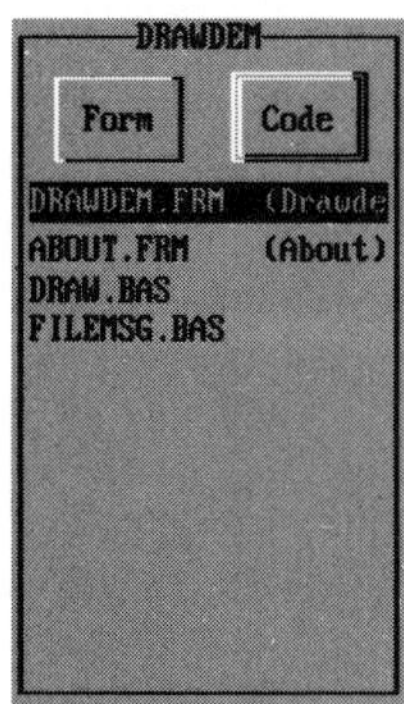

Figure 7-4.
DRAWDEM project list.

Source code for DRAW.BI

```
'=====================================================
' DRAW.BI
' Include file for accessing DRAW.BAS
'=================================================

DECLARE FUNCTION DoDraw (d$, Gmode%) AS INTEGER
```

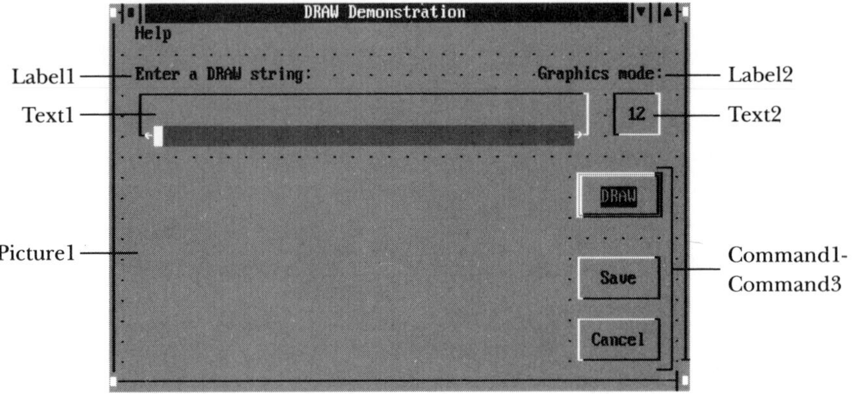

Figure 7-5.
DRAWDEM.FRM during development.

DRAWDEM.FRM Menu Design Window Entries

Caption	CtlName	Indentation
&Help	menHelp	0
&Help on DrawDem	menHelpDrawDem	1
&About DrawDem...	menAboutDrawDem	1
-	menSep	1
E&xit	menExit	1

DRAWDEM.FRM Form and Control Properties

Property	Value
Form:	
Caption	DRAW Demonstration
FormName	Drawdem
Label1:	
Caption	Enter a DRAW string:
CtlName	Label1
Label2:	
Caption	Graphics mode:
CtlName	Label2

(continued)

DRAWDEM.FRM Form and Control Properties *continued*

Property	Value
Text1:	
CtlName	Text1
MultiLine	True
ScrollBars	1 - Horizontal
Text2:	
CtlName	Text2
Picture1:	
BorderStyle	0 - None
CtlName	Picture1
Command1:	
Caption	DRAW
CtlName	Command1
Default	True
Command2:	
Caption	Save
CtlName	Command2
Command3:	
Cancel	True
Caption	Cancel
CtlName	Command3

Source code for DRAWDEM.FRM

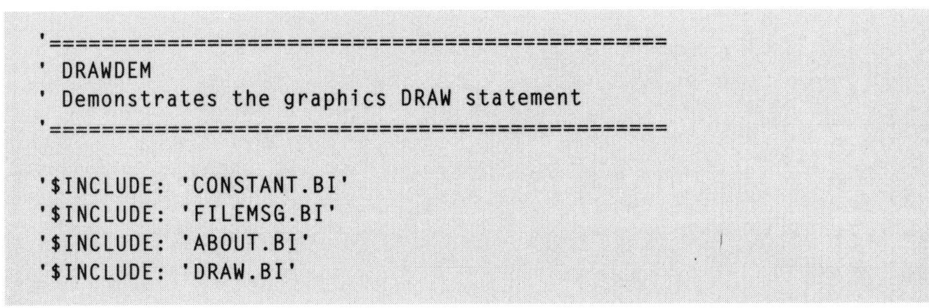

```
'================================================
' DRAWDEM
' Demonstrates the graphics DRAW statement
'================================================

'$INCLUDE: 'CONSTANT.BI'
'$INCLUDE: 'FILEMSG.BI'
'$INCLUDE: 'ABOUT.BI'
'$INCLUDE: 'DRAW.BI'
```

(continued)

DRAWDEM.FRM *continued*

```
SUB Command1_Click ()
    d$ = Text1.Text
    Gmode% = VAL(Text2.Text)
    SCREEN.HIDE
    Ret% = DoDraw(d$, Gmode%)
    SCREEN.SHOW

    IF Ret% THEN
        BEEP
        NL$ = CHR$(13) + CHR$(10)
        Title$ = "ERROR"
        Msg$ = "Check the graphics mode" + NL$
        Msg$ = Msg$ + "Check the DRAW string"
        MSGBOX Msg$, 0, Title$
    END IF
END SUB

SUB Command2_Click ()
    Prompt$ = "Enter a comment for this DRAW string"
    Title$ = "Saving DRAW string"
    Comment$ = INPUTBOX$(Prompt$, Title$)

    OPEN "DRAW.STR" FOR APPEND AS #1
    PRINT #1, ""
    PRINT #1, "' " + Comment$
    PRINT #1, Text1.Text
    CLOSE #1
END SUB

SUB Command3_Click ()
    UNLOAD DrawDem
END SUB

SUB Form_Load ()
    'Center the form on the screen
    DrawDem.Left = (Screen.Width - DrawDem.Width) \ 2
    DrawDem.Top = (Screen.Height - DrawDem.Height) \ 2

    Picture1.AutoRedraw = TRUE
    Picture1.PRINT "                  Cn      Color"
    Picture1.PRINT " H   U   E        Mx,y    Move absolute"
    Picture1.PRINT "   \ ¦ /          M+¦-x,y Move relative"
    Picture1.PRINT " L -   - R        An      Angle (1=90,2=180...)"
    Picture1.PRINT "   / ¦ \          TAn     Turn angle (-360 to
 360)"
    Picture1.PRINT " G   D   F        Sn      Scale factor"
    Picture1.PRINT "                  Pc,b    Paint (color, border)"
```

(continued)

DRAWDEM.FRM *continued*

```
    Picture1.PRINT "Optional prefix B       Move, but no plotting"
    Picture1.PRINT "Optional prefix N       Plot, but snap back"
END SUB

SUB menAboutDrawDem_Click ()
    About.Label1.Caption = "DRAWDEM"
    About.SHOW MODAL
END SUB

SUB menExit_Click ()
    UNLOAD DrawDem
END SUB

SUB menHelpDrawDem_Click ()
    FileMsg "DRAWDEM.MSG", 1
END SUB
```

Source code for DRAW.BAS

```
'================================================
' DRAW.BAS
' Graphics module for DRAWDEM application
'================================================

'$INCLUDE: 'DRAW.BI'

FUNCTION DoDraw (d$, Gmode%) AS INTEGER
    'Trap errors
    ON LOCAL ERROR GOTO BadDraw

    'Set the graphics mode
    SCREEN Gmode%

    'Draw using the string
    DRAW d$

    'Wait for a key press
    DO
    LOOP WHILE INKEY$ = ""

ExitDraw:
    'Reset text mode and quit
    SCREEN 0
    EXIT FUNCTION

BadDraw:
    DoDraw = ERR
    RESUME ExitDraw
END FUNCTION
```

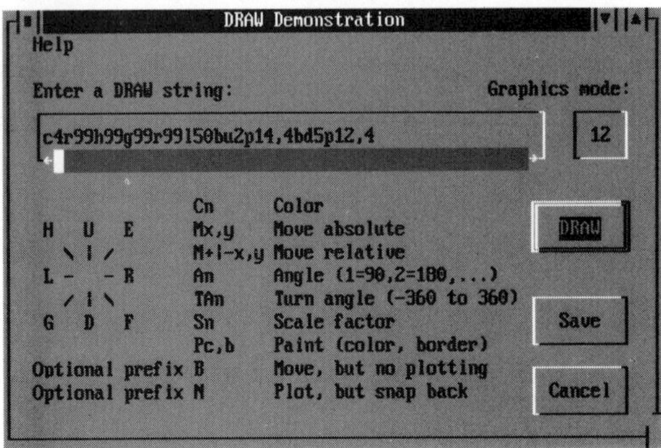

Figure 7-6.
DRAWDEM.FRM in action.

The GRAPHDEM Application

The GRAPHDEM application demonstrates some of the powerful graphics commands available with Visual Basic for MS-DOS. Each command button starts a demonstration of the graphics command associated with the button. For example, the user can click the LINE command button to see the application draw random lines followed by random unfilled and filled boxes (created by a variation of the *LINE* command).

The application isolates the graphics commands in a separate BAS module. As I mentioned in Chapter 3, Visual Basic for MS-DOS interprets the *CLS* and *PRINT* keywords as form or control methods when the keywords reside in the code of a form. If you want the keywords to be compatible with previous versions of QuickBasic, you must isolate them in a separate nonform (BAS) module.

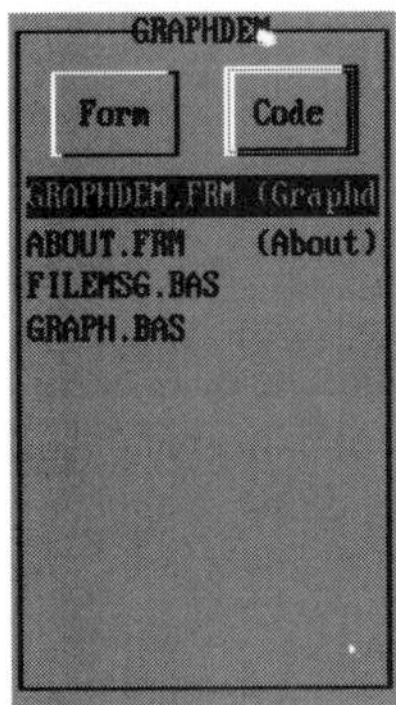

Figure 7-7.
GRAPHDEM project list.

The files for the GRAPHDEM application are included on the companion disk. To load the files into Visual Basic for MS-DOS, choose the File Open Project command and type *C:\VBDWSHOP\GRAPHDEM.MAK*. This opens the project and enables you to view and modify the forms and code. The following figures, tables, and code give the details of the application's creation.

Source code for GRAPH.BI

```
'================================================
' GRAPH.BI
' Include file for accessing GRAPH.BAS
'================================================

DECLARE FUNCTION SetMode () AS INTEGER
DECLARE SUB WaitForKey ()
DECLARE SUB DoPSet ()
DECLARE SUB DoLine ()
DECLARE SUB DoPaint ()
DECLARE SUB DoGetPut ()
DECLARE SUB DoCircle ()
```

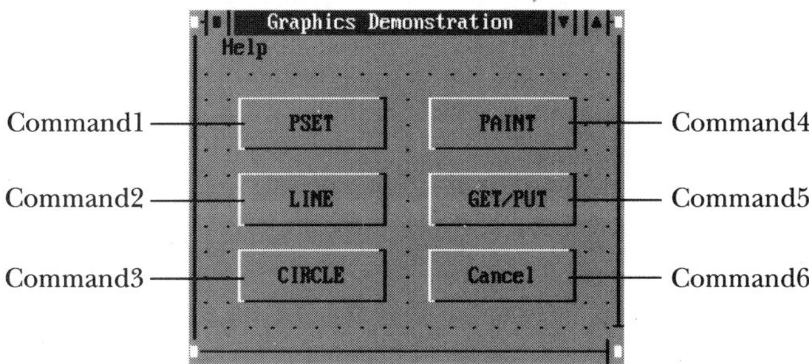

Figure 7-8.
GRAPHDEM.FRM during development.

GRAPHDEM.FRM Menu Design Window Entries

Caption	CtlName	Indentation
&Help	menHelp	0
&Help on GraphDem	menHelpGraphDem	1
&About GraphDem...	menAboutGraphDem	1
-	menSep	1
E&xit	menExit	1

GRAPHDEM.FRM Form and Control Properties

Property	Value
Form:	
Caption	Graphics Demonstration
FormName	Graphdem
Command1:	
Caption	PSET
CtlName	Command1
Command2:	
Caption	LINE
CtlName	Command2
Command3:	
Caption	CIRCLE
CtlName	Command3
Command4:	
Caption	PAINT
CtlName	Command4
Command5:	
Caption	GET/PUT
CtlName	Command5
Command6:	
Cancel	True
Caption	Cancel
CtlName	Command6

Source code for GRAPHDEM.FRM

```
'===============================================
' GRAPHDEM
' Demonstrates graphics commands
'===============================================
```

(continued)

GRAPHDEM.FRM *continued*

```
'$INCLUDE: 'CONSTANT.BI'
'$INCLUDE: 'FILEMSG.BI'
'$INCLUDE: 'ABOUT.BI'
'$INCLUDE: 'GRAPH.BI'

SUB Command1_Click ()
    SCREEN.HIDE
    DoPSet
    SCREEN.SHOW
END SUB

SUB Command2_Click ()
    SCREEN.HIDE
    DoLine
    SCREEN.SHOW
END SUB

SUB Command3_Click ()
    SCREEN.HIDE
    DoCircle
    SCREEN.SHOW
END SUB

SUB Command4_Click ()
    SCREEN.HIDE
    DoPaint
    SCREEN.SHOW
END SUB

SUB Command5_Click ()
    SCREEN.HIDE
    DoGetPut
    SCREEN.SHOW
END SUB

SUB Command6_Click ()
    UNLOAD GraphDem
END SUB

SUB menAboutGraphDem_Click ()
    About.Label1.Caption = "GRAPHDEM"
    About.SHOW MODAL
END SUB

SUB menExit_Click ()
    UNLOAD GraphDem
END SUB
```

(continued)

GRAPHDEM.FRM *continued*

```
SUB menHelpGraphDem_Click ()
    FileMsg "GRAPHDEM.MSG", 1
END SUB
```

Source code for GRAPH.BAS

```
'================================================
' GRAPH.BAS
' Demonstrates graphics commands
'================================================

'$INCLUDE: 'CONSTANT.BI'
'$INCLUDE: 'GRAPH.BI'

SUB DoCircle ()
    Ret% = SetMode
    IF Ret% THEN EXIT SUB

    PRINT "CIRCLE (round)"
    PRINT "Press any key to continue"
    DO
        Clr = INT(RND * 16)
        CIRCLE (0, 0), RND * .7, Clr
        IF INKEY$ <> "" THEN EXIT DO
    LOOP

    CLS
    PRINT "CIRCLE (aspect ratio less than 1)"
    PRINT "Press any key to continue"
    DO
        Clr = INT(RND * 16)
        CIRCLE (0, 0), .7, Clr, , , RND
        IF INKEY$ <> "" THEN EXIT DO
    LOOP

    CLS
    PRINT "CIRCLE (aspect ratio greater than 1)"
    PRINT "Press any key to continue"
    DO
        Clr = INT(RND * 16)
        CIRCLE (0, 0), .7, Clr, , , 1 / RND
        IF INKEY$ <> "" THEN EXIT DO
    LOOP

    SCREEN 0
END SUB
```

(continued)

GRAPH.BAS *continued*

```
SUB DoGetPut ()
    Ret% = SetMode
    IF Ret% THEN EXIT SUB

    DO
        CLS
        PRINT "GET/PUT"
        PRINT "Press any key to continue"

        RadPerDeg = ATN(1) / 45

        Clr = INT(RND * 15) + 1
        FOR Angle = 0 TO 358 STEP 2
            Radians = Angle * RadPerDeg
            x = COS(Radians)
            y = SIN(Radians)
            LINE (-.8, 0)-(x - .8, y), Clr
        NEXT Angle

        REDIM Ary%(900)
        x = RND - .95
        y = RND - .5
        GET (x, y)-(x + .2, y + .2), Ary%
        PUT (x, y), Ary%

        FOR i = 1 TO 17
            PUT ((RND * .8) * 2 - 1, (RND * .8) * 2 - 1), Ary%
        NEXT i

        TimeEnd = TIMER + 2
        DO
            IF INKEY$ <> "" THEN
                QuitFlag% = TRUE
                EXIT DO
            END IF
        LOOP WHILE TIMER < TimeEnd

    LOOP UNTIL QuitFlag%

    SCREEN 0
END SUB

SUB DoLine ()
    Ret% = SetMode
    IF Ret% THEN EXIT SUB

    PRINT "LINE (random endpoints)"
    PRINT "Press any key to continue"
```

(continued)

GRAPH.BAS *continued*

```
    DO
        x1 = RND + RND - 1
        y1 = RND + RND - 1
        x2 = RND + RND - 1
        y2 = RND + RND - 1
        Clr = INT(RND * 16)
        LINE (x1, y1)-(x2, y2), Clr
        IF INKEY$ <> "" THEN EXIT DO
    LOOP

    CLS
    PRINT "LINE (boxes)"
    PRINT "Press any key to continue"
    DO
        x1 = RND + RND - 1
        y1 = RND + RND - 1
        x2 = RND + RND - 1
        y2 = RND + RND - 1
        Clr = INT(RND * 16)
        LINE (x1, y1)-(x2, y2), Clr, B
        IF INKEY$ <> "" THEN EXIT DO
    LOOP

    CLS
    PRINT "LINE (filled boxes)"
    PRINT "Press any key to continue"
    DO
        x1 = RND + RND - 1
        y1 = RND + RND - 1
        x2 = RND + RND - 1
        y2 = RND + RND - 1
        Clr = INT(RND * 16)
        LINE (x1, y1)-(x2, y2), Clr, BF
        IF INKEY$ <> "" THEN EXIT DO
    LOOP

    SCREEN 0
END SUB

SUB DoPaint ()
    Ret% = SetMode
    IF Ret% THEN EXIT SUB

    DO
        CLS
        PRINT "PAINT"
        PRINT "Press any key to continue"
```

(continued)

GRAPH.BAS *continued*

```
        'Select a random color for the lines
        Clr = INT(RND * 15) + 1
        LINE (-1, 1)-(1, 1), Clr

        'Generate a random set of vertical lines
        FOR x = -1 TO 1 STEP .013
            LINE (x, -RND * .95)-(x, RND * .95), Clr
        NEXT x

        'Draw one diagonal line
        LINE (-.95, RND + RND - 1)-(.95, RND + RND - 1), Clr

        'Find a blank point between the lines
        DO
            x = RND + RND - 1
            y = RND + RND - 1
        LOOP UNTIL POINT(x, y) <> Clr

        'Pour the paint
        PAINT (x, y), INT(RND * 15) + 1, Clr

        'Quit when a key is pressed
        IF INKEY$ <> "" THEN EXIT DO

    LOOP

    'Reset text mode
    SCREEN 0
END SUB

SUB DoPSet ()
    Ret% = SetMode
    IF Ret% THEN EXIT SUB

    PRINT "PSET"
    PRINT "Press any key to continue"

    DO
        Clr = INT(RND * 16)
        PSET (RND + RND - 1, RND + RND - 1), Clr
        IF INKEY$ <> "" THEN EXIT DO
    LOOP

    SCREEN 0
END SUB

FUNCTION SetMode () AS INTEGER
    'Find a valid graphics mode
    ON LOCAL ERROR GOTO BadGraphicsMode
```

(continued)

GRAPH.BAS *continued*

```
    'Try VGA mode first
    ScrMode% = 12
    SCREEN ScrMode%

    'Try EGA if neccessary
    IF ScrMode% = 0 THEN
        ScrMode% = 9
        SCREEN ScrMode%
    END IF

    'Try CGA if necessary
    IF ScrMode% = 0 THEN
        ScrMode% = 1
        SCREEN ScrMode%
    END IF

    'No graphics mode found
    IF ScrMode% = 0 THEN
        PRINT "No graphics modes available"
        EXIT FUNCTION
    END IF

    'Scale the screen for convenient plotting
    WINDOW (-1, -1)-(1, 1.2)

    'Shuffle the random numbers
    RANDOMIZE TIMER

    'All done
    EXIT FUNCTION

BadGraphicsMode:
    ScrMode% = 0
    RESUME NEXT
END FUNCTION

SUB WaitForKey ()
    'Prompt the user
    PRINT "Press any key to continue";

    'Clear the keyboard buffer
    DO
    LOOP UNTIL INKEY$ = ""

    'Wait for a key press
    DO
    LOOP WHILE INKEY$ = ""
END SUB
```

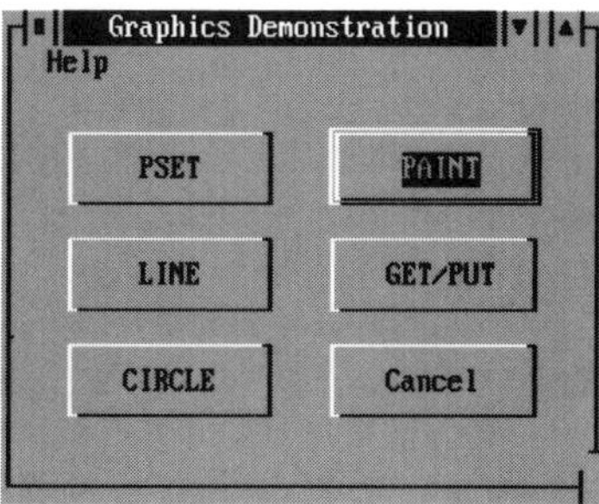

Figure 7-9.
GRAPHDEM.FRM in action.

The INPUTBOX Application

The *INPUTBOX$* function in Visual Basic for MS-DOS supplements the *INPUT$* function in previous versions of Basic. Like the *MSGBOX* statement (which supplements the *PRINT* statement), *INPUTBOX$* is powerful and easy to use. You don't have to predefine a form to contain the program's prompt and the user's response because *INPUTBOX$* creates a standard dialog box that interacts with the user.

The INPUTBOX application uses *INPUTBOX$* to prompt the user for several parameters that the application uses in a call to *INPUTBOX$*. After the user enters all the parameters of the function, a call to *INPUTBOX$* displays the resulting dialog box.

The application also presents a simple technique that changes the appearance of the running application dramatically. The INPUTBOX.FRM form provides a solid-colored full-screen background for the running program. All interaction with the user is through *INPUTBOX$* dialog boxes appearing on the INPUTBOX.FRM form. This is accomplished by setting the background color of the form to solid blue and by setting the form's MaxButton, MinButton, and ControlBox properties to *False*. The form's WindowState property is set to *2 - Maximized*, which causes the form to fill the entire screen when the program loads. When you run the program, the solid blue background adds a touch of intensity to the application.

The files for the INPUTBOX application are included on the companion disk. To load the files into Visual Basic for MS-DOS, choose the File Open Project command and type *C:\VBDWSHOP\INPUTBOX.MAK*. This opens the project and enables you to view and modify the forms and code. The following figures, tables, and code give the details of the application's creation.

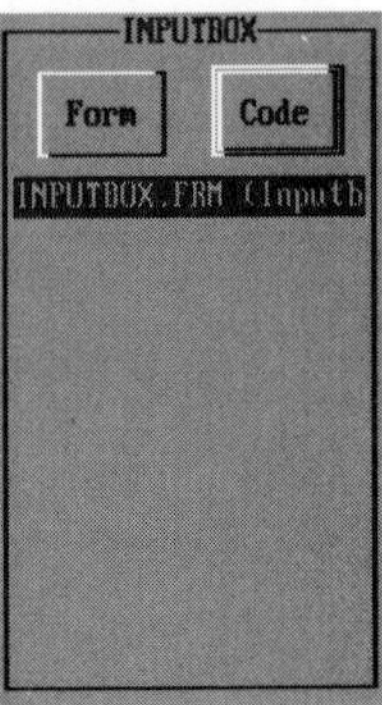

Figure 7-10.
INPUTBOX project list.

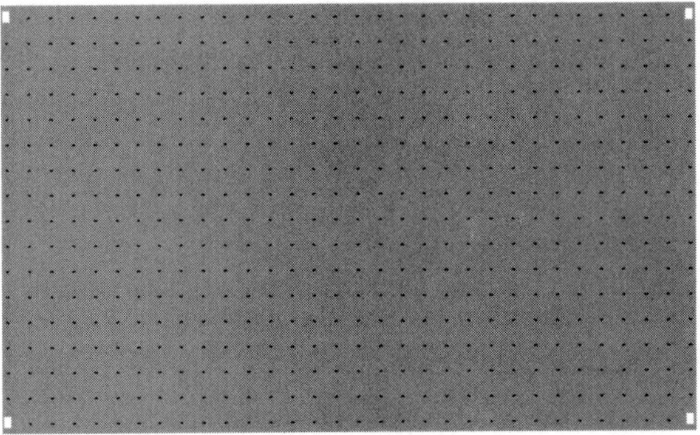

Figure 7-11.
INPUTBOX.FRM during development.

INPUTBOX.FRM Form Properties

Property	Value
Form:	
BackColor	9 - Bright Blue
Caption	*(none)*
ControlBox	False
FormName	Inputbox
MaxButton	False
MinButton	False

Source code for INPUTBOX.FRM

```
'================================================
' INPUTBOX
' Demonstrates the INPUTBOX$ function
'================================================

'$INCLUDE: 'CONSTANT.BI'

SUB Form_GotFocus ()
   NL$ = CHR$(13) + CHR$(10)

   Msg$ = "This program demonstrates the INPUTBOX$" + NL$
   Msg$ = Msg$ + "function. You'll be prompted for several" + NL$
   Msg$ = Msg$ + "parameters, and then the INPUTBOX$ function" +
 NL$
   Msg$ = Msg$ + "you've defined will display a dialog box." + NL$
 + NL$
   Msg$ = Msg$ + "Notice that INPUTBOX$ is called to prompt" + NL$
   Msg$ = Msg$ + "you for each of the parameters." + NL$ + NL$
   Msg$ = Msg$ + "Click OK to continue."
   MSGBOX Msg$

   Prompt$ = "Enter the prompt text"
   Title$ = "INPUTBOX$ Function Demonstration"
   DefaultPrompt$ = "This is the default prompt"
   NewPrompt$ = INPUTBOX$(Prompt$, Title$, DefaultPrompt$)

   Prompt$ = "Enter the title"
   DefaultPrompt$ = "This is the default title"
   NewTitle$ = INPUTBOX$(Prompt$, Title$, DefaultPrompt$)

   Prompt$ = "Enter the input text"
   DefaultPrompt$ = "This is the default input text"
   NewDefault$ = INPUTBOX$(Prompt$, Title$, DefaultPrompt$)

   Prompt$ = "Enter the column position for" + NL$
   Prompt$ = Prompt$ + "the input box or -1 to center" + NL$
   Prompt$ = Prompt$ + "the box"
   DefaultPrompt$ = "-1"
   NewXpos% = VAL(INPUTBOX$(Prompt$, Title$, DefaultPrompt$))

   IF NewXpos% <> -1 THEN
      Prompt$ = "Enter the row position"
      DefaultPrompt$ = "0"
      NewYpos% = VAL(INPUTBOX$(Prompt$, Title$, DefaultPrompt$))
   END IF
```

(continued)

INPUTBOX.FRM *continued*

```
    Msg$ = "Click OK to see your new INPUTBOX$"
    MSGBOX Msg$

    IF NewXpos% = -1 THEN
       Result$ = INPUTBOX$(NewPrompt$, NewTitle$, NewDefault$)
    ELSE
       Result$ = INPUTBOX$(NewPrompt$, NewTitle$, NewDefault$,
  NewXpos%, NewYpos%)
    END IF

    Msg$ = "Result$ returned by INPUTBOX$:" + NL$ + NL$
    Msg$ = Msg$ + Result$
    MSGBOX Msg$

    UNLOAD InputBox
END SUB

SUB Form_Load ()
     InputBox.WindowState = 2
END SUB
```

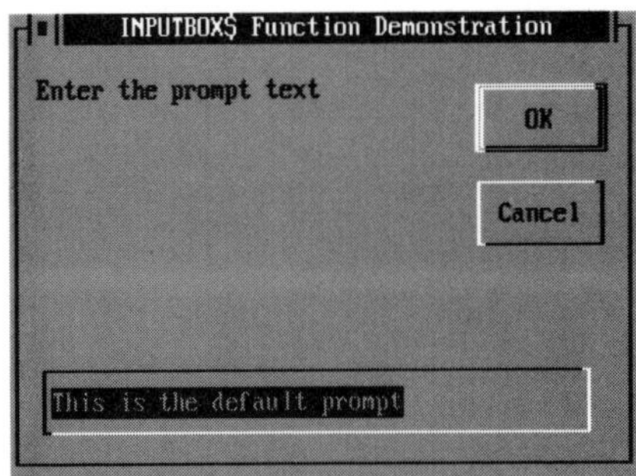

Figure 7-12.
INPUTBOX.FRM in action.

The KEYEVNTS Application

The KEYEVNTS application interactively demonstrates various keyboard events. It is similar to the MOUSEVNT application appearing later in this chapter, except that in this case messages appear when the user presses or releases keys.

The application monitors three keyboard events: KeyDown, KeyPress, and KeyUp. In other applications, you normally need to attach code for only one, or perhaps two, of these events. Here you'll see how all three events occur each time the user presses or releases a key.

The KeyPress event occurs whenever the user presses an ASCII character key. In many applications, this is the only event for which you need to prepare. Special-purpose keys (such as the function and Shift keys), however, do not generate KeyPress events. To catch *all* keyboard activity, you must attach code for the KeyDown and KeyUp events. Each KeyDown event, for example, provides a *KeyCode* parameter that uniquely identifies each key on the keyboard.

As you run this application, press some keys to see how the application handles the various events. Notice that holding down a key generates a series of KeyDown and KeyPress events but generates only one KeyUp event—when the key is finally released. Double-click the control box to quit the application.

The files for the KEYEVNTS application are included on the companion disk. To load the files into Visual Basic for MS-DOS, choose the File Open Project command and type *C:\VBDWSHOP\KEYEVNTS.MAK*. This opens the project and enables you to view and modify the forms and code. The following figures, tables, and code give the details of the application's creation.

Figure 7-13.
KEYEVNTS project list.

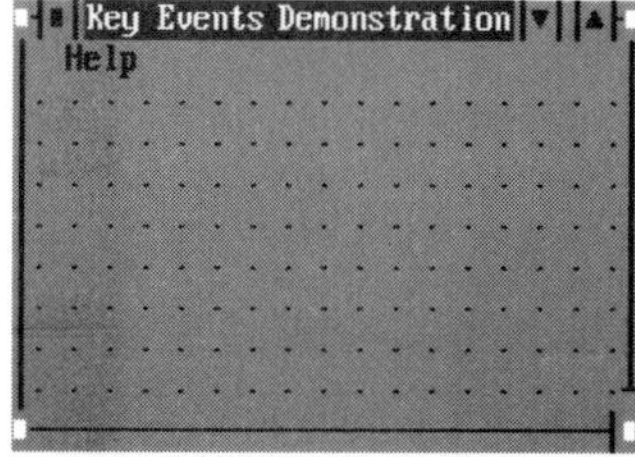

Figure 7-14.
KEYEVNTS.FRM during development.

KEYEVNTS.FRM Menu Design Window Entries

Caption	CtlName	Indentation
&Help	menHelp	0
&Help on KeyEvnts	menHelpKeyEvnts	1
&About KeyEvnts...	menAboutKeyEvnts	1
-	menSep	1
E&xit	menExit	1

KEYEVNTS.FRM Form Properties

Property	Value
Form:	
Caption	Key Events Demonstration
FormName	Keyevnts

Source code for KEYEVNTS.FRM

```
'================================================
' KEYEVNTS
' Demonstrates key events
'================================================

'$INCLUDE: 'CONSTANT.BI'
'$INCLUDE: 'FILEMSG.BI'
'$INCLUDE: 'ABOUT.BI'

DECLARE SUB Position ()

SUB Form_KeyDown (KeyCode AS INTEGER, Shift AS INTEGER)
    PRINT "KeyDown", KeyCode; Shift
    Position
END SUB

SUB Form_KeyPress (KeyAscii AS INTEGER)
    PRINT "KeyPress", KeyAscii; CHR$(KeyAscii)
    Position
END SUB
```

(continued)

KEYEVNTS.FRM *continued*

```
SUB Form_KeyUp (KeyCode AS INTEGER, Shift AS INTEGER)
    PRINT "KeyUp", KeyCode; Shift
    Position
END SUB

SUB Form_Load ()
    KeyEvnts.Height = Screen.Height * .8

    KeyEvnts.Left = (Screen.Width - KeyEvnts.Width) \ 2
    KeyEvnts.Top = (Screen.Height - KeyEvnts.Height) \ 2
END SUB

SUB menAboutKeyEvnts_Click ()
    About.Label1.Caption = "KEYEVNTS"
    About.SHOW MODAL
END SUB

SUB menExit_Click ()
    UNLOAD KeyEvnts
END SUB

SUB menHelpKeyEvnts_Click ()
    FileMsg "KEYEVNTS.MSG", 1
END SUB

SUB Position ()
    IF CurrentY > ScaleHeight THEN
        CLS
    END IF
END SUB
```

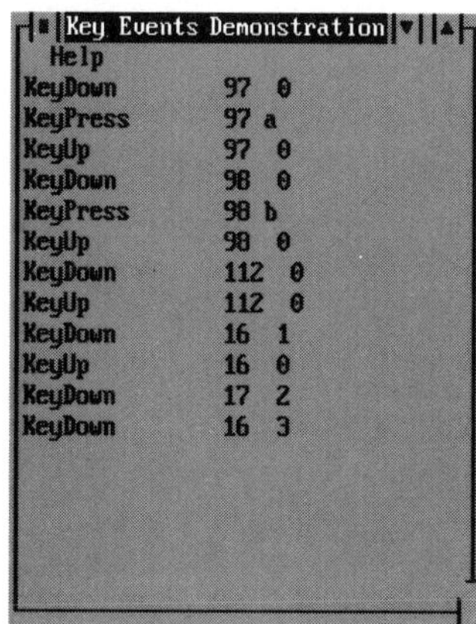

Figure 7-15.
KEYEVNTS.FRM in action.

The MENUDEM Application

The MENUDEM application demonstrates menu properties. Most of the applications in this book use a relatively simple menu that provides standardized online Help and About dialog box capabilities. This application exercises many more of the settings and capabilities of the Visual Basic for MS-DOS menu system.

MENUDEM has two menus: Test and Help. On the Help menu are the standard Help, About, and Exit menu items. On Test are several new menu items that you should investigate.

The Test menu includes two items labeled *First Test Item* and *Second Test Item*. *Hot keys* are set for these two items, allowing the user to select them from the keyboard by using either the Ctrl-F or Ctrl-S key combination. Toggle the check box labeled *Checked* to see how these two menu items appear when their Checked property is set.

The Visible and Enabled properties affect the entire Test menu. When the user clicks the Visible check box, the Test menu disappears and the menu bar collapses so that only the Help menu is shown. The user can click Visible again to redisplay the Test menu. When the user clicks the Enabled check box, the Test menu items dim and cannot be selected. This is how you can arrange to disable menu items and yet still allow the user to view the items. Click Enabled again to re-enable the Test menu.

The third item on the Test menu demonstrates *cascading menus*. You can create up to six levels of cascading menus.

The remainder of the menu items on the Test menu demonstrate menu arrays, which let you dynamically add and remove menu items. Click Menu Array Add to add menu items to the bottom of the menu. Click Menu Array Delete to remove menu items, one at a time. Each of these menu items shares the same control name but has a unique Index setting, resulting in an array of controls. When the user clicks these menu items, a common subprogram activates, and the index of the menu array choice passes to the subprogram to allow identification of the selection.

The files for the MENUDEM application are included on the companion disk. To load the files into Visual Basic for MS-DOS, choose the File Open Project command and type *C:\VBDWSHOP\MENUDEM.MAK*. This opens the project and enables you to view and modify the forms and code. The following figures, tables, and code give the details of the application's creation.

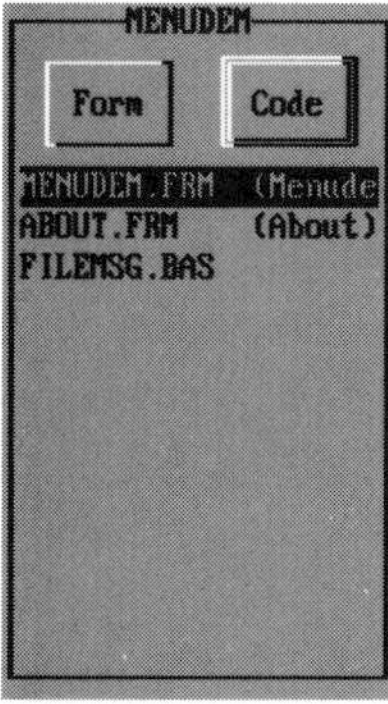

Figure 7-16.
MENUDEM project list.

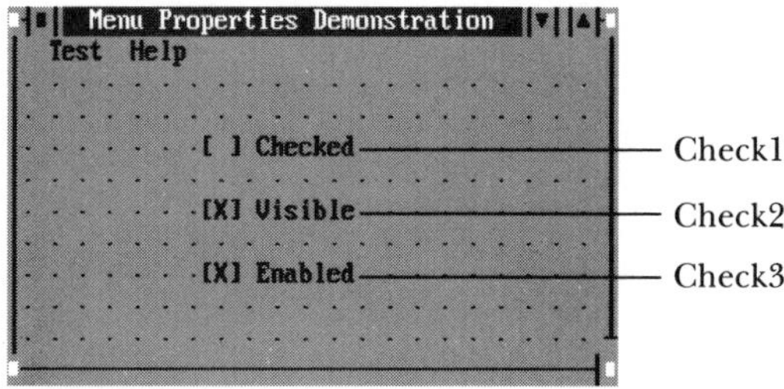

Figure 7-17.
MENUDEM.FRM during development.

MENUDEM.FRM Menu Design Window Entries

Caption	CtlName	Indentation	Shortcut Key	Index
&Test	menTest	0		
&First test item	menFirst	1	Ctrl+F	
&Second test item	menSecond	1	Ctrl+S	
&Cascading menu	menSub	1		
Cascading menu item &1	menSub1	2		
Cascading menu item &2	menSub2	2		
-	menSep1	1		

(continued)

MENUDEM.FRM Menu Design Window Entries *continued*

Caption	CtlName	Indentation	Shortcut Key	Index
Menu Array &Delete	menAryDel	1		
Menu Array &Add	menAryAdd	1		
-	menSep2	1		
Menu Array 1	menAry	1		1
&Help	menHelp	0		
&Help on MenuDem	menHelpMenuDem	1		
&About MenuDem...	menAboutMenuDem	1		
-	menSep3	1		
E&xit	menExit	1		

MENUDEM.FRM Form and Control Properties

Property	Value
Form:	
Caption	Menu Properties Demonstration
FormName	Menudem
Check1:	
Caption	Checked
CtlName	Check1
Value	0 - Unchecked
Check2:	
Caption	Visible
CtlName	Check2
Value	1 - Checked
Check3:	
Caption	Enabled
CtlName	Check3
Value	1 - Checked

Source code for MENUDEM.FRM

```
'================================================
' MENUDEM
' Demonstrates menu properties
'================================================

'$INCLUDE: 'CONSTANT.BI'
'$INCLUDE: 'FILEMSG.BI'
'$INCLUDE: 'ABOUT.BI'

DIM SHARED MenAryCount%

SUB Check1_Click ()
    IF Check1.Value = CHECKED THEN
        menFirst.Checked = TRUE
        menSecond.Checked = TRUE
    ELSE
        menFirst.Checked = FALSE
        menSecond.Checked = FALSE
    END IF
END SUB

SUB Check2_Click ()
    IF Check2.Value = CHECKED THEN
        menTest.Visible = TRUE
    ELSE
        menTest.Visible = FALSE
    END IF
END SUB

SUB Check3_Click ()
    IF Check3.Value = CHECKED THEN
        menTest.Enabled = TRUE
    ELSE
        menTest.Enabled = FALSE
    END IF
END SUB

SUB Form_Load ()
    'Center the form on the screen
    MenuDem.Left = (Screen.Width - MenuDem.Width) \ 2
    MenuDem.Top = (Screen.Height - MenuDem.Height) \ 2

    'Initialize the menu array
    MenAryCount% = 1
    MenAryDel.Enabled = FALSE
END SUB
```

(continued)

MENUDEM.FRM *continued*

```
SUB menAboutMenuDem_Click ()
    About.Label1.Caption = "MENUDEM"
    About.SHOW MODAL
END SUB

SUB menAryAdd_Click ()
    MenAryCount% = MenAryCount% + 1
    LOAD MenAry(MenAryCount%)
    MenAry(MenAryCount%).Caption = "Menu Array" +
 STR$(MenAryCount%)
    MenAryDel.Enabled = TRUE
END SUB

SUB menAryDel_Click ()
    IF MenAryCount% > 1 THEN
        UNLOAD MenAry(MenAryCount%)
        MenAryCount% = MenAryCount% - 1
    ELSE
        BEEP
    END IF

    IF MenAryCount% = 1 THEN
        MenAryDel.Enabled = FALSE
    END IF
END SUB

SUB menExit_Click ()
    UNLOAD MenuDem
END SUB

SUB menFirst_Click ()
    MSGBOX "First test item clicked"
END SUB

SUB menHelpMenuDem_Click ()
    FileMsg "MENUDEM.MSG", 1
END SUB

SUB menSecond_Click ()
    MSGBOX "Second test item clicked"
END SUB

SUB menSub1_Click ()
    MSGBOX "Cascading menu item 1 selected"
END SUB

SUB menSub2_Click ()
    MSGBOX "Cascading menu item 2 selected"
END SUB
```

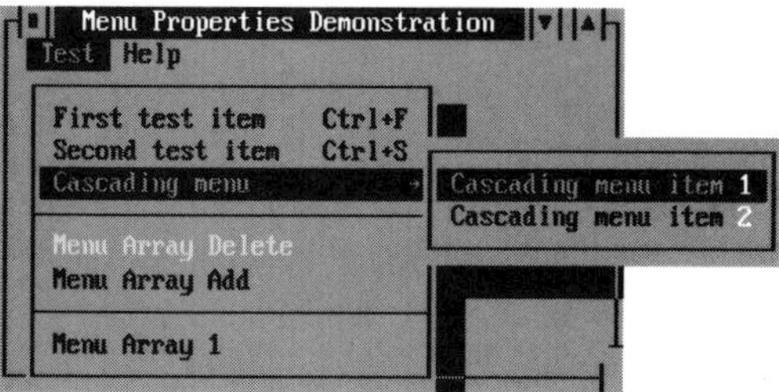

Figure 7-18.
MENUDEM.FRM in action.

The MOUSEPNT Application

The MOUSEPNT application displays all the available mouse pointers. Click each of the option buttons to see each mouse pointer. The mouse pointer changes immediately when the user clicks an option button.

Each form and most objects have a property named MousePointer. The default MousePointer property is *0*, which causes the mouse pointer to appear in its default shape when the user positions the mouse pointer over each form or object. You can set the MousePointer property to any number from *0* through *12*, however, resulting in many different mouse-pointer shapes. For example, assigning the value *11* to the MousePointer property results in the standard hourglass mouse-pointer shape.

These mouse pointers have the same uses as the mouse pointers available in Visual Basic for Windows, but Visual Basic for MS-DOS uses special ASCII and extended character set symbols instead of graphics images to display the mouse pointer. For example, the standard hourglass pointer is simply an uppercase *X*. The default mouse pointer is not a specific character, it instead appears as the reversal of the foreground and background colors of the character underneath the mouse pointer.

The files for the MOUSEPNT application are included on the companion disk. To load the files into Visual Basic for MS-DOS, choose the File Open Project command and type *C:\VBDWSHOP\MOUSEPNT.MAK*. This opens the project and enables you to view and modify the forms and code. The following figures, tables, and code give the details of the application's creation.

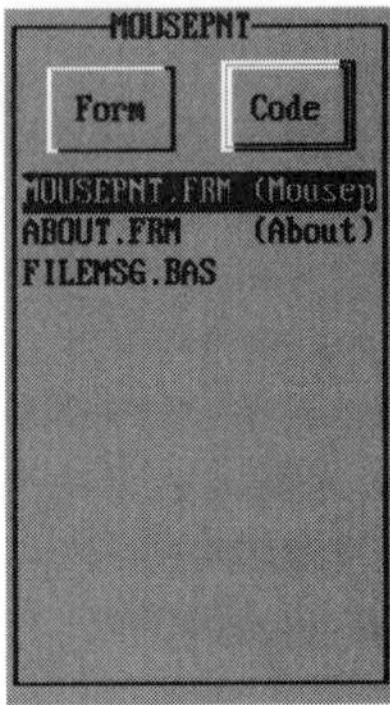

Figure 7-19.
MOUSEPNT project list.

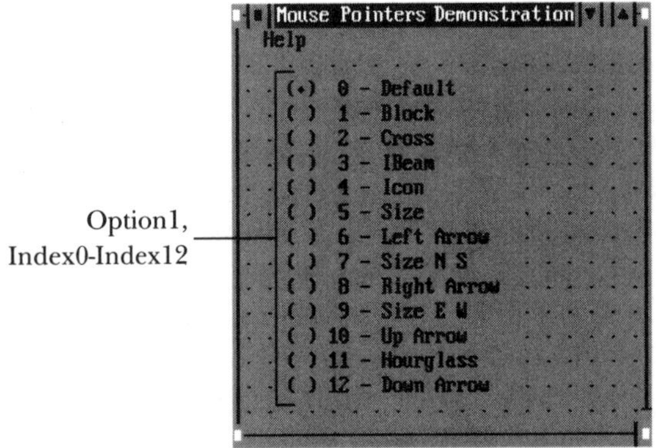

Figure 7-20.
MOUSEPNT.FRM during development.

MOUSEPNT.FRM Menu Design Window Entries

Caption	CtlName	Indentation
&Help	menHelp	0
&Help on MousePnt	menHelpMousePnt	1
&About MousePnt...	menAboutMousePnt	1
-	menSep	1
E&xit	menExit	1

MOUSEPNT.FRM Form and Control Properties

Property	Value
Form:	
Caption	Mouse Pointers Demonstration
FormName	Mousepnt
Option1:	
Caption	0 - Default
CtlName	Option1
Index	0
Option1:	
Caption	1 - Block
CtlName	Option1
Index	1
Option1:	
Caption	2 - Cross
CtlName	Option1
Index	2
Option1:	
Caption	3 - IBeam
CtlName	Option1
Index	3
Option1:	
Caption	4 - Icon
CtlName	Option1
Index	4
Option1:	
Caption	5 - Size
CtlName	Option1
Index	5

(continued)

MOUSEPNT.FRM Form and Control Properties *continued*

Property	Value
Option1:	
Caption	6 - Left Arrow
CtlName	Option1
Index	6
Option1	
Caption	7 - Size N S
CtlName	Option1
Index	7
Option1:	
Caption	8 - Right Arrow
CtlName	Option1
Index	8
Option1:	
Caption	9 - Size E W
CtlName	Option1
Index	9
Option1:	
Caption	10 - Up Arrow
CtlName	Option1
Index	10
Option1:	
Caption	11 - Hourglass
CtlName	Option1
Index	11
Option1:	
Caption	12 - Down Arrow
CtlName	Option1
Index	12

Source code for MOUSEPNT.FRM

```
'================================================
' MOUSEPNT
' Demonstrates the various mouse pointers
'================================================

'$INCLUDE: 'CONSTANT.BI'
'$INCLUDE: 'FILEMSG.BI'
'$INCLUDE: 'ABOUT.BI'

SUB Form_Load ()
    'Center the form on the screen
    MousePnt.Left = (Screen.Width - MousePnt.Width) \ 2
    MousePnt.Top = (Screen.Height - MousePnt.Height) \ 2
END SUB

SUB menAboutMousePnt_Click ()
    About.Label1.Caption = "MOUSEPNT"
    About.SHOW MODAL
END SUB

SUB menExit_Click ()
    UNLOAD MousePnt
END SUB

SUB menHelpMousePnt_Click ()
    FileMsg "MOUSEPNT.MSG", 1
END SUB

SUB Option1_Click (Index AS INTEGER)
    MousePnt.Mousepointer = Index
END SUB
```

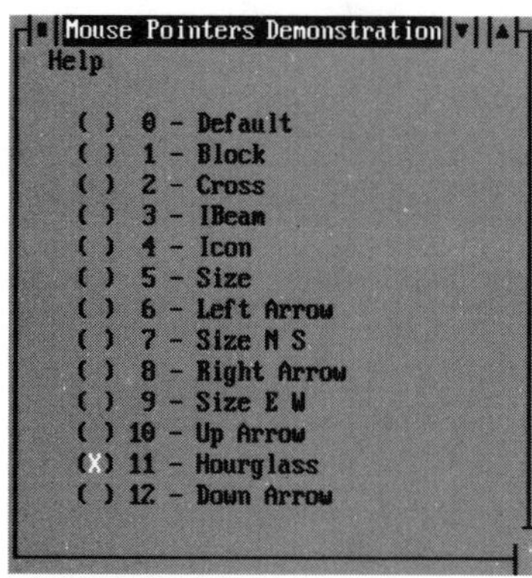

Figure 7-21.
MOUSEPNT.FRM in action.

The MOUSEVNT Application

The MOUSEVNT application demonstrates the mouse events that mouse movement and mouse clicks generate. The MOUSEVNT form handles five mouse events; each event causes a message to appear on the form. The *Form_MouseMove* subprogram activates most often—whenever the user moves the mouse while the mouse pointer is on the form. MouseDown, MouseUp, and Click events occur whenever the user clicks one or both mouse buttons. The DblClick event occurs whenever the user double-clicks a mouse button.

Several controls appear on the form. Their only purpose is to show that mouse events for the form do not occur when the mouse pointer is over these controls. Mouse events for these controls are separate from those for the form. For the program to act on mouse events for these controls, you must create a similar (but unique) set of subprograms for each control.

Notice that the form's height during development is less than it is when the application is running. The *Form_Load* subprogram contains a statement that sets the form's Height property to 80 percent of the screen's height. Other statements in *Form_Load* center the form on the screen. These techniques are useful for creating applications to run on screens with an unpredictable number of display lines. For example, the application centers this form and fills most of the display equally well whether the user's display is set to 25, 43, or 50 lines of text.

The files for the MOUSEVNT application are included on the companion disk. To load the files into Visual Basic for MS-DOS, choose the File Open Project command and type *C:\VBDWSHOP\MOUSEVNT.MAK*. This opens the project and enables you to view and modify the forms and code. The following figures, tables, and code give the details of the application's creation.

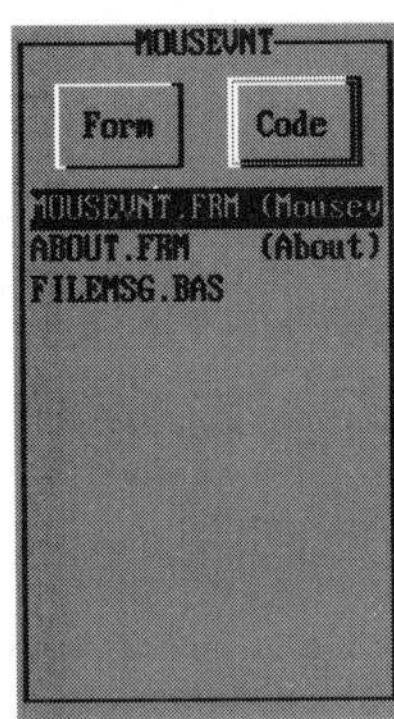

Figure 7-22.
MOUSEVNT project list.

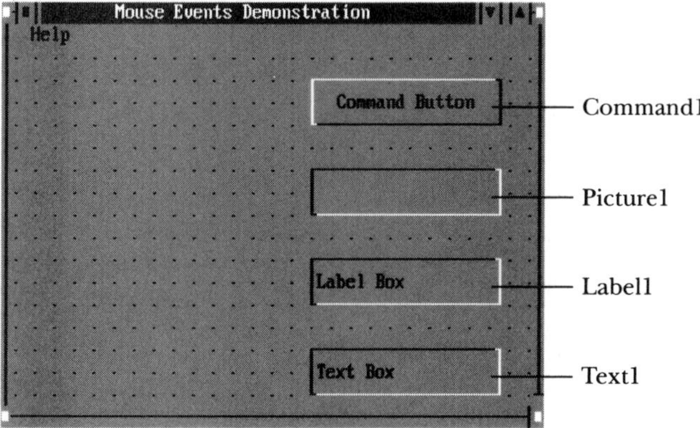

Figure 7-23.
MOUSEVNT.FRM during development.

MOUSEVNT.FRM Menu Design Window Entries

Caption	CtlName	Indentation
&Help	menHelp	0
&Help on MousEvnt	menHelpMousEvnt	1
&About MousEvnt...	menAboutMousEvnt	1
-	menSep	1
E&xit	menExit	1

MOUSEVNT.FRM Form and Control Properties

Property	Value
Form:	
Caption	Mouse Events Demonstration
FormName	Mousevnt
Command1:	
Caption	Command Button
CtlName	Command1
Picture1:	
CtlName	Picture1

(continued)

MOUSEVNT.FRM Form and Control Properties *continued*

Property	Value
Label1:	
BorderStyle	1 - Single Line
Caption	Label Box
CtlName	Label1
Text1:	
Caption	Text Box
CtlName	Text1

Source code for MOUSEVNT.FRM

```
'=================================================
' MOUSEVNT
' Demonstrates mouse events
'=================================================

'$INCLUDE: 'CONSTANT.BI'
'$INCLUDE: 'FILEMSG.BI'
'$INCLUDE: 'ABOUT.BI'

DECLARE SUB CheckFormBottom ()

SUB CheckFormBottom ()
    IF CurrentY > ScaleHeight THEN
        CLS
    END IF
END SUB

SUB Form_Click ()
    PRINT "Click"
    CheckFormBottom
END SUB

SUB Form_DblClick ()
    PRINT "DblClick"
    CheckFormBottom
END SUB
```

(continued)

MOUSEVNT.FRM *continued*

```
SUB Form_Load ()
    'Size form at 80 percent of screen height
    MousEvnt.Height = .8 * Screen.Height

    'Center the form on the screen
    MousEvnt.Left = (Screen.Width - MousEvnt.Width) \ 2
    MousEvnt.Top = (Screen.Height - MousEvnt.Height) \ 2
END SUB

SUB Form_MouseDown (Button AS INTEGER, Shift AS INTEGER, X AS
 SINGLE, Y AS SINGLE)
    PRINT "MouseDown"; Button; Shift; X; Y
    CheckFormBottom
END SUB

SUB Form_MouseMove (Button AS INTEGER, Shift AS INTEGER, X AS
 SINGLE, Y AS SINGLE)
    PRINT "MouseMove"; Button; Shift; X; Y
    CheckFormBottom
END SUB

SUB Form_MouseUp (Button AS INTEGER, Shift AS INTEGER, X AS
 SINGLE, Y AS SINGLE)
    PRINT "MouseUp"; Button; Shift; X; Y
    CheckFormBottom
END SUB

SUB menAboutMousEvnt_Click ()
    About.Label1.Caption = "MOUSEVNT"
    About.SHOW MODAL
END SUB

SUB menExit_Click ()
    UNLOAD MousEvnt
END SUB

SUB menHelpMousEvnt_Click ()
    FileMsg "MOUSEVNT.MSG", 1
END SUB

SUB Picture1_Paint ()
    Picture1.PRINT "Picture Box"
END SUB
```

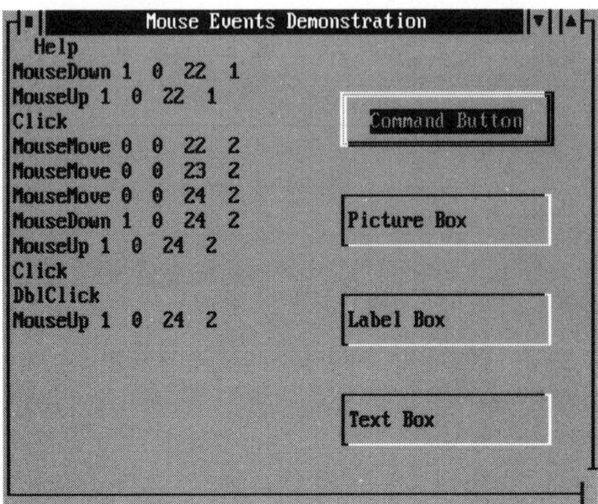

Figure 7-24.
MOUSEVNT.FRM in action.

The MSGBOXES Application

Message boxes created with the *MSGBOX* statement are not only easy to use, they are useful for programming in Visual Basic for MS-DOS. In previous versions of Basic, the *PRINT* statement was the workhorse for simple text output. The *MSGBOX* statement is the equivalent workhorse for text output in Visual Basic for MS-DOS. The MSGBOXES application interactively demonstrates the variety of configurations for message boxes created with the *MSGBOX* statement.

MSGBOXES also provides a good example of how to use groups of option-button controls. Two arrays of option buttons allow you to select the parameters for the *MSGBOX* statements. Because the application requires more than one group of option buttons, you must separate the groups by placing them in picture boxes or frames so that the user can select only one option button from each group. (See "The FRAMOPT Application" in Chapter 6 for more information about grouping option buttons.) If you don't separate the two arrays of buttons, the user can select only one button at a time from all the option buttons on the form. The MSGBOXES application uses frames to enclose the two groups. Each option button in a group has a unique index value that identifies the button when the associated Click event subprogram runs. Visual Basic for MS-DOS handles the details of ensuring the selection of only one option button at a time from a group.

Select one option button from each group to define a message box. The application passes two strings to *MSGBOX* statements, *Title$* and *Message$*. Near the bottom of the MSGBOXES form are text boxes in which the user can enter new strings for these items. The application uses default strings if the user doesn't enter a new title or message.

The files for the MSGBOXES application are included on the companion disk. To load the files into Visual Basic for MS-DOS, choose the File Open Project command and type *C:\VBDWSHOP\MSGBOXES.MAK*. This opens the project and enables you to view and modify the forms and code. The following figures, tables, and code give the details of the application's creation.

Figure 7-25.
MSGBOXES project list.

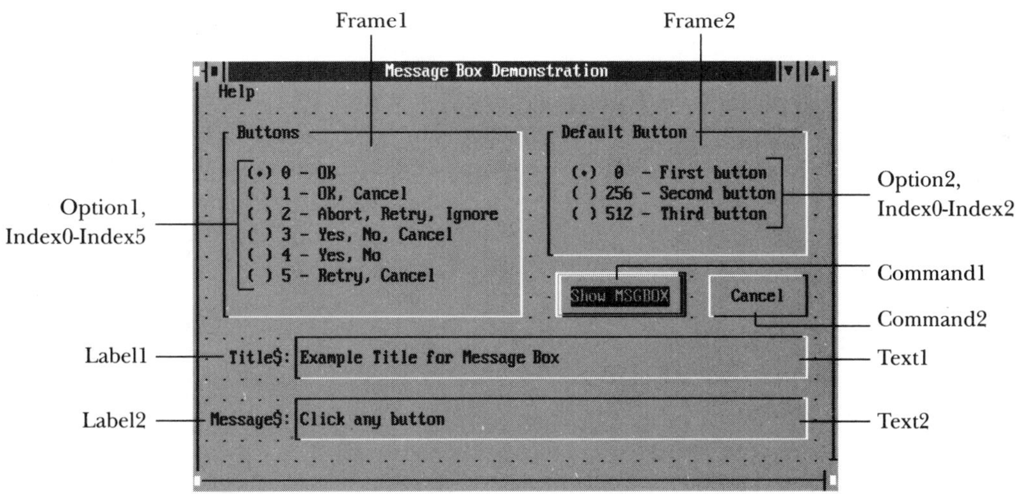

Figure 7-26.
MSGBOXES.FRM during development.

MSGBOXES.FRM Menu Design Window Entries

Caption	CtlName	Indentation
&Help	menHelp	0
&Help on MsgBoxes	menHelpMsgBoxes	1
&About MsgBoxes...	menAboutMsgBoxes	1
-	menSep	1
E&xit	menExit	1

MSGBOXES.FRM Form and Control Properties

Property	Value
Form:	
Caption	Message Box Demonstration
FormName	Msgboxes
Frame1:	
Caption	Buttons
CtlName	Frame1
Frame2:	
Caption	Default Button
CtlName	Frame2
Option1:	
Caption	0 - OK
CtlName	Option1
Index	0
Option1:	
Caption	1 - OK, Cancel
CtlName	Option1
Index	1
Option1:	
Caption	2 - Abort, Retry, Ignore
CtlName	Option1
Index	2

(continued)

MSGBOXES.FRM Form and Control Properties *continued*

Property	Value
Option1:	
Caption	3 - Yes, No, Cancel
CtlName	Option1
Index	3
Option1:	
Caption	4 - Yes, No
CtlName	Option1
Index	4
Option1:	
Caption	5 - Retry, Cancel
CtlName	Option1
Index	5
Option2:	
Caption	0 - First Button
CtlName	Option2
Index	0
Option2:	
Caption	256 - Second Button
CtlName	Option2
Index	1
Option2:	
Caption	512 - Third Button
CtlName	Option2
Index	2
Command1:	
Caption	Show MSGBOX
CtlName	Command1
Default	True

(continued)

MSGBOXES.FRM Form and Control Properties *continued*

Property	Value
Command2:	
Cancel	True
Caption	Cancel
CtlName	Command2
Label1:	
Alignment	1 - Right Justify
Caption	Title$:
CtlName	Label1
Label2:	
Alignment	1 - Right Justify
Caption	Message$:
CtlName	Label2
Text1:	
CtlName	Text1
Text	Example Title for Message Box
Text2:	
CtlName	Text2
Text	Click any button

Source code for MSGBOXES.FRM

```
'================================================
' MSGBOXES
' Demonstrates the MSGBOX statement
'================================================

'$INCLUDE: 'CONSTANT.BI'
'$INCLUDE: 'FILEMSG.BI'
'$INCLUDE: 'ABOUT.BI'

DIM SHARED ButtonType%
DIM SHARED DefaultButton%

SUB Command1_Click ()
    Index% = ButtonType% + DefaultButton%
```

(continued)

MSGBOXES.FRM *continued*

```
    Title$ = Text1.Text
    Msg$ = Text2.Text

    SELECT CASE MSGBOX(Msg$, Index%, Title$)
    CASE 1
        MSGBOX "OK button was clicked"
    CASE 2
        MSGBOX "Cancel button was clicked"
    CASE 3
        MSGBOX "Abort button was clicked"
    CASE 4
        MSGBOX "Retry button was clicked"
    CASE 5
        MSGBOX "Ignore button was clicked"
    CASE 6
        MSGBOX "Yes button was clicked"
    CASE 7
        MSGBOX "No button was clicked"
    CASE ELSE
        MSGBOX "Unknown button was clicked"
    END SELECT
END SUB

SUB Command2_Click ()
    UNLOAD MsgBoxes
END SUB

SUB Form_Load ()
    'Center the form on the screen
    MsgBoxesForm.Left = (Screen.Width - MsgBoxesForm.Width) \ 2
    MsgBoxesForm.Top = (Screen.Height - MsgBoxesForm.Height) \ 2
END SUB

SUB menAboutMsgBoxes_Click ()
    About.Label1.Caption = "MSGBOXES"
    About.SHOW MODAL
END SUB

SUB menExit_Click ()
    UNLOAD MsgBoxes
END SUB

SUB menHelpMsgBoxes_Click ()
    FileMsg "MSGBOXES.MSG", 1
END SUB

SUB Option1_Click (Index AS INTEGER)
    ButtonType% = Index
END SUB

SUB Option2_Click (Index AS INTEGER)
    DefaultButton% = Index * 256
END SUB
```

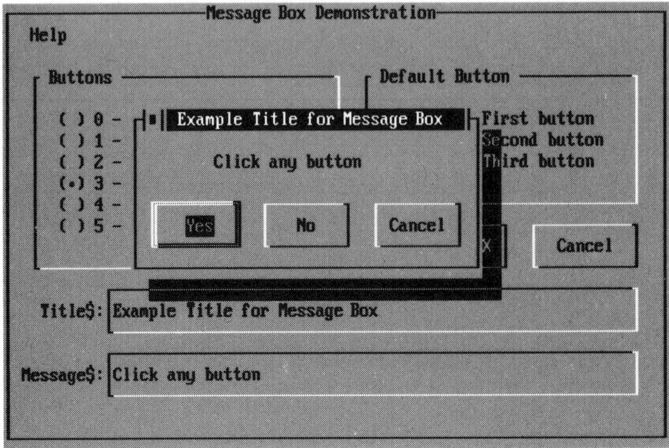

Figure 7-27.
MSGBOXES.FRM in action.

The AUDIODEM Application

The AUDIODEM application lets you build and experiment with the sound-generation capabilities of Visual Basic for MS-DOS. You can save *PLAY* sound strings in a file to include later in other programs.

The simplest sound that Visual Basic for MS-DOS generates is created by the *BEEP* statement. Click the BEEP command button to hear this standard sound.

Next in complexity is the *SOUND* statement. You use frequency and duration parameters to control the *SOUND* statement's output. The frequency is in standard hertz (Hz), or cycles per second, and the duration is in clock-tick units. There are 18.2 clock ticks per second, so setting the duration to *18* results in roughly 1 second of sound.

The most flexible sound-generation statement in Visual Basic for MS-DOS is *PLAY*. The *PLAY* command is an entire music-command language, not unlike the entire graphics language offered by the graphics *DRAW* command. See Visual Basic for MS-DOS's online Help or the Visual Basic for MS-DOS manual for more details and information about the rich command set available with the *PLAY* command.

The AUDIODEM application lets you experiment as much as you want with the *PLAY* command. Edit the *PLAY* string and click the PLAY button to try out your musical creations. At any time, you can append the PLAY string to a file named PLAY.DAT by clicking the Save button, which makes it easy to add these strings later to other programs.

The files for the AUDIODEM application are included on the companion disk. To load the files into Visual Basic for MS-DOS, choose the File Open Project command and type *C:\VBDWSHOP\AUDIODEM.MAK*. This opens the project and enables you to view and modify the forms and code. The following figures, tables, and code give the details of the application's creation.

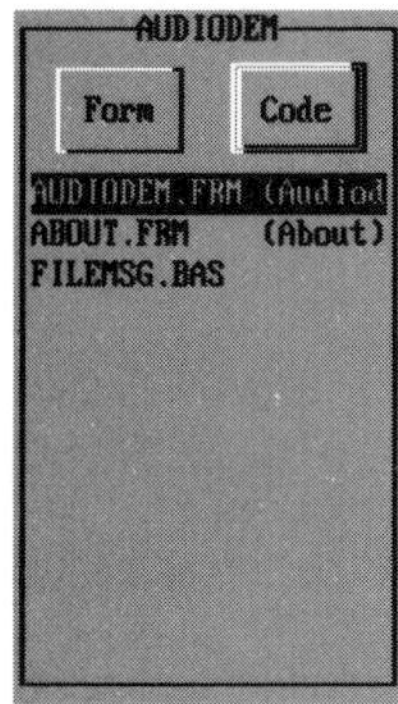

Figure 7-28.
AUDIODEM project list.

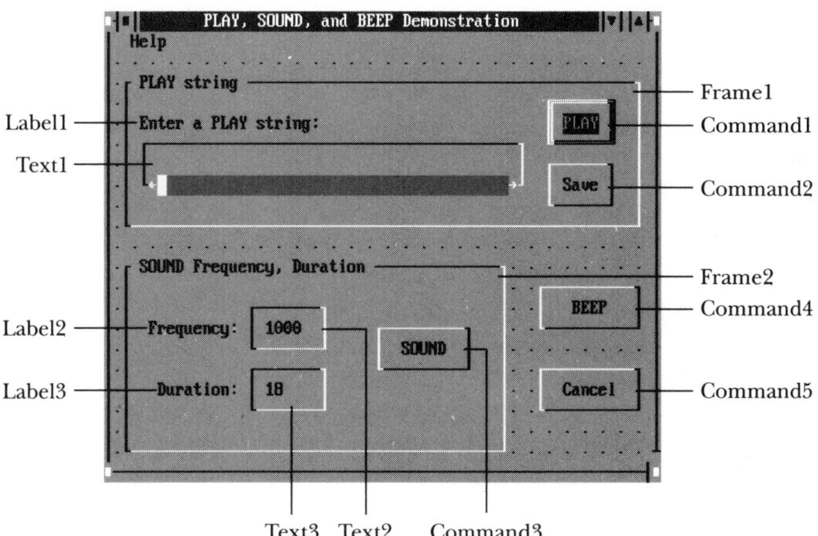

Figure 7-29.
AUDIODEM.FRM during development.

AUDIODEM.FRM Menu Design Window Entries

Caption	CtlName	Indentation
&Help	menHelp	0
&Help on AudioDem	menHelpAudioDem	1
&About AudioDem...	menAboutAudioDem	1
-	menSep	1
E&xit	menExit	1

AUDIODEM.FRM Form and Control Properties

Property	Value
Form:	
Caption	PLAY, SOUND, and BEEP Demonstration
FormName	Audiodem
Frame1:	
Caption	PLAY string
CtlName	Frame1
Frame2:	
Caption	SOUND Frequency, Duration
CtlName	Frame2
Label1:	
Caption	Enter a PLAY string:
CtlName	Label1
Label2:	
Alignment	1 - Right Justify
Caption	Frequency:
CtlName	Label2
Label3:	
Alignment	1 - Right Justify
Caption	Duration:
CtlName	Label3

(continued)

AUDIODEM.FRM Form and Control Properties *continued*

Property	Value
Text1:	
CtlName	Text1
MultiLine	True
ScrollBars	1 - Horizontal
Text	*(blank)*
Text2:	
CtlName	Text2
Text	1000
Text3:	
CtlName	Text3
Text	18
Command1:	
Caption	PLAY
CtlName	Command1
Default	True
Command2:	
Caption	Save
CtlName	Command2
Command3:	
Caption	SOUND
CtlName	Command3
Command4:	
Caption	BEEP
CtlName	Command4
Command5:	
Cancel	True
Caption	Cancel
CtlName	Command5

Source code for AUDIODEM.FRM

```
'==================================================
' AUDIODEM
' Demonstrates PLAY, SOUND, and BEEP commands
'==================================================

'$INCLUDE: 'CONSTANT.BI'
'$INCLUDE: 'FILEMSG.BI'
'$INCLUDE: 'ABOUT.BI'

SUB Command1_Click ()
    ON LOCAL ERROR GOTO BadPlay

    PLAY "MB" + Text1.Text

ExitPlay:
    EXIT SUB

BadPlay:
    MSGBOX "Illegal PLAY string"
    RESUME ExitPlay
END SUB

SUB Command2_Click ()
    OPEN "PLAY.DAT" FOR APPEND AS #1
    PRINT #1, "'PLAY " + CHR$(34) + Text1.Text + CHR$(34)
    CLOSE #1
    MSGBOX "PLAY string appended to PLAY.DAT"
END SUB

SUB Command3_Click ()
    ON LOCAL ERROR GOTO BadSound

    Frequency = VAL(Text2.Text)
    Duration = VAL(Text3.Text)

    SOUND Frequency, Duration

ExitSound:
    EXIT SUB

BadSound:
    MSGBOX "Illegal SOUND parameters"
    RESUME ExitSound
END SUB
```

(continued)

AUDIODEM.FRM *continued*

```
SUB Command4_Click ()
    BEEP
END SUB

SUB Command5_Click ()
    UNLOAD AudioDem
END SUB

SUB Form_Load ()
    'Center the form on the screen
    AudioDem.Left = (Screen.Width - AudioDem.Width) \ 2
    AudioDem.Top = (Screen.Height - AudioDem.Height) \ 2
END SUB

'SUB menAboutAudioDem_Click ()
    About.Label1.Caption = "AUDIODEM"
    About.SHOW MODAL
END SUB

SUB menExit_Click ()
    UNLOAD AudioDem
END SUB

SUB menHelpAudioDem_Click ()
    FileMsg "AUDIODEM.MSG", 1
END SUB
```

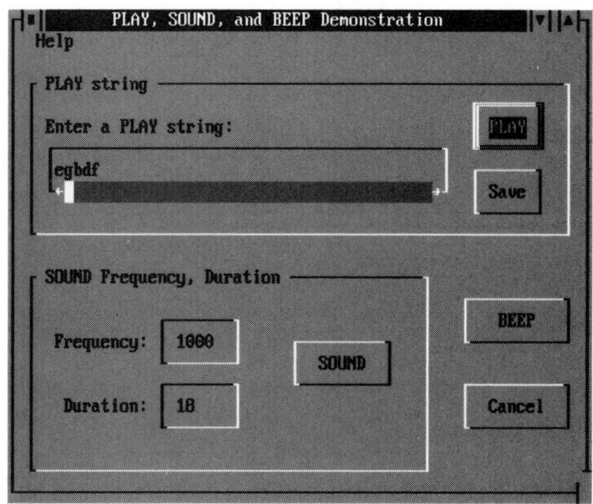

Figure 7-30.
AUDIODEM.FRM in action.

The CTRLPANL Application

The CTRLPANL application lets you interactively experiment with the 18 global property settings that affect the overall appearance of your applications.

The application displays a list of the ControlPanel properties, showing the current setting for each. The user can click anywhere on the string description of a property to cycle through the range of settings for the indicated property. For example, the user can click anywhere on *Active border background color (0–15)* to see the next color setting for the form's border.

The desktop fill pattern is a special case. Because you can use any number in the range 0 through 255 to set the desktop fill pattern, you can use an input box to prompt the user for a value when he or she clicks on this line. Note that the default desktop fill property is *176*. Some of the settings for this property result in a harsh or "busy" background that can be quite distracting. To restore the original desktop fill pattern, set the desktop fill property back to *176* after you have finished experimenting.

The files for the CTRLPANL application are included on the companion disk. To load the files into Visual Basic for MS-DOS, choose the File Open Project command and type *C:\VBDWSHOP\CTRLPANL.MAK*. This opens the project and enables you to view and modify the forms and code. The following figures, tables, and code give the details of the application's creation.

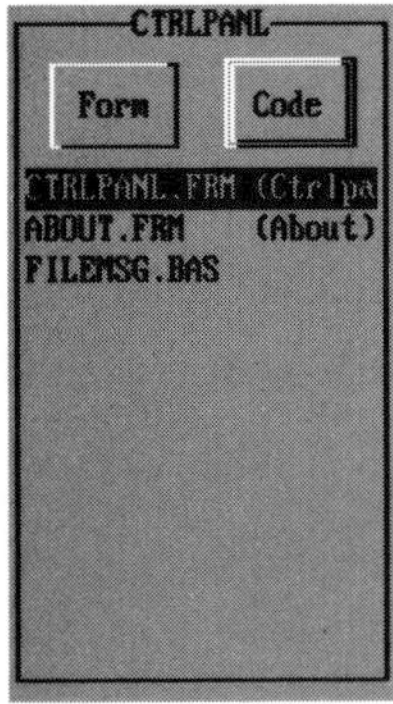

Figure 7-31.
CTRLPANL project list.

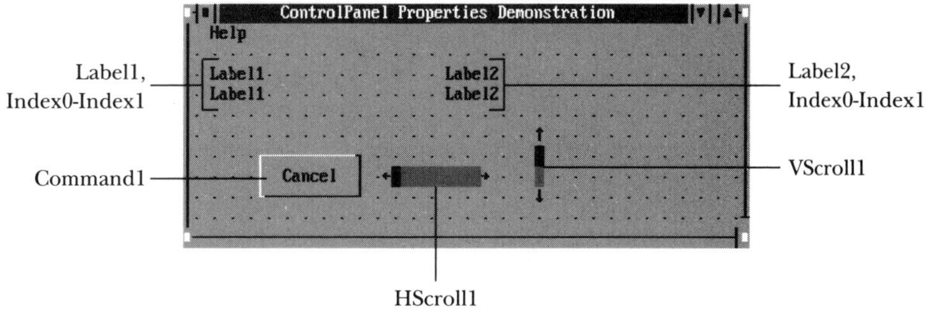

Figure 7-32.
CTRLPANL.FRM during development.

CTRLPANL.FRM Menu Design Window Entries

Caption	CtlName	Indentation
&Help	menHelp	0
&Help on CtrlPanl	menHelpCtrlPanl	1
&About CtrlPanl...	menAboutCtrlPanl	1
-	menSep	1
E&xit	menExit	1

CTRLPANL.FRM Form and Control Properties

Property	Value
Form:	
Caption	ControlPanel Properties Demonstration
FormName	Ctrlpanl
Label1:	
CtlName	Label1
Index	0
Label1:	
CtlName	Label1
Index	1

(continued)

CTRLPANL.FRM Form and Control Properties *continued*

Property	Value
Label2:	
CtlName	Label2
Index	0
Label2:	
CtlName	Label2
Index	1
HScroll1:	
CtlName	HScroll1
VScroll1:	
CtlName	VScroll1
Command1:	
Cancel	True
Caption	Cancel
CtlName	Command1

Source code for CTRLPANL.FRM

```
'================================================
' CTRLPANL
' Demonstrates ControlPanel properties
'================================================

'$INCLUDE: 'CONSTANT.BI'
'$INCLUDE: 'FILEMSG.BI'
'$INCLUDE: 'ABOUT.BI'

SUB Command1_Click ()
    UNLOAD CtrlPanl
END SUB

SUB Form_Load ()
    'Expand the first label array
    FOR i% = 2 TO 17
        LOAD Label1(i%)
        Label1(i%).Top = i% + 1
```

(continued)

CTRLPANL.FRM *continued*

```
        Label1(i%).Visible = TRUE
        Label1(i%).AutoSize = TRUE
    NEXT i%

    'Fill the first label array
    FOR i% = 0 TO 17
        SELECT CASE i%
        CASE 0
            Tmp$ = "Access key foreground color (0-15)"
        CASE 1
            Tmp$ = "Active border background color (0-15)"
        CASE 2
            Tmp$ = "Active border foreground color (0-15)"
        CASE 3
            Tmp$ = "Active window shadow effect (Boolean)"
        CASE 4
            Tmp$ = "Command-button foreground color (0-15)"
        CASE 5
            Tmp$ = "Desktop background color (0-15)"
        CASE 6
            Tmp$ = "Desktop foreground color (0-15)"
        CASE 7
            Tmp$ = "Desktop fill pattern (ASCII 0-255)"
        CASE 8
            Tmp$ = "Disabled menu/dialog item foregrd color (0-15)"
        CASE 9
            Tmp$ = "Menu background color (0-15)"
        CASE 10
            Tmp$ = "Menu foreground color (0-15)"
        CASE 11
            Tmp$ = "Menu item selected background color (0-15)"
        CASE 12
            Tmp$ = "Menu item selected foreground color (0-15)"
        CASE 13
            Tmp$ = "Scroll bar background color (0-15)"
        CASE 14
            Tmp$ = "Scroll bar foreground color (0-15)"
        CASE 15
            Tmp$ = "3-D effect for controls with borders (Boolean)"
        CASE 16
            Tmp$ = "Title bar background color (0-15)"
        CASE 17
            Tmp$ = "Title bar foreground color (0-15)"
        END SELECT
        Label1(i%).Caption = Tmp$
    NEXT i%
```

(continued)

CTRLPANL.FRM *continued*

```
    'Expand the second label array
    FOR i% = 2 TO 17
        LOAD Label2(i%)
        Label2(i%).Visible = TRUE
        Label2(i%).AutoSize = TRUE
    NEXT i%

    'Display current Control Panel values
    FOR i% = 0 TO 17
        Label2(i%).Top = i% + 1
        Label2(i%).Left = 50
        Tmp$ = STR$(Screen.ControlPanel(i%))
        Label2(i%).Caption = Tmp$
    NEXT i%

    'Move the command button
    Command1.Top = 15
    Command1.Left = 55

    'Move the horizontal scroll bar
    HScroll1.Top = 13
    HScroll1.Left = 55

    'Move and resize the vertical scroll bar
    VScroll1.Top = 2
    VScroll1.Left = 61
    VScroll1.Height = 10

    'Set the form's size
    CtrlPanl.Height = 23
    CtrlPanl.Width = 70

    'Center the form on the screen
    CtrlPanl.Left = (Screen.Width - CtrlPanl.Width) \ 2
    CtrlPanl.Top = (Screen.Height - CtrlPanl.Height) \ 2
END SUB

SUB Label1_Click (Index AS INTEGER)
    Tmp% = Screen.ControlPanel(Index)

    SELECT CASE Index
    CASE 0 TO 2, 4 TO 6, 8 TO 14, 16 TO 17
        Tmp% = (Tmp% + 1) MOD 16
    CASE 7
        Prompt$ = "Enter ASCII value (0-255) for desktop fill
 character"
```

(continued)

CTRLPANL.FRM *continued*

```
        Title$ = "Desktop Fill Character"
        Defalt$ = "176"
        DO
            Tmp% = VAL(INPUTBOX$(Prompt$, Title$, Defalt$))
        LOOP UNTIL Tmp% >= 0 AND Tmp% < 256
    CASE 3, 15
        Tmp% = NOT Tmp%
    END SELECT

    Screen.ControlPanel(Index) = Tmp%
    Label2(Index).Caption = STR$(Tmp%)
END SUB

SUB menAboutCtrlPanl_Click ()
    About.Label1.Caption = "CTRLPANL"
    About.SHOW MODAL
END SUB

SUB menExit_Click ()
    UNLOAD CtrlPanl
END SUB

SUB menHelpCtrlPanl_Click ()
    FileMsg "CTRLPANL.MSG", 1
END SUB
```

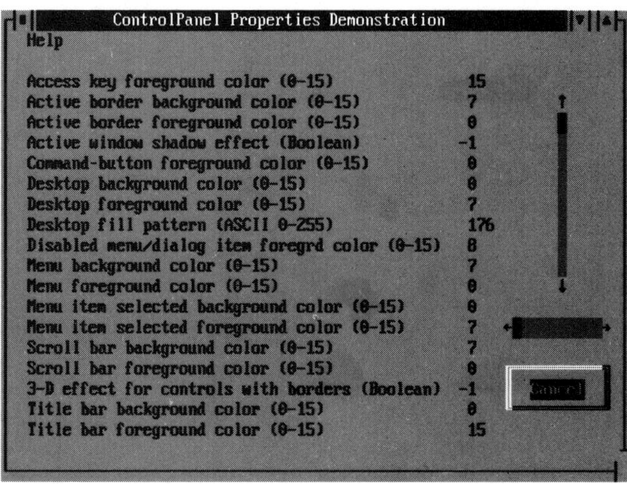

Figure 7-33.
CTRLPANL.FRM in action.

CHAPTER EIGHT

CALENDARS AND TIME

Visual Basic for MS-DOS has a rich set of built-in functions for both date and time computations. The applications in this chapter demonstrate several of these functions. The NISTTIME application also demonstrates how to use serial communications routines to phone the National Institute of Standards and Technology to accurately set your computer's clock.

The CALENDAR Application

The CALENDAR application demonstrates several of the date and time functions in Visual Basic for MS-DOS by displaying a one-month calendar page and letting the user select a day of the month. Scroll bars at the bottom of the form enable the user to select any year or month that is within the legal range of the application. The program highlights one day of the displayed month, and either double-clicking on that day or clicking the OK button selects that date.

When the program starts, it creates an array of labels to hold the numbers for each day of the month. You can set the ForeColor and BackColor properties of each label individually in the array, which is a convenient means of highlighting the date the user has selected.

Visual Basic for MS-DOS provides functions that simplify calendar programming tasks considerably. *DATESERIAL* and *NOW* are built-in functions that return a serial number. (A *serial number* is a date/time code used by Visual Basic for MS-DOS.) *DATESERIAL* returns a serial number that represents the date of the arguments passed to the function, and *NOW* returns a serial number that represents the current system date and time, within the range of years 1753 through 2078. The built-in functions *MONTH, DAY, YEAR,* and *WEEKDAY* operate on any serial number to extract information from the number.

The files for the CALENDAR application are included on the companion disk. To load the files into Visual Basic for MS-DOS, choose the File Open Project command and type *C:\VBDWSHOP\CALENDAR.MAK.* This opens the project and enables you to view and modify the forms and code. The following figures, tables, and code give the details of the application's creation.

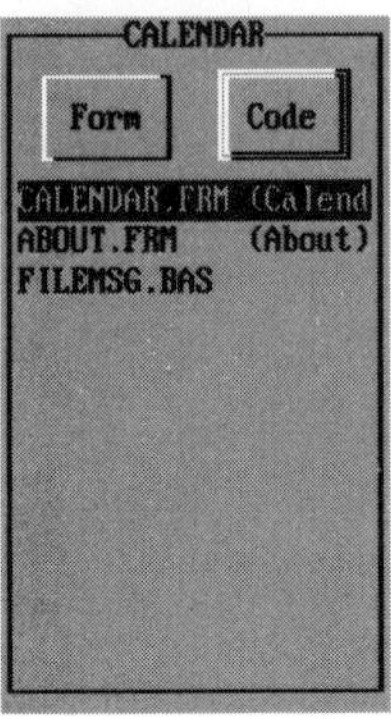

Figure 8-1.
CALENDAR project list.

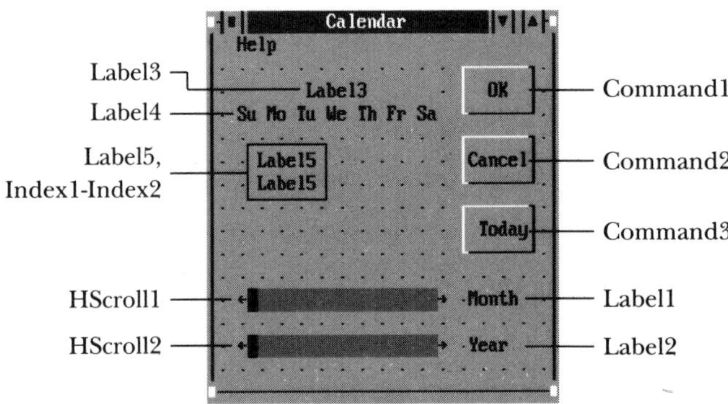

Figure 8-2.
CALENDAR.FRM during development.

CALENDAR.FRM Menu Design Window Entries

Caption	CtlName	Indentation
&Help	menHelp	0
&Help on Calendar	menHelpCalendar	1
&About Calendar...	menAboutCalendar	1
-	menSep	1
E&xit	menExit	1

CALENDAR.FRM Form and Control Properties

Property	Value
Form:	
BorderStyle	1 - Fixed Single
Caption	Calendar
FormName	Calendar
Label1:	
Caption	Month
CtlName	Label1
Label2:	
Caption	Year
CtlName	Label2
Label3:	
Caption	Label3
CtlName	Label3
Label4:	
Caption	Su Mo Tu We Th Fr Sa
CtlName	Label4
Label5:	
Caption	Label5
CtlName	Label5
Index	1
Label5:	
Caption	Label5
CtlName	Label5
Index	2
HScroll1:	
CtlName	HScroll1
LargeChange	3
Max	12
Min	1

(continued)

CALENDAR.FRM Form and Control Properties *continued*

Property	Value
HScroll2:	
CtlName	HScroll2
LargeChange	10
Max	2077
Min	1753
Command1:	
Caption	OK
CtlName	Command1
Default	True
Command2:	
Cancel	True
Caption	Cancel
CtlName	Command2
Command3:	
Caption	Today
CtlName	Command3

Source code for CALENDAR.FRM

```
'================================================
' CALENDAR
' Displays a monthly calendar
'================================================

'$INCLUDE: 'CONSTANT.BI'
'$INCLUDE: 'FILEMSG.BI'
'$INCLUDE: 'ABOUT.BI'

DECLARE SUB SplitSerial ()
DECLARE SUB UpdateTitle ()
DECLARE SUB MakeSerial ()
DECLARE SUB Command3_Click ()
DECLARE SUB UpdateNumbers ()
```

(continued)

CALENDAR.FRM *continued*

```
DECLARE SUB Highlight ()
DECLARE SUB HScroll2_Change ()
DECLARE SUB Command1_Click ()

DIM SHARED YearNum%
DIM SHARED MonthNum%
DIM SHARED DayNum%
DIM SHARED SerialNum
DIM SHARED AryIndex%

SUB Command1_Click ()
    Title$ = "Date Selected"
    Msg$ = Label3.Caption
    n% = INSTR(Msg$, ",")
    Msg$ = LEFT$(Msg$, n% - 1) + STR$(DayNum%) + MID$(Msg$, n%)
    MSGBOX Msg$, 0, Title$
END SUB

SUB Command2_Click ()
    UNLOAD Calendar
END SUB

SUB Command3_Click ()
    SerialNum = NOW
    SplitSerial
    IF HScroll2.Value <> YearNum% OR HScroll1.Value <> MonthNum%
 THEN
        HScroll2.Value = YearNum%
        HScroll1.Value = MonthNum%
    ELSE
        HScroll2_Change
    END IF
END SUB

SUB Form_Load ()
    'Center the form on the screen
    Calendar.Left = (Screen.Width - Calendar.Width) \ 2
    Calendar.Top = (Screen.Height - Calendar.Height) \ 2

    'Expand the day numbers label array
    FOR i% = 3 TO 37
        LOAD Label5(i%)
    NEXT i%
```

(continued)

CALENDAR.FRM *continued*

```
    'Initialize the day numbers label array
    FOR i% = 1 TO 37
        Label5(i%).Left = ((i% - 1) MOD 7) * 3 + 2
        Label5(i%).Top = ((i% - 1) \ 7) + 3
        Label5(i%).Width = 2
        Label5(i%).Visible = TRUE
        Label5(i%).Alignment = CENTER
    NEXT i%

    'Initialize using today's date
    Command3_Click
END SUB

SUB Highlight ()
    'Highlight the selected date
    FOR i% = 1 TO 37
        IF i% = AryIndex% THEN
            Label5(i%).ForeColor = YELLOW
            Label5(i%).BackColor = BLUE
        ELSE
            Label5(i%).ForeColor = BLACK
            Label5(i%).BackColor = WHITE
        END IF
    NEXT i%
END SUB

SUB HScroll1_Change ()
    MonthNum% = HScroll1.Value
    HScroll2_Change
END SUB

SUB HScroll2_Change ()
    YearNum% = HScroll2.Value
    MakeSerial
    UpdateTitle
    UpdateNumbers
    Highlight
END SUB

SUB Label5_Click (Index AS INTEGER)
    'Don't do anything if not a numbered day
    n% = VAL(Label5(Index).Caption)
    IF n% = 0 THEN EXIT SUB

    'Update the currently selected date
    DayNum% = n%
    MakeSerial
```

(continued)

CALENDAR.FRM *continued*

```
    'Highlight the selected date
    AryIndex% = Index
    Highlight
END SUB

SUB Label5_DblClick (Index AS INTEGER)
    'Don't do anything if not a numbered day
    n% = VAL(Label5(Index).Caption)
    IF n% = 0 THEN EXIT SUB

    Command1_Click
END SUB

SUB MakeSerial ()
    SerialNum = DATESERIAL(YearNum%, MonthNum%, DayNum%)
END SUB

SUB menAboutCalendar_Click ()
    About.Label1.Caption = "CALENDAR"
    About.SHOW MODAL
END SUB

SUB menExit_Click ()
    UNLOAD Calendar
END SUB

SUB menHelpCalendar_Click ()
    FileMsg "CALENDAR.MSG", 1
END SUB

SUB SplitSerial ()
    MonthNum% = MONTH(SerialNum)
    DayNum% = DAY(SerialNum)
    YearNum% = YEAR(SerialNum)
END SUB

SUB UpdateNumbers ()
    'Get day of week for the first of month
    Day1 = DATESERIAL(YearNum%, MonthNum%, 1)
    Wkdy% = WEEKDAY(Day1)

    'Get number of days in current month
    Day2 = DATESERIAL(YearNum%, MonthNum% + 1, 1)
    Ndays% = Day2 - Day1
```

(continued)

CALENDAR.FRM *continued*

```
    'Put spaces or day numbers on display
    FOR i% = 1 TO 37
        IF i% < Wkdy% OR n% >= Ndays% THEN
            Label5(i%).Caption = " "
        ELSE
            n% = n% + 1
            IF n% < 10 THEN
                Label5(i%).Caption = STR$(n%)
            ELSE
                Label5(i%).Caption = LTRIM$(STR$(n%))
            END IF
            IF n% = 1 OR n% = DayNum% THEN
                AryIndex% = i%
            END IF
        END IF
    NEXT i%

    'Reset the day number
    DayNum% = VAL(Label5(AryIndex%).Caption)
END SUB

SUB UpdateTitle ()
    SELECT CASE MonthNum%
    CASE 1
        Tmp$ = "January"
    CASE 2
        Tmp$ = "February"
    CASE 3
        Tmp$ = "March"
    CASE 4
        Tmp$ = "April"
    CASE 5
        Tmp$ = "May"
    CASE 6
        Tmp$ = "June"
    CASE 7
        Tmp$ = "July"
    CASE 8
        Tmp$ = "August"
    CASE 9
        Tmp$ = "September"
    CASE 10
        Tmp$ = "October"
    CASE 11
        Tmp$ = "November"
```

(continued)

CALENDAR.FRM *continued*

```
    CASE 12
        Tmp$ = "December"
    CASE ELSE
        Tmp$ = "???"
    END SELECT

    Label3.Caption = Tmp$ + "," + STR$(YearNum%)
END SUB
```

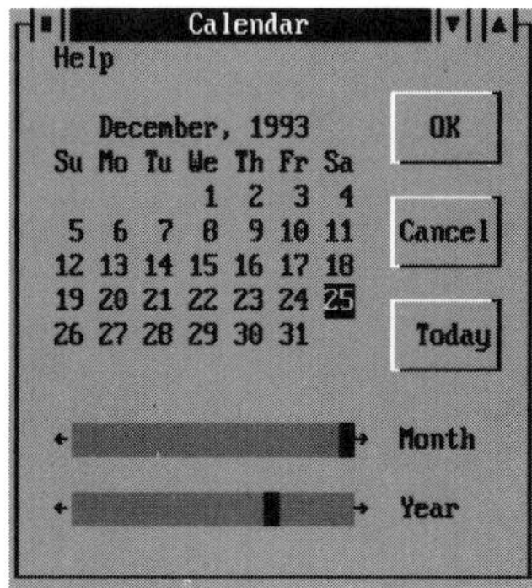

Figure 8-3.
CALENDAR.FRM in action.

The CLOCKDEM Application

The CLOCKDEM application demonstrates a simple clock form that you can easily add to your programs. This small clock displays the current system time while the calling form continues to interact with the user. In this application, CLOCKDEM is the start-up form that demonstrates the second form, CLOCK.

A timer control triggers the code to update the clock once each second. At first, setting the Interval property to *1000 milliseconds* (1 second) might appear to be the ideal way to kick off the time-keeping code. Because of Visual Basic for MS-DOS processing delays, however, the actual interval generated by the 1000 millisecond setting stretches to a little more than 1 second. As a result, the clock occasionally "stutters," or seems to skip a beat. The solution is to set the timer interval to an interval much shorter than 1 second, such as 50 milliseconds (which will make the code activate about 20 times per second), and to check the elapsed system time since the previous activation of the code. If 1 second has not passed, the *Timer1_Timer* event code exits. As soon as 1 second passes, the application updates the display. This makes the clock operate much more smoothly.

The files for the CLOCKDEM application are included on the companion disk. To load the files into Visual Basic for MS-DOS, choose the File Open Project command and type *C:\VBDWSHOP\CLOCKDEM.MAK*. This opens the project and enables you to view and modify the forms and code. The following figures, tables, and code give the details of the application's creation.

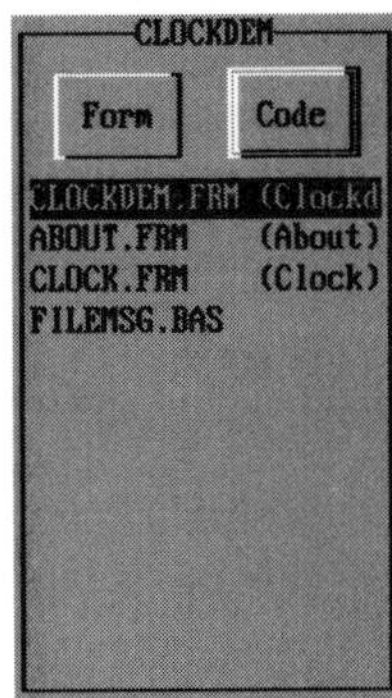

Figure 8-4.
CLOCKDEM project list.

Source code for CLOCK.BI

```
'=====================================================
' CLOCK.BI
' Include file for accessing CLOCK.FRM
'=====================================================
' $FORM Clock
```

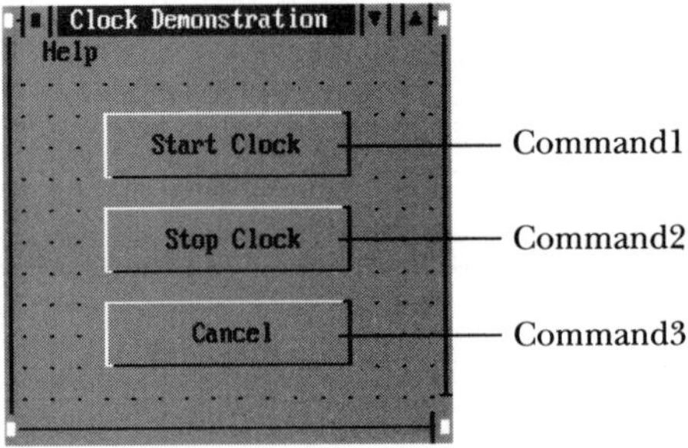

Figure 8-5.
CLOCKDEM.FRM during development.

CLOCKDEM.FRM Menu Design Window Entries

Caption	CtlName	Indentation
&Help	menHelp	0
&Help on ClockDem	menHelpClockDem	1
&About ClockDem...	menAboutClockDem	1
-	menSep	1
E&xit	menExit	1

CLOCKDEM.FRM Form and Control Properties

Property	Value
Form:	
Caption	Clock Demonstration
FormName	Clockdem
Command1:	
Caption	Start Clock
CtlName	Command1
Command2:	
Caption	Stop Clock
CtlName	Command2
Command3:	
Cancel	True
CtlName	Command3
Caption	Cancel

Source code for CLOCKDEM.FRM

```
'===============================================
' CLOCKDEM
' Demonstrates the CLOCK form
'===============================================

'$INCLUDE: 'CONSTANT.BI'
'$INCLUDE: 'FILEMSG.BI'
'$INCLUDE: 'ABOUT.BI'
'$INCLUDE: 'CLOCK.BI'
```

(continued)

CLOCKDEM.FRM *continued*

```
SUB Command1_Click ()
    Clock.SHOW MODELESS
    SETFOCUS
END SUB

SUB Command2_Click ()
    UNLOAD Clock
END SUB

SUB Command3_Click ()
    UNLOAD ClockDem
END SUB

SUB Form_Load ()
    'Center the form on the screen
    ClockDem.Left = (Screen.Width - ClockDem.Width) \ 2
    ClockDem.Top = (Screen.Height - ClockDem.Height) \ 2
END SUB

SUB Form_Unload (CANCEL AS INTEGER)
    UNLOAD Clock
END SUB

SUB menAboutClockDem_Click ()
    About.Label1.Caption = "CLOCK"
    About.SHOW MODAL
END SUB

SUB menExit_Click ()
    UNLOAD ClockDem
END SUB

SUB menHelpClockDem_Click ()
    FileMsg "CLOCK.MSG", 1
END SUB
```

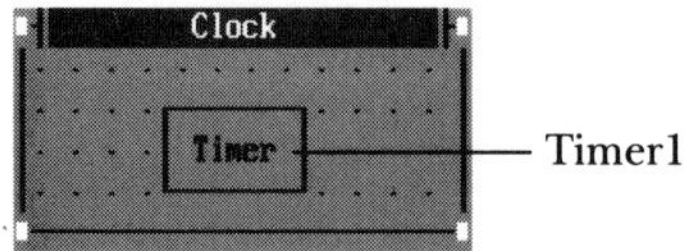

Figure 8-6.
CLOCK.FRM during development.

CLOCK.FRM Form and Control Properties

Property	Value
Form:	
Caption	Clock
FormName	Clock
Timer1:	
CtlName	Timer1
Enabled	True
Interval	50

Source code for CLOCK.FRM

```
'==================================================
' CLOCK
' Displays a simple clock
'==================================================

' Notes:
' Add $INCLUDE: 'CLOCK.BI' to the calling module.
' Load CLOCK.FRM into your project.
'
' Example of use:
'    Clock.SHOW MODELESS
'    SETFOCUS

SUB Form_Load ()
    Width = 10
    Height = 2
    Left = 3
    Top = 2
END SUB

SUB Timer1_Timer ()
    STATIC TimerLast

    IF TIMER <> TimerLast THEN
        TimerLast = TIMER
        CurrentX = 0
        CurrentY = 0
        PRINT TIME$
    END IF
END SUB
```

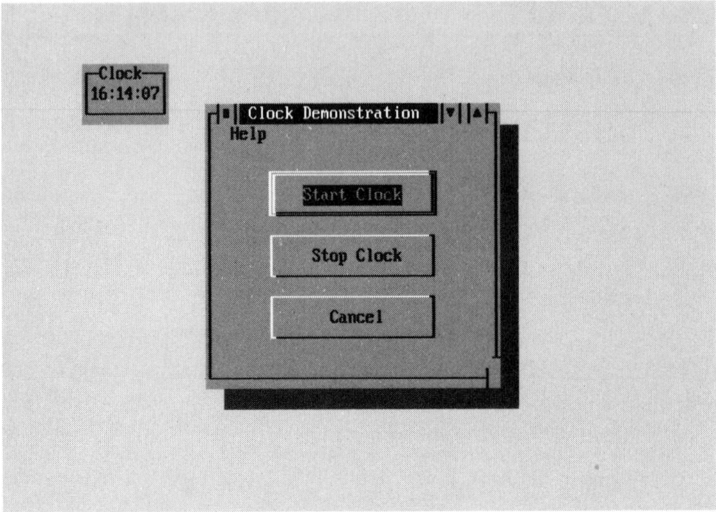

Figure 8-7.
CLOCKDEM.FRM and CLOCK.FRM in action.

The SIDEREAL Application

The SIDEREAL application displays Greenwich mean sidereal time given the current time, time-zone, and daylight saving time settings. The application also displays the current system time for easy reference. Sidereal time is useful for astronomical observations.

This application demonstrates several controls and how to use profile strings, as described in the PROFDEM program in Chapter 5. The SIDEREAL application uses profile strings to save the current time-zone and daylight saving time settings. The *Form_Load* and *Form_Unload* subprograms are ideal for automatically reading the previous time settings and then saving the current settings until the next time the user runs the application. Take a look at these subprograms to see how the application reads and writes profile strings.

A timer drives the display of the current system time and the calculated Greenwich mean sidereal time. Every 10 milliseconds, the timer-event code recalculates Greenwich mean sidereal time, based on the value of *NOW*, a Visual Basic for MS-DOS function that returns the current system date and time as a serial number. The value of *NOW* changes with each clock tick, or about 18.2 times each second. The application updates the displayed Greenwich mean sidereal time every second. Because of the fine resolution of *NOW*, the update can happen "between" the seconds of system time. The system time and Greenwich mean sidereal time appear to run independently of each other, and indeed in reality they do: 24 hours on a sidereal clock is equivalent to about 23 hours, 56 minutes, and 4.09 seconds of conventional (or Greenwich mean) clock time.

This program provides a good working demonstration of a combo box. Here the combo box is used to provide a list of time zones and to display the currently selected time-zone setting.

The files for the SIDEREAL application are included on the companion disk. To load the files into Visual Basic for MS-DOS, choose the File Open Project command and type *C:\VBDWSHOP\SIDEREAL.MAK*. This opens the project and enables you to view and modify the forms and code. The following figures, tables, and code give the details of the application's creation.

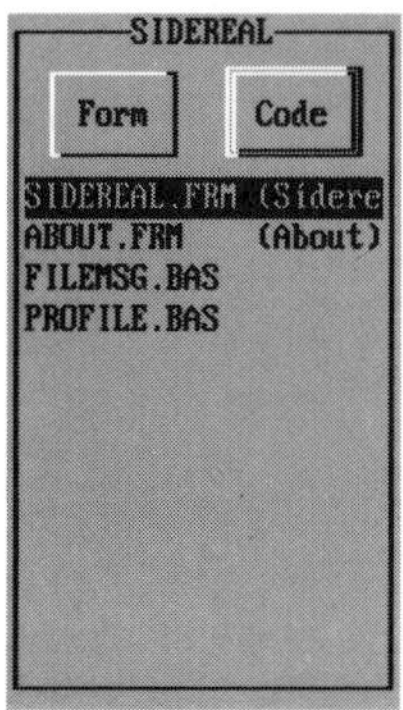

Figure 8-8.
SIDEREAL project list.

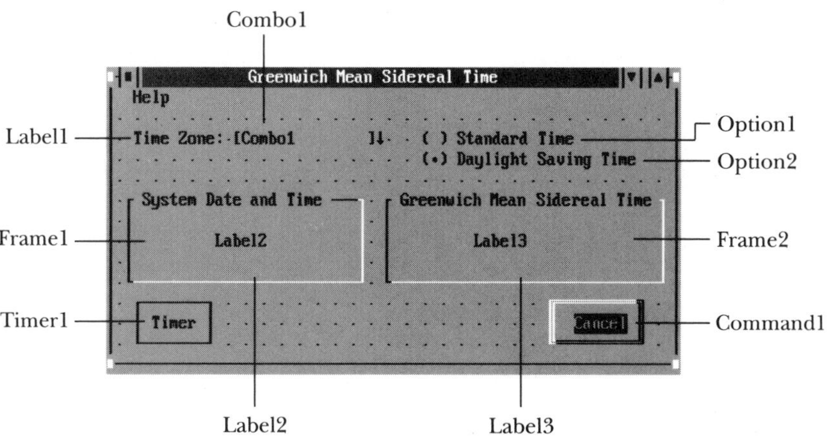

Figure 8-9.
SIDEREAL.FRM during development.

SIDEREAL.FRM Menu Design Window Entries

Caption	CtlName	Indentation
&Help	menHelp	0
&Help on Sidereal	menHelpSidereal	1
&About Sidereal...	menAboutSidereal	1
-	menSep	1
E&xit	menExit	1

SIDEREAL.FRM Form and Control Properties

Property	Value
Form:	
BorderStyle	1 - Fixed Single
Caption	Greenwich Mean Sidereal Time
FormName	Sidereal
Label1:	
Alignment	1 - Right Justify
Caption	Time Zone:
CtlName	Label1
Combo1:	
CtlName	Combo1
Style	0 - Dropdown Combo
Option1:	
Caption	Standard Time
CtlName	Option1
Option2:	
Caption	Daylight Saving Time
CtlName	Option2
Frame1:	
Caption	System Date and Time
CtlName	Frame1

(continued)

SIDEREAL.FRM Form and Control Properties *continued*

Property	Value
Frame2:	
Caption	Greenwich Mean Sidereal Time
CtlName	Frame2
Label2:	
Alignment	2 - Center
CtlName	Label2
Label3:	
Alignment	2 - Center
CtlName	Label3
Timer1:	
CtlName	Timer1
Interval	10
Command1:	
Cancel	True
Caption	Cancel
CtlName	Command1
Default	True

Source code for SIDEREAL.FRM

```
'=============================================
' SIDEREAL
' Displays local sidereal time
'=============================================

'$INCLUDE: 'CONSTANT.BI'
'$INCLUDE: 'ABOUT.BI'
'$INCLUDE: 'FILEMSG.BI'
'$INCLUDE: 'PROFILE.BI'

DECLARE FUNCTION SiderealTime$ (Ghours%, Daylight%)
```

(continued)

SIDEREAL.FRM *continued*

```
SUB Command1_Click ()
    UNLOAD Sidereal
END SUB

SUB Form_Load ()
    'Center the form on screen
    Sidereal.Left = (Screen.Width - Sidereal.Width) \ 2
    Sidereal.Top = (Screen.Height - Sidereal.Height) \ 2

    'Load the time-zone combo box
    Combo1.ADDITEM "Atlantic"
    Combo1.ADDITEM "Eastern"
    Combo1.ADDITEM "Central"
    Combo1.ADDITEM "Mountain"
    Combo1.ADDITEM "Pacific"
    Combo1.ADDITEM "Alaska"
    Combo1.ADDITEM "Hawaii-Aleutian"

    'Get the previous setting for time-zone index
    Last$ = ProfileRead("sidereal.ini", "settings", "timezoneindex")
    Combo1.ListIndex = VAL(Last$)

    'Get the previous setting for standard or daylight saving time
    Last$ = ProfileRead("sidereal.ini", "settings", "savingsflag")
    Option2.Value = VAL(Last$)
END SUB

SUB Form_Unload (CANCEL AS INTEGER)
    'Save the current setting for time-zone index
    ProfileStr$ = STR$(Combo1.ListIndex)
    ProfileWrite "sidereal.ini", "settings", "timezoneindex",
 ProfileStr$

    'Save the current setting for standard or daylight saving time
    ProfileStr$ = STR$(Option2.Value)
    ProfileWrite "sidereal.ini", "settings", "savingsflag",
 ProfileStr$
END SUB

SUB menAboutSidereal_Click ()
    About.Label1.Caption = "SIDEREAL"
    About.SHOW MODAL
END SUB

SUB menExit_Click ()
    UNLOAD Sidereal
END SUB
```

(continued)

SIDEREAL.FRM *continued*

```
SUB menHelpSidereal_Click ()
    FileMsg "SIDEREAL.MSG", 1
END SUB

FUNCTION SiderealTime$ (Ghours%, Daylight%)
    TimeZone = Ghours% + Daylight%
    JD# = NOW + TimeZone / 24 + 2415018.5#
    T# = (JD# - 2451545#) / 36525#
    t1# = 280.46061837#
    t2# = 360.98564736629#
    t3# = 2451545#
    t4# = .000387933#
    t5# = 38710000
    Deg# = t1# + t2# * (JD# - t3#) + t4# * T# ^ 2 - T# ^ 3 / t5#
    Deg# = (Deg# - 360# * INT(Deg# / 360#))
    Dy# = Deg# / 15# / 24#
    SiderealTime$ = FORMAT$(Dy#, "hh:mm:ss")
END FUNCTION

SUB Timer1_Timer ()
    Label3.Caption = DATE$ + SPACE$(3) + TIME$
    Ghours% = Combo1.ListIndex + 4
    Daylight% = Option2.Value
    Label4.Caption = SiderealTime$(Ghours%, Daylight%)
END SUB
```

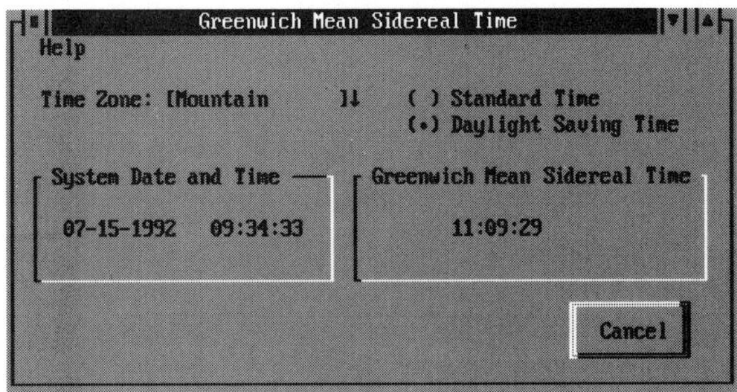

Figure 8-10.
SIDEREAL.FRM in action.

The NISTTIME Application

The NISTTIME application uses Visual Basic for MS-DOS serial I/O communications functions to phone the National Institute of Standards and Technology (NIST) for information to set the system clock accurately.

NISTTIME sets the minute and second accurately but does not set the date or hour information, so the user should be sure the system clock is set to the correct date and hour before running the application. NISTTIME sets the minute and second information to within about a second of the correct time.

Once each second, the phone call to the National Institute of Standards and Technology returns a string that ends with an asterisk. This asterisk arrives at the user's computer almost exactly when the indicated second occurs. NIST even includes compensation for the expected phone-line and modem delays.

This application runs by going through several processing "states." With each activation of the *Timer* subprogram, the application checks the current state and the appropriate operations take place. One of the advantages of this technique is that the application can easily monitor the elapsed time for certain critical states. For example, if a connection takes place (signified by *CONNECT* appearing on the screen) but the correct time information strings aren't received within a reasonable amount of time, the connection is broken and the program aborts. This mechanism makes it reasonably safe to use this program as part of an unattended batch file (of the kind you might run in the middle of the night, for instance).

The *Form_Load* subprogram checks the command-line arguments, which are passed in *COMMAND$*, and immediately dials for the time if any parameters at all are present. In a batch file, use a command such as *NIST GO* to cause immediate operation. If *COMMAND$* is null, the start-up form displays the current system time and waits for the user to click the Dial NIST button before progressing. Likewise, as soon as the time is reset, the program immediately terminates and returns to MS-DOS if any command-line parameters were present or returns to the start-up form to display the accurate time if no command-line parameters were included.

If you live in the Denver area, be sure to modify the long-distance telephone number to make it a local call. Several *CONST* strings are declared at the module level, including the telephone dialing string. These strings are set up for standard modem operation at 1200 baud. If you have any trouble connecting, take a look at the commands in these strings to see whether they're compatible with your hardware. The National Institute of Standards and Technology equipment can connect at 300 baud, but the strings NIST returns at this rate are different, and so you must make changes to this program for the program to operate properly.

The files for the NISTTIME application are included on the companion disk. To load the files into Visual Basic for MS-DOS, choose the File Open Project command and type *C:\VBDWSHOP\NISTTIME.MAK*. This opens the project and enables you to view and modify the forms and code. The following figures, tables, and code give the details of the application's creation.

Figure 8-11.
NISTTIME project list.

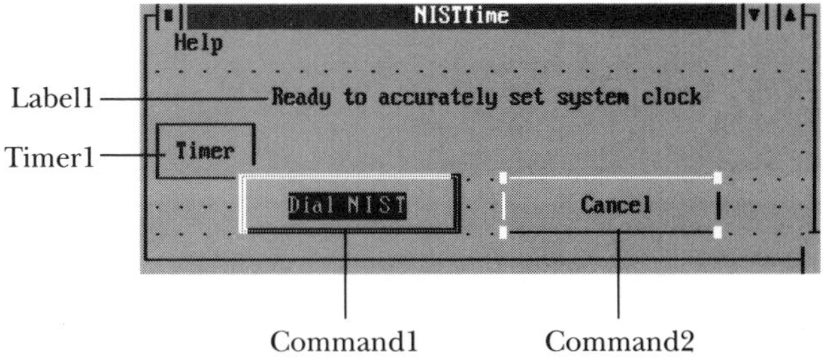

Figure 8-12.
NISTTIME.FRM during development.

NISTTIME.FRM Menu Design Window Entries

Caption	CtlName	Indentation
&Help	menHelp	0
&Help on NISTTime	menHelpNISTTime	1
&About NISTTime...	menAboutNISTTime	1
-	menSep	1
E&xit	menExit	1

NISTTIME.FRM Form and Control Properties

Property	Value
Form:	
Caption	NISTTime
FormName	NistTime
Timer1:	
CtlName	Timer1
Interval	2000
Label1:	
Caption	Ready to accurately set system clock
CtlName	Label1
Height	3
Command1:	
Caption	Dial NIST
CtlName	Command1
Default	True
Command2:	
Cancel	True
Caption	Cancel
CtlName	Command2

Source code for NISTTIME.FRM

```
'================================================
' NISTTIME
' Dials the National Institute of Standards and
' Technology and synchronizes system clock
'================================================

'$INCLUDE: 'CONSTANT.BI'
'$INCLUDE: 'FILEMSG.BI'
'$INCLUDE: 'ABOUT.BI'

DECLARE SUB HangUp ()
DECLARE SUB SetTime (A$)
```

(continued)

NISTTIME.FRM *continued*

```
DECLARE SUB Process (t$)
DECLARE SUB Send (A$)
DECLARE SUB Command1_Click ()
DECLARE SUB Command2_Click ()

CONST COMM$ = "COM1:1200,N,8,1,OP0,DS0"
CONST SEND1$ = "ATZ"
CONST SEND2$ = "ATE0 S7=60 S11=55 V1 X1 L0 S0=0"
CONST SEND3$ = "ATDT 1-303-494-4774"
CONST EXITSTATE = 999

DIM SHARED UserFlag AS INTEGER
DIM SHARED State AS INTEGER

SUB Command1_Click ()
    'Dial NIST only when ready
    IF State = 0 THEN
        State = 1
    END IF
END SUB

SUB Command2_Click ()
    'Prepare to exit program
    State = EXITSTATE
END SUB

SUB Form_Load ()
    'Dial immediately if any command-line parameters are present
    IF COMMAND$ <> "" THEN
        Command1.Visible = FALSE
        UserFlag = FALSE
        State = 1
    ELSE
        UserFlag = TRUE
    END IF
END SUB

SUB menAboutNISTTime_Click ()
    About.Label1.Caption = "NISTTIME"
    About.SHOW MODAL
END SUB

SUB menExit_Click ()
    Command2_Click
END SUB

SUB menHelpNISTTime_Click ()
    FileMsg "NISTTIME.MSG", 1
END SUB
```

(continued)

NISTTIME.FRM *continued*

```
SUB Process (t$)
    STATIC A$

    'Concatenate incoming characters to work string
    A$ = A$ + t$
    t$ = ""

    'Has asterisk not yet arrived?
    IF LEFT$(A$, 1) <> "!" THEN

        'Check whether asterisk just arrived
        Pstar = INSTR(A$, "*")

        'If yes, replace it with "!"
        IF Pstar THEN
            A$ = MID$(A$, Pstar)
            MID$(A$, 1, 1) = "!"
        END IF

    'Asterisk arrived previously
    ELSE

        'Watch for next asterisk to arrive
        Pstar = INSTR(A$, "*")

        'Then set the system clock
        IF Pstar THEN
            SetTime A$
            A$ = ""
            State = State + 1
        END IF

    END IF
END SUB

SUB Send (A$)
    'Append a carriage-return character
    A$ = A$ + CHR$(13)

    'Send the string to the COM port
    PUT #1, , A$
END SUB

SUB SetTime (A$)
    'This is the format of the NIST string (A$):
    '!..48690 92-03-09 20:45:37 78 0 -.3 045.0 UTC(NIST) *
    '12345678901234567890123456789012345678901234567890123
    '         1         2         3         4         5

    'Extract the minute and second numbers
    mi = VAL(MID$(A$, 22, 2))
    se = VAL(MID$(A$, 25, 2))
```

(continued)

NISTTIME.FRM *continued*

```
    'Determine the system hour
    ho$ = LEFT$(TIME$, 2)

    'Build strings for the new minute and second numbers
    mi$ = CHR$((mi \ 10) + 48) + CHR$((mi MOD 10) + 48)
    se$ = CHR$((se \ 10) + 48) + CHR$((se MOD 10) + 48)

    'Set system clock
    TIME$ = ho$ + ":" + mi$ + ":" + se$
END SUB

SUB Timer1_Timer ()
    STATIC Tim$
    STATIC MaxTime AS SINGLE
    STATIC DspTime AS SINGLE
    STATIC ConnectFlag AS INTEGER

    NL$ = CHR$(13) + CHR$(10)

    SELECT CASE State

    'Waiting for user input
    CASE 0
        IF TIME$ <> Tim$ THEN
            Tim$ = TIME$
            Label1.Caption = "Time: " + Tim$
            Timer1.Interval = 1
        END IF

    'Dial the phone number
    CASE 1
        OPEN COMM$ FOR RANDOM AS #1 LEN = 256
        Tmp$ = "Dialing" + NL$
        Tmp$ = Tmp$ + "National Institute of Standards and
  Technology" + NL$
        Tmp$ = Tmp$ + "Telephone Time Service"
        Label1.Caption = Tmp$
        Send SEND1$
        Send SEND2$
        Send SEND3$
        MaxTime = TIMER + 50
        DspTime = TIMER + 4
        State = State + 1

    'Display message while waiting for phone connection
    CASE 2
        IF TIMER > DspTime THEN
            State = State + 1
        END IF
        EXIT SUB
```

(continued)

NISTTIME.FRM *continued*

```
        'Wait for connection and data to arrive
        CASE 3
            IF TIMER > MaxTime THEN
                State = EXITSTATE
                EXIT SUB
            END IF
            IF NOT EOF(1) THEN
                IF ConnectFlag = FALSE THEN
                    Label1.Caption = "Attempting to connect"
                    ConnectFlag = TRUE
                END IF
                t$ = INPUT$(LOC(1), #1)
                IF INSTR(t$, "*") THEN
                    Label1.Caption = "Processing time data"
                END IF
                Process t$
            END IF

        'Disconnect and finish up
        CASE 4
            Label1.Caption = "Hanging up"
            CLOSE
            Tim$ = TIME$
            IF UserFlag = TRUE THEN
                State = 0
                Command2.SETFOCUS
            ELSE
                State = EXITSTATE
                Timer1.Interval = 1000
            END IF

        'End program
        CASE ELSE
            UNLOAD NistTime

        END SELECT
    END SUB
```

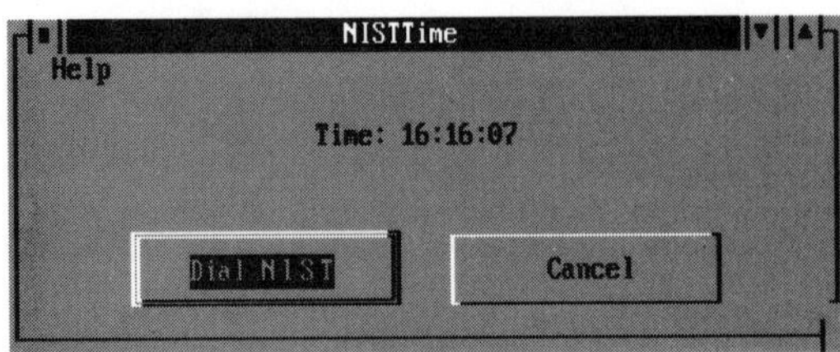

Figure 8-13.
NISTTIME.FRM in action.

CHAPTER NINE

SCREEN SAVERS AND GRAPHICS

This chapter demonstrates two programs: a screen saver program and a program that draws phases of the moon using both text and graphics modes.

The DOODLE Application

This application fills the screen with shifting colored lines in a kaleidoscopic pattern. Option button groups let the user select one from a number of standard types of graphics hardware, choose whether to draw lines or boxes, and choose whether to split the screen into quadrants (with a separate set of lines in each quadrant) or to fill the entire screen (using one set of lines only). Each combination of these settings produces interesting and unique results.

The code for this program is self-contained in DOODLE.FRM. Notice that none of the graphics commands used in the form conflicts with form methods. In particular, no *CLS* or *PRINT* statements are necessary for the graphics subprograms. As I've said before, if your graphics programs require these types of statements you must isolate the code in a separate BAS module.

The lines are drawn in a *DO-LOOP* construct until the user presses any key. This lets the graphics progress as fast as possible, yet provides a simple mechanism for exiting to the main window.

This application is not a "true" screen saver program because the user must start the program manually, rather than set it to start automatically after a period of keyboard and mouse inactivity. Ideally, a screen saver program starts after no keyboard or mouse activity has occurred for a few minutes. If any command-line parameters are passed to the DOODLE application, however, the start-up form immediately begins the graphics activity. This allows you to place a command in a batch file to cause this screen saver to begin after a sequence of tasks has been completed.

The files for the DOODLE application are included on the companion disk. To load the files into Visual Basic for MS-DOS, choose the File Open Project command and type *C:\VBDWSHOP\DOODLE.MAK*. This opens the project and enables you to view and modify the forms and code. The following figures, tables, and code give the details of the application's creation.

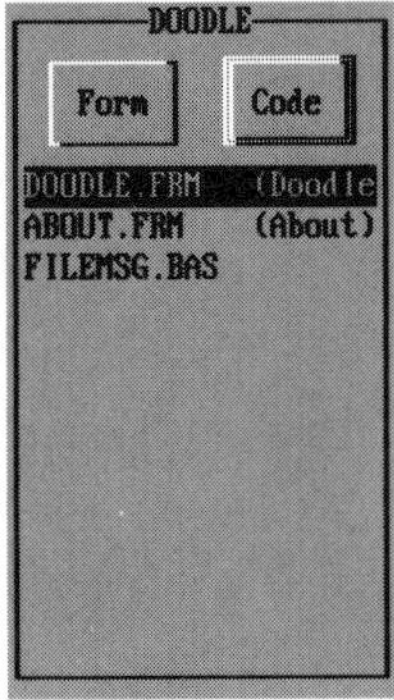

Figure 9-1.
DOODLE project list.

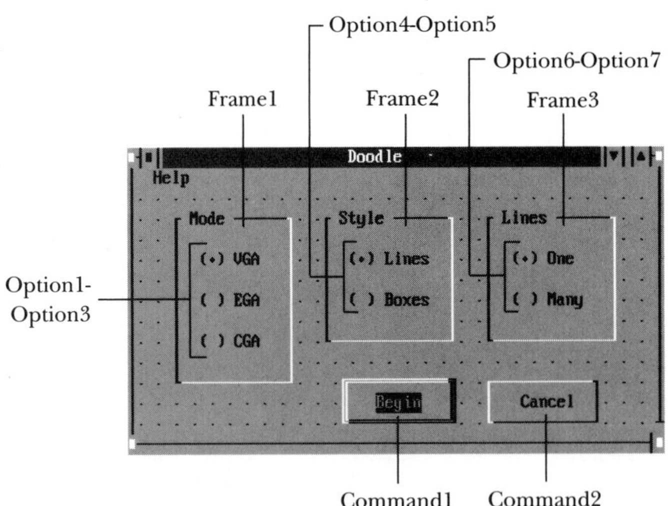

Figure 9-2.
DOODLE.FRM during development.

DOODLE.FRM Menu Design Window Entries

Caption	CtlName	Indentation
&Help	menHelp	0
&Help on Doodle	menHelpDoodle	1
&About Doodle...	menAboutDoodle	1
-	menSep	1
E&xit	menExit	1

DOODLE.FRM Form and Control Properties

Property	Value
Form:	
Caption	Doodle
FormName	Doodle
Frame1:	
Caption	Mode
CtlName	Frame1
Frame2:	
Caption	Style
CtlName	Frame2
Frame3:	
Caption	Lines
CtlName	Frame3
Option1:	
Caption	VGA
CtlName	Option1
Option2:	
Caption	EGA
CtlName	Option2

(continued)

DOODLE.FRM Form and Control Properties *continued*

Property	Value
Option3:	
Caption	CGA
CtlName	Option3
Option4:	
Caption	Lines
CtlName	Option4
Option5:	
Caption	Boxes
CtlName	Option5
Option6:	
Caption	One
CtlName	Option6
Option7:	
Caption	Many
CtlName	Option7
Command1:	
Caption	Begin
CtlName	Command1
Default	True
Command2:	
Cancel	True
Caption	Cancel
CtlName	Command2

Source code for DOODLE.FRM

```
'=====================================================
' DOODLE
' Demonstrates a screen saver
'=====================================================
```

(continued)

DOODLE.FRM *continued*

```
DEFINT A-Z

'$INCLUDE: 'CONSTANT.BI'
'$INCLUDE: 'FILEMSG.BI'
'$INCLUDE: 'ABOUT.BI'

DECLARE SUB SetMode ()
DECLARE SUB Doodle1 ()
DECLARE SUB Doodle2 ()
DECLARE SUB Command1_Click ()

DEFINT A-Z
'
SUB Command1_Click ()
    SCREEN.HIDE
    SetMode

    IF Option7.Value = TRUE THEN
        Doodle1
    ELSE
        Doodle2
    END IF

    SCREEN 0
    WIDTH 80
    SCREEN.SHOW
END SUB

DEFINT A-Z
'
SUB Command2_Click ()
    UNLOAD Doodle
END SUB

DEFINT A-Z
'
SUB Doodle1 ()
    CONST LineCount = 5
    CONST Xmax = 300
    CONST Ymax = 300
    CONST Inc = 5

    REDIM Dx1(LineCount), Dx2(LineCount)
    REDIM Dy1(LineCount), Dy2(LineCount)
    REDIM Xa(LineCount), Xb(LineCount)
    REDIM Ya(LineCount), Yb(LineCount)
    REDIM ColorNum(LineCount)
```

(continued)

DOODLE.FRM *continued*

```
    FOR I = 0 TO LineCount
        IF Option3.Value = TRUE THEN
            ColorNum(I) = INT(RND * 3 + 1)
        ELSE
            ColorNum(I) = INT(RND * 15 + 1)
        END IF
    NEXT I

    WINDOW (-Xmax, -Ymax)-(Xmax, Ymax)

    DO
        FOR I = 0 TO LineCount

            IF RND < .01 THEN
                IF Option3.Value = TRUE THEN
                    ColorNum(I) = INT(RND * 3 + 1)
                ELSE
                    ColorNum(I) = INT(RND * 15 + 1)
                END IF
            END IF

            IF Xa(I) <= 0 THEN
               Dx1(I) = Inc * RND
            END IF

            IF Xb(I) <= 0 THEN
               Dx2(I) = Inc * RND
            END IF

            IF Ya(I) <= 0 THEN
               Dy1(I) = Inc * RND
            END IF

            IF Yb(I) <= 0 THEN
               Dy2(I) = Inc * RND
            END IF

            IF Xa(I) >= Xmax THEN
               Dx1(I) = -Inc * RND
            END IF

            IF Xb(I) >= Xmax THEN
               Dx2(I) = -Inc * RND
            END IF
```

(continued)

DOODLE.FRM *continued*

```
          IF Ya(I) >= Ymax THEN
             Dy1(I) = -Inc * RND
          END IF

          IF Yb(I) >= Ymax THEN
             Dy2(I) = -Inc * RND
          END IF

          Xa(I) = Xa(I) + Dx1(I)
          Xb(I) = Xb(I) + Dx2(I)
          Ya(I) = Ya(I) + Dy1(I)
          Yb(I) = Yb(I) + Dy2(I)

          IF Option5.Value = TRUE THEN
              LINE (Xa(I), Ya(I))-(Xb(I), Yb(I)), ColorNum(I), B
              LINE (-Xa(I), -Ya(I))-(-Xb(I), -Yb(I)),
 ColorNum(I), B
              LINE (-Xa(I), Ya(I))-(-Xb(I), Yb(I)), ColorNum(I),
 B
              LINE (Xa(I), -Ya(I))-(Xb(I), -Yb(I)), ColorNum(I),
 B
          ELSE
              LINE (Xa(I), Ya(I))-(Xb(I), Yb(I)), ColorNum(I)
              LINE (-Xa(I), -Ya(I))-(-Xb(I), -Yb(I)), ColorNum(I)
              LINE (-Xa(I), Ya(I))-(-Xb(I), Yb(I)), ColorNum(I)
              LINE (Xa(I), -Ya(I))-(Xb(I), -Yb(I)), ColorNum(I)
          END IF

       NEXT I

    LOOP WHILE INKEY$ = ""
END SUB

DEFINT A-Z
'
SUB Doodle2 ()
    CONST Lines = 50
    CONST Xmax = 500
    CONST Ymax = 500
    CONST Inc = 7

    REDIM x1(Lines), y1(Lines), x2(Lines), y2(Lines)

    WINDOW (0, 0)-(Xmax, Ymax)
    COLOR INT(RND * 15 + 1)
```

(continued)

DOODLE.FRM *continued*

```
    DO

        FOR I = 0 TO Lines

            IF Option5.Value = TRUE THEN
                LINE (x1(I), y1(I))-(x2(I), y2(I)), 0, B
            ELSE
                LINE (x1(I), y1(I))-(x2(I), y2(I)), 0
            END IF

            IF Xa <= 0 THEN
               Dx1 = Inc * RND
            END IF

            IF Xb <= 0 THEN
               Dx2 = Inc * RND
            END IF

            IF Ya <= 0 THEN
               Dy1 = Inc * RND
            END IF

            IF Yb <= 0 THEN
               Dy2 = Inc * RND
            END IF

            IF Xa >= Xmax THEN
               Dx1 = -Inc * RND
            END IF

            IF Xb >= Xmax THEN
               Dx2 = -Inc * RND
            END IF

            IF Ya >= Ymax THEN
               Dy1 = -Inc * RND
            END IF

            IF Yb >= Ymax THEN
               Dy2 = -Inc * RND
            END IF

            Xa = Xa + Dx1
            Xb = Xb + Dx2
            Ya = Ya + Dy1
            Yb = Yb + Dy2
```

(continued)

DOODLE.FRM *continued*

```
            x1(I) = Xa
            y1(I) = Ya
            x2(I) = Xb
            y2(I) = Yb

            IF Option5.Value = TRUE THEN
                LINE (Xa, Ya)-(Xb, Yb), , B
            ELSE
                LINE (Xa, Ya)-(Xb, Yb)
            END IF

        NEXT I

        IF RND < .1 THEN
            COLOR INT(RND * 15 + 1)
        END IF

    LOOP WHILE INKEY$ = ""
END SUB

DEFINT A-Z
'
SUB Form_Load ()
    'Unique doodles every time
    RANDOMIZE TIMER

    'Center the form on the screen
    Doodle.Left = (Screen.Width - Doodle.Width) \ 2
    Doodle.Top = (Screen.Height - Doodle.Height) \ 2

    'Set desired default here
    Option5.Value = TRUE
    Option6.Value = TRUE

    'Start drawing if any command-line parameters are present
    IF COMMAND$ <> "" THEN
        Command1_Click
    END IF
END SUB

DEFINT A-Z
'
SUB menAboutDoodle_Click ()
    About.Label1.Caption = "DOODLE"
    About.SHOW MODAL
END SUB
```

(continued)

DOODLE.FRM *continued*

```
DEFINT A-Z
'
SUB menExit_Click ()
    UNLOAD Doodle
END SUB

DEFINT A-Z
'
SUB menHelpDoodle_Click ()
    FileMsg "DOODLE.MSG", 1
END SUB

DEFINT A-Z
'
SUB SetMode ()
    ON LOCAL ERROR GOTO BadMode

    IF Option1.Value = TRUE THEN
        SCREEN 12
    ELSEIF Option2.Value = TRUE THEN
        SCREEN 9
    ELSE
        SCREEN 1
    END IF

AllDone:
    EXIT SUB

BadMode:
    MSGBOX "Bad Graphics Mode"
    RESUME AllDone
END SUB
```

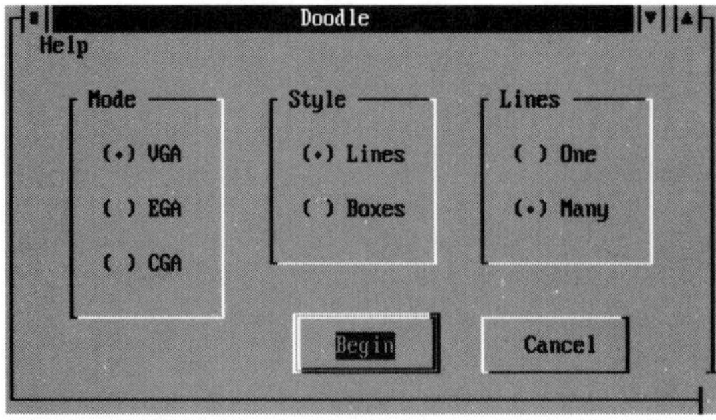

Figure 9-3.
DOODLE.FRM form in action.

Figure 9-4.
DOODLE.FRM graphics in action.

The MOON Application

The MOON application graphically shows the phase of the moon for any date from 1753 through 2078 (the range of valid dates for the calendar-related functions of Visual Basic for MS-DOS). The moon's elliptical orbit and the tilt of its path around the earth is quite complicated and is not incorporated here, so the simple calculation presented here is accurate only to about +/–1 day. This should still be accurate enough, however, for planting potatoes, planning fishing trips, or demonstrating some interesting Visual Basic for MS-DOS graphics.

This program demonstrates how you can creatively use special text characters as pseudo-graphics on a form. The form's BackColor property is set to blue to simulate the night sky, and solid horizontal bars formed by strings of characters (ASCII 223) are used to fill the lit portion of the moon's face. The dark portion of the face of the moon is constructed of single quotation mark characters. Look in the *Form_Paint* subprogram to see how the *STRING$* function is used to create the desired length of solid white bars from these characters.

For a direct comparison of text-mode graphics and graphics-mode graphics, this program can also create the moon's image in graphics mode. Choose Graphics Mode from the Options menu to generate the graphics-mode version of the MOON application. In graphics mode, I was able to add more interesting details, such as a sprinkling of stars in the background. Press any key to return to text mode.

When MOON starts, it uses the current date from your system's clock to generate an image of the current moon phase. Choose New Date from the Options menu to select another date. The *INPUTBOX$* function is used to prompt the user for the new date.

The files for the MOON application are included on the companion disk. To load the files into Visual Basic for MS-DOS, choose the File Open Project command and type *C:\VBDWSHOP\MOON.MAK*. This opens the project and enables you to view and modify the forms and code. The following figures, tables, and code give the details of the application's creation.

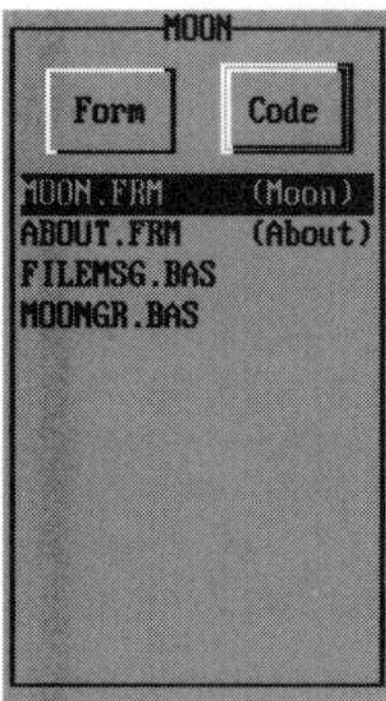

Figure 9-5.
MOON project list.

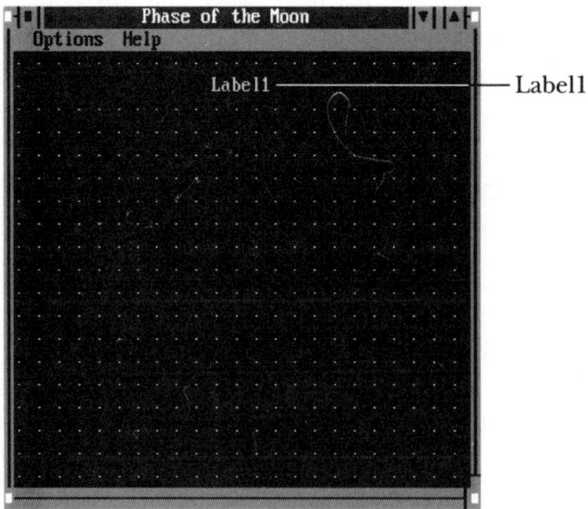

Figure 9-6.
MOON.FRM during development.

MOON.FRM Menu Design Window Entries

Caption	CtlName	Indentation
&Options	menOptions	0
&Graphics Mode	menGraphicsMode	1
&New Date...	menNewDate	1
-	menSep	1
E&xit	menExit	1
&Help	menHelp	0
&Help on Moon	menHelpMoon	1
&About Moon...	menAboutMoon	1

MOON.FRM Form and Control Properties

Property	Value
Form:	
BackColor	1 - Blue
Caption	Phase of the Moon
FormName	Moon
Label1:	
Alignment	2 - Center
BackColor	1 - Blue
CtlName	Label1
ForeColor	14 - Yellow

Source code for MOON.FRM

```
'=================================================
' MOON
' Generates the phase of the moon for the current
' date or for any date from 1753 through 2078
'=================================================

'$INCLUDE: 'CONSTANT.BI'
'$INCLUDE: 'FILEMSG.BI'
'$INCLUDE: 'ABOUT.BI'
```

(continued)

MOON.FRM *continued*

```
COMMON SHARED /comMoon/ Phase, MoonDate$

DECLARE SUB GetMoonDate ()
DECLARE SUB Form_Paint ()
DECLARE SUB GraphicsMoon ()

SUB Form_Load ()
    'Center the form on the screen
    Moon.Left = (Screen.Width - Moon.Width) \ 2
    Moon.Top = (Screen.Height - Moon.Height) \ 2

    'Get current date
    GetMoonDate
END SUB

SUB Form_Paint ()
     'Update label
    IF Phase < .5 THEN
        Tmp$ = "n"
    ELSE
        Tmp$ = "x"
    END IF
    Label1.Caption = "The wa" + Tmp$ + "ing moon on " + MoonDate$

    'Draw the moon
    FOR y = -8 TO 8 STEP 1
        x = SQR(1 - y * y / 8 / 8)
        xLen% = 2 * 17 * x
        xLen% = xLen% + xLen% MOD 2
        xPos% = 23 - xLen% / 2
        IF Phase < .5 THEN
            x1% = 2 * Phase * xLen%
            x2% = xLen% - x1%
            t$ = STRING$(x2%, 223) + STRING$(x1%, "'")
        ELSE
            x1% = 2 * (1 - Phase) * xLen%
            x2% = xLen% - x1%
            t$ = STRING$(x1%, "'") + STRING$(x2%, 223)
        END IF
        Moon.CurrentX = xPos%
        Moon.CurrentY = CINT(10 + y)
        Moon.PRINT t$
    NEXT y
END SUB
```

(continued)

MOON.FRM *continued*

```
SUB GetMoonDate ()
    STATIC NotFirstTimeFlag AS INTEGER

TryAgain:

    'Don't ask user for date the first time
    IF NotFirstTimeFlag = TRUE THEN

        'Set parameters for INPUTBOX$
        Prompt$ = "Enter a date from 1753 through 2078 in this
 format: mm-dd-yyyy"
        Title$ = "Phase of the Moon"
        DefaultDate$ = DATE$

        'Ask user for date
        MoonDate$ = INPUTBOX$(Prompt$, Title$, DefaultDate$)

    ELSE

        'Use current date the first time
        MoonDate$ = DATE$

        'Set flag the first time
        NotFirstTimeFlag = TRUE

    END IF

    'Check for "Cancel"
    IF MoonDate$ = "" THEN
        MoonDate$ = DATE$
    END IF

    'Extract the date numbers from the string
    MonthNum = VAL(LEFT$(MoonDate$, 2))
    DayNum = VAL(MID$(MoonDate$, 4, 2))
    YearNum = VAL(MID$(MoonDate$, 7, 4))

    'Get the serial number for the entered date
    ON LOCAL ERROR GOTO ErrorTrap
    SerialNum = DATESERIAL(YearNum, MonthNum, DayNum)

    'Extract the date numbers from the serial number
    Mtst = MONTH(SerialNum)
    Dtst = DAY(SerialNum)
    Ytst = YEAR(SerialNum)
```

(continued)

MOON.FRM *continued*

```
    'Verify the entered date
    IF Mtst <> MonthNum OR Dtst <> DayNum OR Ytst <> YearNum THEN
        ERROR 1
    END IF

    'Calculate the astronomical Julian day number
    Julian = SerialNum + 2415019

    'Calculate the approximate phase of the moon
    Phase = (Julian + 4.867) / 29.53059
    Phase = Phase - INT(Phase)

    'All done
    EXIT SUB

ErrorTrap:

    BEEP
    MSGBOX "Invalid date... " + MoonDate$, 48, "Moon"
    RESUME TryAgain
END SUB

SUB menAboutMoon_Click ()
    About.Label1.Caption = "MOON"
    About.SHOW MODAL
END SUB

SUB menExit_Click ()
    UNLOAD Moon
END SUB

SUB menGraphicsMode_Click ()
    SCREEN.HIDE
    GraphicsMoon
    SCREEN.SHOW
END SUB

SUB menHelpMoon_Click ()
    FileMsg "MOON.MSG", 1
END SUB

SUB menNewDate_Click ()
    GetMoonDate
    Form_Paint
END SUB
```

Source code for MOONGR.BAS

```
'==================================================
' MOONGR.BAS
' Displays moon using graphics mode
'==================================================

COMMON SHARED /comMoon/ Phase, MoonDate$

'$INCLUDE: 'CONSTANT.BI'

SUB GraphicsMoon ()
    'Find a valid graphics mode
    ON LOCAL ERROR GOTO BadGraphicsMode

    'Try VGA mode first
    ScrMode% = 12
    SCREEN ScrMode%

    'Try EGA if neccessary
    IF ScrMode% = 0 THEN
        ScrMode% = 9
        SCREEN ScrMode%
    END IF

    'Try CGA if necessary
    IF ScrMode% = 0 THEN
        ScrMode% = 1
        SCREEN ScrMode%
    END IF

    'No graphics mode found
    IF ScrMode% = 0 THEN
        PRINT "No graphics mode found"
        EXIT SUB
    ELSE
        SELECT CASE ScrMode%
        CASE 12
            PixelsX% = 640
            PixelsY% = 480
        CASE 9
            PixelsX% = 640
            PixelsY% = 350
        CASE 1
            PixelsX% = 320
            PixelsY% = 200
        END SELECT
    END IF
```

(continued)

MOONGR.BAS *continued*

```
'Scale the screen for convenient plotting
xMax = 8 / 3
yMax = 2
WINDOW (-xMax, -yMax)-(xMax, yMax)

'Color the sky
IF ScrMode% <> 1 THEN
    PAINT (0, 0), BLUE
ELSE
    CLS
END IF

'Sprinkle a few stars around
IF ScrMode% <> 1 THEN COLOR BRIGHT_WHITE
FOR i% = 1 TO 500
    x = xMax * (2 * RND - 1)
    y = yMax * (2 * RND - 1)
    PSET (x, y)
NEXT i%

'Update label
IF Phase < .5 THEN
    Tmp$ = "n"
ELSE
    Tmp$ = "x"
END IF
IF ScrMode% <> 1 THEN
    COLOR YELLOW
    LOCATE 2, 25
ELSE
    LOCATE 2, 4
END IF
PRINT " The wa" + Tmp$ + "ing moon on " + MoonDate$ + " "

'Draw the moon
FOR y = 0 TO 1 STEP 4 / PixelsY%
    x = SQR(1 - y * y)

    'Black out any stars behind the moon
    LINE (-x, y)-(x, y), BLACK
    LINE (-x, -y)-(x, -y), BLACK

    'Determine the edges of the lit portion
    r = 2 * x
    IF Phase < .5 THEN
        x1 = -x
        x2 = r - 2 * Phase * r - x
    ELSE
        x1 = x
        x2 = x - 2 * Phase * r + r
    END IF
```

(continued)

MOONGR.BAS *continued*

```
        'Draw the lit portion of the moon
        LINE (x1, y)-(x2, y), BRIGHT_WHITE
        LINE (x1, -y)-(x2, -y), BRIGHT_WHITE

    NEXT y

    'Wait for a key press
    DO
    LOOP WHILE INKEY$ = ""

    'All done
    SCREEN 0
    WIDTH 80
    EXIT SUB

BadGraphicsMode:
    ScrMode% = 0
    RESUME NEXT
END SUB
```

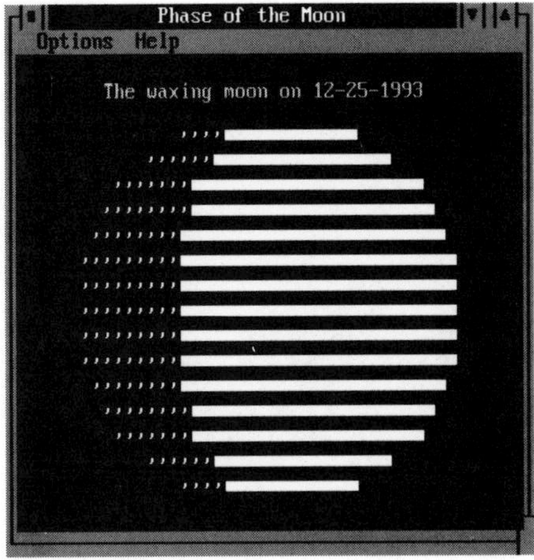

Figure 9-7.
MOON.FRM in action, text mode.

Figure 9-8.
MOON.FRM in action, graphics mode.

CHAPTER TEN

RANDOM-NUMBER APPLICATIONS

Visual Basic for MS-DOS has a simple built-in random-number generator, suitable for use in many applications. This chapter presents a program that uses the random-number generator of Visual Basic for MS-DOS to help the user pick lottery numbers and a second program that demonstrates alternative fast and efficient random-number–generation functions.

The LOTTERY Application

Using the LOTTERY application is a "just-for-fun" way to select lottery numbers. (Of course, if you win, you might be generous enough to forward the author a small but significant percentage of the proceeds!) This program is modeled after the Colorado state lottery, but I've tried to construct the program so that changes are easy to make. For example, I have included *CONST* statements at the module level for parameters that are likely to change. MAXNUMBER, for instance, is the highest number printed on the lottery machine's numbered balls. In the Colorado lottery, MAXNUMBER's value is 42. Other state lotteries are probably different, however, so change this constant to match your own lottery.

The LOTTERY application works by generating an array of 42 numbers that are shuffled into a random order using the *RND* function of Visual Basic for MS-DOS. The application displays these numbers repeatedly in the same order, waiting for the user to "grab" the currently displayed number by clicking the Grab Number button. The application deletes grabbed numbers from the list to prevent duplicates. As the application grabs the six numbers, it displays them in numeric order in the label box.

The rate at which the application displays numbers is controlled by the constant DISPLAYMS. You'll want this rate to be fast enough to prevent the user from consciously selecting the numbers as they flash by and yet slow enough to allow the user's subconscious to perhaps grab the right numbers. (Sounds good in theory, anyway!)

The files for the LOTTERY application are included on the companion disk. To load the files into Visual Basic for MS-DOS, choose the File Open Project command and type *C:\VBDWSHOP\LOTTERY.MAK*. This opens the project and enables you to view and modify the forms and code. The following figures, tables, and code give the details of the application's creation.

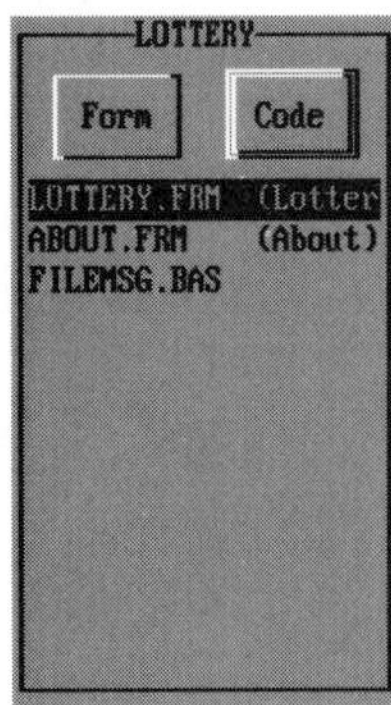

Figure 10-1.
LOTTERY project list.

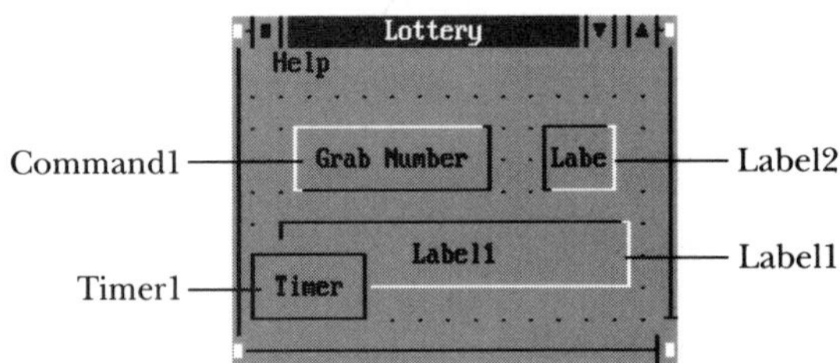

Figure 10-2.
LOTTERY.FRM during development.

LOTTERY.FRM Menu Design Window Entries

Caption	CtlName	Indentation
&Help	menHelp	0
&Help on Lottery	menHelpLottery	1
&About Lottery...	menAboutLottery	1
-	menSep	1
E&xit	menExit	1

LOTTERY.FRM Form and Control Properties

Property	Value
Form:	
Caption	Lottery
FormName	Lottery
Timer1:	
CtlName	Timer1
Interval	50
Command1:	
Caption	Grab Number
CtlName	Command1
Label1:	
CtlName	Label1
Label2:	
CtlName	Label2

Source code for LOTTERY.FRM

```
'==================================================
' LOTTERY
' Helps pick lottery numbers
'==================================================

'$INCLUDE: 'CONSTANT.BI'
'$INCLUDE: 'FILEMSG.BI'
'$INCLUDE: 'ABOUT.BI'

CONST MAXNUMBER = 42
CONST GRABCOUNT = 6
CONST DISPLAYMS = 100

DECLARE SUB Form_Load ()

DIM SHARED c, x
DIM SHARED a(GRABCOUNT), n(MAXNUMBER)
```

(continued)

LOTTERY.FRM *continued*

```
SUB Command1_Click ()
    'Start over after full set selected
    IF c = GRABCOUNT THEN
        BEEP
        Form_Load
        EXIT SUB
    END IF

    'Increase the count of numbers selected
    c = c + 1

    'Grab the currently displayed number
    a(c) = n(x)

    'Zap the number from the list
    n(x) = 0

    'Sort the list of selected numbers
    IF c > 1 THEN
        FOR i = 1 TO c - 1
            FOR j = i + 1 TO c
                IF a(i) > a(j) THEN
                    SWAP a(i), a(j)
                END IF
            NEXT j
        NEXT i
    END IF

    'Build the list of numbers to display
    FOR i = 1 TO c
        t$ = t$ + RIGHT$("   " + STR$(a(i)), 4)
    NEXT i

    'Put the numbers on display
    Label1.Caption = LTRIM$(RTRIM$(t$))

    'If enough numbers have been selected, halt the action
    IF c = GRABCOUNT THEN
        Timer1.Enabled = FALSE
        Label2.Caption = "----"
    END IF
END SUB

SUB Form_Load ()
    'Center the form on the screen
    Lottery.Left = (Screen.Width - Lottery.Width) \ 2
    Lottery.Top = (Screen.Height - Lottery.Height) \ 2
```

(continued)

LOTTERY.FRM *continued*

```
    'Display message in Label1
    Label1.Caption = "Ready - Go for it!"

    'Paint numbers on the balls
    FOR i = 1 TO MAXNUMBER
        n(i) = i
    NEXT i

    'Shuffle the random numbers
    RANDOMIZE TIMER

    'Shuffle the order of the numbered balls
    FOR i = 1 TO MAXNUMBER
        j = INT(RND * MAXNUMBER) + 1
        SWAP n(i), n(j)
    NEXT i

    'Start the numbered balls tumbling
    c = 0
    Timer1.Interval = DISPLAYMS
    Timer1.Enabled = TRUE
END SUB

SUB menAboutLottery_Click ()
    About.Label1.Caption = "LOTTERY"
    About.SHOW MODAL
END SUB

SUB menExit_Click ()
    UNLOAD Lottery
END SUB

SUB menHelpLottery_Click ()
    FileMsg "LOTTERY.MSG", 1
END SUB

SUB Timer1_Timer ()
    'Cycle through the list of numbered balls
    DO
        x = x + 1
        IF x > MAXNUMBER THEN x = 1
    LOOP UNTIL n(x)

    'Display the shuffled numbers sequentially
    Label2.Caption = RIGHT$(SPACE$(3) + STR$(n(x)) + " ", 4)
END SUB
```

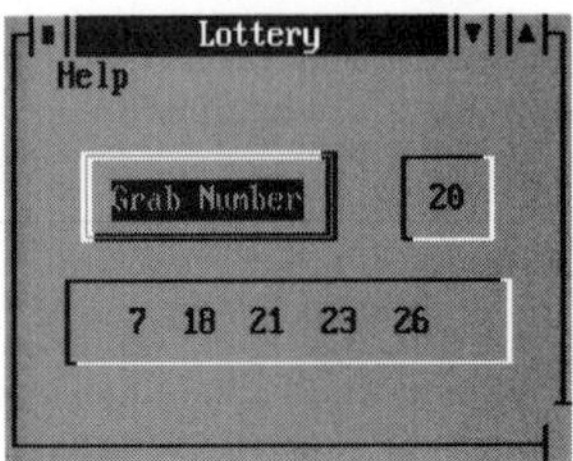

Figure 10-3.
LOTTERY.FRM in action.

The RANDOMS Application

The RANDOM.BAS module provides the subprograms and functions for generating six types of random numbers. This module consists of code only and is intended to be loaded into another project to provide a source of random numbers. A separate form module demonstrates the types of random numbers.

RandShuffle is the subprogram that seeds the random-number generator to a given sequence. Any string that is passed to this subprogram provides the information to randomize the generator, and every unique string creates a unique sequence. To guarantee a new sequence every time, have your program create the string using the system date and time. For example, the string *DATE$ + TIME$* is unique for every second, and *DATE$ + TIME$ + STR$(TIMER)* is unique for every tick of the system clock (18.2 times per second).

To generate the same sequence each time, have your program pass the same string to *RandShuffle*. For example, whenever you pass the string *SEQUENCE 1* to *RandShuffle*, the generator always creates the same sequence.

The *Rand* function returns a random long integer in the range 0 through 999999999. This function is very fast because it does not use multiplication or division operations (only addition and subtraction). The resulting sequence is very long because a table of 55 long integers interacts in a cyclic pattern and another table of 42 long integers further shuffles the results. *Rand* is called by each of the other functions in the module, which modify the resulting random integer to create the other types of random-number sequences.

RandFrac returns a single-precision number in the range between 0 and 1. This function is similar to the *RND* function of Visual Basic for MS-DOS.

RandInteger returns a random integer in the range specified by the parameters *a%* and *b%*, which contain any integer in the range –32768 through 32767.

RandReal returns a value in the range specified by the parameters *x!* and *y!*, which contain single-precision floating-point values. For example, the call *RandReal (0.0, 1.0)* would return the same type of random number as *RandFrac* would return.

RandExponential returns a random number from an exponential distribution with a given mean.

RandNormal returns a number from a normal distribution given the mean and standard deviations.

RANDOMS.FRM demonstrates the random-number–generation functions available in the RANDOM.BAS module. The Options menu provides selections for shuffling the random numbers, using either the system clock or a string the user has entered, and provides a choice of the type of random numbers to be generated and displayed. The generated numbers appear on the form.

The files for the RANDOMS application are included on the companion disk. To load the files into Visual Basic for MS-DOS, choose the File Open Project command and type *C:\VBDWSHOP\RANDOMS.MAK*. This opens the project and enables you to view and modify the form and code. The following figures, tables, and code give the details of the application's creation.

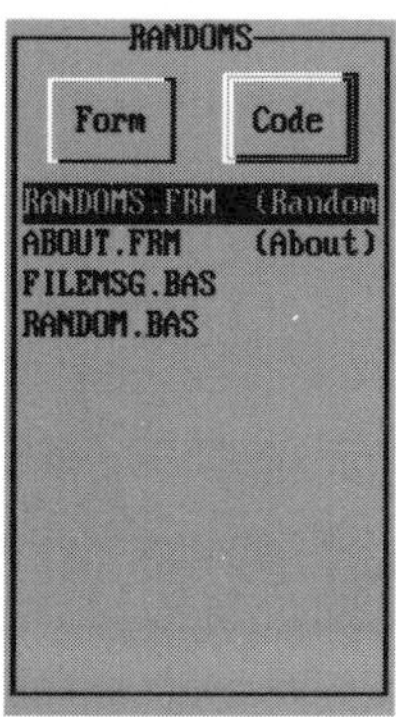

Figure 10-4.
RANDOMS project list.

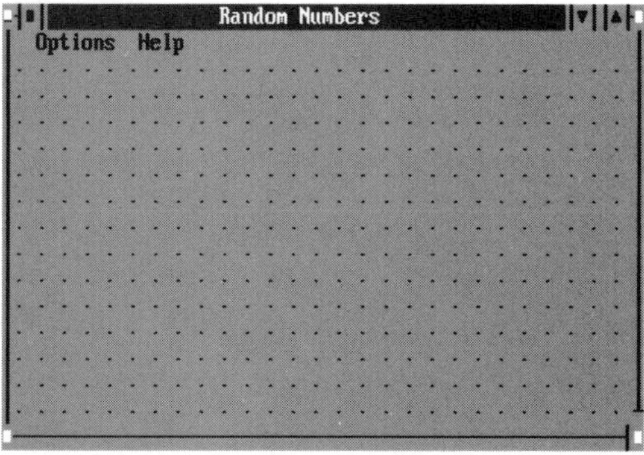

Figure 10-5.
RANDOMS.FRM during development.

RANDOMS.FRM Menu Design Window Entries

Caption	CtlName	Indentation
&Options	menOptions	0
&Shuffle	menShuffle	1
&Use System Time	menRanTime	2
&Enter a String	menRanString	2
&Generate	menGen	1
&Rand	menRLong	2
Rand&Integer	menRInteger	2
Rand&Fraction	menRFrac	2
RandRea&l	menRReal	2
Rand&Normal	menRNormal	2
Rand&Exponential	menRExponential	2
-	menSep	1
E&xit	menExit	1
&Help	menHelp	0
&Help on Randoms	menHelpRandoms	1
&About Randoms...	menAboutRandoms	1

RANDOMS.FRM Form Properties

Property	Value
Form:	
Caption	Random Numbers
FormName	Randoms

Source code for RANDOM.BI

```
'================================================
' RANDOM.BI
' Include file for accessing RANDOM.BAS
'================================================

DECLARE SUB RandShuffle (Key$)
```

(continued)

RANDOM.BI *continued*

```
DECLARE FUNCTION Rand& ()
DECLARE FUNCTION RandExponential! (mean!)
DECLARE FUNCTION RandFrac! ()
DECLARE FUNCTION RandInteger% (a%, b%)
DECLARE FUNCTION RandNormal! (mean!, stddev!)
DECLARE FUNCTION RandReal! (x!, y!)

DIM SHARED r&(100)
```

Source code for RANDOMS.FRM

```
'=================================================
' RANDOMS
' Demonstrates the RANDOM.BAS module
'=================================================

'$INCLUDE: 'CONSTANT.BI'
'$INCLUDE: 'FILEMSG.BI'
'$INCLUDE: 'ABOUT.BI'
'$INCLUDE: 'RANDOM.BI'

SUB Form_Load ()
    'Be sure random numbers are shuffled at least once
    RandShuffle DATE$ + TIME$

    'Center the form on the screen
    Randoms.Left = (Screen.Width - Randoms.Width) \ 2
    Randoms.Top = (Screen.Height - Randoms.Height) \ 2
END SUB

SUB menAboutRandoms_Click ()
    About.Label1.Caption = "RANDOMS"
    About.SHOW MODAL
END SUB

SUB menExit_Click ()
    UNLOAD Randoms
END SUB

SUB menHelpRandoms_Click ()
    FileMsg "RANDOMS.MSG", 1
END SUB

SUB menRanString_Click ()
    NL$ = CHR$(13) + CHR$(10)
    Key$ = INPUTBOX$("Enter a string for randomizing...",
```

(continued)

RANDOMS.FRM *continued*

```
 "Randomizing", "default string")
    IF Key$ <> "" THEN
        MSGBOX "Randomizing string: " + NL$ + Key$
        RandShuffle Key$
    END IF
END SUB

SUB menRanTime_Click ()
    NL$ = CHR$(13) + CHR$(10)
    Key$ = DATE$ + SPACE$(1) + TIME$ + STR$(TIMER)
    MSGBOX "Randomizing string: " + NL$ + Key$
    RandShuffle Key$
END SUB

SUB menRExponential_Click ()
    CLS
    NL$ = CHR$(13) + CHR$(10)
    PRINT NL$ + "Random exponentials, Mean = 10" + NL$ + NL$
    FOR i% = 1 TO 10
        FOR j% = 1 TO 4
            PRINT FORMAT$(RandExponential(10), "###.###"),
        NEXT j%
        PRINT
    NEXT i%
END SUB

SUB menRFrac_Click ()
    CLS
    NL$ = CHR$(13) + CHR$(10)
    PRINT NL$ + "Random fractions between 0.0 and 1.0" + NL$ + NL$
    FOR i% = 1 TO 10
        FOR j% = 1 TO 4
            PRINT FORMAT$(RandFrac(), "#.#########"),
        NEXT j%
        PRINT
    NEXT i%
END SUB

SUB menRInteger_Click ()
    CLS
    NL$ = CHR$(13) + CHR$(10)
    PRINT NL$ + "Random integers between 0 and 100" + NL$ + NL$
    FOR i% = 1 TO 10
        FOR j% = 1 TO 12
            PRINT FORMAT$(RandInteger(0, 100), "####  ");
        NEXT j%
        PRINT
    NEXT i%
END SUB
```

(continued)

RANDOMS.FRM *continued*

```
SUB menRLong_Click ()
    CLS
    NL$ = CHR$(13) + CHR$(10)
    PRINT NL$ + "Random long integers between 0 and 1E9" + NL$ +
NL$
    FOR i% = 1 TO 10
        PRINT Rand(), Rand(), Rand(), Rand()
    NEXT i%
END SUB

SUB menRNormal_Click ()
    CLS
    NL$ = CHR$(13) + CHR$(10)
    PRINT NL$ + "Random normals, Mean = 100, StdDev = 5" + NL$ +
NL$
    FOR i% = 1 TO 10
        FOR j% = 1 TO 4
            PRINT FORMAT$(RandNormal(100, 5), "###.###"),
        NEXT j%
        PRINT
    NEXT i%
END SUB

SUB menRReal_Click ()
    CLS
    NL$ = CHR$(13) + CHR$(10)
    PRINT NL$ + "Random reals between -1.0 and 1.0" + NL$ + NL$
    FOR i% = 1 TO 10
        FOR j% = 1 TO 4
            PRINT FORMAT$(RandReal(-1, 1), "#.#########"),
        NEXT j%
        PRINT
    NEXT i%
END SUB
```

Source code for RANDOM.BAS

```
'================================================
' RANDOM.BAS
' Generates various types of random numbers
'================================================

' Notes:
' Add $INCLUDE: 'RANDOM.BI' to the calling module.
' Load RANDOM.BAS into your project.
'
```

(continued)

RANDOM.BAS *continued*

```
' Example of use:
'    RandShuffle Key$
'    n% = RandInteger(0, 100)

'$INCLUDE: 'RANDOM.BI'

FUNCTION Rand& ()
    'Get the pointers into the table
    i% = r&(98)
    j% = r&(99)

    'Subtract the two table values
    t& = r&(i%) - r&(j%)

    'Adjust result if less than 0
    IF t& < 0 THEN
        t& = t& + 1000000000
    END IF

    'Replace table entry with new random number
    r&(i%) = t&

    'Decrement first index, keeping in range 1 through 55
    IF i% > 1 THEN
        r&(98) = i% - 1
    ELSE
        r&(98) = 55
    END IF

    'Decrement second index, keeping in range 1 through 55
    IF j% > 1 THEN
        r&(99) = j% - 1
    ELSE
        r&(99) = 55
    END IF

    'Use last random number to index into shuffle table
    i% = r&(100) MOD 42 + 56

    'Grab random number from table as current random number
    r&(100) = r&(i%)

    'Put new calculated random number in table
    r&(i%) = t&

    'Return random number grabbed from table
    Rand& = r&(100)
END FUNCTION
```

(continued)

RANDOM.BAS *continued*

```
FUNCTION RandExponential! (mean!)
    RandExponential! = -mean! * LOG(RandFrac!())
END FUNCTION

FUNCTION RandFrac! ()
    RandFrac! = Rand&() / 1E+09
END FUNCTION

FUNCTION RandInteger% (a%, b%)
    RandInteger% = a% + (Rand&() MOD (b% - a% + 1))
END FUNCTION

FUNCTION RandNormal! (mean!, stddev!)
    u1! = RandFrac!()
    u2! = RandFrac!()
    x! = SQR(-2! * LOG(u1!)) * COS(6.283185 * u2)
    RandNormal! = mean! + stddev! * x!
END FUNCTION

FUNCTION RandReal! (x!, y!)
    RandReal! = x! + (y! - x!) * (Rand&() / 1E+09)
END FUNCTION

SUB RandShuffle (Key$)
    'Form 97-character string, with Key$ as part of it
    Tmp$ = LEFT$("Abracadabra" + Key$ + SPACE$(86), 97)

    'Use each character to seed table
    FOR i% = 1 TO 97
        r&(i%) = ASC(MID$(Tmp$, i%, 1)) * 8171717 + i% * 997&
    NEXT i%

    'Preserve string space
    Tmp$ = ""

    'Initialize pointers into table
    i% = 97
    j% = 12

    'Randomize table to get it warmed up
    FOR k% = 1 TO 997

        'Subtract entries pointed to by i% and j%
        r&(i%) = r&(i%) - r&(j%)

        'Adjust result if less than 0
        IF r&(i%) < 0 THEN
            r&(i%) = r&(i%) + 1000000000
        END IF
```

(continued)

RANDOM.BAS *continued*

```
        'Decrement first index, keeping in range 1 through 97
        IF i% > 1 THEN
            i% = i% - 1
        ELSE
            i% = 97
        END IF

        'Decrement second index, keeping in range 1 through 97
        IF j% > 1 THEN
            j% = j% - 1
        ELSE
            j% = 97
        END IF

    NEXT k%

    'Initialize pointers for use by Rand& function
    r&(98) = 55
    r&(99) = 24

    'Initialize pointer for shuffle table lookup by Rand& function
    r&(100) = 77
END SUB
```

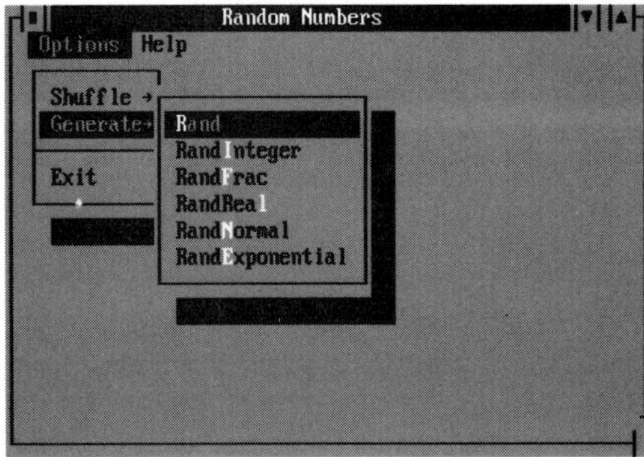

Figure 10-6.
RANDOMS.FRM in action (menu).

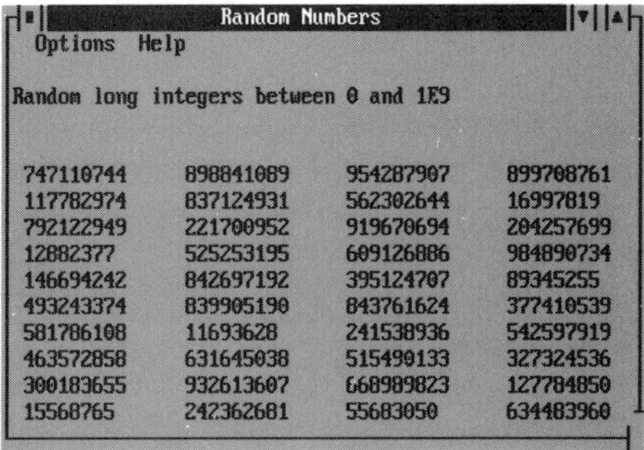

Figure 10-7.
RANDOMS.FRM in action (Rand).

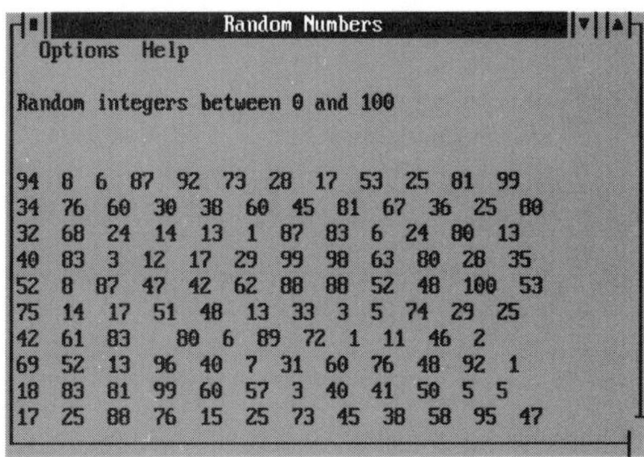

Figure 10-8.
RANDOMS.FRM in action (RandInteger).

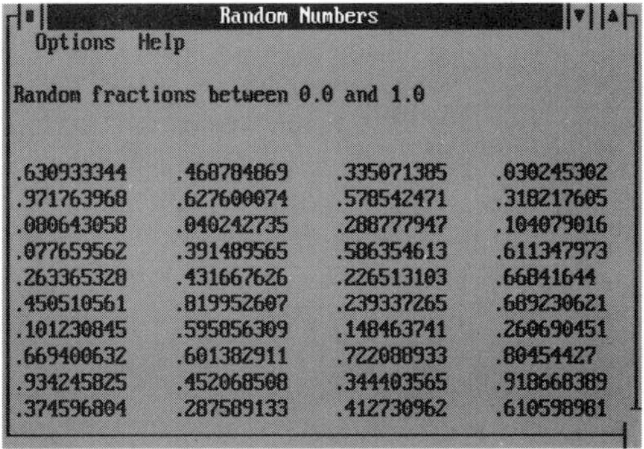

Figure 10-9.
RANDOMS.FRM in action (RandFrac).

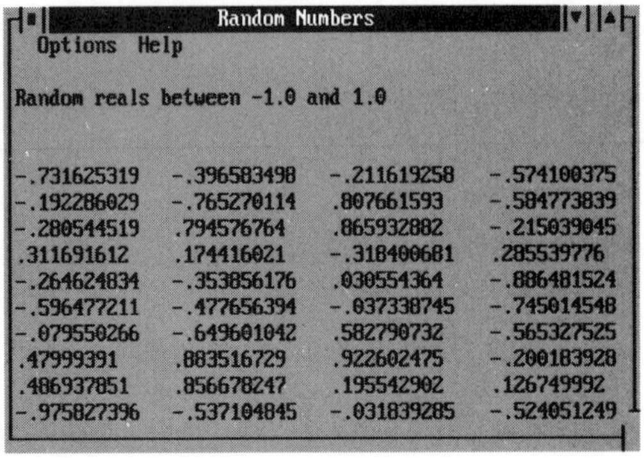

Random Numbers

Options Help

Random reals between -1.0 and 1.0

-.731625319	-.396583498	-.211619258	-.574100375
-.192286029	-.765270114	.807661593	-.584773839
-.280544519	.794576764	.865932882	-.215039045
.311691612	.174416021	-.318400681	.285539776
-.264624834	-.353856176	.030554364	-.886481524
-.596477211	-.477656394	-.037338745	-.745014548
-.079550266	-.649601042	.582790732	-.565327525
.47999391	.883516729	.922602475	-.200183928
.486937851	.856678247	.195542902	.126749992
-.975827396	-.537104845	-.031839285	-.524051249

Figure 10-10.
RANDOMS.FRM in action (RandReal).

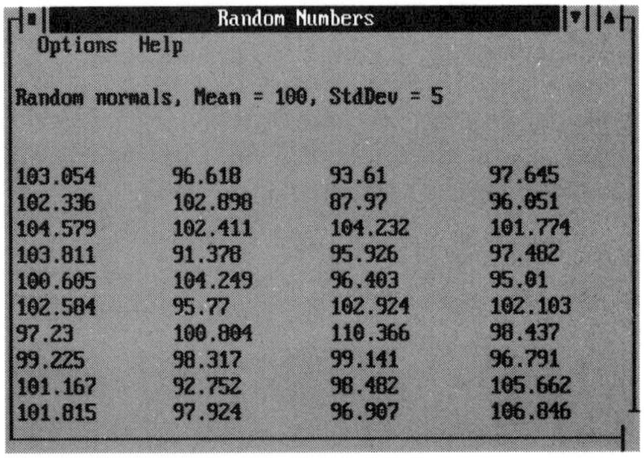

Random Numbers

Options Help

Random normals, Mean = 100, StdDev = 5

103.054	96.618	93.61	97.645
102.336	102.898	87.97	96.051
104.579	102.411	104.232	101.774
103.811	91.378	95.926	97.482
100.605	104.249	96.403	95.01
102.584	95.77	102.924	102.103
97.23	100.804	110.366	98.437
99.225	98.317	99.141	96.791
101.167	92.752	98.482	105.662
101.815	97.924	96.907	106.846

Figure 10-11.
RANDOMS.FRM in action (RandNormal).

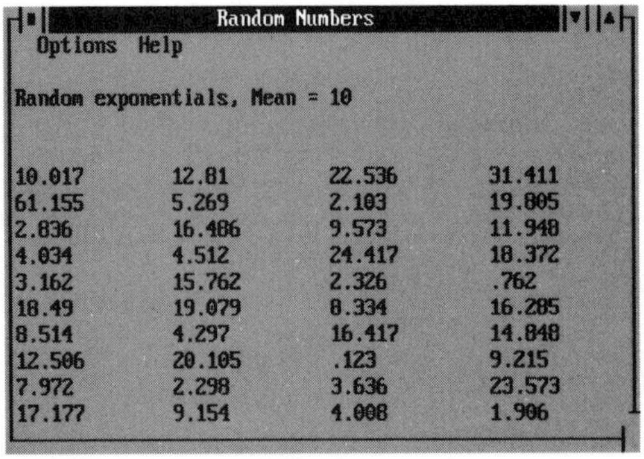

Random Numbers

Options Help

Random exponentials, Mean = 10

10.017	12.81	22.536	31.411
61.155	5.269	2.103	19.805
2.836	16.486	9.573	11.948
4.034	4.512	24.417	18.372
3.162	15.762	2.326	.762
18.49	19.079	8.334	16.285
8.514	4.297	16.417	14.848
12.506	20.105	.123	9.215
7.972	2.298	3.636	23.573
17.177	9.154	4.008	1.906

Figure 10-12.
RANDOMS.FRM in action (RandExponential).

CHAPTER ELEVEN

UTILITY APPLICATIONS

The FILEFACT Application

The FILEFACT application displays a collection of facts about a file. This program uses four forms and so provides a good example of multiform programming. The main form contains a menu and five command buttons for selecting a file and displaying information about the file. The ABOUT form provides the standard About dialog box, and the GETFILE form selects a file. (See the ABOUTDEM and GETDEMO applications in Chapter 5 for more information about these forms.) The FILFACT2 form, which appears when the user clicks the ASCII Count button, displays a scrollable list that shows the count of each ASCII (and extended ASCII) character in the selected file.

The Word Count button provides a count of the words in the file; the Checksum button displays a *checksum* (a calculated value that a program uses to test whether a file has been copied correctly); the Length button provides the number of bytes in the selected file; and the Cancel button unloads the form and ends the program.

When the user clicks the Length button, the file opens in random-access mode (although any mode would work for this purpose), and the *LOF* function immediately returns the length of the file. The application does not read any data from the file and closes the file immediately after it determines the length. (The user must select a file before clicking the ASCII Count, Word Count, Checksum, or Length button. The application beeps and displays a reminder if the user clicks one of these buttons before selecting a file.)

To calculate the word count, the application opens the selected file for sequential input and reads in one line of text at a time, using the *LINE INPUT* statement. The application parses each string from the file to determine a word count and then displays the total word count when the application reaches the end of the file.

The checksum and character-count subprograms access the file in similar ways. The application opens the file in binary mode and then reads large chunks of bytes from the file using the *GET* statement. The checksum computation processes one byte at a time from the string buffers; it also tallies the total byte count one byte at a time. Notice that the checksum subprogram, named *Checksm_Click*, uses a *GOSUB* statement. This statement lets you build subroutines that are local to a particular subprogram or function, which can prevent the duplication of code.

The FILFACT2.FRM form displays a table of character counts. The application builds the table as a single string displayed in a scrollable text box. This is the same technique I used in the EDITDEMO application in Chapter 5 and in other applications in this book.

I brought this application into the Visual Basic for MS-DOS environment from the Visual Basic for Windows environment with only minimal changes. The application first appeared in my previous book *The Microsoft Visual Basic Workshop*. (And so you'll notice that the control names in the FILEFACT application look a little different from the rest of the control names appearing throughout this book.)

Visual Basic for MS-DOS provides a utility form conversion program named FT.EXE. I used this program to translate the original Visual Basic for Windows forms into Visual Basic for MS-DOS format. With only a little resizing, the forms were ready to go. See your Visual Basic for MS-DOS documentation for instructions on how to use this and other development tools.

The files for the FILEFACT application are included on the companion disk. To load the files into Visual Basic for MS-DOS, choose the File Open Project command and type *C:\VBDWSHOP\FILEFACT.MAK*. This opens the project and enables you to view and modify the forms and code. The following figures, tables, and code give the details of the application's creation.

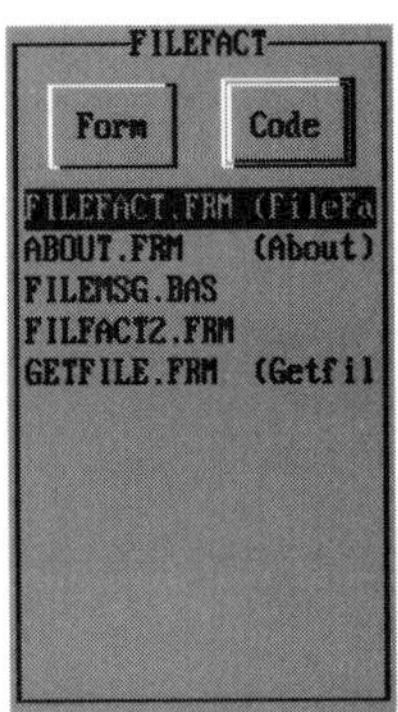

Figure 11-1.
FILEFACT project list.

Source code for FILEFACT.BI

```
'==================================================
' FILEFACT.BI
' Include file for accessing FILEFACT.FRM
'==================================================

'$FORM FilFact2

DECLARE SUB ExitFileFact_Click ()
DECLARE FUNCTION WordCount% (A$, Sep$)
DECLARE SUB ByteCount (Chunk$)
DECLARE SUB NoFile ()
```

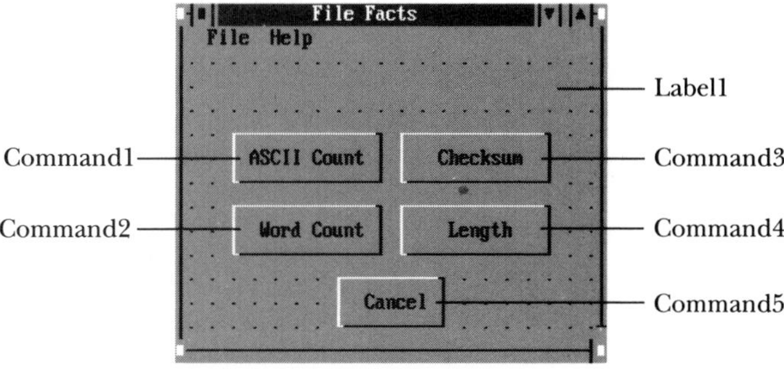

Figure 11-2.
FILEFACT.FRM during development.

FILEFACT.FRM Menu Design Window Entries

Caption	CtlName	Indentation
&File	menFileTop	0
&Select a File...	menSelectFile	1
-	menSep	1
E&xit	menExit	1
&Help	menHelpTop	0
&Help on FileFact	menHelpFileFact	1
&About FileFact...	menAboutFileFact	1

FILEFACT.FRM Form and Control Properties

Property	Value
Form:	
Caption	File Facts
FormName	FileFact
Label1:	
Alignment	2 - Center
Caption	*(blank)*
CtlName	Label1
Command1:	
Caption	ASCII Count
CtlName	ASCIICnt
Command2:	
Caption	Word Count
CtlName	WordCnt
Command3:	
Caption	Checksum
CtlName	Checksm
Command4:	
Caption	Length
CtlName	Length
Command5:	
Caption	Cancel
CtlName	Cancel
Cancel	True

Source code for FILEFACT.FRM

```
'================================================
' FILEFACT
' Displays information about a file
'================================================
```

(continued)

FILEFACT.FRM *continued*

```
'$INCLUDE: 'CONSTANT.BI'
'$INCLUDE: 'GETFILE.BI'
'$INCLUDE: 'FILEMSG.BI'
'$INCLUDE: 'ABOUT.BI'
'$INCLUDE: 'FILEFACT.BI'

DIM SHARED Cnt&(0 TO 255)
DIM SHARED FileSelected AS INTEGER

SUB menAboutFileFact_Click ()
    About.Label1.Caption = "FILEFACT"
    About.SHOW MODAL
END SUB

SUB ASCIICnt_Click ()
    'Be sure a file was selected
    IF FileSelected = FALSE THEN
        BEEP
        NoFile
        EXIT SUB
    END IF

    'Change mouse pointer to hourglass shape
    MousePointer = 11

    'Open the file in binary mode
    OPEN FullPath FOR BINARY AS #1

    'Determine size of the file for reading chunks
    ChunkSize% = 32000
    N1& = LOF(1)
    N2% = N1& \ ChunkSize%
    N3% = N1& MOD ChunkSize%

    'Read in and process each big chunk
    Chunk$ = SPACE$(ChunkSize%)
    FOR i% = 1 TO N2%
        GET #1, , Chunk$
        ByteCount Chunk$
    NEXT i%

    'Read smaller leftover chunk
    Chunk$ = SPACE$(N3%)
    GET #1, , Chunk$
    ByteCount Chunk$
```

(continued)

FILEFACT.FRM *continued*

```
    'Close the file
    CLOSE #1

    'Build string to display the ASCII count
    NL$ = CHR$(13) + CHR$(10)
    StrShow$ = " Dec   Hex   Count" + NL$ + NL$
    FOR i% = 0 TO 255
        IF Cnt&(i%) THEN
            t1$ = RIGHT$(SPACE$(2) + STR$(i%), 3)
            t2$ = RIGHT$(SPACE$(5) + HEX$(i%), 6)
            t3$ = RIGHT$(SPACE$(7) + STR$(Cnt&(i%)), 8)
            StrShow$ = StrShow$ + t1$ + t2$ + t3$ + NL$
        END IF
    NEXT i%

    'Change the mouse pointer back to default shape
    MousePointer = 0

    'Display the results
    FilFact2.Text1.Text = StrShow$
    FilFact2.SHOW MODAL

    'Zero the counts for the next time
    FOR i% = 0 TO 255
        Cnt&(i%) = 0
    NEXT i%
END SUB

SUB ByteCount (Chunk$)
    FOR i% = 1 TO LEN(Chunk$)
        j% = ASC(MID$(Chunk$, i%, 1))
        Cnt&(j%) = Cnt&(j%) + 1
    NEXT i%
END SUB

SUB Cancel_Click ()
     UNLOAD FileFact
END SUB

SUB Checksm_Click ()
    CONST Chunk = 10000

    'Be sure a file was selected
    IF FileSelected = FALSE THEN
        BEEP
        NoFile
        EXIT SUB
    END IF
```

(continued)

FILEFACT.FRM *continued*

```
    'Change mouse pointer to hourglass shape
    MousePointer = 11

    'Open the file in binary mode
    OPEN FullPath FOR BINARY AS #1

    'Process all the bytes of the file
    LenFil& = LOF(1)
    A$ = SPACE$(Chunk)
    DO WHILE LenFil& > Chunk
        GET #1, , A$
        GOSUB ProcessString
        LenFil& = LenFil& - Chunk
    LOOP

    A$ = SPACE$(LenFil&)
    GET #1, , A$
    GOSUB ProcessString

    'Close the file
    CLOSE #1

    'Change the mouse pointer back to default shape
    MousePointer = 0

    'Display the resulting checksum
    Msg$ = "File checksum is" + STR$(Checksum%)
    MSGBOX Msg$, 64, ""

    EXIT SUB

ProcessString:

    FOR i% = 1 TO LEN(A$)
        Checksum% = Checksum% XOR (ASC(MID$(A$, i%, 1)) + i%)
    NEXT i%

    RETURN
END SUB

SUB menExit_Click ()
    UNLOAD FileFact
END SUB

SUB Form_Load ()
    FileSelected = FALSE

    'Center the form on the screen
    FileFact.Left = (Screen.Width - FileFact.Width) \ 2
    FileFact.Top = (Screen.Height - FileFact.Height) \ 2
END SUB
```

(continued)

FILEFACT.FRM *continued*

```
SUB menHelpFileFact_Click ()
    FileMsg "FILEFACT.MSG", 1
END SUB

SUB Length_Click ()
    'Be sure a file was selected
    IF FileSelected = FALSE THEN
        BEEP
        NoFile
        EXIT SUB
    END IF

    'Change mouse pointer to hourglass shape
    MousePointer = 11

    'Open file in random-access mode and calculate its length
    OPEN FullPath FOR RANDOM AS #1
    FilLen& = LOF(1)

    'Close the file
    CLOSE #1

    'Change the mouse pointer back to default shape
    MousePointer = 0

    'Display the length of the file
    Msg$ = "Length of the file is" + STR$(FilLen&) + " bytes"
    MSGBOX Msg$, 64, ""
END SUB

SUB NoFile ()
    Msg$ = "You must select a file first"
    MSGBOX Msg$, 48, ""
END SUB

SUB menSelectFile_Click ()
    FullPath = ""
    WildCard = "*.*"
    GetFile.SHOW MODAL
    Label1.Caption = FullPath
    FileSelected = PathFlag
END SUB

SUB WordCnt_Click ()
    'Be sure a file was selected
    IF FileSelected = FALSE THEN
        BEEP
        NoFile
        EXIT SUB
    END IF
```

(continued)

FILEFACT.FRM *continued*

```
        'Change mouse pointer to hourglass shape
        MousePointer = 11

        'Open the file in sequential input mode
        OPEN FullPath FOR INPUT AS #1

        'Set the word-separating characters to space, tab, and comma
        Sep$ = " " + CHR$(9) + ","

        'Read in and process each line
        DO
            LINE INPUT #1, A$
            TotalCount& = TotalCount& + WordCount%(A$, Sep$)
        LOOP UNTIL EOF(1)

        'Close the file
        CLOSE #1

        'Change the mouse pointer back to default shape
        MousePointer = 0

        'Display the word count
        Msg$ = "Number of words is" + STR$(TotalCount&)
        MSGBOX Msg$, 64, ""
END SUB

FUNCTION WordCount% (A$, Sep$)
    Count% = 0
    Flag% = 0
    LenStr% = LEN(A$)

    IF LenStr% > 0 AND Sep$ <> "" THEN
        FOR i% = 1 TO LenStr%
            IF INSTR(Sep$, MID$(A$, i%, 1)) THEN
                IF Flag% THEN
                    Flag% = 0
                    Count% = Count% + 1
                END IF
            ELSE
                Flag% = 1
            END IF
        NEXT i%
    END IF

    WordCount% = Count% + Flag%
END FUNCTION
```

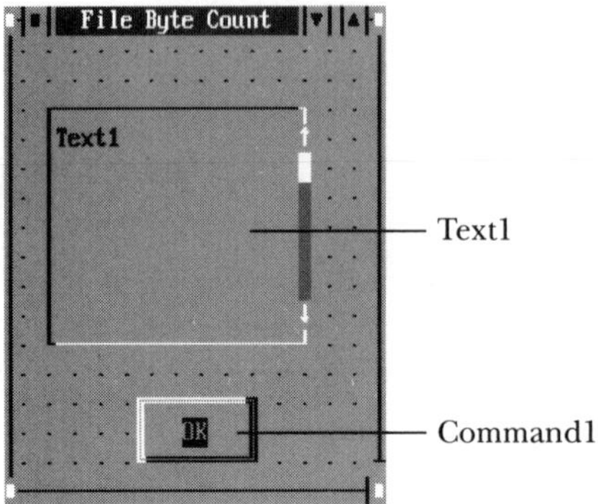

Figure 11-3.
FILFACT2.FRM during development.

FILFACT2.FRM Form and Control Properties

Property	Value
Form:	
Caption	File Byte Count
FormName	FilFact2
Text1:	
CtlName	Text1
MultiLine	True
ScrollBars	2 - Vertical
Command1:	
Cancel	True
Caption	OK
CtlName	Command1
Default	True

Source code for FILFACT2.FRM

```
'=================================================
' FILFACT2
' Displays ASCII count for the FILEFACT program
'=================================================
```

(continued)

FILFACT2.FRM *continued*

```
DECLARE SUB Form_Resize ()

SUB Command1_Click ()
    UNLOAD FilFact2
END SUB

SUB Form_Load ()
    Form_Resize
END SUB

SUB Form_Resize ()
    'Size text box in form window
    Text1.Top = 0
    Text1.Left = 0
    Text1.Width = ScaleWidth
    Text1.Height = ScaleHeight - 3
END SUB

SUB Text1_GotFocus ()
    Command1.SETFOCUS
END SUB
```

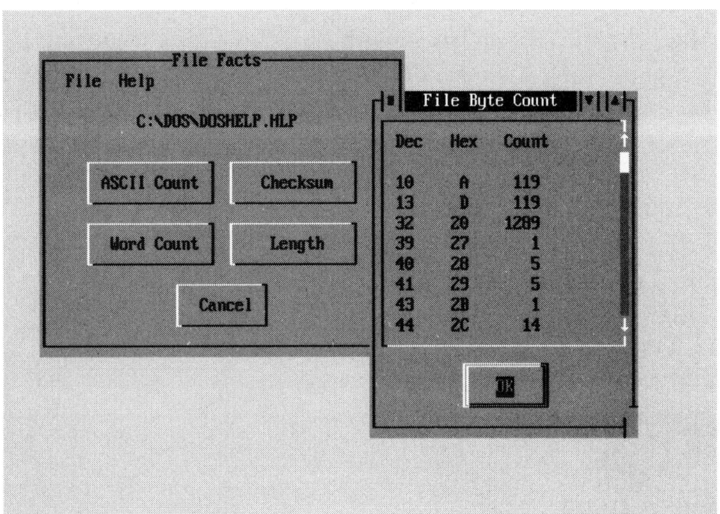

Figure 11-4.
FILEFACT.FRM and FILFACT2.FRM in action.

The FILEPACK Application

The FILEPACK application converts files to and from hexadecimal format or packed ASCII format. These formats are useful for sending a file in printed output form or for sending a file via a modem in nonbinary form.

When a file is converted to hexadecimal format from binary format, the resulting file is roughly twice the size of the original. This size increase occurs because the application converts each byte of a binary file to a two-character string; the string represents the hexadecimal value of the byte. A few extra formatting characters that are added to the output file, such as spaces, carriage-returns, and linefeed characters, actually make the hexadecimal file slightly larger than twice the size of the original binary file. When the application converts a file back from hexadecimal form to binary form, the application ignores all extraneous characters (those not in the range 0–9 or A–F).

The packed ASCII format is a little more compact than the hexadecimal format. The application converts groups of three bytes to groups of four ASCII characters from the range of printable characters. The resulting file contains a wider diversity of characters than does the hexadecimal file, but all the characters are printable and displayable. The packed ASCII file is slightly larger than—about $1\frac{1}{3}$ the size of—the original.

The files for the FILEPACK application are included on the companion disk. To load the files into Visual Basic for MS-DOS, choose the File Open Project command and type *C:\VBDWSHOP\FILEPACK.MAK*. This opens the project and enables you to view and modify the forms and code. The following figures, tables, and code give the details of the application's creation.

Figure 11-5.
FILEPACK project list.

Source code for FILEPACK.BI

```
'==================================================
' FILEPACK.BI
' Include file for FILEPACK
'==================================================

DECLARE SUB FromHex (InFile$, OutFile$)
DECLARE SUB ToHex (InFile$, OutFile$)
DECLARE SUB ToAsc (InFile$, OutFile$)
DECLARE SUB FromAsc (InFile$, OutFile$)
```

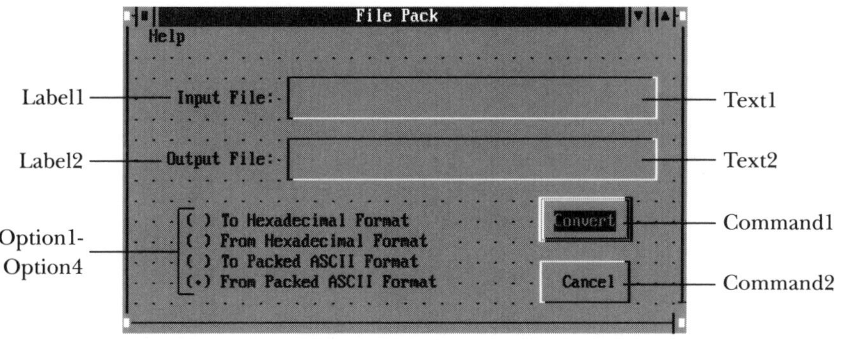

Figure 11-6.
FILEPACK.FRM during development.

FILEPACK.FRM Menu Design Window Entries

Caption	CtlName	Indentation
&Help	menHelp	0
&Help on FilePack	menHelpFilePack	1
&About FilePack...	menAboutFilePack	1
-	menSep	1
E&xit	menExit	1

FILEPACK.FRM Form and Control Properties

Property	Value
Form:	
Caption	File Pack
FormName	Filepack
Label1:	
Alignment	1 - Right Justify
Caption	Input File:
CtlName	Label1
Label2:	
Alignment	1 - Right Justify
Caption	Output File:
CtlName	Label2
Text1:	
CtlName	Text1
Text	*(blank)*
Text2:	
CtlName	Text2
Text	*(blank)*
Option1:	
Caption	To Hexadecimal Format
CtlName	Option1
Option2:	
Caption	From Hexadecimal Format
CtlName	Option2
Option3:	
Caption	To Packed ASCII Format
CtlName	Option3

(continued)

FILEPACK.FRM Form and Control Properties *continued*

Property	Value
Option4:	
Caption	From Packed ASCII Format
CtlName	Option4
Command1:	
Caption	Convert
CtlName	Command1
Default	True
Command2:	
Cancel	True
Caption	Cancel
CtlName	Command2

Source code for FILEPACK.FRM

```
'==================================================
' FILEPACK
' Converts any file to or from hexadecimal format
' or packed ASCII format
'==================================================

'$INCLUDE: 'CONSTANT.BI'
'$INCLUDE: 'FILEMSG.BI'
'$INCLUDE: 'ABOUT.BI'
'$INCLUDE: 'FILEPACK.BI'

SUB Command1_Click ()
    'Get the filenames
    InFile$ = Text1.Text
    OutFile$ = Text2.Text

    IF Option1.Value = TRUE THEN
        ToHex InFile$, OutFile$
    ELSEIF Option2.Value = TRUE THEN
        FromHex InFile$, OutFile$
    ELSEIF Option3.Value = TRUE THEN
        ToAsc InFile$, OutFile$
```

(continued)

FILEPACK.FRM *continued*

```
    ELSEIF Option4.Value = TRUE THEN
        FromAsc InFile$, OutFile$
    END IF
END SUB

SUB Command2_Click
    UNLOAD FilePack
END SUB

SUB Form_Load ()
    FilePack.Top = (Screen.Height - FilePack.Height) \ 2
    FilePack.Left = (Screen.Width - FilePack.Width) \ 2
END SUB

SUB FromAsc (InFile$, OutFile$)
    'Trap filename errors
    ON LOCAL ERROR GOTO BadFile_FromAsc

    'Open both files
    f1% = FREEFILE
    OPEN InFile$ FOR INPUT AS #f1%
    f2% = FREEFILE
    OPEN OutFile$ FOR BINARY AS #f2%

    'Resume normal error trapping
    ON LOCAL ERROR GOTO 0

    'Get the byte count
    INPUT #f1%, Count&

    'Process the input file
    DO UNTIL EOF(f1%)
        LINE INPUT #f1%, A$

        'Process groups of four characters
        FOR i% = 1 TO LEN(A$) STEP 4
            B$ = MID$(A$, i%, 4)
            C1& = (ASC(MID$(B$, 1, 1)) - 48) * &H40000
            C2& = (ASC(MID$(B$, 2, 1)) - 48) * &H1000&
            C3& = (ASC(MID$(B$, 3, 1)) - 48) * &H40&
            C4& = ASC(MID$(B$, 4, 1)) - 48

            'Output groups of three binary bytes
            C$ = LEFT$(MKL$(C1& + C2& + C3& + C4&), 3)
            IF Count& >= 3 THEN
                Count& = Count& - 3
                PUT #f2%, , C$
            ELSE
                C$ = LEFT$(C$, Count&)
                PUT #f2%, , C$
                EXIT DO
            END IF
```

(continued)

FILEPACK.FRM *continued*

```
        NEXT i%
    LOOP

    MSGBOX "File converted successfully"

Exit_FromAsc:
    CLOSE #f1%, #f2%
    EXIT SUB

BadFile_FromAsc:
    MSGBOX "Bad Filename"
    RESUME Exit_FromAsc
END SUB

SUB FromHex (InFile$, OutFile$)
    'Trap filename errors
    ON LOCAL ERROR GOTO BadFile_FromHex

    'Open both files
    f1% = FREEFILE
    OPEN InFile$ FOR INPUT AS #f1%
    f2% = FREEFILE
    OPEN OutFile$ FOR BINARY AS #f2%

    'Resume normal error trapping
    ON LOCAL ERROR GOTO 0

    'Process the input file
    DO UNTIL EOF(f1%)
        INPUT #f1%, A$
        A$ = UCASE$(A$)
        Ndx% = 1
        DO WHILE Ndx% <= LEN(A$)
            B$ = MID$(A$, Ndx%, 1)
            Ndx% = Ndx% + 1

            'Process only hexadecimal characters
            IF INSTR("0123456789ABCDEF", B$) THEN
                IF LEN(C$) THEN
                    Byte$ = CHR$(VAL(C$ + B$))
                    PUT #f2%, , Byte$
                    C$ = ""
                ELSE
                    C$ = "&H" + B$
                END IF
            END IF

        LOOP
    LOOP
```

(continued)

FILEPACK.FRM *continued*

```
    MSGBOX "File converted successfully"

Exit_FromHex:
    CLOSE #f1%, #f2%
    EXIT SUB

BadFile_FromHex:
    MSGBOX "Bad Filename"
    RESUME Exit_FromHex
END SUB

SUB menAboutFilePack_Click ()
    About.Label1.Caption = "FILEPACK"
    About.SHOW MODAL
END SUB

SUB menExit_Click ()
    UNLOAD FilePack
END SUB

SUB menHelpFilePack_Click ()
    FileMsg "FILEPACK.MSG", 1
END SUB

SUB ToAsc (InFile$, OutFile$)
    'Trap filename errors
    ON LOCAL ERROR GOTO BadFile_ToAsc

    'Open both files
    f1% = FREEFILE
    OPEN InFile$ FOR BINARY AS #f1%
    f2% = FREEFILE
    OPEN OutFile$ FOR OUTPUT AS #f2%

    'Resume normal error trapping
    ON LOCAL ERROR GOTO 0

    'Output the byte count
    PRINT #f2%, LTRIM$(STR$(LOF(1)))

    'Process groups of three bytes
    A$ = SPACE$(3)
    DO
        GET #f1%, , A$
        A& = CVL(A$ + CHR$(0))
```

(continued)

FILEPACK.FRM *continued*

```
        C1% = (A& AND &HFC0000) \ &H40000 + 48
        C2% = (A& AND &H3F000) \ &H1000 + 48
        C3% = (A& AND &HFC0) \ &H40 + 48
        C4% = (A& AND &H3F) + 48
        B$ = CHR$(C1%) + CHR$(C2%) + CHR$(C3%) + CHR$(C4%)
        C$ = C$ + B$
        IF LEN(C$) > 70 THEN
            PRINT #f2%, C$
            C$ = ""
        END IF
    LOOP UNTIL EOF(f1%)
    IF C$ <> "" THEN
        PRINT #f2%, C$
        C$ = ""
    END IF

    MSGBOX "File converted successfully"

Exit_ToAsc:
    CLOSE #f1%, #f2%
    EXIT SUB

BadFile_ToAsc:
    MSGBOX "Bad Filename"
    RESUME Exit_ToAsc
END SUB

SUB ToHex (InFile$, OutFile$)
    'Trap filename errors
    ON LOCAL ERROR GOTO BadFile_ToHex

    'Open both files
    f1% = FREEFILE
    OPEN InFile$ FOR BINARY AS #f1%
    f2% = FREEFILE
    OPEN OutFile$ FOR OUTPUT AS #f2%

    'Resume normal error trapping
    ON LOCAL ERROR GOTO 0

    'Process each byte
    A$ = SPACE$(1)
    DO
        GET #f1%, , A$
        IF EOF(f1%) THEN EXIT DO
        PRINT #f2%, RIGHT$("0" + HEX$(ASC(A$)), 2);
```

(continued)

FILEPACK.FRM *continued*

```
        Count% = Count% + 1
        SELECT CASE Count%
        CASE 8, 24
            PRINT #f2%, SPACE$(1);
        CASE 16
            PRINT #f2%, SPACE$(2);
        CASE 32
            PRINT #f2%, ""
            Count% = 0
        END SELECT
    LOOP UNTIL EOF(1)

    MSGBOX "File converted successfully"

Exit_ToHex:
    CLOSE #f1%, #f2%
    EXIT SUB

BadFile_ToHex:
    MSGBOX "Bad Filename"
    RESUME Exit_ToHex
END SUB
```

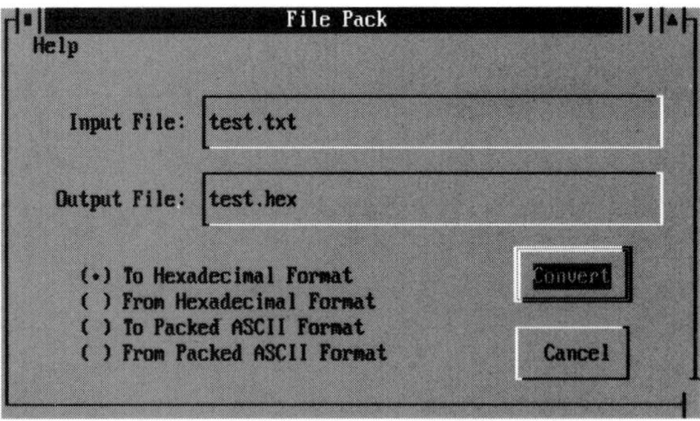

Figure 11-7.
FILEPACK.FRM in action.

```
This is a short test file
for the FILEPACK program.
```

Figure 11-8.
Test file before conversion.

```
5468697320697320 612073686F727420  746573742066696C 650D0A666F722074
68652046494C4550 41434B2070726F67  72616D2E0D0A
```

Figure 11-9.
Test file in hexadecimal format.

```
54
JFQDJB1cHB1cJ7<PM79_IG@P87AcK6UV2PeULVmVJ7@PAR1UADa9@d5@L21;IfmbKF5b2Pd^
0000
```

Figure 11-10.
Test file in packed ASCII format.

The QUICKDEM Application

The QUICKDEM application demonstrates a BAS module that provides subprograms for sorting arrays of several types of data. These subprograms use the quicksort algorithm. To use these sort subprograms in your own program, simply add the QUICKSRT.BAS module to your project list and include QUICKSRT.BI in the calling module. Instructions to remind you about these steps are included in the comment lines at the start of the QUICKSRT.BAS file.

When you run this program, first type a few words in the scrollable text box. Notice that the application automatically converts spaces to carriage-return and linefeed characters so that each line in the text box contains only one word. Take a look at the *Text1_KeyPress* subprogram to see how the application intercepts and preprocesses key presses as you enter the text. Note that this technique is very useful for processing key presses as they occur. For example, if an integer is to be entered in a text field, a similar subprogram could be set to ignore any key presses except the digits 0–9. (To ignore a key press completely, simply set the variable *KeyAscii* to *0*.)

After you've entered a few words, click Sort to sort the words into alphanumeric order. The QUICKDEM application calls and demonstrates the *QuicksortSTR* subprogram (which sorts strings), but I have also provided other similar subprograms to sort arrays of most other types of variables.

The files for the QUICKDEM application are included on the companion disk. To load the files into Visual Basic for MS-DOS, choose the File Open Project command and type *C:\VBDWSHOP\QUICKDEM.MAK*. This opens the project and enables you to view and modify the forms and code. The following figures, tables, and code give the details of the application's creation.

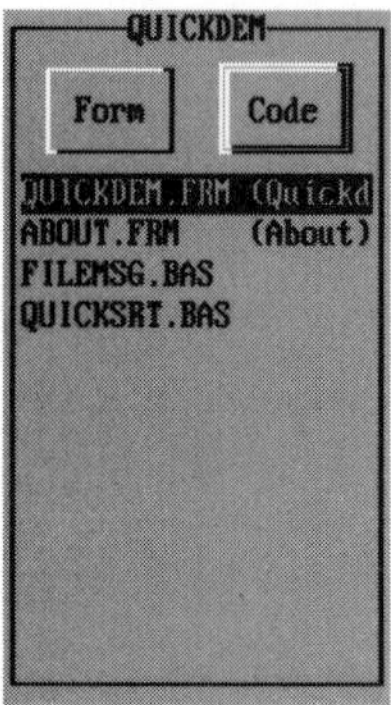

Figure 11-11.
QUICKDEM project list.

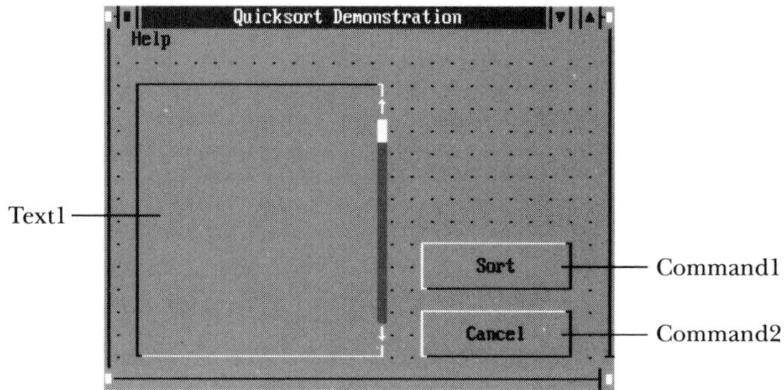

Figure 11-12.
QUICKDEM.FRM during development.

QUICKDEM.FRM Menu Design Window Entries

Caption	CtlName	Indentation
&Help	menHelp	0
&Help on QuickDem	menHelpQuickDem	1
&About QuickDem...	menAboutQuickDem	1
-	menSep	1
E&xit	menExit	1

QUICKDEM.FRM Form and Control Properties

Property	Value
Form:	
Caption	Quicksort Demonstration
FormName	Quickdem
Text1:	
CtlName	Text1
MultiLine	True
ScrollBars	2 - Vertical
Command1:	
Caption	Sort
CtlName	Command1
Default	True
Command2:	
Cancel	True
Caption	Cancel
CtlName	Command2

Source code for QUICKSRT.BI

```
'================================================
' QUICKSRT.BI
' Include file for accessing QUICKSRT.BAS
'================================================

DECLARE SUB QuicksortSTR (X$())
DECLARE SUB QuicksortDBL (X#())
DECLARE SUB QuicksortSNG (X!())
DECLARE SUB QuicksortLNG (X&())
DECLARE SUB QuicksortINT (X%())
```

Source code for QUICKDEM.FRM

```
'==================================================
' QUICKDEM
' Demonstrates the QUICKSRT module
'==================================================

'$INCLUDE: 'CONSTANT.BI'
'$INCLUDE: 'FILEMSG.BI'
'$INCLUDE: 'ABOUT.BI'
'$INCLUDE: 'QUICKSRT.BI'

DIM SHARED SortedFlag%

SUB Command1_Click ()
    'Initialize some variables
    NL$ = CHR$(13) + CHR$(10)
    NLPos% = 1
    A$ = Text1.Text

    'Be sure the string ends with a newline character
    IF RIGHT$(A$, 1) <> NL$ THEN
        A$ = A$ + NL$
    END IF

    'Build a string array of the words
    DO
        NLPos% = INSTR(A$, NL$)
        IF NLPos% = 0 THEN EXIT DO
        IF NLPos% > 1 THEN
            Count% = Count% + 1
            REDIM PRESERVE Ary$(1 TO Count%)
            Ary$(Count%) = LEFT$(A$, NLPos%)
        END IF
        A$ = MID$(A$, NLPos% + 2)
    LOOP

    'Sort the string array
    QuickSortSTR Ary$()

    'Build display string
    FOR i% = 1 TO Count%
        B$ = B$ + Ary$(i%)
    NEXT i%

    'Redisplay the sorted words
    Text1.Text = B$

    'Note that the sort has occurred
    SortedFlag% = TRUE
END SUB
```

(continued)

QUICKDEM.FRM *continued*

```
SUB Command2_Click ()
    UNLOAD QuickDem
END SUB

SUB Form_Load ()
    'Center the form on the screen
    QuickDem.Left = (Screen.Width - QuickDem.Width) \ 2
    QuickDem.Top = (Screen.Height - QuickDem.Height) \ 2
END SUB

SUB menAboutQuickDem_Click ()
    About.Label1.Caption = "QUICKDEM"
    About.SHOW MODAL
END SUB

SUB menExit_Click ()
    UNLOAD QuickDem
END SUB

SUB menHelpQuickDem_Click ()
    FileMsg "QUICKDEM.MSG", 1
END SUB

SUB Text1_KeyPress (KeyAscii AS INTEGER)
    'Force each word to start a new line
    IF KeyAscii = 32 THEN
        KeyAscii = 13
    END IF

    'If just sorted, start over
    IF SortedFlag% = TRUE THEN
        SortedFlag% = FALSE
        Text1.Text = ""
    END IF
END SUB
```

Source code for QUICKSRT.BAS

```
'================================================
' QUICKSRT.BAS
' Sorts data arrays into ascending order
'================================================

' Notes:
' Add $INCLUDE: 'QUICKSRT.BI' to the calling module.
' Load QUICKSRT.BAS into your project.
```

(continued)

QUICKSRT.BAS *continued*

```
'
' Example of use:
'     QuicksortSTR A$()

SUB QuicksortDBL (X#())
    AuxSize% = 17
    REDIM L%(1 TO AuxSize%), R%(1 TO AuxSize%)

    S% = 1
    L%(S%) = LBOUND(X#)
    R%(S%) = UBOUND(X#)

    DO
        L% = L%(S%)
        R% = R%(S%)
        S% = S% - 1

        DO
            i% = L%
            j% = R%
            V# = X#((L% + R%) \ 2)

            DO

                DO WHILE X#(i%) < V#
                    i% = i% + 1
                LOOP

                DO WHILE V# < X#(j%)
                    j% = j% - 1
                LOOP

                IF i% <= j% THEN
                    SWAP X#(i%), X#(j%)
                    i% = i% + 1
                    j% = j% - 1
                END IF

            LOOP UNTIL i% > j%

            IF j% - L% < R% - i% THEN
                IF i% < R% THEN
                    S% = S% + 1
                    L%(S%) = i%
                    R%(S%) = R%
                END IF
                R% = j%
```

(continued)

QUICKSRT.BAS *continued*

```
            ELSE
                IF L% < j% THEN
                    S% = S% + 1
                    L%(S%) = L%
                    R%(S%) = j%
                END IF
                L% = i%
            END IF

        LOOP WHILE L% < R%

    LOOP UNTIL S% = 0
END SUB

SUB QuicksortINT (X%())
    AuxSize% = 17
    REDIM L%(1 TO AuxSize%), R%(1 TO AuxSize%)

    S% = 1
    L%(S%) = LBOUND(X%)
    R%(S%) = UBOUND(X%)

    DO
        L% = L%(S%)
        R% = R%(S%)
        S% = S% - 1

        DO
            i% = L%
            j% = R%
            V% = X%((L% + R%) \ 2)

            DO

                DO WHILE X%(i%) < V%
                    i% = i% + 1
                LOOP

                DO WHILE V% < X%(j%)
                    j% = j% - 1
                LOOP

                IF i% <= j% THEN
                    SWAP X%(i%), X%(j%)
                    i% = i% + 1
                    j% = j% - 1
                END IF
```

(continued)

QUICKSRT.BAS *continued*

```
                LOOP UNTIL i% > j%

                IF j% - L% < R% - i% THEN
                    IF i% < R% THEN
                        S% = S% + 1
                        L%(S%) = i%
                        R%(S%) = R%
                    END IF
                    R% = j%
                ELSE
                    IF L% < j% THEN
                        S% = S% + 1
                        L%(S%) = L%
                        R%(S%) = j%
                    END IF
                    L% = i%
                END IF

            LOOP WHILE L% < R%

        LOOP UNTIL S% = 0
    END SUB

    SUB QuicksortLNG (X&())
        AuxSize% = 17
        REDIM L%(1 TO AuxSize%), R%(1 TO AuxSize%)

        S% = 1
        L%(S%) = LBOUND(X&)
        R%(S%) = UBOUND(X&)

        DO
            L% = L%(S%)
            R% = R%(S%)
            S% = S% - 1

            DO
                i% = L%
                j% = R%
                V& = X&((L% + R%) \ 2)

                DO

                    DO WHILE X&(i%) < V&
                        i% = i% + 1
                    LOOP

                    DO WHILE V& < X&(j%)
                        j% = j% - 1
                    LOOP
```

(continued)

QUICKSRT.BAS *continued*

```
                IF i% <= j% THEN
                    SWAP X&(i%), X&(j%)
                    i% = i% + 1
                    j% = j% - 1
                END IF

            LOOP UNTIL i% > j%

            IF j% - L% < R% - i% THEN
                IF i% < R% THEN
                    S% = S% + 1
                    L%(S%) = i%
                    R%(S%) = R%
                END IF
                R% = j%
            ELSE
                IF L% < j% THEN
                    S% = S% + 1
                    L%(S%) = L%
                    R%(S%) = j%
                END IF
                L% = i%
            END IF

        LOOP WHILE L% < R%

    LOOP UNTIL S% = 0
END SUB

SUB QuicksortSNG (X!())
    AuxSize% = 17
    REDIM L%(1 TO AuxSize%), R%(1 TO AuxSize%)

    S% = 1
    L%(S%) = LBOUND(X!)
    R%(S%) = UBOUND(X!)

    DO
        L% = L%(S%)
        R% = R%(S%)
        S% = S% - 1

        DO
            i% = L%
            j% = R%
            V! = X!((L% + R%) \ 2)
```

(continued)

QUICKSRT.BAS *continued*

```
            DO

                DO WHILE X!(i%) < V!
                    i% = i% + 1
                LOOP

                DO WHILE V! < X!(j%)
                    j% = j% - 1
                LOOP

                IF i% <= j% THEN
                    SWAP X!(i%), X!(j%)
                    i% = i% + 1
                    j% = j% - 1
                END IF

            LOOP UNTIL i% > j%

            IF j% - L% < R% - i% THEN
                IF i% < R% THEN
                    S% = S% + 1
                    L%(S%) = i%
                    R%(S%) = R%
                END IF
                R% = j%
            ELSE
                IF L% < j% THEN
                    S% = S% + 1
                    L%(S%) = L%
                    R%(S%) = j%
                END IF
                L% = i%
            END IF

        LOOP WHILE L% < R%

    LOOP UNTIL S% = 0
END SUB

SUB QuicksortSTR (X$())

    AuxSize% = 17
    REDIM L%(1 TO AuxSize%), R%(1 TO AuxSize%)

    S% = 1
    L%(S%) = LBOUND(X$)
    R%(S%) = UBOUND(X$)
```

(continued)

QUICKSRT.BAS *continued*

```
    DO
        L% = L%(S%)
        R% = R%(S%)
        S% = S% - 1

        DO
            i% = L%
            j% = R%
            V$ = X$((L% + R%) \ 2)

            DO

                DO WHILE X$(i%) < V$
                    i% = i% + 1
                LOOP

                DO WHILE V$ < X$(j%)
                    j% = j% - 1
                LOOP

                IF i% <= j% THEN
                    SWAP X$(i%), X$(j%)
                    i% = i% + 1
                    j% = j% - 1
                END IF

            LOOP UNTIL i% > j%

            IF j% - L% < R% - i% THEN
                IF i% < R% THEN
                    S% = S% + 1
                    L%(S%) = i%
                    R%(S%) = R%
                END IF
                R% = j%
            ELSE
                IF L% < j% THEN
                    S% = S% + 1
                    L%(S%) = L%
                    R%(S%) = j%
                END IF
                L% = i%
            END IF

        LOOP WHILE L% < R%

    LOOP UNTIL S% = 0
END SUB
```

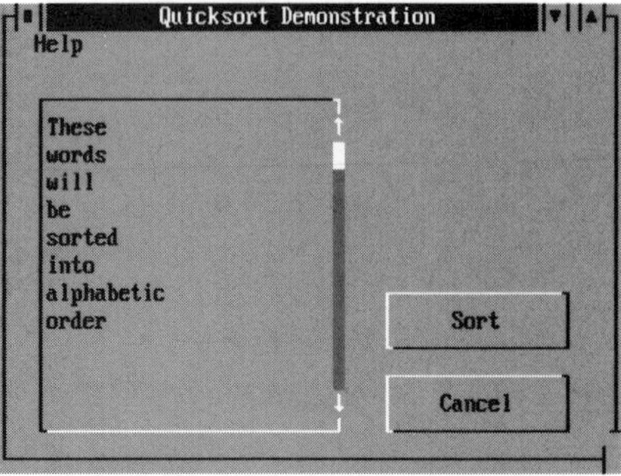

Figure 11-13.
QUICKDEM.FRM in action. At this point, words have been entered but not yet sorted.

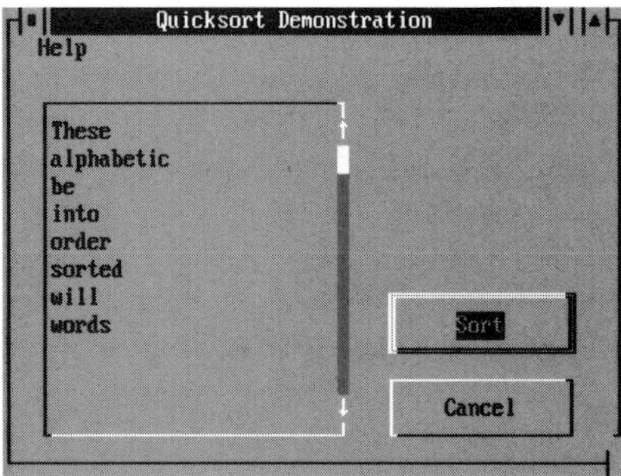

Figure 11-14.
QUICKDEM.FRM in action. At this point, words have been entered and sorted.

The FRACTION Application

The FRACTION application is a calculator designed to solve problems involving fractions. The application can add, subtract, multiply, and divide whole numbers, fractions, and mixed numbers. In addition, the application reduces the results of the calculations to their lowest terms.

The FRACTION application uses a Reverse Polish Notation (RPN) stack to store the numbers the user has entered as well as the intermediate results of calculations. Four text boxes form the *X, Y, Z,* and *T registers,* in which the application stores numbers. As the user clicks buttons to enter a number, the application stores the number in the X register. Operations (such as addition) work with the numbers in the X and Y registers and then store the results in the X register. Because the numbers stored in all four registers are visible, the operation of the stack manipulations is easy to follow.

The user employs the eight buttons in the top-right corner of the form to manipulate the stack. The user can move numbers from any register into the X register, or the user can rotate the numbers in all four registers. The Undo and Last X buttons are handy for backing up a step or recovering a previous number.

When entering numbers, the user can employ three special buttons in addition to the buttons for the 10 digits. The – button changes the sign of the number. The / button inserts the slash character to separate the numerator and denominator portions of a fraction, and the Spc button inserts a space to separate the whole part of a number from the fractional part. For example, a user who wanted to enter a fractional number equivalent to 2.75 would click *2*, *Spc*, *3*, */*, and *4*. The X register would then display $2\,{}^{3}/_{4}$.

The Reduce key operates on a single quantity—the number in the X register—reducing the number to its lowest terms. For example, ${}^{123}/_{456}$ reduces to ${}^{41}/_{152}$, and ${}^{1955}/_{289}$ reduces to $6\,{}^{13}/_{17}$.

The files for the FRACTION application are included on the companion disk. To load the files into Visual Basic for MS-DOS, choose the File Open Project command and type *C:\VBDWSHOP\FRACTION.MAK*. This opens the project and enables you to view and modify the forms and code. The following figures, tables, and code give the details of the application's creation.

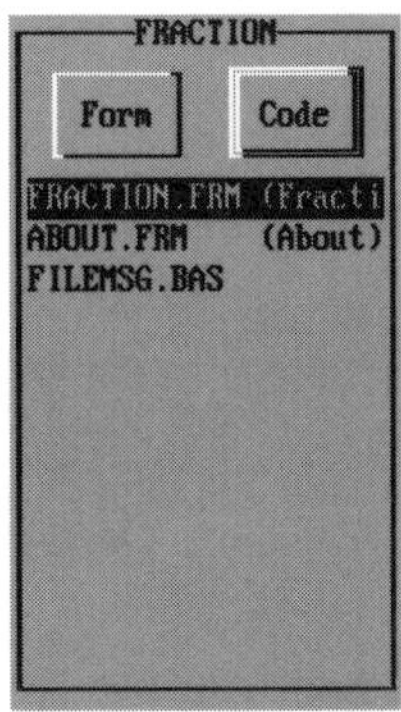

Figure 11-15.
FRACTION project list.

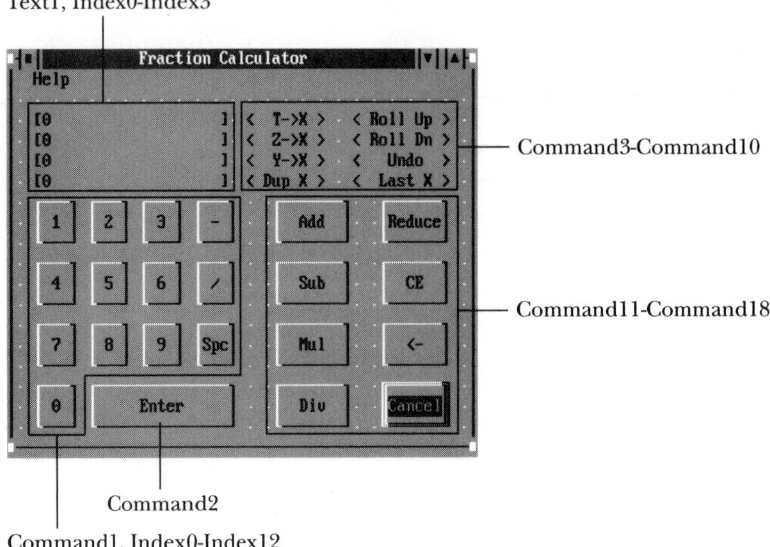

Figure 11-16.
FRACTION.FRM during development.

FRACTION.FRM Menu Design Window Entries

Caption	CtlName	Indentation
&Help	menHelp	0
&Help on Fraction	menHelpFraction	1
&About Fraction...	menAboutFraction	1
-	menSep	1
E&xit	menExit	1

FRACTION.FRM Form and Control Properties

Property	Value
Form:	
Caption	Fraction Calculator
FormName	Fraction

(continued)

FRACTION.FRM Form and Control Properties *continued*

Property	Value
Text1:	
CtlName	Text1 (array)
Caption	0
Index	3 (T register)
Caption	0
Index	2 (Z register)
Caption	0
Index	1 (Y register)
Caption	0
Index	0 (X register)
Command1:	
CtlName	Button (array)
Caption	0
Index	0
Caption	1
Index	1
Caption	2
Index	2
Caption	3
Index	3
Caption	4
Index	4
Caption	5
Index	5
Caption	6
Index	6
Caption	7
Index	7

(continued)

FRACTION.FRM Form and Control Properties *continued*

Property	Value
Caption	8
Index	8
Caption	9
Index	9
Caption	–
Index	10
Caption	/
Index	11
Caption	Spc
Index	12
Command2:	
Caption	Enter
CtlName	Entr
Command3:	
Caption	T–>X
CtlName	TX
Command4:	
Caption	Z–>X
CtlName	ZX
Command5:	
Caption	Y–>X
CtlName	YX
Command6:	
Caption	Dup X
CtlName	DupX
Command7:	
Caption	Roll Up
CtlName	RollUp

(continued)

FRACTION.FRM Form and Control Properties *continued*

Property	Value
Command8:	
Caption	Roll Dn
CtlName	RollDn
Command9:	
Caption	Undo
CtlName	Undo
Command10:	
Caption	Last X
CtlName	LastX
Command11:	
Caption	Add
CtlName	Add
Command12:	
Caption	Sub
CtlName	Subtract
Command13:	
Caption	Mul
CtlName	Multiply
Command14:	
Caption	Div
CtlName	Divide
Command15:	
Caption	Reduce
CtlName	Reduce
Command16:	
Caption	CE
CtlName	ClearEntry

(continued)

FRACTION.FRM Form and Control Properties *continued*

Property	Value
Command17:	
Caption	<–
CtlName	Backspace
Command18:	
Cancel	True
Caption	Cancel
CtlName	Cancel

Source code for FRACTION.FRM

```
'===================================================
' FRACTION
' Calculator for fractional-number calculations
'===================================================

DEFLNG A-Z

'$INCLUDE: 'CONSTANT.BI'
'$INCLUDE: 'FILEMSG.BI'
'$INCLUDE: 'ABOUT.BI'

DECLARE SUB Extract (X$, Num&, Den&)
DECLARE SUB DropStack ()
DECLARE SUB LiftStack ()
DECLARE SUB SaveStack ()
DECLARE SUB RestoreStack ()
DECLARE SUB LowestTerms (Num&, Den&)

DECLARE FUNCTION Build$ (Num&, Den&)

DIM SHARED LiftFlag AS INTEGER
DIM SHARED DegFlag AS INTEGER
DIM SHARED LastStack(3) AS STRING

DEFLNG A-Z
'
SUB Add_Click ()
    Extract (Text1(0).Text), N1, D1
    Extract (Text1(1).Text), N2, D2
    N = N1 * D2 + N2 * D1
```

(continued)

FRACTION.FRM *continued*

```
    D = D1 * D2
    IF D = 0 THEN EXIT SUB
    SaveStack
    DropStack
    Text1(0).Text = Build$(N, D)
    LiftFlag = TRUE
END SUB

DEFLNG A-Z
'
SUB Backspace_Click ()
     IF LEN(Text1(0).Text) > 0 THEN
        Text1(0).Text = LEFT$(Text1(0).Text, LEN(Text1(0).Text) - 1)
    END IF
 END SUB

DEFLNG A-Z
'
FUNCTION Build$ (Num, Den)
    Sign = SGN(Num) * SGN(Den)
    Num = ABS(Num)
    Den = ABS(Den)

    LowestTerms Num, Den

    Whole = INT(Num / Den)
    Num = Num - Whole * Den

    IF Whole <> 0 THEN
        X$ = LTRIM$(STR$(Whole))
        IF Num <> 0 THEN
            X$ = X$ + " " + STR$(Num) + "/" + LTRIM$(STR$(Den))
        END IF
    ELSE
        IF Num <> 0 THEN
            X$ = LTRIM$(STR$(Num)) + "/" + LTRIM$(STR$(Den))
        ELSE
            X$ = "0"
        END IF
    END IF

    IF Sign = -1 THEN X$ = "-" + X$

    Build$ = X$
END FUNCTION
```

(continued)

FRACTION.FRM *continued*

```
DEFLNG A-Z
'
SUB Button_Click (Index AS INTEGER)
     IF LiftFlag = TRUE THEN
        LiftStack
        LiftFlag = FALSE
    END IF

    X$ = Text1(0).Text

    SELECT CASE Index
    CASE 0 TO 9
        X$ = X$ + CHR$(48 + Index)
    CASE 10
        IF LEFT$(X$, 1) = "-" THEN
            X$ = MID$(X$, 2)
        ELSE
            X$ = "-" + X$
        END IF
    CASE 11
        IF INSTR(X$, "/") = 0 THEN
            X$ = X$ + "/"
        ELSE BEEP
        END IF
    CASE 12
        IF INSTR(X$, " ") = 0 AND INSTR(X$, "/") = 0 THEN
            X$ = X$ + " "
        ELSE BEEP
        END IF
    END SELECT

    DO WHILE LEFT$(X$, 1) = " " OR LEFT$(X$, 1) = "0"
        X$ = MID$(X$, 2)
    LOOP

    DO WHILE LEFT$(X$, 2) = "-0"
        X$ = "-" + MID$(X$, 3)
    LOOP

    IF X$ = "" THEN X$ = "0"

    Text1(0).Text = X$
END SUB

DEFLNG A-Z
'
SUB Cancel_Click ()
     UNLOAD Fraction
END SUB
```

(continued)

FRACTION.FRM *continued*

```
DEFLNG A-Z
'
SUB ClearEntry_Click ()
     Text1(0).Text = "0"
END SUB

DEFLNG A-Z
'
SUB Divide_Click ()
    Extract (Text1(0).Text), N1, D1
    Extract (Text1(1).Text), N2, D2
    N = N2 * D1
    D = N1 * D2
    IF D = 0 THEN EXIT SUB
    SaveStack
    DropStack
    Text1(0).Text = Build$(N, D)
    LiftFlag = TRUE
END SUB

DEFLNG A-Z
'
SUB DropStack ()
     FOR i% = 0 TO 2
        Text1(i%).Text = Text1(i% + 1).Text
    NEXT i%
END SUB

DEFLNG A-Z
'
SUB DupX_Click ()
    SaveStack
    LiftStack
    Text1(0).Text = Text1(1).Text
END SUB

DEFLNG A-Z
'
SUB Entr_Click ()
    SaveStack
    Text1(3).Text = Text1(2).Text
    Text1(2).Text = Text1(1).Text
    Text1(1).Text = Text1(0).Text
    Text1(0).Text = " 0"
    LiftFlag = FALSE
END SUB
```

(continued)

FRACTION.FRM *continued*

```
DEFLNG A-Z
'
SUB Extract (X$, Num, Den)
    X$ = LTRIM$(X$)
    IF INSTR(X$, " ") = 0 THEN
        IF INSTR(X$, "/") THEN
            X$ = "0 " + X$
        ELSE
            X$ = X$ + "/1"
        END IF
    ELSEIF INSTR(X$, "/") = 0 THEN
        X$ = X$ + "/0"
    END IF

    Spos = INSTR(X$, " ")
    Whole = VAL(LEFT$(X$, Spos))
    Num = VAL(MID$(X$, Spos + 1))
    Den = VAL(MID$(X$, INSTR(X$, "/") + 1))

    IF Whole < 0 THEN
        Num = -Num
    END IF

    Num = Num + Whole * Den

    IF Den = 0 THEN
        MSGBOX "Undefined fraction, den = 0", 48, "Fraction"
    END IF
END SUB

DEFLNG A-Z
'
SUB Form_Load ()
    LiftFlag = FALSE
    SaveStack

    'Center the form on the screen
    Fraction.Left = (Screen.Width - Fraction.Width) \ 2
    Fraction.Top = (Screen.Height - Fraction.Height) \ 2
END SUB

DEFLNG A-Z
'
SUB LastX_Click ()
    LiftStack
    Text1(0).Text = LastStack(0)
END SUB
```

(continued)

FRACTION.FRM *continued*

```
DEFLNG A-Z
'
SUB LiftStack ()
    FOR i% = 3 TO 1 STEP -1
        Text1(i%).Text = Text1(i% - 1).Text
    NEXT i%
    Text1(0).Text = "0"
END SUB

DEFLNG A-Z
'
SUB LowestTerms (Num, Den)
    s = Num
    t = Den
    DO
        u = INT(s / t) * t
        u = s - u
        s = t
        t = u
    LOOP WHILE u > 0
    Num = Num / s
    Den = Den / s
END SUB

DEFLNG A-Z
'
SUB menAboutFraction_Click ()
    About.Label1.Caption = "FRACTION"
    About.SHOW MODAL
END SUB

DEFLNG A-Z
'
SUB menExit_Click ()
    UNLOAD Fraction
END SUB

DEFLNG A-Z
'
SUB menHelpFraction_Click ()
    FOR i% = 1 TO 3
        FileMsg "FRACTION.MSG", i%
    NEXT i%
END SUB
```

(continued)

FRACTION.FRM *continued*

```
DEFLNG A-Z
'
SUB Multiply_Click ()
    Extract (Text1(0).Text), N1, D1
    Extract (Text1(1).Text), N2, D2
    N = N1 * N2
    D = D1 * D2
    IF D = 0 THEN EXIT SUB
    SaveStack
    DropStack
    Text1(0).Text = Build$(N, D)
    LiftFlag = TRUE
END SUB

DEFLNG A-Z
'
SUB Reduce_Click ()
    Extract (Text1(0).Text), N, D
    IF D = 0 THEN EXIT SUB
    SaveStack
    Text1(0).Text = Build$(N, D)
    LiftFlag = TRUE
END SUB

DEFLNG A-Z
'
SUB RestoreStack ()
    FOR i% = 0 TO 3
        Text1(i%).Text = LastStack(i%)
    NEXT i%
END SUB

DEFLNG A-Z
'
SUB RollDn_Click ()
    SaveStack
    DropStack
    Text1(3).Text = LastStack(0)
END SUB

DEFLNG A-Z
'
SUB RollUp_Click ()
    SaveStack
    LiftStack
    Text1(0).Text = LastStack(3)
END SUB
```

(continued)

FRACTION.FRM *continued*

```
DEFLNG A-Z
'
SUB SaveStack ()
    FOR i% = 0 TO 3
        LastStack(i%) = Text1(i%).Text
    NEXT i%
END SUB

DEFLNG A-Z
'
SUB Subtract_Click ()
    Extract (Text1(0).Text), N1, D1
    Extract (Text1(1).Text), N2, D2
    N = N2 * D1 - N1 * D2
    D = D1 * D2
    IF D = 0 THEN EXIT SUB
    SaveStack
    DropStack
    Text1(0).Text = Build$(N, D)
    LiftFlag = TRUE
END SUB

DEFLNG A-Z
'
SUB Text1_KeyPress (Index AS INTEGER, KeyAscii AS INTEGER)
    KeyAscii = 0
END SUB

DEFLNG A-Z
'
SUB TX_Click ()
    SaveStack
    Tmp$ = Text1(3).Text
    Text1(3).Text = Text1(2).Text
    Text1(2).Text = Text1(1).Text
    Text1(1).Text = Text1(0).Text
    Text1(0).Text = Tmp$
END SUB

DEFLNG A-Z
'
SUB Undo_Click ()
    RestoreStack
END SUB
```

(continued)

FRACTION.FRM *continued*

```
DEFLNG A-Z
'
SUB YX_Click ()
    SaveStack
    Tmp$ = Text1(1).Text
    Text1(1).Text = Text1(0).Text
    Text1(0).Text = Tmp$
END SUB

DEFLNG A-Z
'
SUB ZX_Click ()
    SaveStack
    Tmp$ = Text1(2).Text
    Text1(2).Text = Text1(1).Text
    Text1(1).Text = Text1(0).Text
    Text1(0).Text = Tmp$
END SUB
```

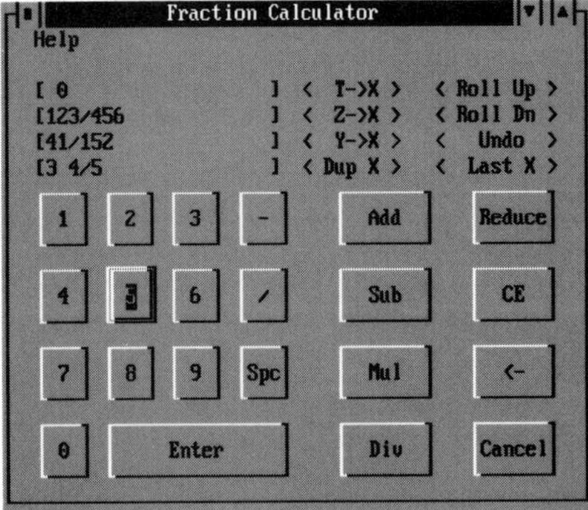

Figure 11-17.
FRACTION.FRM in action.

PART III

ADVANCED PROGRAMMING CONCEPTS

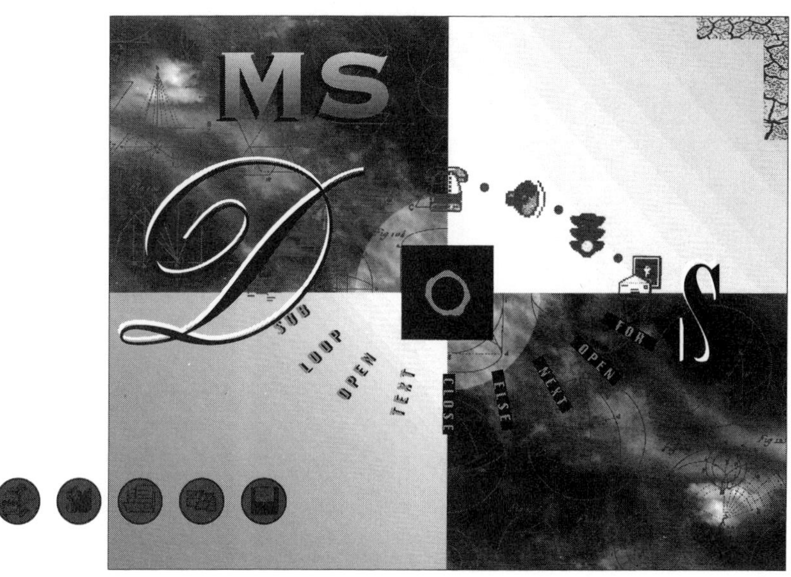

CHAPTER TWELVE

MANAGING LARGE PROJECTS

The FILESORT Application

Visual Basic for MS-DOS provides several mechanisms for creating and managing large projects. The FILESORT application demonstrates how to organize a group of subprograms and functions into a Quick Library. Loading a Quick Library into the Visual Basic for MS-DOS environment provides a convenient way for you to extend the language.

You can build a Quick Library from one or several modules. For the FILESORT application, we'll first create a Quick Library named MYLIB.QLB. MYLIB.QLB contains four modules that I have used in many of the applications in this book. In fact, if you plan to use the ABOUT, GETFILE, FILEMSG, or QUICKSRT modules in your own projects, you might want to simply use the MYLIB Quick Library, as shown in the FILESORT application, to save time and effort. After you create and start to use a Quick Library, you'll find that the subprograms and functions involved are so easy to use that they soon seem to become part of the language to you. By carefully tailoring a suite of software tools to your project, you can turn Visual Basic for MS-DOS into a customized development system.

Creating a Quick Library is easy. Start Visual Basic for MS-DOS and load the four modules listed in Figure 12-1 on the following page. (I've presented all of these modules earlier in this book—look for them in the table of contents and index if you don't remember the chapters in which they are located.) Choose File Save Project and name your new project *MYLIB*. Then, to create the Quick Library, choose Run Make Library. Enter *MYLIB.QLB* for the library's name. Click on Make Library and Exit. Visual Basic for MS-DOS compiles the modules and then links them to form two files, MYLIB.QLB and MYLIB.LIB. The MYLIB.QLB library file is in a special format suitable for loading into the Visual Basic for MS-DOS environment, and the MYLIB.LIB file is used by the system whenever you compile and link a program as a stand-alone EXE file that uses MYLIB.QLB. These two types of files, QLB and LIB, work hand in hand to form a Quick Library's two principal components.

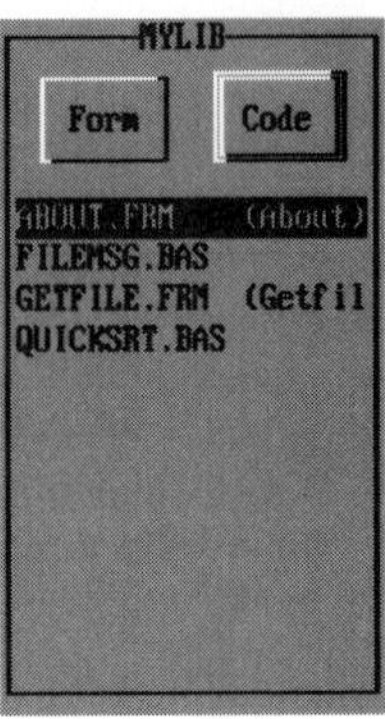

Figure 12-1.
MYLIB.MAK project list.

To use a Quick Library, you must first load it when you start Visual Basic for MS-DOS. A special command-line option loads the library from the MS-DOS prompt. Add */L MYLIB.QLB* to your command line, as shown:

```
VBDOS /L MYLIB.QLB
```

You should add the following MYLIB.BI include file to your projects that use MYLIB.QLB. The MYLIB.BI include file simply includes the appropriate include files for each of the four modules. Visual Basic for MS-DOS lets you nest include files in this way, a convenient feature of using Quick Libraries. Each of the include files provides declarations for the subprograms and functions in the MYLIB Quick Library. While developing an application using MYLIB.QLB, you might want to review these include files to remind yourself of the parameters and syntax for the available calls.

Source code for MYLIB.BI

```
'================================================
' MYLIB.BI
' Include file for accessing MYLIB.QLB/LIB
'================================================
'
' Note that MYLIB.BI contains two forms and two
' BAS modules, as implied by the following
' include files.  To use this library in other
' programs:
'    Include MYLIB.BI at the module level.
'    Load MYLIB.QLB into the environment when you
'    start Visual Basic for MS-DOS, as follows:
'          VBDOS /L MYLIB.QLB
```

(continued)

MYLIB.BI *continued*

```
'$INCLUDE: 'QUICKSRT.BI'
'$INCLUDE: 'GETFILE.BI'
'$INCLUDE: 'FILEMSG.BI'
'$INCLUDE: 'ABOUT.BI'
```

The FILESORT application is contained in a single module (called FILESORT.FRM), although the application makes several calls to the subprograms in MYLIB.BI. (You could also create the FILESORT project by loading the four other modules one at a time into the Visual Basic for MS-DOS environment, but using MYLIB.BI simplifies and modularizes the development process.) The FILESORT.FRM source-code listing shows how to include MYLIB.BI in other programs and how to make calls to the MYLIB Quick Library.

To use the FILESORT application, first choose File Open to select any file. (Ideally, you should use readable ASCII files, although you can also use a binary file.) After selecting a file, choose File Sort to sort the lines in the file into ascending order based on the ASCII values of the characters in each line. Notice that almost all the program's tasks—such as selecting a file, sorting the lines, and displaying Help—are performed by the code and forms provided in the MYLIB Quick Library.

No special steps are required to create a stand-alone EXE file for this project. Simply choose Run Make EXE File, exactly as if you were creating an executable file without a Quick Library. Visual Basic for MS-DOS already knows that MYLIB.QLB has been loaded into the development environment and proceeds to link the program with MYLIB.LIB.

The files for the FILESORT application are included on the companion disk. To load the files into Visual Basic for MS-DOS, choose the File Open Project command and type *C:\VBDWSHOP\FILESORT.MAK.* This opens the project and enables you to view and modify the forms and code. The following figures, tables, and code give the details of the application's creation.

Figure 12-2.
FILESORT project list.

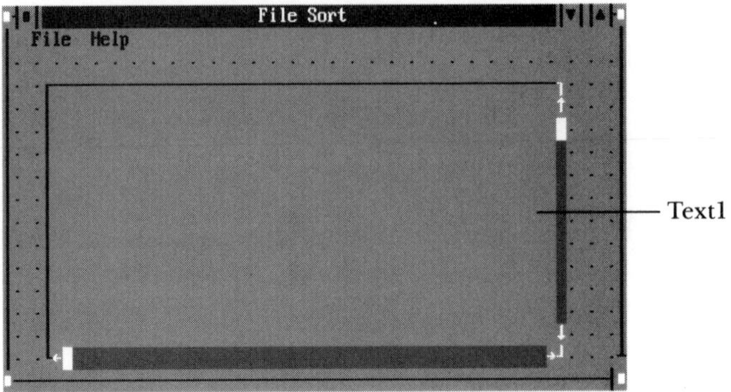

Figure 12-3.
FILESORT.FRM during development.

FILESORT.FRM Menu Design Window Entries

Caption	CtlName	Indentation
&File	menFile	0
&Open	menOpen	1
&Sort	menSort	1
-	menSep	1
E&xit	menExit	1
&Help	menHelp	0
&Help on FileSort	menHelpFileSort	1
&About FileSort...	menAboutFileSort	1

FILESORT.FRM Form and Control Properties

Property	Value
Form:	
Caption	File Sort
FormName	Filesort
Text1:	
CtlName	Text1
MultiLine	True
ScrollBars	3 - Both
Text	*(none)*

Source code for FILESORT.FRM

```
'===============================================
' FILESORT
' Demonstrates how to use a Quick Library
'===============================================

'$INCLUDE: 'CONSTANT.BI'
'$INCLUDE: 'MYLIB.BI'

SUB Form_Load ()
    'Center the form on the screen
    FileSort.Left = (Screen.Width - FileSort.Width) \ 2
    FileSort.Top = (Screen.Height - FileSort.Height) \ 2
END SUB

SUB Form_Resize ()
    'Resize the text box on the form
    Text1.MOVE 0, 0, ScaleWidth, ScaleHeight
END SUB

SUB menAboutFileSort_Click ()
    About.Label1.Caption = "FILESORT"
    About.SHOW MODAL
END SUB

SUB menExit_Click ()
    UNLOAD FileSort
END SUB

SUB menHelpFileSort_Click ()
    FileMsg "FILESORT.MSG", 1
END SUB

SUB menOpen_Click ()
    'Build a newline string
    NL$ = CHR$(13) + CHR$(10)

    'Use the GETFILE form to get a filename
    FullPath = ""
    WildCard = "*.*"
    GetFile.SHOW MODAL
    IF PathFlag = FALSE THEN EXIT SUB

    'Read in the file contents
    OPEN FullPath FOR INPUT AS #1
```

(continued)

FILESORT.FRM *continued*

```
    DO UNTIL EOF(1)
        LINE INPUT #1, A$
        Tmp$ = Tmp$ + A$ + NL$
    LOOP
    CLOSE #1

    'Display the file contents
    Text1.Text = Tmp$

    'Time to enable the Sort menu choice
    menSort.Enabled = TRUE
END SUB

SUB menSort_Click ()
    'Create newline string
    NL$ = CHR$(13) + CHR$(10)

    'Get a working copy of the displayed strings
    Tmp$ = Text1.Text

    'Split string into an array of strings
    DO
        i% = INSTR(Tmp$, NL$)
        IF i% = 0 THEN EXIT DO
        IF i% > 1 THEN
            REDIM PRESERVE Ary$(n%)
            Ary$(n%) = LEFT$(Tmp$, i% - 1)
            n% = n% + 1
        END IF
        Tmp$ = MID$(Tmp$, i% + 2)
    LOOP

    'Sort the array of strings
    QuicksortSTR Ary$()

    'Rebuild the displayable string
    FOR i% = 0 TO n% - 1
        Tmp$ = Tmp$ + Ary$(i%) + NL$
    NEXT i%

    'Display the sorted strings
    Text1.Text = Tmp$
END SUB
```

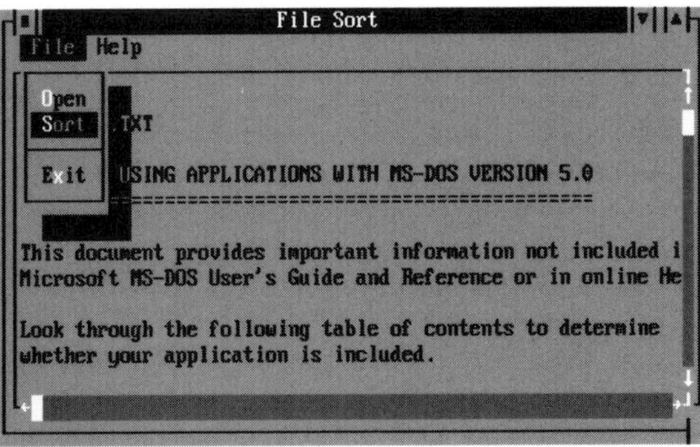

Figure 12-4.
FILESORT.FRM in action.

The HUGEARRY Application

Huge arrays are arrays that require more than 64 KB of memory. Visual Basic for MS-DOS provides a means of dimensioning those data arrays that would normally cause an error because of their size. The HUGEARRY program demonstrates the use of some huge arrays.

To signal that you want to be able to dimension huge arrays, add */Ah* to the command line when you start Visual Basic for MS-DOS, as follows:

```
VBDOS /Ah
```

Huge arrays must be *dynamic:* The program allocates the memory for the array while the program is running rather than having the compiler allocate the memory while you're building the program. A very straightforward way to create dynamic arrays is to use the *REDIM* statement instead of the *DIM* statement. The HUGEARRY program uses the *REDIM* statement to create the huge arrays.

Because any index for an array is limited to a maximum of 32,767 values, the huge array that is "grown" to its maximum size in the subprogram *menFindBiggestArray_Click* is two dimensional and has two indexes. Each row in the *BigAry%* integer array contains 1000 integers. When a new row is created (using the *REDIM* statement), a total of 2000 more bytes is allocated to the array. If *BigAry%* had only one dimension, the index limitation would probably be reached before the maximum huge array size could be found.

This program also creates a huge string array, *HugeAry*. Each element of this dynamic string array is allocated space for a fixed length string of 50 characters. As a demonstration of how to use this type of array, I've arranged for prime numbers 1 through 100,000 to be generated by storing *0* and *1* characters in the array. The huge string array stores the prime numbers found by the Sieve of Eratosthenes algorithm.

The files for the HUGEARRAY application are included on the companion disk. To load the files into Visual Basic for MS-DOS, choose the File Open Project command and type *C:\VBDWSHOP\HUGEARRY.MAK*. This opens the project and enables you to view and modify the forms and code. The following figures, tables, and code give the details of the application's creation.

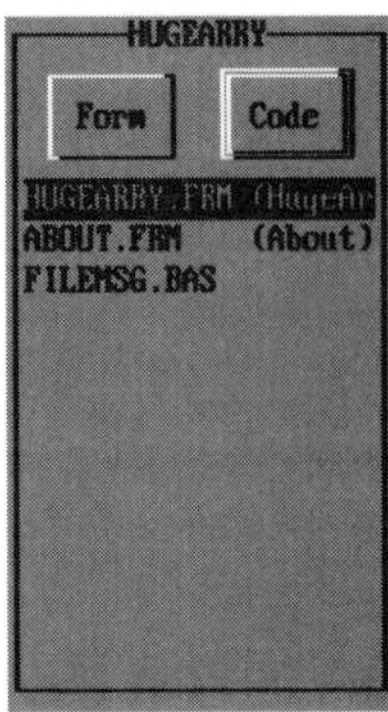

Figure 12-5.
HUGEARRY project list.

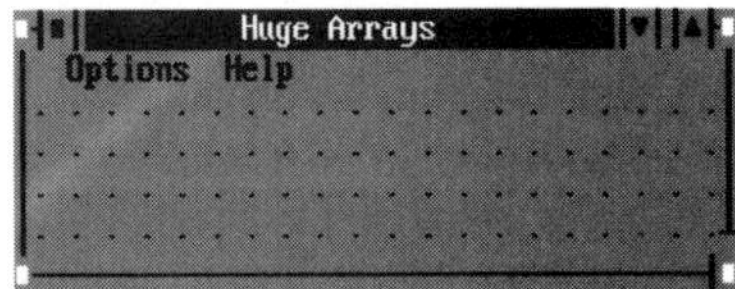

Figure 12-6.
HUGEARRY.FRM during development.

HUGEARRY.FRM Menu Design Window Entries

Caption	CtlName	Indentation
&Options	menOptions	0
&Find Biggest Array	menFindBiggestArray	1
&Primes Between 99,000 and 100,000	menPrimes	1
-	menSep	1

(continued)

HUGEARRY.FRM Menu Design Window Entries *continued*

Caption	CtlName	Indentation
E&xit	menExit	1
&Help	menHelp	0
&Help on Huge Arrays	menHelpHugeArry	1
&About Huge Arrays...	menAboutHugeArry	1

HUGEARRY.FRM Form Properties

Property	Value
Form:	
Caption	Huge Arrays
FormName	HugeArry

Source code for HUGEARRY.FRM

```
'================================================
' HUGEARRY
' Demonstrates huge arrays
'================================================

'$INCLUDE: 'CONSTANT.BI'
'$INCLUDE: 'FILEMSG.BI'
'$INCLUDE: 'ABOUT.BI'

SUB menAboutHugeArry_Click ()
    About.Label1.Caption = "HUGEARRY"
    About.SHOW MODAL
END SUB

SUB menExit_Click ()
    UNLOAD HugeArry
END SUB

SUB menFindBiggestArray_Click ()
    'Stop when array becomes too large
    ON LOCAL ERROR GOTO ErrorTrap
```

(continued)

HUGEARRY.FRM *continued*

```
    'Generate a huge array
    DO
        i& = i& + 1
        REDIM BigAry%(1000, i&)
    LOOP

ErrorTrap:
    RESUME FinishUp

FinishUp:
    CLS
    Width = 50
    Height = 8
    CurrentY = 1
    PRINT "  Biggest array... REDIM BigAry%( 1000,";
    PRINT i& - 1; ")"
    PRINT "  (about ";
    PRINT FORMAT$((i& - 1) * 2, "###,###,###,###");
    PRINT "KB)"
END SUB

SUB menHelpHugeArry_Click ()
    FileMsg "HUGEARRY.MSG", 1
END SUB

SUB menPrimes_Click ()
    'Create a huge dynamic array
    REDIM HugeAry(2000) AS STRING * 50

    'Initialize the array
    NL$ = CHR$(13) + CHR$(10)
    FirstFlag% = TRUE
    CLS
    PRINT
    PRINT "Initializing array"

    'Fill array with "1" characters
    FOR i% = 1 TO 2000
        HugeAry(i%) = STRING$(50, "1")
    NEXT i%

    'Use the Sieve of Eratosthenes algorithm to find primes
    FOR i& = 2 TO 100000
        j% = (i& - 1) \ 50 + 1
        k% = ((i& - 1) MOD 50) + 1
        IF MID$(HugeAry(j%), k%, 1) = "1" THEN
            FOR m& = i& + i& TO 100000 STEP i&
                n% = (m& - 1) \ 50 + 1
                p% = ((m& - 1) MOD 50) + 1
```

(continued)

HUGEARRY.FRM *continued*

```
                MID$(HugeAry(n%), p%, 1) = "0"
            NEXT m&
            IF i& > 99000 THEN
                IF FirstFlag% = TRUE THEN
                    FirstFlag% = FALSE
                    CLS
                    MOVE 11, 4, Screen.Width - 22, Screen.Height -
 10
                    PRINT "Primes between 99,000 and 100,000..."
                END IF
                PRINT i&;
                IF CurrentX > 55 THEN PRINT
            ELSE
                CurrentY = 1
                PRINT "Found prime number:" + STR$(i&)
            END IF
            IF DOEVENTS() = 0 THEN EXIT SUB
        END IF
    NEXT i&
END SUB
```

Figure 12-7.
HUGEARRY.FRM in action, displaying the biggest array available.

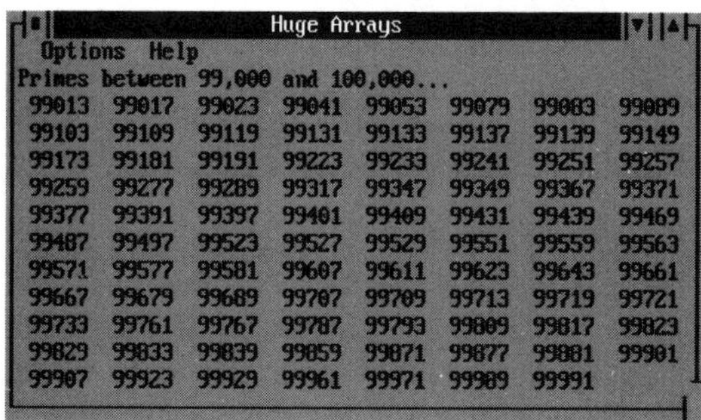

Figure 12-8.
HUGEARRY.FRM in action, displaying large prime numbers.

CHAPTER THIRTEEN

MDI PROGRAMMING

The FILECOMP Application

The FILECOMP application provides a working example of a Multiple Document Interface (MDI) form. To create an MDI application, set the main form's FormType property to *1 - MDI.* An MDI form automatically maximizes to fill the screen, and the Move, Size, Minimize, and Restore commands on the form's Control menu are disabled. You can't add controls to an MDI form, but you can add controls to the child forms of an MDI form. The MDI form's menus take on added importance because child forms do not have their own menu bars. (When a child window is active, its menus replace the menus on the MDI form's menu bar.) For more detailed information about MDI forms, see your Visual Basic for MS-DOS documentation.

The FILECOMP program lets the user open, display, and compare up to four files simultaneously. Four child forms, named FILE1, FILE2, FILE3, and FILE4, display the files' contents. Menu commands on the main MDI form allow you to rearrange the layout of the child forms. You can cascade, tile, or stack the forms; the program adjusts the algorithm for each of these arrangements according to the number of forms that are currently displayed. Experiment by opening several files and choosing the Cascade, Tile, and Stack commands from the main MDI form's Window menu.

In this application, all four child forms are nearly identical in functionality and appearance. (MDI child forms, however, can be unique.) You can load dialog boxes, windows, and any variety of forms into the MDI form.

The files for the FILECOMP application are included on the companion disk. To load the files into Visual Basic for MS-DOS, choose the File Open Project command and type *C:\VBDWSHOP\FILECOMP.MAK.* This opens the project and enables you to view and modify the forms and code. The following figures, tables, and code give the details of the application's creation.

Figure 13-1.
FILECOMP project list.

Source code for FILECOMP.BI

```
'================================================
' FILECOMP.BI
' Include file for FILECOMP program
'================================================

'$FORM FileComp
'$FORM File1
'$FORM File2
'$FORM File3
'$FORM File4

COMMON SHARED /comFileComp/ FocusNum%
```

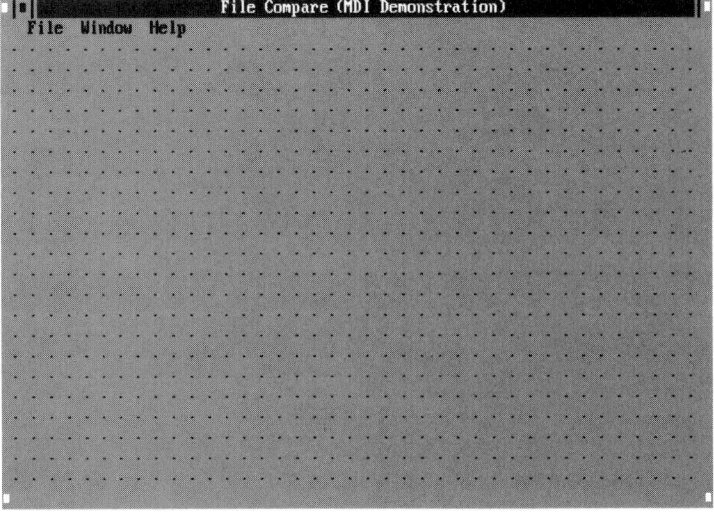

Figure 13-2.
FILECOMP.FRM during development.

FILECOMP.FRM Menu Design Window Entries

Caption	CtlName	Indentation
&File	menFile	0
&Open	menOpen	1
&Close	menClose	1
-	menSep	1
E&xit	menExit	1
&Window	menWindow	0
&Cascade	menCascade	1
&Tile	menTile	1
&Stack	menStack	1
&Help	menHelp	0
&Help on FileComp	menHelpFileComp	1
&About FileComp...	menAboutFileComp	1

FILECOMP.FRM Form Properties

Property	Value
Form:	
Caption	File Compare (MDI Demonstration)
FormName	Filecomp
FormType	1 - MDI

Source code for FILECOMP.FRM

```
'==================================================
' FILECOMP
' Demonstrates an MDI form
'==================================================

'$INCLUDE: 'CONSTANT.BI'
'$INCLUDE: 'FILECOMP.BI'
'$INCLUDE: 'FILEMSG.BI'
'$INCLUDE: 'ABOUT.BI'
'$INCLUDE: 'GETFILE.BI'
```

(continued)

FILECOMP.FRM *continued*

```
SUB Form_Load ()
    'Turn off the form shadows
    Screen.ControlPanel(ACTIVE_WINDOW_SHADOW) = FALSE
END SUB

SUB menAboutFileComp_Click ()
    About.Label1.Caption = "FILECOMP"
    About.SHOW MODAL
END SUB

SUB menCascade_Click ()
    W% = ScaleWidth - 7
    H% = ScaleHeight - 4

    IF File1.Visible = TRUE THEN
        File1.WindowState = NORMAL
        File1.MOVE N%, N%, W%, H%
        File1.SETFOCUS
        N% = N% + 1
    END IF

    IF File2.Visible = TRUE THEN
        File2.WindowState = NORMAL
        File2.MOVE N%, N%, W%, H%
        File2.SETFOCUS
        N% = N% + 1
    END IF

    IF File3.Visible = TRUE THEN
        File3.WindowState = NORMAL
        File3.MOVE N%, N%, W%, H%
        File3.SETFOCUS
        N% = N% + 1
    END IF

    IF File4.Visible = TRUE THEN
        File4.WindowState = NORMAL
        File4.MOVE N%, N%, W%, H%
        File4.SETFOCUS
        N% = N% + 1
    END IF
END SUB

SUB menClose_Click ()
    SELECT CASE FocusNum%
    CASE 1
        UNLOAD File1
```

(continued)

FILECOMP.FRM *continued*

```
    CASE 2
        UNLOAD File2
    CASE 3
        UNLOAD File3
    CASE 4
        UNLOAD File4
    END SELECT
END SUB

SUB menExit_Click ()
    UNLOAD FileComp
END SUB

SUB menHelpFileComp_Click ()
    FileMsg "FILECOMP.MSG", 1
END SUB

SUB menOpen_Click ()
    CONST MAXSTR = 32000

    'Build newline character string
    NL$ = CHR$(13) + CHR$(10)

    'Determine first "empty" window
    IF File1.Visible = FALSE THEN
        N% = 1
    ELSEIF File2.Visible = FALSE THEN
        N% = 2
    ELSEIF File3.Visible = FALSE THEN
        N% = 3
    ELSEIF File4.Visible = FALSE THEN
        N% = 4
    ELSE
        BEEP
        EXIT SUB
    END IF

    'Get filename from user
    FullPath = ""
    WildCard = "*.*"
    GetFile.SHOW MODAL
    IF PathFlag = FALSE THEN
        EXIT SUB
    END IF

    'Load the file for displaying
    FileNum% = FREEFILE
    OPEN FullPath FOR INPUT AS #FileNum%
```

(continued)

FILECOMP.FRM *continued*

```
    DO UNTIL EOF(FileNum%)
        LINE INPUT #FileNum%, A$
        Tmp$ = Tmp$ + A$ + NL$
        IF LEN(Tmp$) > MAXSTR THEN EXIT DO
    LOOP

    'Prepare to move and size the window
    W% = .7 * ScaleWidth
    H% = .6 * ScaleHeight
    L% = (Width - W%) \ 2
    T% = (Height - H%) \ 2

    'Display the selected window
    SELECT CASE N%
    CASE 1
        File1.Caption = FullPath
        File1.Text1.Text = Tmp$
        File1.MOVE L%, T%, W%, H%
        File1.SHOW
    CASE 2
        File2.Caption = FullPath
        File2.Text1.Text = Tmp$
        File2.MOVE L%, T%, W%, H%
        File2.SHOW
    CASE 3
        File3.Caption = FullPath
        File3.Text1.Text = Tmp$
        File3.MOVE L%, T%, W%, H%
        File3.SHOW
    CASE 4
        File4.Caption = FullPath
        File4.Text1.Text = Tmp$
        File4.MOVE L%, T%, W%, H%
        File4.SHOW
    END SELECT
END SUB

SUB menStack_Click ()
    REDIM L%(1 TO 4)
    REDIM T%(1 TO 4)
    REDIM W%(1 TO 4)
    REDIM H%(1 TO 4)

    IF File1.Visible = TRUE THEN N% = N% + 1
    IF File2.Visible = TRUE THEN N% = N% + 1
    IF File3.Visible = TRUE THEN N% = N% + 1
    IF File4.Visible = TRUE THEN N% = N% + 1
```

(continued)

FILECOMP.FRM *continued*

```
SELECT CASE N%
CASE 1
    W%(1) = ScaleWidth
    H%(1) = ScaleHeight
CASE 2
    W%(1) = ScaleWidth
    H%(1) = ScaleHeight \ 2
    T%(2) = H%(1)
    W%(2) = W%(1)
    H%(2) = ScaleHeight - H%(1)
CASE 3
    W%(1) = ScaleWidth
    H%(1) = ScaleHeight \ 3
    T%(2) = H%(1)
    W%(2) = W%(1)
    H%(2) = H%(1)
    T%(3) = H%(1) + H%(2)
    W%(3) = W%(1)
    H%(3) = ScaleHeight - H%(1) - H%(2)
CASE 4
    W%(1) = ScaleWidth
    H%(1) = ScaleHeight \ 4
    T%(2) = H%(1)
    W%(2) = W%(1)
    H%(2) = H%(1)
    T%(3) = H%(1) + H%(2)
    W%(3) = W%(1)
    H%(3) = H%(1)
    T%(4) = H%(1) + H%(2) + H%(3)
    W%(4) = W%(1)
    H%(4) = ScaleHeight - H%(1) - H%(2) - H%(3)
END SELECT

IF File1.Visible = TRUE THEN
    j% = j% + 1
    File1.WindowState = NORMAL
    File1.MOVE L%(j%), T%(j%), W%(j%), H%(j%)
END IF

IF File2.Visible = TRUE THEN
    j% = j% + 1
    File2.WindowState = NORMAL
    File2.MOVE L%(j%), T%(j%), W%(j%), H%(j%)
END IF

IF File3.Visible = TRUE THEN
    j% = j% + 1
    File3.WindowState = NORMAL
    File3.MOVE L%(j%), T%(j%), W%(j%), H%(j%)
END IF
```

(continued)

FILECOMP.FRM *continued*

```
    IF File4.Visible = TRUE THEN
        j% = j% + 1
        File4.WindowState = NORMAL
        File4.MOVE L%(j%), T%(j%), W%(j%), H%(j%)
    END IF
END SUB

SUB menTile_Click ()
    REDIM L%(1 TO 4)
    REDIM T%(1 TO 4)
    REDIM W%(1 TO 4)
    REDIM H%(1 TO 4)

    IF File1.Visible = TRUE THEN N% = N% + 1
    IF File2.Visible = TRUE THEN N% = N% + 1
    IF File3.Visible = TRUE THEN N% = N% + 1
    IF File4.Visible = TRUE THEN N% = N% + 1

    SELECT CASE N%
    CASE 1
        W%(1) = ScaleWidth
        H%(1) = ScaleHeight
    CASE 2
        W%(1) = ScaleWidth \ 2
        H%(1) = ScaleHeight
        L%(2) = W%(1) + 1
        W%(2) = ScaleWidth - W%(1)
        H%(2) = H%(1)
    CASE 3
        W%(1) = ScaleWidth \ 2
        H%(1) = ScaleHeight \ 2
        L%(2) = W%(1)
        W%(2) = ScaleWidth - W%(1)
        H%(2) = H%(1)
        T%(3) = H%(2)
        W%(3) = ScaleWidth
        H%(3) = ScaleHeight - H%(1)
    CASE 4
        W%(1) = ScaleWidth \ 2
        H%(1) = ScaleHeight \ 2
        L%(2) = W%(1)
        W%(2) = ScaleWidth - W%(1)
        H%(2) = H%(1)
        T%(3) = H%(1)
        W%(3) = W%(1)
        H%(3) = ScaleHeight - H%(1)
        L%(4) = L%(2)
```

(continued)

FILECOMP.FRM *continued*

```
        T%(4) = T%(3)
        W%(4) = W%(2)
        H%(4) = H%(3)
    END SELECT

    IF File1.Visible = TRUE THEN
        j% = j% + 1
        File1.WindowState = NORMAL
        File1.MOVE L%(j%), T%(j%), W%(j%), H%(j%)
    END IF

    IF File2.Visible = TRUE THEN
        j% = j% + 1
        File2.WindowState = NORMAL
        File2.MOVE L%(j%), T%(j%), W%(j%), H%(j%)
    END IF

    IF File3.Visible = TRUE THEN
        j% = j% + 1
        File3.WindowState = NORMAL
        File3.MOVE L%(j%), T%(j%), W%(j%), H%(j%)
    END IF

    IF File4.Visible = TRUE THEN
        j% = j% + 1
        File4.WindowState = NORMAL
        File4.MOVE L%(j%), T%(j%), W%(j%), H%(j%)
    END IF
END SUB
```

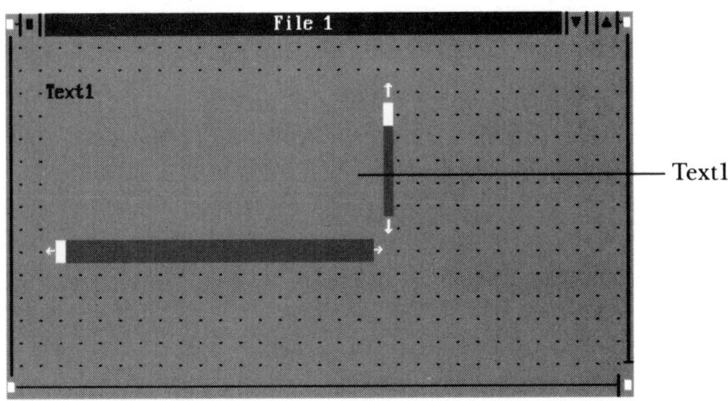

Figure 13-3.
FILE1.FRM during development.

FILE1.FRM Form and Control Properties

Property	Value
Form:	
Caption	File 1
FormName	File1
Text1:	
CtlName	Text1
MultiLine	True
ScrollBars	3 - Both

NOTE

With the exception of their Caption and FormName properties, FILE2.FRM, FILE3.FRM, and FILE4.FRM are identical to FILE1.FRM.

Source code for FILE1.FRM

```
'==================================================
' FILE1.FRM
' MDI child form that displays a file
'==================================================

'$INCLUDE: 'CONSTANT.BI'
'$INCLUDE: 'FILECOMP.BI'

SUB Form_Resize ()
    IF ScaleWidth <> 0 AND ScaleHeight <> 0 THEN
        Text1.MOVE 0, 0, ScaleWidth, ScaleHeight
    END IF
END SUB

SUB Text1_GotFocus ()
    FocusNum% = 1
END SUB
```

Source code for FILE2.FRM

```
'=================================================
' FILE2.FRM
' MDI child form that displays a file
'=================================================

'$INCLUDE: 'CONSTANT.BI'
'$INCLUDE: 'FILECOMP.BI'

SUB Form_Resize ()
    IF ScaleWidth <> 0 AND ScaleHeight <> 0 THEN
        Text1.MOVE 0, 0, ScaleWidth, ScaleHeight
    END IF
END SUB

SUB Text1_GotFocus ()
    FocusNum% = 2
END SUB
```

Source code for FILE3.FRM

```
'=================================================
' FILE3.FRM
' MDI child form that displays a file
'=================================================

'$INCLUDE: 'CONSTANT.BI'
'$INCLUDE: 'FILECOMP.BI'

SUB Form_Resize ()
    IF ScaleWidth <> 0 AND ScaleHeight <> 0 THEN
        Text1.MOVE 0, 0, ScaleWidth, ScaleHeight
    END IF
END SUB

SUB Text1_GotFocus ()
    FocusNum% = 3
END SUB
```

Source code for FILE4.FRM

```
'================================================
' FILE4.FRM
' MDI child form that displays a file
'================================================

'$INCLUDE: 'CONSTANT.BI'
'$INCLUDE: 'FILECOMP.BI'

SUB Form_Resize ()
    IF ScaleWidth <> 0 AND ScaleHeight <> 0 THEN
        Text1.MOVE 0, 0, ScaleWidth, ScaleHeight
    END IF
END SUB

SUB Text1_GotFocus ()
    FocusNum% = 4
END SUB
```

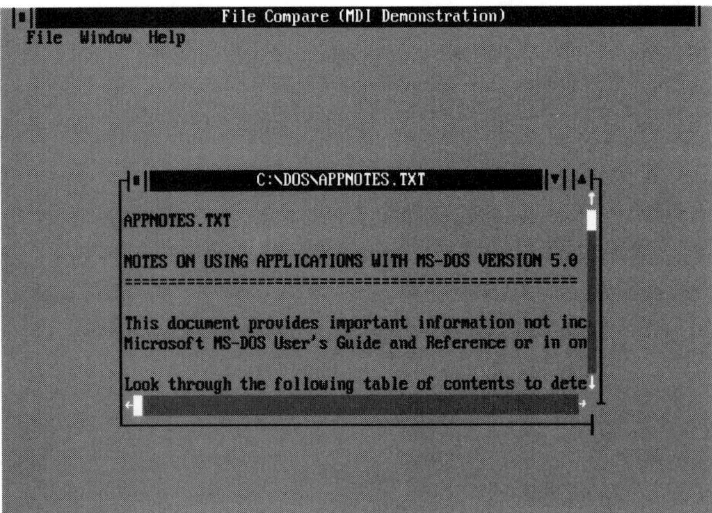

Figure 13-4.
FILECOMP.FRM in action with one file open.

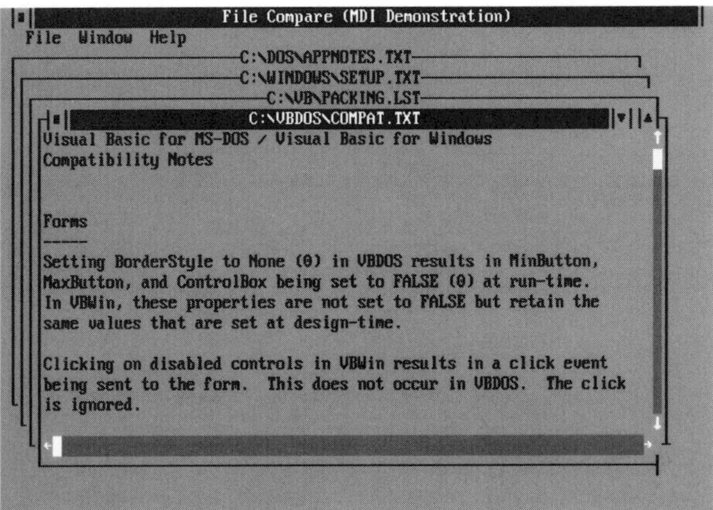

Figure 13-5.
FILECOMP.FRM in action with cascaded files.

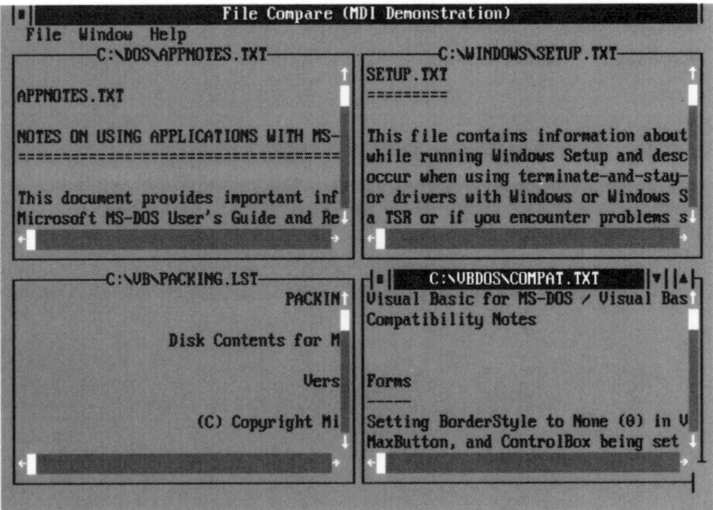

Figure 13-6.
FILECOMP.FRM in action with tiled files.

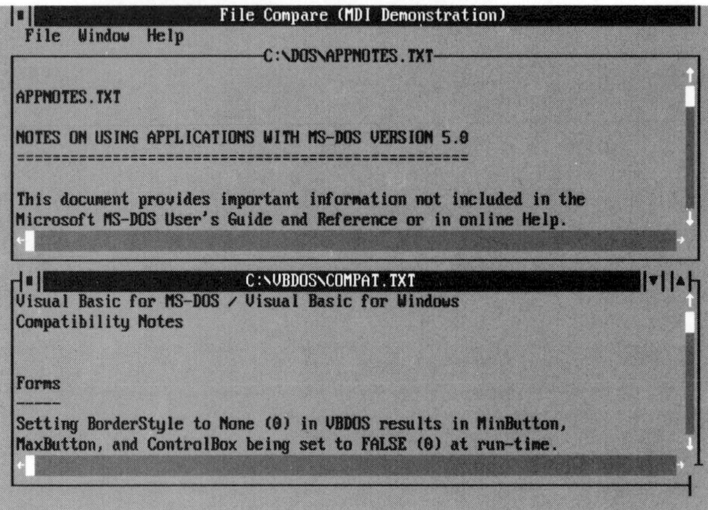

Figure 13-7.
FILECOMP.FRM in action with stacked files.

CHAPTER FOURTEEN

BIOS AND MS-DOS INTERRUPTS

Visual Basic for MS-DOS comes with a special Quick Library, VBDOS.QLB (and its associated file, VBDOS.LIB), that provides subprograms for calling BIOS and MS-DOS interrupts. These interrupts let you call low-level system functions that provide useful services at the machine and operating-system levels. Although providing a complete description of the available interrupts is beyond the scope of this book, the following two applications provide working examples of how to use these interrupts and demonstrate the power afforded by these techniques. (See Chapter 12 for an introduction to Quick Libraries.)

The BIOSCALL Application

The BIOSCALL application shows how to use BIOS interrupts in your programs to access low-level information, such as ascertaining the states of the Shift keys. Another interrupt returns information about hardware equipment currently available, such as printers and serial ports.

To use the VBDOS Quick Library, be sure to load it when you start Visual Basic for MS-DOS. Type the following command line at the MS-DOS prompt:

```
VBDOS /L VBDOS.QLB
```

The include file VBDOS.BI also comes with Visual Basic for MS-DOS. Include this file in applications that use the VBDOS Quick Library. You can find declarations and notes about the VBDOS Quick Library in VBDOS.BI, and you should review this file's contents. Notice that the BIOSCALL application includes this file in the first few lines of the application's source code.

The files for the BIOSCALL application are included on the companion disk. To load the files into Visual Basic for MS-DOS, choose the File Open Project command and type *C:\VBDWSHOP\BIOSCALL.MAK*. This opens the project and enables you to view and modify the forms and code. The following figures, tables, and code give the details of the application's creation.

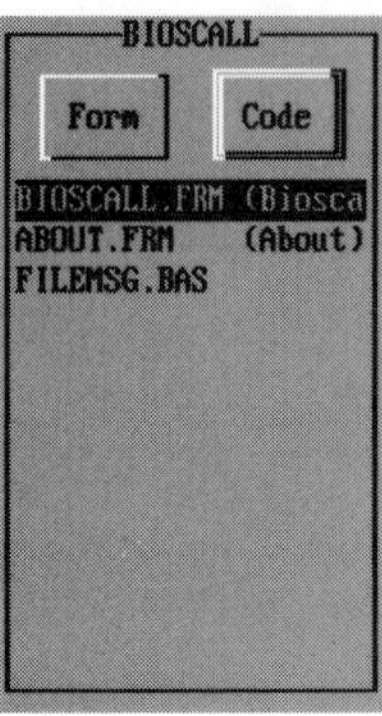

Figure 14-1.
BIOSCALL project list.

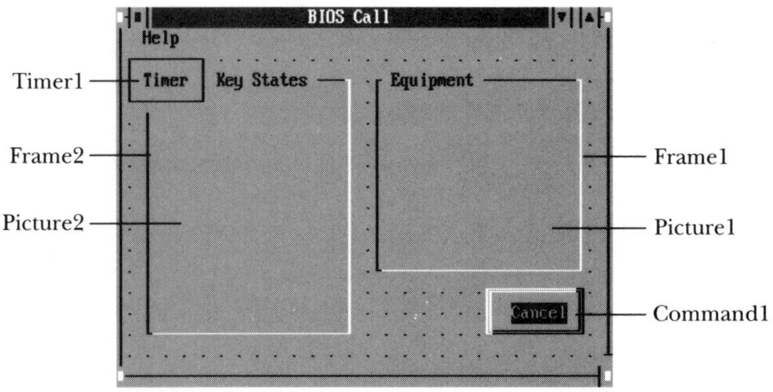

Figure 14-2.
BIOSCALL.FRM during development.

BIOSCALL.FRM Menu Design Window Entries

Caption	CtlName	Indentation
&Help	menHelp	0
&Help on BIOSCall	menHelpBIOSCall	1
&About BIOSCall...	menAboutBIOSCall	1
-	menSep	1
E&xit	menExit	1

BIOSCALL.FRM Form and Control Properties

Property	Value
Form:	
Caption	BIOS Call
FormName	Bioscall
Timer1:	
CtlName	Timer1
Enabled	True
Interval	1
Frame1:	
Caption	Equipment
CtlName	Frame1
Frame2:	
Caption	Shift Key States
CtlName	Frame2
Picture1 (inside Frame1):	
AutoRedraw	True
BorderStyle	0 - None
CtlName	Picture1
Picture2 (inside Frame2):	
AutoRedraw	True
BorderStyle	0 - None
CtlName	Picture2
Command1:	
Cancel	True
Caption	Cancel
CtlName	Command1
Default	True

Source code for BIOSCALL.FRM

```
'===============================================
' BIOSCALL
' Demonstrates BIOS interrupts
'===============================================

'$INCLUDE: 'VBDOS.BI'
'$INCLUDE: 'CONSTANT.BI'
'$INCLUDE: 'ABOUT.BI'
'$INCLUDE: 'FILEMSG.BI'

DECLARE SUB Picture1_Paint ()

SUB Command1_Click ()
    UNLOAD BIOSCall
END SUB

SUB Form_Load ()
    'Center the form on the screen
    BIOSCall.Left = (Screen.Width - BIOSCall.Width) \ 2
    BIOSCall.Top = (Screen.Height - BIOSCall.Height) \ 2
END SUB

SUB menAboutBIOSCall_Click ()
    About.Label1.Caption = "BIOSCALL"
    About.SHOW MODAL
END SUB

SUB menExit_Click ()
    UNLOAD BIOSCall
END SUB

SUB menHelpBIOSCall_Click ()
    FileMsg "BIOSCALL.MSG", 1
END SUB

SUB Picture1_Paint ()
    DIM Regs AS RegType

    'BIOS interrupt to get equipment information
    INTERRUPT &H11, Regs, Regs

    'Display equipment information
    Picture1.CurrentY = 1
    Picture1.PRINT "No. printers", (Regs.ax AND &HC000&) \ 16384
    Picture1.PRINT "Game adapter", (Regs.ax AND &H1000) \ 4096
```

(continued)

BIOSCALL.FRM *continued*

```
    Picture1.PRINT "Serial ports", (Regs.ax AND &HE00) \ 512
    Picture1.PRINT "No. floppies", (Regs.ax AND &HC0) \ 64 + 1
    Picture1.PRINT "Video mode  ", (Regs.ax AND &H30) \ 16
    Picture1.PRINT "Coprocessor ", (Regs.ax AND &H2) \ 2
END SUB

SUB Timer1_Timer ()
    DIM Regs AS RegType
    STATIC EquipFlag%

    'Get equipment information once only
    IF EquipFlag% = 0 THEN
        EquipFlag% = 1
        Picture1_Paint
    END IF

    'Get the Shift key states every time
    Regs.ax = &H200            'AH = 2, AL = 0
    INTERRUPT &H16, Regs, Regs

    Picture2.CurrentY = 1
    Picture2.PRINT "Right Shift", Regs.ax AND 1
    Picture2.PRINT "Left Shift ", (Regs.ax AND 2) \ 2
    Picture2.PRINT "Ctrl       ", (Regs.ax AND 4) \ 4
    Picture2.PRINT "Alt        ", (Regs.ax AND 8) \ 8
    Picture2.PRINT ""
    Picture2.PRINT "Scroll Lock", (Regs.ax AND 16) \ 16
    Picture2.PRINT "Num Lock   ", (Regs.ax AND 32) \ 32
    Picture2.PRINT "Caps Lock  ", (Regs.ax AND 64) \ 64
    Picture2.PRINT "Insert     ", (Regs.ax AND 128) \ 128
END SUB
```

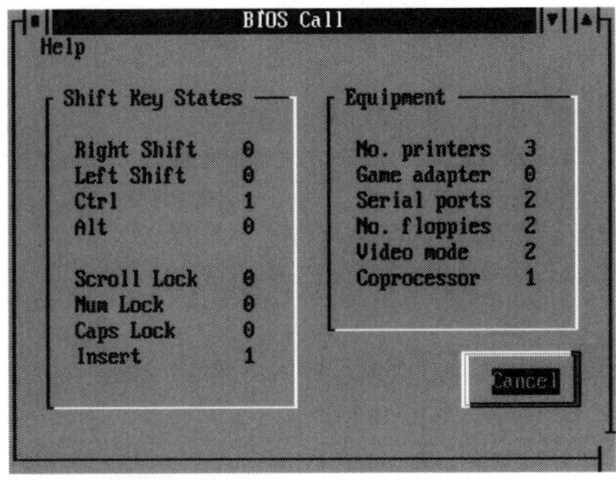

Figure 14-3.
BIOSCALL.FRM in action.

The DOSCALL Application

The DOSCALL application demonstrates several MS-DOS interrupts. MS-DOS interrupts are called in the same manner as BIOS interrupts; you place values in the CPU registers and call a specific interrupt number. MS-DOS–interrupt code is installed from disk files whenever the computer boots and so is updated whenever the user updates the version of DOS the computer uses. Because the application program interface (API) for MS-DOS interrupts is well defined, in general the interrupts work as expected. New versions of MS-DOS often provide new system-level functions.

The MS-DOS interrupts that this application demonstrates provide information about the current version of DOS, the complete path to the current working directory, and the remaining space on the default disk drive. This is only a sample of some of the useful information and services provided by MS-DOS interrupts.

Be sure to load the VBDOS Quick Library when you start Visual Basic for MS-DOS. Type the following command line at the MS-DOS prompt:

```
VBDOS /L VBDOS.QLB
```

Also be sure to include the VBDOS.BI file in any application that calls the *Interrupt* or *InterruptX* subprograms.

The files for the DOSCALL application are included on the companion disk. To load the files into Visual Basic for MS-DOS, choose the File Open Project command and type *C:\VBDWSHOP\DOSCALL.MAK*. This opens the project and enables you to view and modify the forms and code. The following figures, tables, and code give the details of the application's creation.

Figure 14-4.
DOSCALL project list.

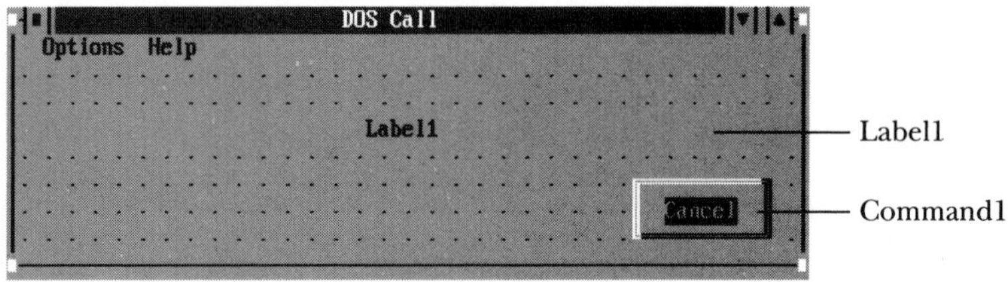

Figure 14-5.
DOSCALL.FRM during development.

DOSCALL.FRM Menu Design Window Entries

Caption	CtlName	Indentation
&Options	menOptions	0
&DOS Version	menDOSVersion	1
&Current Path	menCurrentPath	1
&Free Disk Space	menFreeDiskSpace	1
&Help	menHelp	0
&Help on DOSCall	menHelpDOSCall	1
&About DOSCall...	menAboutDOSCall	1

DOSCALL.FRM Form and Control Properties

Property	Value
Form:	
Caption	DOS Call
FormName	Doscall
Label1:	
Alignment	2 - Center
CtlName	Label1
Command1:	
Cancel	True
Caption	Cancel
CtlName	Command1
Default	True

Source code for DOSCALL.FRM

```
'===============================================
' DOSCALL
' Demonstrates MS-DOS interrupts
'===============================================

'$INCLUDE: 'VBDOS.BI'
'$INCLUDE: 'CONSTANT.BI'
'$INCLUDE: 'ABOUT.BI'
'$INCLUDE: 'FILEMSG.BI'

SUB Command1_Click ()
    UNLOAD DosCall
END SUB

SUB Form_Load ()
    'Center the form on the screen
    DosCall.Left = (Screen.Width - DosCall.Width) \ 2
    DosCall.Top = (Screen.Height - DosCall.Height) \ 2

    Label1.Caption = "Choose items from the Options menu"
END SUB

SUB menAboutDOSCall1_Click ()
    About.Label1.Caption = "DOSCALL"
    About.SHOW MODAL
END SUB

SUB menCurrentPath_Click ()
    DIM Regs AS RegType
    DIM RegX AS RegTypeX

    'Get the drive number
    Regs.ax = &H1900             'AH = 19, AL = 0
    INTERRUPT &H21, Regs, Regs
    Drive% = (Regs.ax AND &HFF) + 1

    'Convert to a drive character designation
    Drive$ = CHR$(Drive% + 64) + ":"

    'Get the current working directory
    RegX.ax = &H4700             'AH = 47, AL = 0
    RegX.dx = Drive%
    Path$ = SPACE$(64)
    RegX.ds = SSEG(Path$)
    RegX.si = SADD(Path$)
    INTERRUPTX &H21, RegX, RegX
```

(continued)

DOSCALL.FRM *continued*

```
    'Truncate the string at the 0 byte
    Path$ = LEFT$(Path$, INSTR(Path$, CHR$(0)) - 1)

    'Add the drive to the path
    Path$ = Drive$ + "\" + Path$

    Label1.Caption = "Current path is " + Path$
END SUB

SUB menDOSVersion_Click ()
    DIM Regs AS RegType

    'Get the DOS version number
    Regs.ax = &H3000              'AH = 30, AL = 0
    INTERRUPT &H21, Regs, Regs

    'Extract the major and minor DOS version numbers
    Major% = Regs.ax MOD 256
    Minor% = Regs.ax \ 256

    'Combine as standard version number
    DOSVersion = Major% + Minor / 100!

    Label1.Caption = "DOS version is " + FORMAT$(DOSVersion,
 "0.00")
END SUB

SUB menFreeDiskSpace_Click ()
    DIM Regs AS RegType

    'Get the drive designation
    Regs.ax = &H1900              'AH = 19, AL = 0
    INTERRUPT &H21, Regs, Regs
    Drive% = (Regs.ax AND &HFF) + 1

    'Convert to a drive character designation
    Drive$ = CHR$(Drive% + 64)

    'Get the free disk space information
    Regs.ax = &H3600              'AH = 36, AL = 0
    Regs.dx = Drive%
    INTERRUPT &H21, Regs, Regs

    'Extract the disk space numbers
    SectorsPerCluster = Regs.ax
    AvailableClusters& = Regs.bx
```

(continued)

DOSCALL.FRM *continued*

```
    BytesPerSector = Regs.cx
    ClustersPerDrive = Regs.dx

    'Adjust signed integers
    IF AvailableClusters& < 0 THEN
        AvailableClusters& = AvailableClusters& + 65535
    END IF
    IF ClustersPerDrive < 0 THEN
        ClustersPerDrive = ClustersPerDrive + 65535
    END IF

    'Calculate the total bytes available on the drive
    Bytes& = AvailableClusters& * SectorsPerCluster * BytesPerSector
    Bytes$ = FORMAT$(Bytes&, "###,###,###,###,###")

    Tmp$ = "There are " + Bytes$
    Tmp$ = Tmp$ + " bytes available on drive " + Drive$
    Label1.Caption = Tmp$
END SUB

SUB menHelpDOSCall_Click ()
    FileMsg "DOSCALL.MSG", 1
END SUB
```

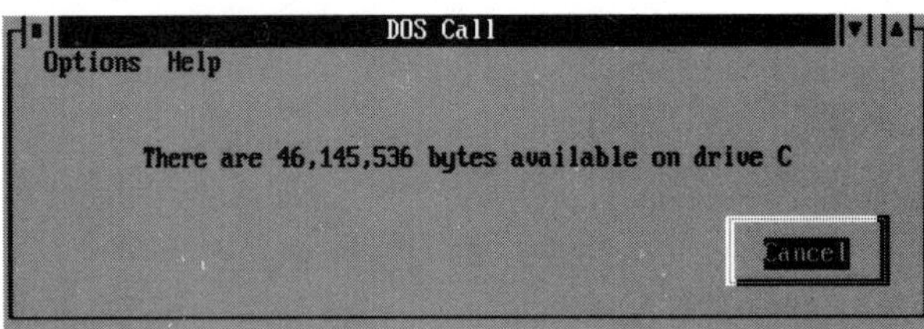

Figure 14-6.
DOSCALL.FRM in action.

CHAPTER FIFTEEN

MIXED-LANGUAGE PROGRAMMING

Visual Basic for MS-DOS applications can call subprograms and functions written in other programming languages, such as C, macro assembler, Pascal, and FORTRAN. Combining different types of code in an application in this way is called *mixed-language programming.*

The MIXED Quick Library

The MIXED application, described later in this chapter, includes C, macro assembler, and Visual Basic for MS-DOS code. You first compile the C and macro assembler subprograms and then combine them into a Quick Library that Visual Basic for MS-DOS can use. After it's loaded into the Visual Basic for MS-DOS environment, this Quick Library provides fast and efficient extensions to Visual Basic for MS-DOS code by using the other programming languages' code.

The first module in the MIXED Quick Library, BITS.C, provides several functions that manipulate the bits in integer variables. The *BitCount* function returns the number of bits set to 1 in a given integer value. The value *BitCount* returns is always in the range 0 through 16. The *BitSet, BitClr,* and *BitGet* functions allow manipulation of individual bits in an array of integers. For every integer in the array, 16 bits are available for the application to individually set, clear, or read. For example, an integer array dimensioned to contain 1000 integers allows access to bit numbers 0 through 15,999. We'll use these functions in our sample Visual Basic for MS-DOS application to find prime numbers in the range 1 through 1000 quickly and efficiently.

The next three sections explain how to create MIXED.QLB, a Quick Library used by the MIXED application. Creating the BITS.OBJ and BYTES.OBJ modules used in MIXED.QLB requires Microsoft C 7.0 or later and Microsoft MASM 5.1 or later. If you don't have these products or if you want to use the MIXED.QLB file provided on the companion disk, you can skip ahead to the section titled "The MIXED Application."

The BITS.C Module

The following command line compiles BITS.C using Microsoft C 6.0 or later to create BITS.OBJ. (This command assumes that the Microsoft C compiler is in your computer's search path. Use the BITS.OBJ file included on the companion disk if you don't have Microsoft C 7.0 or later or if you do not want to compile the BITS.C program.) Later we'll link this object module with others to form a Quick Library.

```
cl /c /AM /Ox /Gs /FoBITS.OBJ BITS.C
```

Source code for BITS.C

```
//==========================================
// BITS.C
//==========================================

int BitCount( unsigned int x )
{
   int i, n = 0;

   for ( i = 0; i < 16; i++ )
   {
      n += x & 1;
      x >>= 1;
   }

   return( n );
}

void BitSet( unsigned ArySeg, unsigned AryOfs, int BitNum )
{
   char far *AryPtr;

   AryPtr = (char far *)(( (unsigned long)ArySeg << 16 ) + AryOfs );
   AryPtr[BitNum >> 3] |= ( 1 << ( BitNum & 7 ));
}

void BitClr( unsigned ArySeg, unsigned AryOfs, int BitNum )
{
   char far *AryPtr;

   AryPtr = (char far *)( (unsigned long)ArySeg << 16 + AryOfs );
   AryPtr[BitNum >> 3] &= ~( 1 << ( BitNum & 7 ));
}
```

(continued)

BITS.C *continued*

```
int BitGet( unsigned ArySeg, unsigned AryOfs, int BitNum )
{
   char far *AryPtr;

   AryPtr = (char far *)( (unsigned long)ArySeg << 16 + AryOfs );
   return(( AryPtr[BitNum >> 3] & ( 1 << ( BitNum & 7 ))) ? 1 : 0 );
}
```

The BYTES.ASM Module

The BYTES.ASM module contains macro assembler code to be linked into our mixed-language Quick Library. I've included two subprograms that pack and unpack bytes into an integer variable. For example, packing a value of 255 into both the high-order and low-order bytes of an integer results in an integer value of –1. Because Visual Basic for MS-DOS provides only signed integers, it can be tricky to extract the high-order byte from certain integer values, such as –1000. The subprograms, however, let you access these byte values quickly and efficiently.

Use the following command line to assemble the BYTES.ASM source code to create BYTES.OBJ. (This command assumes that MASM is in your computer's search path. Use the BYTES.OBJ file included on the companion disk if you don't have Microsoft MASM 5.1 or later or if you do not want to assemble the BYTES.ASM program.)

```
MASM BYTES;
```

Source code for BYTES.ASM

```
; **********************************************
; ** BYTES.ASM
; **********************************************
;

.MODEL  MEDIUM
.CODE
        public  GetBytes
        public  PutBytes

GetBytes        proc

; Standard entry
        push    bp
        mov     bp,sp
```

(continued)

BYTES.ASM *continued*

```
; Put X% into AX register
        mov     bx,[bp+10]
        mov     ax,[bx]

; Copy X% into CX
        mov     cx,ax

; Isolate the low-order byte
        xor     ah,ah

; Put the low-order byte integer into Lo%
        mov     bx,[bp+6]
        mov     [bx],ax

; Isolate the high-order byte
        mov     al,ch

; Put the high-order byte integer into Hi%
        mov     bx,[bp+8]
        mov     [bx],ax

; Standard exit, which assumes three parameters
        pop     bp
        ret     6

GetBytes        endp

;==========================================

PutBytes        proc

; Standard entry
        push    bp
        mov     bp,sp

; Put Hi% into AX register
        mov     bx,[bp+8]
        mov     ax,[bx]

; Copy X% into CX
        mov     cx,ax

; Put Lo% into AX register
        mov     bx,[bp+6]
        mov     ax,[bx]

; Combine the two bytes
        mov     ah,cl
```

(continued)

BYTES.ASM *continued*

```
; Put the integer into X%
        mov     bx,[bp+10]
        mov     [bx],ax

; Standard exit, which assumes three parameters
        pop     bp
        ret     6

PutBytes        endp

;==========================================

end
```

Forming a Quick Library

After you've created BITS.OBJ and BYTES.OBJ, the next step is to link these modules to form a Quick Library. The following command lines link the modules to create MIXED.QLB and its associated file, MIXED.LIB:

```
LINK /Q BYTES.OBJ BITS.OBJ, MIXED.QLB,,VBDOSQLB.LIB;

LIB MIXED.LIB BITS.OBJ+BYTES.OBJ;
```

For more information about the *LINK* and *LIB* commands, see your Visual Basic for MS-DOS manual.

The MIXED Application

The MIXED application uses the MIXED Quick Library file. Be sure to load this Quick Library when you start Visual Basic for MS-DOS. Type the following command line at the MS-DOS prompt:

```
VBDOS /L MIXED.QLB
```

The MIXED application must include the MIXED.BI include file. Notice that MIXED.BI provides the declarations to make the connection with the MIXED.QLB and MIXED.LIB Quick Library files, which are already loaded. These declarations demonstrate several new keywords, such as *CDECL* and *BYVAL*. Your Visual Basic for MS-DOS documentation explains the syntax and possible variations of the *DECLARE* statement in detail. These variations let you control the order of parameter passing on the stack and the method by which the application passes a variable's contents.

The MIXED application provides scroll bars that change the values of two bytes. The application combines these bytes to form an integer and then counts the number of bits that are set to 1 in the resulting integer. With each scroll bar Change event, the application calls the mixed-language subprograms to update the integer values. A command button, labeled *Primes*, quickly generates and displays a table of prime numbers in the range 1 through 1000, using the bit-manipulation subprograms provided in the mixed-language Quick Library.

The files for the MIXED application are included on the companion disk. To load the files into Visual Basic for MS-DOS, choose the File Open Project command and type *C:\VBDOSWSHOP\MIXED.MAK*. This opens the project and enables you to view and modify the forms and code. The following figures, tables, and code give the details of the application's creation.

Figure 15-1.
MIXED project list.

Source code for MIXED.BI

```
'==================================================
' MIXED.BI
' Include file for accessing MIXED.QLB/LIB
'==================================================

'Subprograms found in BYTES.ASM
DECLARE SUB GetBytes (X%, Hi%, Lo%)
DECLARE SUB PutBytes (X%, Hi%, Lo%)

'Functions and subprograms found in BITS.C
DECLARE FUNCTION BitCount CDECL (BYVAL X%) AS INTEGER
DECLARE FUNCTION BitGet% CDECL (BYVAL Sgm%, BYVAL Ofs%, BYVAL Bit%)
DECLARE SUB BitSet CDECL (BYVAL Sgm%, BYVAL Ofs%, BYVAL Bit%)
DECLARE SUB BitClr CDECL (BYVAL Sgm%, BYVAL Ofs%, BYVAL Bit%)

'Subprogram found in MIXED.FRM
DECLARE SUB Process ()
```

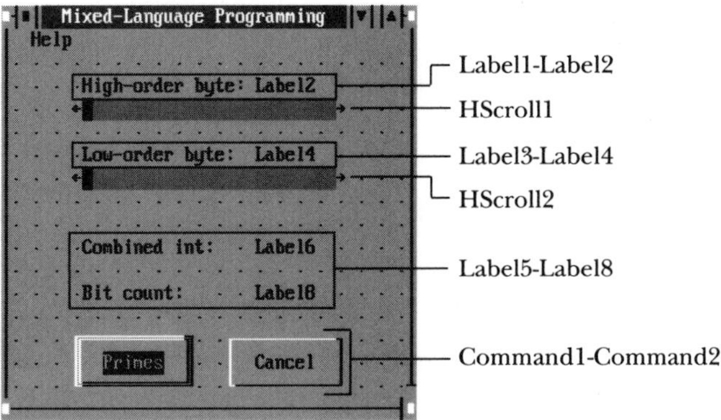

Figure 15-2.
MIXED.FRM during development.

MIXED.FRM Menu Design Window Entries

Caption	CtlName	Indentation
&Help	menHelp	0
&Help on Mixed	menHelpMixed	1
&About Mixed...	menAboutMixed	1
-	menSep	1
E&xit	menExit	1

MIXED.FRM Form and Control Properties

Property	Value
Form:	
Caption	Mixed-Language Programming
FormName	Mixed
Label1:	
Caption	High-order byte:
CtlName	Label1
Label2:	
Alignment	2 - Center
CtlName	Label2

(continued)

MIXED.FRM Form and Control Properties *continued*

Property	Value
Label3:	
Caption	Low-order byte:
CtlName	Label3
Label4:	
Alignment	2 - Center
CtlName	Label4
Label5:	
Caption	Combined int:
CtlName	Label5
Label6:	
Alignment	2 - Center
CtlName	Label6
Label7:	
Caption	Bit count:
CtlName	Label7
Label8:	
Alignment	2 - Center
CtlName	Label8
HScroll1:	
CtlName	HScroll1
LargeChange	20
Max	255
Min	0
SmallChange	1
HScroll2:	
CtlName	HScroll2
LargeChange	20
Max	255
Min	0
SmallChange	1

(continued)

MIXED.FRM Form and Control Properties *continued*

Property	Value
Command1:	
Caption	Cancel
Cancel	True
CtlName	Command1
Command2:	
Caption	Primes
CtlName	Command2
Default	True

Source code for MIXED.FRM

```
'================================================
' MIXED
' Demonstrates mixed-language programming
'================================================

'$INCLUDE: 'MIXED.BI'
'$INCLUDE: 'FILEMSG.BI'
'$INCLUDE: 'ABOUT.BI'

SUB Command1_Click ()
    UNLOAD Mixed
END SUB

SUB Command2_Click ()
    REDIM B%(62)

    'Set all 1000 bits
    FOR i% = 1 TO 1000
        BitSet VARSEG(B%(0)), VARPTR(B%(0)), i%
    NEXT i%

    'Sieve of Eratosthenes algorithm
    FOR i% = 2 TO 500
        IF BitGet(VARSEG(B%(0)), VARPTR(B%(0)), i%) THEN
            FOR j% = i% + i% TO 1000 STEP i%
                BitClr VARSEG(B%(0)), VARPTR(B%(0)), j%
            NEXT j%
        END IF
    NEXT i%
```

(continued)

MIXED.FRM *continued*

```
    'Build list of primes
    FOR i% = 1 TO 1000
        IF BitGet(VARSEG(B%(0)), VARPTR(B%(0)), i%) THEN
            t$ = t$ + RIGHT$(SPACE$(3) + STR$(i%), 4)
            n% = n% + 1
            IF n% > 15 THEN
                n% = 0
                t$ = t$ + CHR$(13) + CHR$(10)
            END IF
        END IF
    NEXT i%

    'Display the primes
    MSGBOX t$, 0, "Prime Numbers Less Than 1000"
END SUB

SUB Form_Load ()
    'Center the form on the screen
    Mixed.Left = (Screen.Width - Mixed.Width) \ 2
    Mixed.Top = (Screen.Height - Mixed.Height) \ 2

    'Initialize displayed data
    Label2.Caption = STR$(0)
    Label4.Caption = STR$(0)
    Label6.Caption = STR$(0)
    Label8.Caption = STR$(0)
END SUB

SUB HScroll1_Change ()
    Process
END SUB

SUB HScroll2_Change ()
    Process
END SUB

SUB menAboutMixed_Click ()
    About.Label1.Caption = "MIXED"
    About.SHOW MODAL
END SUB

SUB menExit_Click ()
    UNLOAD Mixed
END SUB
```

(continued)

MIXED.FRM *continued*

```
SUB menHelpMixed_Click ()
    FileMsg "MIXED.MSG", 1
END SUB

SUB Process ()
    'Get the current scroll bar values
    Hi% = HScroll1.Value
    Lo% = HScroll2.Value

    'Display the byte values
    Label2.Caption = STR$(Hi%)
    Label4.Caption = STR$(Lo%)

    'Combine the bytes into an integer
    PutBytes X%, Hi%, Lo%
    Label6.Caption = STR$(X%)

    'Extract bytes to verify code
    GetBytes X%, H%, L%
    IF H% <> Hi% OR L% <> Lo% THEN
        MSGBOX "Problem with GetBytes/PutBytes!"
    END IF

    'Count the number of bits in the integer
    n% = BitCount(X%)
    Label8.Caption = STR$(n%)
END SUB
```

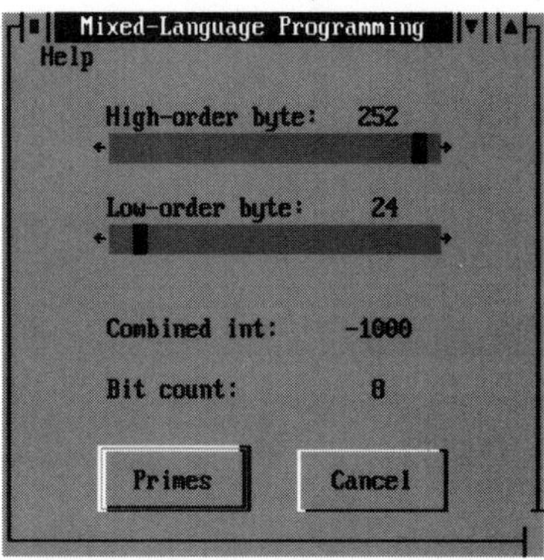

Figure 15-3.
MIXED.FRM in action, manipulating bytes.

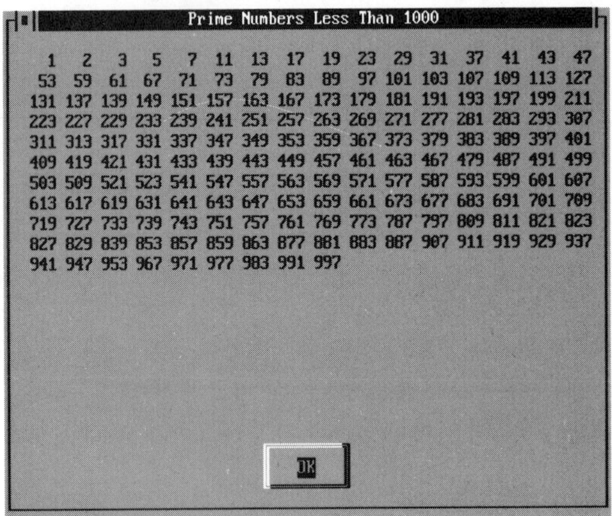

Figure 15-4.
MIXED.FRM in action, calculating primes.

PART IV

VISUAL BASIC FOR MS-DOS PROFESSIONAL EDITION

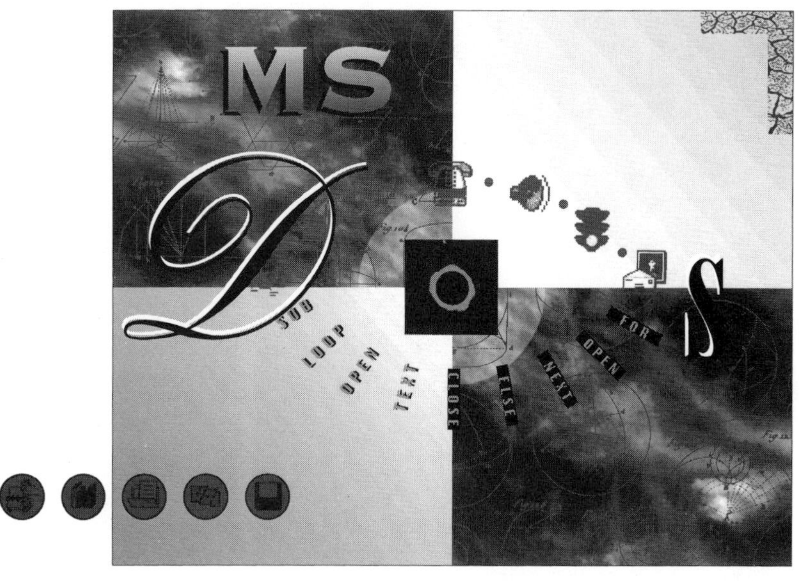

C H A P T E R   S I X T E E N

CUSTOM CONTROLS

The Professional Edition of Visual Basic for MS-DOS provides several toolkits and features for developing advanced applications. In this chapter, we'll take a look at an example custom control, and in the next chapter, we'll use the Professional Edition toolkits to create simple but useful example programs. The Visual Basic for MS-DOS Professional Edition is available separately. For additional information about this product, contact Microsoft Corporation or your local software dealer.

Custom controls extend the language capabilities of Visual Basic for MS-DOS significantly. In fact, many "cottage industry" software businesses have used custom controls as the underpinnings of their software products. You can use custom controls to modify Visual Basic for MS-DOS for specific types of programming tasks or to enhance the operation of almost any program.

Creating custom controls requires several steps. The manual that comes with the Professional Edition provides in-depth explanation of and guidance through these steps. This chapter presents a simple custom control example, walking you through the steps necessary to build and use the control, to give you a taste of both what's possible with custom controls and what's involved in their creation. MASM 5.1 or later is required to create the Quick Library that contains the custom control. If you don't have MASM 5.1 or later or if you do not want to create the Quick Library, you can use the Quick Library provided on the companion disk and skip to the section titled "The CUSTDEMO Application" later in this chapter.

Using CUSTGEN.EXE

Our example control is a Yes/No button. When the focus is on this control, pressing the Y or N key (uppercase or lowercase) or clicking on the displayed *Y* or *N* initiates a custom event that returns either the TRUE or FALSE constant to your application. When the Yes/No button has the focus, its border changes from one to two lines.

The first step in creating the Yes/No control is to run a special utility program named CUSTGEN.EXE, which comes with the Professional Edition. Figure 16-1 on the following page shows this program in action, while the

Yes/No custom control is being created. Note that the CUSTGEN.EXE program itself is a Visual Basic for MS-DOS application.

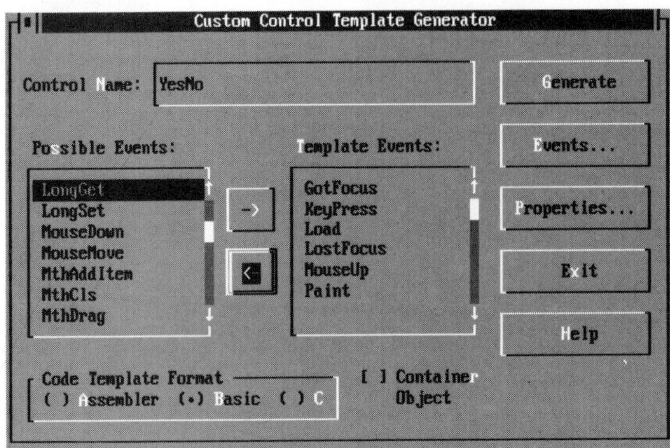

Figure 16-1.
CUSTGEN.EXE in action.

To define the Yes/No control, select the following six events from the Possible Events list and move them to the Template Events list: GotFocus, KeyPress, Load, LostFocus, MouseUp, and Paint. These template events are the ones we want the program to act upon in the custom control code. Type *YesNo* in the Control Name text box and click the Generate button. The Template Names dialog box appears. The CUSTGEN program automatically creates macro assembler and Visual Basic for MS-DOS source-code files for the Yes/No custom control that contains, among other elements, template macro assembler and Visual Basic for MS-DOS subprograms for the selected events. Type *YESNOREG.ASM* and *YESNO.BAS* as the names of the registration/ishandler and code template filenames before clicking OK. These two files are listed on the following pages for reference.

You must edit the six functions (*YesNo_CKeyPress, YesNo_CMouseUp, YesNo_CPaint, YesNo_CLoad, YesNo_CGotFocus,* and *YesNo_CLostFocus*) in the YESNO.BAS file so that they include your code. Add the code for these functions as shown at the end of the YESNO.BAS listing. The CUSTGEN program automatically names these functions to include the control and event names in their titles. For example, the KeyPress event for the Yes/No control is processed by a function named *YesNo_CKeyPress.* You'll probably recognize the other functions based on this pattern.

Source code for YESNO.BAS

```
' ─────────────────────────────────────────
' YESNO.BAS: Custom Control Event Procedures
'
' Custom control event procedure templates created by
' CUSTGEN.EXE (Custom Control Template Generator).
'
' CUSTGEN.EXE is a utility provided to make custom
' control development easier.  It allows you to select
' the events you want your custom control to respond to,
' then generates code templates and a custom control
' registration routine for these events.
'
' Modify the code template file as necessary, then build
' your custom control as follows:
'     ML -c <RegisterFile>          ; Assumes Masm 6.0 compiler
'     BC /o <TemplateFile>;
'     DEL <TemplateFile.LIB>        ; Delete existing library if
exists
'     LIB <TemplateFile.LIB>+<RegisterFile.OBJ>+<TemplateFile.OBJ>
'     LINK /Q <TemplateFile.LIB>,<TemplateFile.QLB>,,VBDOSQLB.LIB;
' You can combine multiple custom controls into one Quick library
for
' use within the programming environment as follows:
'     DEL <CombinedLib.LIB>         ; Delete existing library if
exists
'     LIB <CombinedLib.LIB>+<Cust1.LIB>+<Cust2.LIB>+<CustN.LIB>
'     LINK /Q <CombinedLib.LIB>,<CombinedLib.QLB>,,VBDOSQLB.LIB;
' To create an Alternate Math custom control library (instead of an
' Emulator Math custom control library as shown above), compile the
' TemplateFile with the /FPa switch.  Note, an Altmath library
cannot be
' used to create a Quick Library.
'
'
' Copyright (C) 1982-1992 Microsoft Corporation
'
' You have a royalty-free right to use, modify, reproduce
' and distribute the sample applications and toolkits provided with
' Visual Basic for MS-DOS (and/or any modified version)
' in any way you find useful, provided that you agree that
' Microsoft has no warranty, obligations or liability for
' any of the sample applications or toolkits.
' ─────────────────────────────────────────
```

(continued)

YESNO.BAS *continued*

```
' Include file containing constant definitions for
' Property, Event, Method and ControlType ID numbers.
'$INCLUDE: 'CUSTINCL.BI'

' Turn on option explicit to force all variables to be
' declared before use.  Note, this is an optional debugging aid.
OPTION EXPLICIT


' Declarations for custom control callbacks.
' These callbacks are used to set and get custom control
' properties and invoke custom control methods and events.
'
' ** IMPORTANT: Remove all unused callback declarations
'    to reduce DGROUP consumption.
'
'    AID = Attribute Id - list is found in CUSTINCL include file.
'    CID = Control Id created internally by Visual Basic
'    EID = Event Id - list is found in CUSTINCL include file.
'    MthID = Method Id - list is found in CUSTINCL include file.
'    PID = Property Id - list is found in CUSTINCL include file.

' Declare callbacks for invoking methods and events and getting
' and setting properties.  These callbacks accept a variable number
' and types of arguments depending on the method or event that is
' being invoked.
DECLARE SUB InvokeEvent
DECLARE SUB InvokeMethod
DECLARE SUB GetProperty
DECLARE SUB SetProperty

' Declare callback for getting a control's container object.
' This callback returns a CID for the container object.
DECLARE FUNCTION GetContainer (BYVAL CID AS INTEGER) AS INTEGER

' Declare callback for setting a control's attributes (access key,
' focus availability, arrow key trapping ability, and text cursor
' location).  Refer to the custom control section of the README.TXT
' file for complete information on using this callback.
DECLARE SUB SetAttribute (BYVAL CID AS INTEGER, BYVAL AID AS
 INTEGER, BYVAL Value AS INTEGER)

' Declare unique callbacks for each property datatype for
' setting and getting property values by aliasing the
' GetProperty and SetProperty callbacks which accept any datatype.
' This provides type checking during calls to these procedures.
```

(continued)

YESNO.BAS *continued*

```
DECLARE SUB GetIntProperty    ALIAS "GETPROPERTY" (Value AS INTEGER,
 BYVAL CID AS INTEGER, BYVAL PID AS INTEGER)
DECLARE SUB GetStringProperty ALIAS "GETPROPERTY" (Value AS STRING,
 BYVAL CID AS INTEGER, BYVAL PID AS INTEGER)
DECLARE SUB GetLongProperty   ALIAS "GETPROPERTY" (Value AS LONG,
 BYVAL CID AS INTEGER, BYVAL PID AS INTEGER)
DECLARE SUB SetIntProperty    ALIAS "SETPROPERTY" (BYVAL value AS
 INTEGER, BYVAL CID AS INTEGER, BYVAL PID AS INTEGER)
DECLARE SUB SetStringProperty ALIAS "SETPROPERTY" (Value AS STRING,
 BYVAL CID AS INTEGER, BYVAL PID AS INTEGER)
DECLARE SUB SetLongProperty   ALIAS "SETPROPERTY" (BYVAL value AS
 LONG, BYVAL CID AS INTEGER, BYVAL PID AS INTEGER)

' Declare unique callbacks for invoking each user event
' by aliasing the InvokeEvent callback which accepts a variable
 number
' of arguments and types depending on the event being invoked.
' This provides type checking during calls to these procedures.
DECLARE SUB InvokeChangeEvent       ALIAS "INVOKEEVENT" (BYVAL CID
 AS INTEGER, BYVAL EID AS INTEGER)
DECLARE SUB InvokeClickEvent        ALIAS "INVOKEEVENT" (BYVAL CID
 AS INTEGER, BYVAL EID AS INTEGER)
DECLARE SUB InvokeCustomEvent       ALIAS "INVOKEEVENT" (EventType
 AS INTEGER, BYVAL CID AS INTEGER, BYVAL EID AS INTEGER)
DECLARE SUB InvokeDblClickEvent     ALIAS "INVOKEEVENT" (BYVAL CID
 AS INTEGER, BYVAL EID AS INTEGER)
DECLARE SUB InvokeDragDropEvent     ALIAS "INVOKEEVENT" (BYVAL
 SourceCID AS INTEGER, X AS SINGLE, Y AS SINGLE, BYVAL CID AS
 INTEGER, BYVAL EID AS INTEGER)
DECLARE SUB InvokeDragOverEvent     ALIAS "INVOKEEVENT" (BYVAL
 SourceCID AS INTEGER, X AS SINGLE, Y AS SINGLE, State AS INTEGER,
 BYVAL CID AS INTEGER, BYVAL EID AS INTEGER)
DECLARE SUB InvokeDropDownEvent     ALIAS "INVOKEEVENT" (BYVAL CID
 AS INTEGER, BYVAL EID AS INTEGER)
DECLARE SUB InvokeGotFocusEvent     ALIAS "INVOKEEVENT" (BYVAL CID
 AS INTEGER, BYVAL EID AS INTEGER)
DECLARE SUB InvokeKeyDownEvent      ALIAS "INVOKEEVENT" (KeyCode
 AS INTEGER, Shift AS INTEGER, BYVAL CID AS INTEGER, BYVAL EID AS
 INTEGER)
DECLARE SUB InvokeKeyPressEvent     ALIAS "INVOKEEVENT" (KeyAscii
 AS INTEGER, BYVAL CID AS INTEGER, BYVAL EID AS INTEGER)
DECLARE SUB InvokeKeyUpEvent        ALIAS "INVOKEEVENT" (KeyCode
 AS INTEGER, Shift AS INTEGER, BYVAL CID AS INTEGER, BYVAL EID AS
 INTEGER)
DECLARE SUB InvokeLoadEvent         ALIAS "INVOKEEVENT" (BYVAL CID
 AS INTEGER, BYVAL EID AS INTEGER)
```

(continued)

YESNO.BAS *continued*

```
DECLARE SUB InvokeLostFocusEvent     ALIAS "INVOKEEVENT" (BYVAL CID
 AS INTEGER, BYVAL EID AS INTEGER)
DECLARE SUB InvokeMouseDownEvent     ALIAS "INVOKEEVENT" (Button AS
 INTEGER, Shift AS INTEGER, X AS SINGLE, Y AS SINGLE, BYVAL CID AS
 INTEGER, BYVAL EID AS INTEGER)
DECLARE SUB InvokeMouseMoveEvent     ALIAS "INVOKEEVENT" (Button AS
 INTEGER, Shift AS INTEGER, X AS SINGLE, Y AS SINGLE, BYVAL CID AS
 INTEGER, BYVAL EID AS INTEGER)
DECLARE SUB InvokeMouseUpEvent       ALIAS "INVOKEEVENT" (Button AS
 INTEGER, Shift AS INTEGER, X AS SINGLE, Y AS SINGLE, BYVAL CID AS
 INTEGER, BYVAL EID AS INTEGER)
DECLARE SUB InvokePaintEvent         ALIAS "INVOKEEVENT" (BYVAL CID
 AS INTEGER, BYVAL EID AS INTEGER)
DECLARE SUB InvokePathChangeEvent    ALIAS "INVOKEEVENT" (BYVAL CID
 AS INTEGER, BYVAL EID AS INTEGER)
DECLARE SUB InvokePatternChangeEvent ALIAS "INVOKEEVENT" (BYVAL CID
 AS INTEGER, BYVAL EID AS INTEGER)
DECLARE SUB InvokeResizeEvent        ALIAS "INVOKEEVENT" (BYVAL CID
 AS INTEGER, BYVAL EID AS INTEGER)
DECLARE SUB InvokeTimerEvent         ALIAS "INVOKEEVENT" (BYVAL CID
 AS INTEGER, BYVAL EID AS INTEGER)
DECLARE SUB InvokeUnloadEvent        ALIAS "INVOKEEVENT" (Cancel AS
 INTEGER, BYVAL CID AS INTEGER, BYVAL EID AS INTEGER)

' Declare unique callbacks for invoking each custom control method
' by aliasing the InvokeMethod callback which accepts a variable
 number
' of arguments and types depending on the method being invoked.
' This provides type checking during calls to these procedures.
DECLARE SUB InvokePrintMethod       ALIAS "INVOKEMETHOD" (BYVAL CurrX
 AS INTEGER, BYVAL CurrY AS INTEGER, BYVAL FColor AS INTEGER, BYVAL
 BColor AS INTEGER, Text AS STRING, BYVAL NumArgs AS INTEGER, BYVAL
 CID AS INTEGER, BYVAL MthID AS INTEGER)
DECLARE SUB InvokePrintFormMethod   ALIAS "INVOKEMETHOD" (BYVAL
 NumArgs AS INTEGER, BYVAL CID AS INTEGER, BYVAL MthID AS INTEGER)
DECLARE SUB InvokeCLSMethod         ALIAS "INVOKEMETHOD" (BYVAL
 NumArgs AS INTEGER, BYVAL CID AS INTEGER, BYVAL MthID AS INTEGER)
DECLARE SUB InvokeHideMethod        ALIAS "INVOKEMETHOD" (BYVAL
 NumArgs AS INTEGER, BYVAL CID AS INTEGER, BYVAL MthID AS INTEGER)
DECLARE SUB InvokeShowMethod        ALIAS "INVOKEMETHOD" (BYVAL
 Modal AS INTEGER, BYVAL NumArgs AS INTEGER, BYVAL CID AS INTEGER,
 BYVAL MthID AS INTEGER)
DECLARE SUB InvokeRefreshMethod     ALIAS "INVOKEMETHOD" (BYVAL
 NumArgs AS INTEGER, BYVAL CID AS INTEGER, BYVAL MthID AS INTEGER)
DECLARE SUB InvokeMoveMethod        ALIAS "INVOKEMETHOD" (BYVAL
 mLeft AS INTEGER, BYVAL mTop AS INTEGER, BYVAL mWidth AS INTEGER,
```

(continued)

YESNO.BAS *continued*

```
 BYVAL mHeight AS INTEGER, BYVAL NumArgs AS INTEGER, BYVAL CID
 AS INTEGER, BYVAL MthID AS INTEGER)
DECLARE SUB InvokeSetFocusMethod   ALIAS "INVOKEMETHOD" (BYVAL
 NumArgs AS INTEGER, BYVAL CID AS INTEGER, BYVAL MthID AS INTEGER)
DECLARE SUB InvokeDragMethod       ALIAS "INVOKEMETHOD" (BYVAL
 Action AS INTEGER, BYVAL NumArgs AS INTEGER, BYVAL CID AS INTEGER,
 BYVAL MthID AS INTEGER)


FUNCTION YesNo_CGotFocus(Ctrl as Control, ByVal ControlId as
 Integer) AS INTEGER
    SetIntProperty 2, ControlId, PROP_BorderStyle
    YesNo_CGotFocus = 0
END FUNCTION

FUNCTION YesNo_CKeyPress(Ctrl as Control, ByVal ControlId as
 Integer, KeyAscii as Integer) AS INTEGER
    SELECT CASE KeyAscii
    CASE 89, 121  'Y or y
       InvokeCustomEvent -1, ControlId, EVENT_Custom
    CASE 78, 110  'N or n
       InvokeCustomEvent 0, ControlId, EVENT_Custom
    END SELECT
    YesNo_CKeyPress = 0
END FUNCTION

FUNCTION YesNo_CLostFocus(Ctrl as Control, ByVal ControlId as
 Integer) AS INTEGER
    SetIntProperty 1, ControlId, PROP_BorderStyle
    YesNo_CLostFocus = 0
END FUNCTION

FUNCTION YesNo_CMouseUp(Ctrl as Control, ByVal ControlId as Integer,
 Button as Integer, Shift as Integer, X as Single, Y as Single) AS
 INTEGER
    IF Y = 0 THEN
       IF X = 1 THEN
          InvokeCustomEvent -1, ControlId, EVENT_Custom
       ELSEIF X = 3 THEN
          InvokeCustomEvent 0, ControlId, EVENT_Custom
       ENDIF
    ENDIF
    YesNo_CMouseUp = 0
END FUNCTION
```

(continued)

YESNO.BAS *continued*

```
FUNCTION YesNo_CPaint(Ctrl as Control, ByVal ControlId as Integer)
 AS INTEGER
    Ctrl.CLS
    Ctrl.PRINT " Y/N "
    YesNo_CPaint = 0
END FUNCTION

FUNCTION YesNo_CLoad(Ctrl as Control, ByVal ControlId as Integer)
 AS INTEGER
    SetIntProperty 7, ControlId, PROP_Width
    SetIntProperty 3, ControlId, PROP_Height
    YesNo_CLoad = 0
END FUNCTION
```

Source code for YESNOREG.ASM

```
; ─────────────────────────────────────────
; YESNOREG.ASM: Custom Control Initialization and
; and IsHandler routines.
;
; Initializer segment and IsHandler routine created by
; CUSTGEN.EXE (Custom Control Template Generator).
;
; CUSTGEN.EXE is a utility provided to make custom
; control development easier.  It allows you to select
; the events you want your custom control to respond to,
; then generates code templates and a custom control
; registration routine for these events.
;
; Modify the code template file as necessary, then build
; your custom control as follows:
;     ML -c <RegisterFile>            ; Assumes Masm 6.0 compiler
;     BC /o <TemplateFile>;           ; Use appropriate compiler for
 template source code
;     DEL <TemplateFile.LIB>          ; Delete existing library if
 exists
;     LIB <TemplateFile.LIB>+<RegisterFile.OBJ>+<TemplateFile.OBJ>
;     LINK /Q <TemplateFile.LIB>,<TemplateFile.QLB>,,VBDOSQLB.LIB;
; You can combine multiple custom controls into one Quick library
 for
; use within the programming environment as follows:
;     DEL <CombinedLib.LIB>           ; Delete existing library if
 exists
;     LIB <CombinedLib.LIB>+<Cust1.LIB>+<Cust2.LIB>+<CustN.LIB>
;     LINK /Q <CombinedLib.LIB>,<CombinedLib.QLB>,,VBDOSQLB.LIB;
```

(continued)

YESNOREG.ASM *continued*

```
; To create an Alternate Math custom control library (instead of an
; Emulator Math custom control library as shown above), compile the
; TemplateFile with the /FPa switch.  Note, an Altmath library
 cannot be
; used to create a Quick Library.
;
;
; Copyright (C) 1982-1992 Microsoft Corporation
;
; You have a royalty-free right to use, modify, reproduce
; and distribute the sample applications and toolkits provided with
; Visual Basic for MS-DOS (and/or any modified version)
; in any way you find useful, provided that you agree that
; Microsoft has no warranty, obligations or liability for
; any of the sample applications or toolkits.
; ————————————————————————————————————————————


; Memory model and include files.

.MODEL     medium, basic
INCLUDE    CUSTINCL.INC
; Far externs for the custom control event handlers.

EXTRN    YesNo_CGotFocus:FAR
EXTRN    YesNo_CKeyPress:FAR
EXTRN    YesNo_CLostFocus:FAR
EXTRN    YesNo_CMouseUp:FAR
EXTRN    YesNo_CPaint:FAR
EXTRN    YesNo_CLoad:FAR


   PUBLIC BCC$YESNO                          ; Public declaration to
 pull in necessary
   BCC$YESNO  EQU 5253H                      ; code when linking EXE
 file. Must consist of
                          ; 'BCC$' plus TypeID string or custom
 control
                          ; code will not be linked into program.


; Custom control initializer segment
;
; Note, more than one custom control's initialization
; information can be contained in this segment.  Simply
; provide the required information in correct order for
; each custom control.
```

(continued)

YESNOREG.ASM *continued*

```
DGROUP GROUP XECIB, XECI, XECIE

XECIB  SEGMENT WORD PUBLIC 'DATA'  ; Start of the initializer
 segment
XECIB  ENDS

XECI   SEGMENT WORD PUBLIC 'DATA'
   DW OFFSET YesNoType          ; Custom control TypeID string.
                            ; Must be alphanumeric beginning
                            ; with alphabetic character.
                            ; Near pointer to 0 terminated
                            ; string in data segment
   DW lenYesNoType              ; Length of string (excluding
                            ; terminating zero, max = 25)
   DD YesNoIsHandler            ; Far pointer to IsHandler
   DW 0                     ; Flags (0,1) determines if control
                            ; can be a container object.

   BeginEventMasks          ; Event masks
   EndEventMasks
   BeginPropertyMasks       ; Property masks
   EndPropertyMasks
XECI   ENDS

XECIE  SEGMENT WORD PUBLIC 'DATA'  ; End of the initializer segment.
XECIE  ENDS


.DATA

   YesNoType DB    "YesNo",0h         ; Custom control TypeID string.
                            ; Must be alphanumeric beginning
                            ; with alphabetic character.
   lenYesNoType = $ - YesNoType - 1  ; Length of string (excluding
                            ; terminating zero, max = 25)


.CODE  YesNo_TEXT

   ; Custom control event handler address table.
   ; For use with a table driven IsHandler routine.  Table contains
   ; address of event handler routine for events that will be
   ; handled/intercepted by the custom control.  Table contains a
   ; Long 0 for events that will not be handled/intercepted by the
   ; custom control but passed directly to the user's code where
   ; applicable.
```

(continued)

YESNOREG.ASM *continued*

```
   YesNoTable LABEL DWORD
        DD     0                                            ; Skipped
 table entry: DO NOT REMOVE
        DD     0                                            ;Click
        DD     0                                            ; Skipped
 table entry: DO NOT REMOVE
        DD     0                                            ;DblClick
        DD     0                                            ;DragDrop
        DD     0                                            ;DragOver
        DD     0                                            ; Skipped
 table entry: DO NOT REMOVE
        DD     YesNo_CGotFocus                              ;GotFocus
        DD     0                                            ;KeyDown
        DD     YesNo_CKeyPress                              ;KeyPress
        DD     0                                            ;KeyUp
        DD     0                                            ; Skipped
 table entry: DO NOT REMOVE
        DD     YesNo_CLostFocus                             ;LostFocus
        DD     0                                            ;MouseDown
        DD     0                                            ;MouseMove
        DD     YesNo_CMouseUp                               ;MouseUp
        DD     YesNo_CPaint                                 ;Paint
        DD     0                                            ; Skipped
 table entry: DO NOT REMOVE
        DD     0                                            ; Skipped
 table entry: DO NOT REMOVE
        DD     0                                            ; Skipped
 table entry: DO NOT REMOVE
        DD     0                                            ;Timer
        DD     0                                            ; Skipped
 table entry: DO NOT REMOVE
        DD     YesNo_CLoad                                  ;Load
        DD     0
;IntegerGet
        DD     0
;IntegerSet
        DD     0                                            ;LongGet
        DD     0                                            ;LongSet
        DD     0                                            ;StringGet
        DD     0                                            ;StringSet
        DD     0                                            ;Unload
        DD     0
;MthAddItem
        DD     0                                            ;MthCls
        DD     0                                            ;MthHide
        DD     0                                            ;MthMove
        DD     0                                            ;MthPrint
        DD     0                                            ; Skipped
```

(continued)

YESNOREG.ASM *continued*

```
 table entry: DO NOT REMOVE
         DD    0
;MthRefresh
         DD    0
;MthRemoveItem
         DD    0
;MthSetFocus
         DD    0                                                ;MthShow
         DD    0                                                ; Skipped
 table entry: DO NOT REMOVE
         DD    0                                                ; Skipped
 table entry: DO NOT REMOVE
         DD    0                                                ;MthDrag

    lenYesNoTable = ($ - YesNoTable)/4     ; Number of entries in
table


   ; IsHandler routine for the custom control.  This routine is
   ; called by Visual Basic each time an event occurs for the custom
 control.
   ; The EventID for the event is passed to the IsHandler routine
   ; which returns the address of the custom control's event handler
   ; routine for that event.  If the custom control does not want to
   ; handle/intercept the event, IsHandler returns a Long 0 and the
event
   ; is passed to the user's code if applicable.
   ;
   ; This IsHandler routine uses a table driven approach for
returning
   ; event handler address or 0 (table is defined above).
   ; Different methods can be used to return this information
however.

    PUBLIC   YesNoIsHandler
   YesNoIsHandler PROC , EventId:WORD

      MOV     bx, EventId                    ;[bx] = event Id
      CMP     bx, lenYesNoTable   ; Is value in range?
      JAE     OutOfRange                    ;Break and return 0:0
      ADD     bx, bx
      ADD     bx, bx                       ;[bx] = dword index
      LES     ax, YesNoTable[bx-4]        ;[es:ax] = address of handler
      MOV     dx, es                      ;[dx:ax] = address of handler / 0
      RET
```

(continued)

YESNOREG.ASM *continued*

```
OutOfRange:
        XOR    ax, ax
        CWD
        RET

    YesNoIsHandler ENDP

END
```

I've included a small batch file named MAKEYN.BAT on the companion disk that assembles, compiles, and links these two source-code files to form the YESNO.QLB and YESNO.LIB custom control Quick Libraries. (The batch file assumes that the MASM and Visual Basic for MS-DOS files are in your computer's search path.) Run MAKEYN.BAT, or type and enter these commands at the MS-DOS prompt to create YESNO.LIB:

```
del yes*.??b
ML -c yesnoreg.asm
BC /x/o/d yesno;
LINK /q yesnoreg.obj+yesno.obj,yesno.QLB,,vbdosqlb;
LIB yesno.lib yesnoreg.obj+yesno.obj;
```

The YESNO custom control Quick Library is now complete and ready to try out. You must add a special command-line option to load the YESNO Quick Library when you start Visual Basic for MS-DOS. Add */L YESNO.QLB* to your command line, as follows:

```
VBDOS /L YESNO.QLB
```

The CUSTDEMO Application

The following demonstration program, CUSTDEMO, provides a simple working example of the Yes/No custom control. When you run this program, simply click on the *Y* or *N* in either of the two custom controls, or tab to the controls and press either the Y or N key. A message appears to the right of the control to tell you whether Yes or No has been selected.

The files for the CUSTDEMO application are included on the companion disk. To load the files into Visual Basic for MS-DOS, choose the File Open Project command and type *C:\VBDWSHOP\CUSTDEMO.MAK*. This opens the project and enables you to view and modify the forms and code. The following figures, tables, and code give the details of the application's creation.

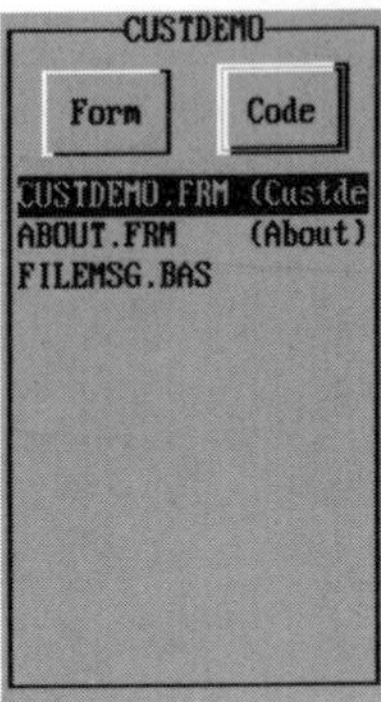

Figure 16-2.
CUSTDEMO project list.

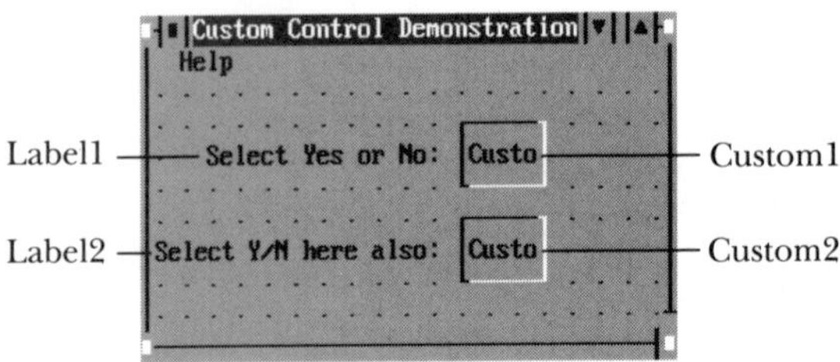

Figure 16-3.
CUSTDEMO.FRM during development.

CUSTDEMO.FRM Menu Design Window Entries

Caption	CtlName	Indentation
&Help	menHelp	0
&Help on CustDemo	menHelpCustDemo	1
&About CustDemo...	menAboutCustDemo	1
-	menSep	1
E&xit	menExit	1

CUSTDEMO.FRM Form and Control Properties

Property	Value
Form:	
Caption	Custom Control Demonstration
FormName	Custdemo
Label1:	
Alignment	1 - Right Justify
Caption	Select Yes or No:
CtlName	Label1
Label2:	
Alignment	1 - Right Justify
Caption	Select Y/N here also:
CtlName	Label2
Custom1:	
CtlName	Custom1
Custom2:	
CtlName	Custom2

Source code for CUSTDEMO.FRM

```
'================================================
' CUSTDEMO
' Demonstrates a custom control
'================================================

'$INCLUDE: 'CONSTANT.BI'
'$INCLUDE: 'FILEMSG.BI'
'$INCLUDE: 'ABOUT.BI'

SUB Custom1_Custom (EventType AS INTEGER)
    IF EventType = TRUE THEN
        Label3.Caption = "(YES)"
    ELSE
        Label3.Caption = "(NO)"
    END IF
END SUB
```

(continued)

CUSTDEMO.FRM *continued*

```
SUB Custom2_Custom (EventType AS INTEGER)
    IF EventType = TRUE THEN
        Label4.Caption = "(YES)"
    ELSE
        Label4.Caption = "(NO)"
    END IF
END SUB

SUB Form_Load ()
    'Center the form on the screen
    CustDemo.Left = (Screen.Width - CustDemo.Width) \ 2
    CustDemo.Top = (Screen.Height - CustDemo.Height) \ 2
END SUB

SUB menAboutCustDemo_Click ()
    About.Label1.Caption = "CUSTDEMO"
    About.SHOW MODAL
END SUB

SUB menExit_Click ()
    UNLOAD CustDemo
END SUB

SUB menHelpCustDemo_Click ()
    FileMsg "CUSTDEMO.MSG", 1
END SUB
```

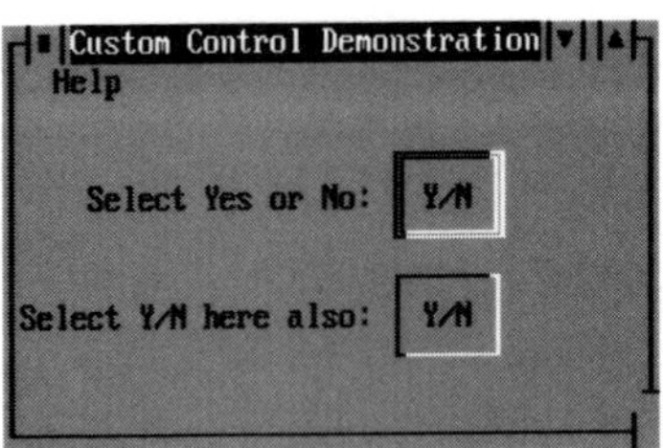

Figure 16-4.
CUSTDEMO.FRM in action.

CHAPTER SEVENTEEN

PROFESSIONAL TOOLKITS

This chapter introduces the following advanced toolkits, which are included with the Visual Basic for MS-DOS Professional Edition:

- ISAM Toolkit
- Presentation Graphics Toolkit
- Matrix Math Toolkit

The commands and functions these toolkits provide extend the Visual Basic for MS-DOS language significantly and support the development of powerful, professional-quality MS-DOS–based applications.

The NAMES Application

The ISAM (Indexed Sequential Access Method) capabilities of Visual Basic for MS-DOS, combined with the language's advanced forms capabilities, provide an excellent way to create applications that use databases of up to 128 MB. The NAMES application provides a simple working example of an ISAM application for you to experiment with or study as a starting point for creating your own more sophisticated ISAM programs.

The NAMES application lets you maintain a database containing names, telephone numbers, and notes. I've limited the program to only three fields to keep the demonstration simple. Later you might want to split the Notes field into City, State, and Zip Code fields, but for now the Notes entry field serves as a catchall for textual data.

Option buttons let you select one of the three fields on which to sort the records. The ISAM database model lets the user access the records efficiently using any of several indexes, so sorting using a different index is simple. When you add new records, the application automatically updates all the indexes using the ISAM engine.

Before you use ISAM commands in Visual Basic for MS-DOS, you must load into memory a special TSR (terminate-and-stay-resident) program. Type the following command at the MS-DOS prompt to enable ISAM capabilities before you start Visual Basic for MS-DOS. (Refer to your Professional Edition manual for more details about command-line options and for other information concerning this TSR.)

```
PROISAMD
```

The NAMES application automatically creates the database file NAMES.MDB if the file doesn't already exist. You'll notice that this file starts out at about 64 KB, which is the standard size for a new ISAM database file. You can add quite a few names to the database before the file grows larger, however.

When you run the NAMES application, click one of the three option buttons to choose a new sort index. This moves you to the first record in the database based on the new sort index.

Click Create to create a new blank record, ready for you to enter new data. The new record is initially inserted before the current record. Click Update after you enter data for a new record to save the record and move it to its proper position. If you don't click Update, any changes you made to the new record are lost when you move to another record. Click Delete to delete the current record.

You can move through the list of records in three ways. Click the Next and Previous buttons to select the next and previous records, based on the current sort index. Click Find and enter the first few characters of a string for which you want to find a matching record. Notice that the application searches for the match based on the current sort index. For example, if you select Notes for the sort index, searching for the string *den* will match a field such as *Denver, CO* in the Notes field.

The files for the NAMES application are included on the companion disk. To load the files into Visual Basic for MS-DOS, choose the File Open Project command and type *C:\VBDWSHOP\NAMES.MAK*. This opens the project and enables you to view and modify the forms and code. The following figures, tables, and code give the details of the application's creation.

Figure 17-1.
NAMES project list.

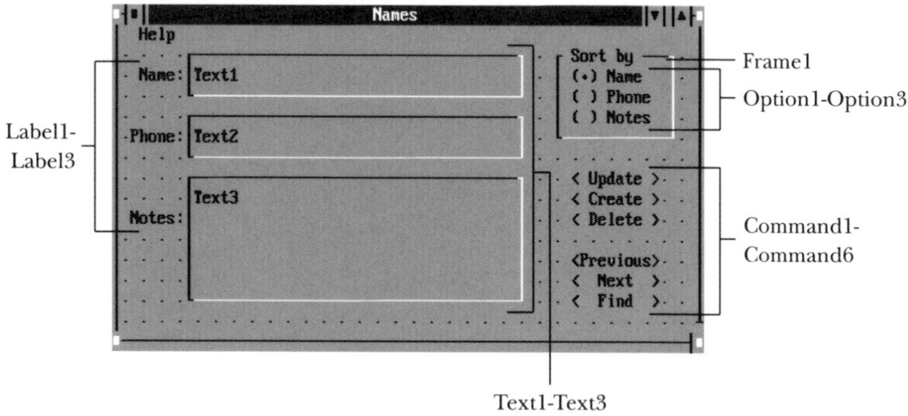

Figure 17-2.
NAMES.FRM during development.

NAMES.FRM Menu Design Window Entries

Caption	CtlName	Indentation
&Help	menHelp	0
&Help on Names	menHelpNames	1
&About Names...	menAboutNames	1
-	menSep	1
E&xit	menExit	1

NAMES.FRM Form and Control Properties

Property	Value
Form:	
Caption	Names
FormName	Names
Label1:	
Alignment	1 - Right Justify
Caption	Name:
CtlName	Label1

(continued)

NAMES.FRM Form and Control Properties *continued*

Property	Value
Label2:	
Alignment	1 - Right Justify
Caption	Phone:
CtlName	Label2
Label3:	
Alignment	1 - Right Justify
Caption	Notes:
CtlName	Label3
Text1:	
CtlName	Text1
Text	Text1
Text2:	
CtlName	Text2
Text	Text2
Text3:	
CtlName	Text3
MultiLine	True
Text	Text3
Frame1:	
Caption	Sort by
CtlName	Frame1
Option1:	
Caption	Name
CtlName	Option1
Option2:	
Caption	Phone
CtlName	Option2

(continued)

NAMES.FRM Form and Control Properties *continued*

Property	Value
Option3:	
Caption	Notes
CtlName	Option3
Command1:	
Caption	Update
CtlName	UpdateBtn
Command2:	
Caption	Create
CtlName	CreateBtn
Command3:	
Caption	Delete
CtlName	DeleteBtn
Command4:	
Caption	Previous
CtlName	PreviousBtn
Command5:	
Caption	Next
CtlName	NextBtn
Command6:	
Caption	Find
CtlName	FindBtn

Source code for NAMES.FRM

```
'================================================
' NAMES
' Demonstrates the ISAM Toolkit
'================================================

'$INCLUDE: 'CONSTANT.BI'
'$INCLUDE: 'FILEMSG.BI'
'$INCLUDE: 'ABOUT.BI'
```

(continued)

NAMES.FRM *continued*

```
CONST NamesFile$ = "NAMES.MDB"
CONST cNames = 1

DECLARE SUB Option1_Click ()
DECLARE SUB ShowFirst ()

TYPE Names
    Nam AS STRING * 40
    Tel AS STRING * 40
    Notes AS STRING * 200
END TYPE

DIM SHARED NameRec AS Names

SUB CreateBtn_Click ()
    Text1.Text = " "
    Text2.Text = " "
    Text3.Text = " "

    NameRec.Nam = Text1.Text
    NameRec.Tel = Text2.Text
    NameRec.Notes = Text3.Text

    INSERT cNames, NameRec

    ShowFirst

    Text1.SETFOCUS
END SUB

SUB DeleteBtn_Click ()
    IF LOF(cNames) > 1 THEN DELETE cNames

    ShowFirst

    Text1.SETFOCUS
END SUB

SUB FindBtn_Click ()
    IF Option1.Value = TRUE THEN Tmp$ = "name"
    IF Option2.Value = TRUE THEN Tmp$ = "telephone"
    IF Option3.Value = TRUE THEN Tmp$ = "notes"

    Prompt$ = "Enter the " + Tmp$ + " to find..."
    Title$ = "Names - Find"
    A$ = INPUTBOX$(Prompt$, Title$)
```

(continued)

NAMES.FRM *continued*

```
    SEEKGE cNames, A$
    IF EOF(cNames) THEN MOVELAST cNames

    RETRIEVE cNames, NameRec

    Text1.Text = NameRec.Nam
    Text2.Text = NameRec.Tel
    Text3.Text = NameRec.Notes
END SUB

SUB Form_Load ()
    'Catch any errors
    ON LOCAL ERROR GOTO FormLoadError

    'Center the form on the screen
    Names.Left = (Screen.Width - Names.Width) \ 2
    Names.Top = (Screen.Height - Names.Height) \ 2

    'Open ISAM file if it exists, or else create it
    IF DIR$(NamesFile$) <> "" THEN
        OPEN NamesFile$ FOR ISAM Names "People" AS cNames
    ELSE
        OPEN NamesFile$ FOR ISAM Names "People" AS cNames
        CREATEINDEX cNames, "NamIndex", 0, "Nam"
        CREATEINDEX cNames, "TelIndex", 0, "Tel"
        CREATEINDEX cNames, "NotesIndex", 0, "Notes"
        INSERT cNames, NameRec
    END IF

    'All done
    EXIT SUB

FormLoadError:

    MSGBOX "Error: " + ERROR$
    UNLOAD Names
END SUB

SUB menAboutNames_Click ()
    About.Label1.Caption = "NAMES"
    About.SHOW MODAL
END SUB

SUB menExit_Click ()
    UNLOAD Names
END SUB

SUB menHelpNames_Click ()
    FileMsg "NAMES.MSG", 1
END SUB
```

(continued)

NAMES.FRM *continued*

```
SUB NextBtn_Click ()
    MOVENEXT cNames
    IF EOF(cNames) THEN MOVELAST cNames

    RETRIEVE cNames, NameRec

    Text1.Text = NameRec.Nam
    Text2.Text = NameRec.Tel
    Text3.Text = NameRec.Notes
END SUB

SUB Option1_Click ()
    'Index by name
    SETINDEX cNames, "NamIndex"

    ShowFirst
END SUB

SUB Option2_Click ()
    'Index by telephone
    SETINDEX cNames, "TelIndex"

    ShowFirst
END SUB

SUB Option3_Click ()
    'Index by notes
    SETINDEX cNames, "NotesIndex"

    ShowFirst
END SUB

SUB PreviousBtn_Click ()
    MOVEPREVIOUS cNames
    IF BOF(cNames) THEN MOVEFIRST cNames

    RETRIEVE cNames, NameRec

    Text1.Text = NameRec.Nam
    Text2.Text = NameRec.Tel
    Text3.Text = NameRec.Notes
END SUB

SUB ShowFirst ()
    'Show the first record
    MOVEFIRST cNames

    RETRIEVE cNames, NameRec
```

(continued)

NAMES.FRM *continued*

```
    Text1.Text = NameRec.Nam
    Text2.Text = NameRec.Tel
    Text3.Text = NameRec.Notes
END SUB

SUB UpdateBtn_Click ()
    NameRec.Nam = Text1.Text
    NameRec.Tel = Text2.Text
    NameRec.Notes = Text3.Text

    UPDATE cNames, NameRec

    IF Option1.Value = TRUE THEN A$ = NameRec.Nam
    IF Option2.Value = TRUE THEN A$ = NameRec.Tel
    IF Option3.Value = TRUE THEN A$ = NameRec.Notes

    SEEKGE cNames, A$
    IF EOF(cNames) THEN MOVELAST cNames

    RETRIEVE cNames, NameRec

    Text1.Text = NameRec.Nam
    Text2.Text = NameRec.Tel
    Text3.Text = NameRec.Notes
END SUB
```

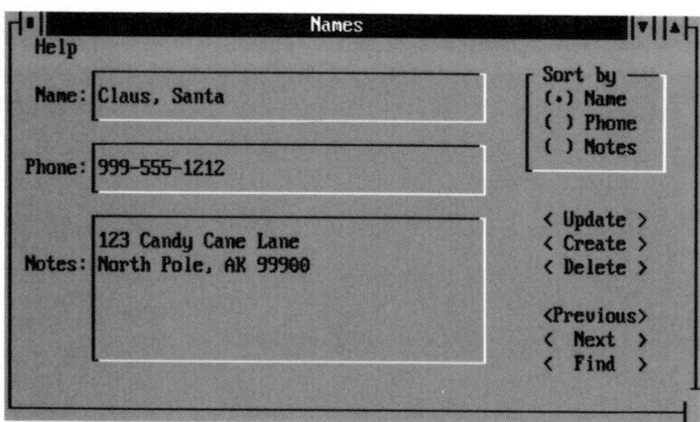

Figure 17-3.
NAMES.FRM in action.

The CHARTDEM Application

The Presentation Graphics Toolkit available with the Professional Edition creates sophisticated charts and graphs and provides several useful graphics mode fonts. The CHARTDEM application creates a bar chart from the data typed into a file named CHART.DAT. The CHARTDEM application is not complex, and it is easy to modify so that you can experiment with other types of charts and graphs.

Most of the important work in CHARTDEM is performed in the *Command1_Click* subprogram. After loading the data title and data arrays from the data file, *Command1_Click* calls the *SetMode* subprogram to set an appropriate graphics mode and then generates the bar chart using the *DefaultChart* and *Chart* commands. You can modify the *DefaultChart* command in *Command1_Click* to set up and try a variety of other types of charts.

The *SetMode* subprogram automatically determines and sets a graphics mode for the CHARTDEM application. Notice that you must use the *ChartScreen* command rather than the standard *SCREEN* command to set the graphics mode for Presentation Graphics Toolkit programs. All the Presentation Graphics Toolkit subprograms must be aware of several internal parameters and settings, but fortunately the *ChartScreen* command takes care of this housekeeping for you behind the scenes.

As listed here, the *SetMode* subprogram first tries VGA graphics mode 13 to determine whether this mode is valid for your system's current graphics hardware. (If you have only EGA or CGA graphics, the *SetMode* subprogram keeps searching until it finds a valid graphics mode.) Mode 13 is VGA's lower resolution, albeit more colorful, mode. To see the bar chart at a higher resolution, change the *Mode%* setting to *12.* A comment line in the listing guides you in making this change.

You can experiment with this program. Try editing CHART.DAT (or create another data file) to see how the resulting chart changes. Each line of CHART.DAT should contain a label, followed by a comma, and end with a numeric value.

The CHART Quick Library is provided with the Professional Edition. You must load this Quick Library when you start Visual Basic for MS-DOS. Type the following command:

```
VBDOS /L CHART.QLB
```

The files for the CHARTDEM application are included on the companion disk. To load the files into Visual Basic for MS-DOS, choose the File Open Project command and type *C:\VBDWSHOP\CHARTDEM.MAK.* This opens the project and enables you to view and modify the forms and code. The following figures, tables, and code give the details of the application's creation.

Data for CHART.DAT

```
Apples, 10
Oranges, 14
Peaches, 12
Grapes, 17
Pears, 9
```

Figure 17-4.
CHARTDEM project list.

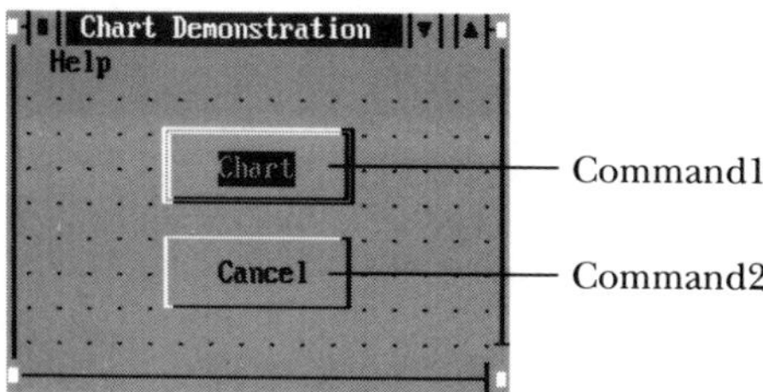

Figure 17-5.
CHARTDEM.FRM during development.

CHARTDEM.FRM Menu Design Window Entries

Caption	CtlName	Indentation
&Help	menHelp	0
&Help on ChartDem	menHelpChartDem	1
&About ChartDem...	menAboutChartDem	1

(continued)

CHARTDEM.FRM Menu Design Window Entries *continued*

Caption	CtlName	Indentation
-	menSep	1
E&xit	menExit	1

CHARTDEM.FRM Form and Control Properties

Property	Value
Form:	
Caption	Chart Demonstration
FormName	Chartdem
Command1:	
Caption	Chart
CtlName	Command1
Default	True
Command2:	
Cancel	True
Caption	Cancel
CtlName	Command2

Source code for CHARTDEM.FRM

```
'================================================
' CHARTDEM
' Demonstrates the Presentation Graphics Toolkit
'================================================

'$INCLUDE: 'CHART.BI'
'$INCLUDE: 'CONSTANT.BI'
'$INCLUDE: 'FILEMSG.BI'
'$INCLUDE: 'ABOUT.BI'

DECLARE SUB SetMode ()

DIM SHARED Env AS ChartEnvironment
```

(continued)

CHARTDEM.FRM *continued*

```
SUB Command1_Click ()
    'Get name of data file
    Prompt$ = "Enter name of data file"
    Title$ = "Chart Demonstration"
    Def$ = "CHART.DAT"
    Fil$ = INPUTBOX$(Prompt$, Title$, Def$)

    IF Fil$ = "" THEN EXIT SUB
    'Read the titles and data values
    OPEN Fil$ FOR INPUT AS #1
    DO
        N% = N% + 1
        REDIM PRESERVE Label$(1 TO N%)
        REDIM PRESERVE Value!(1 TO N%)
        INPUT #1, Label$(N%), Num$
        Value!(N%) = VAL(Num$)
        IF EOF(1) THEN EXIT DO
    LOOP
    CLOSE #1

    'Set the graphics mode
    SetMode

    'Set the chart type
    DefaultChart Env, cBar, cPlain

    'Chart the data
    Chart Env, Label$(), Value!(), N%

    'Wait for user
    DO
    LOOP WHILE INKEY$ = ""

    'Reset text mode for main form
    SCREEN 0
    WIDTH 80
    Screen.SHOW
END SUB

SUB Command2_Click ()
    UNLOAD ChartDem
END SUB

SUB menAboutChartDem_Click ()
    About.Label1.Caption = "CHARTDEM"
    About.SHOW MODAL
END SUB
```

(continued)

CHARTDEM.FRM *continued*

```
SUB menExit_Click ()
    UNLOAD ChartDem
END SUB

SUB menHelpChartDem_Click ()
    FileMsg "CHARTDEM.MSG", 1
END SUB

SUB SetMode ()
    ON LOCAL ERROR GOTO SetModeError

    Mode% = 13
   'Or try starting at 12 for higher resolution...
    Screen.HIDE
    DO
        TestMode% = Mode%
        SCREEN Mode%
    LOOP UNTIL TestMode% = Mode%

    'Set the charting screen mode
    ChartScreen (Mode%)
    EXIT SUB

SetModeError:
    Mode% = Mode% - 1
    IF Mode% THEN RESUME NEXT
    MSGBOX "Graphics problem"
    UNLOAD ChartDem
END SUB
```

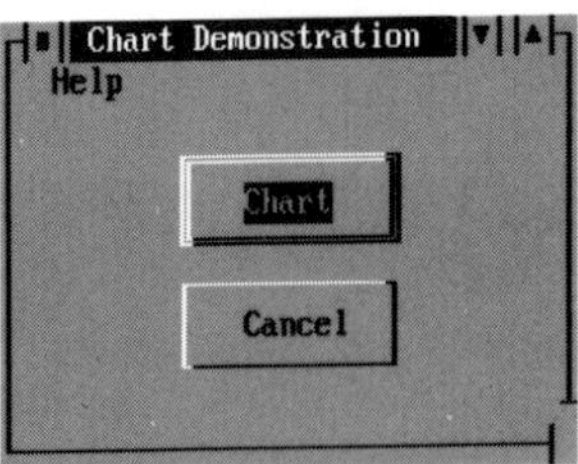

Figure 17-6.
CHARTDEM.FRM in action.

The SIMULT Application

The Professional Edition's Matrix Math Toolkit provides a powerful collection of subprograms for matrix calculations. The SIMULT application uses one of these functions to solve a set of simultaneous equations.

The SIMULT form is set up to solve for a variable number of equations/unknowns. When the program starts, an *INPUTBOX$* function prompts the user for the number of equations/unknowns and dimensions the dynamic arrays accordingly.

A single text box allows the user to enter and review equation coefficients and constants. Command buttons let the user move up, down, left, or right to access any of these matrix values. A label above the text box indicates where the cursor is located among the arrays. To make number entry easier, the user can press Enter after typing each value, and the text box automatically moves to the next column or row in the array. After all the values have been entered, the user can press Enter again or click the Solve button to solve the set of equations. For example, to solve the simultaneous equations

$$2x + 2y = 12$$

$$2x + 7y = 10$$

enter *2* as the number of equations/unknowns. Enter *2* as the coefficient of row 1, column 1; enter *2* as the coefficient of row 1, column 2; enter *12* as the constant for row 1; enter *2* as the coefficient of row 2, column 1; enter *7* as the coefficient of row 2, column 2; enter *10* as the constant for row 2; and then click Solve. The application reports that the first unkown (x) has a value of *6.4* and that the second unknown (y) has a value of *–.4*.

Visual Basic for MS-DOS lets you dynamically change the appearance of a form. In this case, after the user clicks Solve, the left and right command buttons disappear, along with the now unnecessary Solve button, and the remaining command buttons change position to improve the form's appearance.

The Matrix Math Toolkit is provided with the Professional Edition of Visual Basic for MS-DOS in source-code form. To use the Matrix Math Toolkit, simply load MATH.BAS into your project, include MATH.BI at the module level, and call any of the documented functions.

The files for the SIMULT application are included on the companion disk. To load the files into Visual Basic for MS-DOS, choose the File Open Project command and type *C:\VBDWSHOP\SIMULT.MAK*. This opens the project and enables you to view and modify the forms and code. The following figures, tables, and code give the details of the application's creation. For more information about the Matrix Math Toolkit, see your Professional Edition documentation.

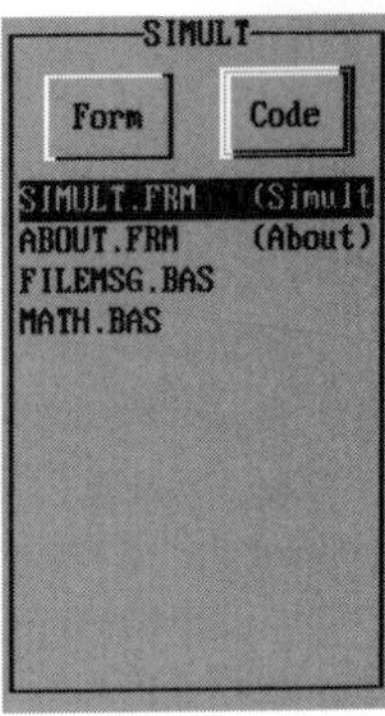

Figure 17-7.
SIMULT project list.

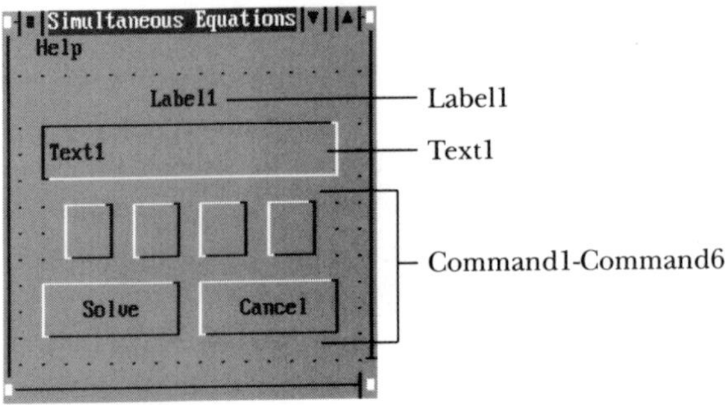

Figure 17-8.
SIMULT.FRM during development.

SIMULT.FRM Menu Design Window Entries

Caption	CtlName	Indentation
&Help	menHelp	0
&Help on Simult	menHelpSimult	1
&About Simult...	menAboutSimult	1
-	menSep	1
E&xit	menExit	1

SIMULT.FRM Form and Control Properties

Property	Value
Form:	
Caption	Simultaneous Equations
FormName	Simult
Label1:	
Alignment	2 - Center
Caption	Label1
CtlName	Label1
Text1:	
Caption	Text1
CtlName	Text1
Command1:	
Caption	*(blank)*
CtlName	Command1
Command2:	
Caption	*(blank)*
CtlName	Command2
Command3:	
Caption	*(blank)*
CtlName	Command3
Command4:	
Caption	*(blank)*
CtlName	Command4
Command5:	
Caption	Solve
CtlName	Command5
Command6:	
Cancel	True
Caption	Cancel
CtlName	Command6

Source code for SIMULT.FRM

```
'================================================
' SIMULT
' Demonstrates the Matrix Math Toolkit
'================================================

'$INCLUDE: 'MATH.BI'
'$INCLUDE: 'CONSTANT.BI'
'$INCLUDE: 'FILEMSG.BI'
'$INCLUDE: 'ABOUT.BI'

DECLARE SUB Command2_Click ()
DECLARE SUB Command3_Click ()
DECLARE SUB Command4_Click ()
DECLARE SUB ShowRowCol ()

DIM SHARED Row%, Col%, State%, Num%
COMMON SHARED /comSimult/ A#(), B#()

SUB Command1_Click ()
    Row% = Row% - 1
    IF Row% = 0 THEN Row% = Num%

    ShowRowCol
END SUB

SUB Command2_Click ()
    Row% = Row% + 1
    IF Row% > Num% THEN Row% = 1

    ShowRowCol
END SUB

SUB Command3_Click ()
    Col% = Col% - 1
    IF Col% = 0 THEN Col% = Num% + 1

    ShowRowCol
END SUB

SUB Command4_Click ()
    Col% = Col% + 1
    IF Col% > Num% + 1 THEN Col% = 1

    ShowRowCol
END SUB
```

(continued)

SIMULT.FRM *continued*

```
SUB Command5_Click ()
    ErrCode% = MatSEqnD%(A#(), B#())
    IF ErrCode% THEN
        BEEP
        MSGBOX "No Solution!"
    ELSE
        State% = 2
        Row% = 1
        Command3.Visible = FALSE
        Command4.Visible = FALSE
        Command5.Visible = FALSE
        Command1.Left = 10
        Command2.Left = 16
        Command6.Left = 9
        ShowRowCol
        Command2.SETFOCUS
    END IF
END SUB

SUB Command6_Click ()
    UNLOAD Simult
END SUB

SUB Form_Load ()
    'Center the form on the screen
    Simult.Left = (Screen.Width - Simult.Width) \ 2
    Simult.Top = (Screen.Height - Simult.Height) \ 2
    Command1.Caption = SPACE$(1) + CHR$(24) + SPACE$(1)
    Command2.Caption = SPACE$(1) + CHR$(25) + SPACE$(1)
    Command3.Caption = SPACE$(1) + CHR$(27) + SPACE$(1)
    Command4.Caption = SPACE$(1) + CHR$(26) + SPACE$(1)

    Row% = 1
    Col% = 1
    State% = 1

    Prompt$ = "Enter number of equations/unknowns"
    Title$ = "Simultaneous Equations"
    Defalt$ = "0"
    DO
        N$ = INPUTBOX$(Prompt$, Title$, Defalt$)
        Num% = VAL(N$)
    LOOP UNTIL Num% > 1 AND Num% < 90

    REDIM A#(1 TO Num%, 1 TO Num%)
    REDIM B#(1 TO Num%)
    ShowRowCol
END SUB
```

(continued)

SIMULT.FRM *continued*

```
SUB menAboutSimult_Click ()
    About.Label1.Caption = "SIMULT"
    About.SHOW MODAL
END SUB

SUB menExit_Click ()
    UNLOAD Simult
END SUB

SUB menHelpSimult_Click ()
    FileMsg "SIMULT.MSG", 1
END SUB

SUB ShowRowCol ()
    IF State% = 1 THEN
        IF Col% <= Num% THEN
            Text1.Text = STR$(A#(Row%, Col%))
            Label1.Caption = "Coeff... Row, Col: " + STR$(Row%) +
 "," + STR$(Col%)
        ELSE
            Text1.Text = STR$(B#(Row%))
            Label1.Caption = "Constant... Row: " + STR$(Row%)
        END IF
        IF Text1.Text = STR$(0) THEN
            Text1.Text = ""
        END IF
    ELSE
        Label1.Caption = "Solution... Unknown: " + STR$(Row%)
        Text1.Text = STR$(B#(Row%))
    END IF
END SUB

SUB Text1_Change ()
    IF Col% <= Num% THEN
        A#(Row%, Col%) = VAL(Text1.Text)
    ELSE
        B#(Row%) = VAL(Text1.Text)
    END IF
END SUB

SUB Text1_KeyPress (KeyAscii AS INTEGER)
    IF KeyAscii = 13 THEN
        KeyAscii = 0
        IF State% = 1 THEN
            IF Col% <= Num% THEN
                Command4_Click
```

(continued)

SIMULT.FRM *continued*

```
                ELSEIF Row% < Num% THEN
                    Col% = 1
                    Command2_Click
                ELSE
                    Row% = 1
                    Col% = 2
                    Command3_Click
                    Command5.SETFOCUS
                END IF
            ELSE
                Command2_Click
            END IF
        END IF
    END SUB
```

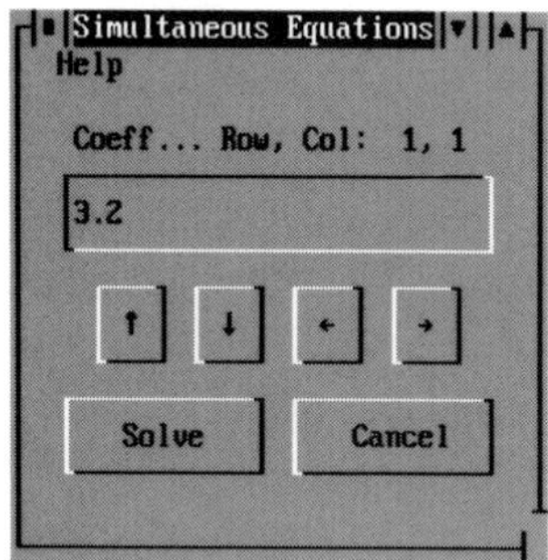

Figure 17-9.
SIMULT.FRM in action.

INDEX

Note: Italicized page numbers refer to figures.

B

C

T

John Clark Craig

Since 1980, John Clark Craig has written several books on computer programming, including *The Microsoft Visual Basic Workshop* (Microsoft Press, 1991), *Microsoft QuickC Programmer's Toolbox* (Microsoft Press, 1990), and *Microsoft QuickBasic Programmer's Toolbox* (Microsoft Press, 1988). He also made substantial contributions to the first and second editions of *Microsoft Mouse Programmer's Reference* (Microsoft Press, 1989, 1991). Craig lives with his family in Castle Rock, Colorado.

The manuscript for this book was prepared and submitted to Microsoft Press in electronic form. Text files were formatted and processed using Microsoft Word.

Principal proofreader/copy editor: Jennifer Harris
Principal typographer: Carolyn Magruder
Interior text designer: Kim Eggleston
Principal illustrator: Peggy Herman
Cover designer: Rebecca Geisler
Cover color separator: Color Control

Text composition by Microsoft Press in Baskerville with display type in Helvetica bold, using Aldus PageMaker 4.0 and the Linotronic 300 laser imagesetter.

Printed on recycled paper stock.

Essential References from Microsoft Press

The Waite Group's MICROSOFT® QUICKBASIC™ BIBLE

The Waite Group

Indispensable reference for beginning or intermediate QuickBasic programmers. Organized by category, this book includes detailed information on every QuickBasic statement, function, and command in QuickBasic, from version 2.0 through version 4.5. Packed with advice, tips, and scores of example programs.

960 pages, softcover $35.00 ($46.95 Canada) Order Code QBBI

THE ESSENTIAL GUIDE TO MS-DOS® 5 PROGRAMMING

Peter G. Aitken

Enhance the power, speed, and flexibility of your programs with this Microsoft-authorized guide to MS-DOS 5 programming. Intermediate to advanced C programmers ready to push MS-DOS to its limits will find this practical, example-packed guide invaluable. The heart of the book provides detailed information on using the MS-DOS services, organized by programming topic. THE ESSENTIAL GUIDE TO MS-DOS 5 PROGRAMMING is the perfect starting point for exploring and understanding MS-DOS programming.

464 pages, softcover $24.95 ($34.95 Canada) Order Code ESGDO5

MICROSOFT® MS-DOS® PROGRAMMER'S REFERENCE

Microsoft Corporation

"If you're a DOS programmer, you need this book." **PC Magazine**

This is the official reference manual to the MS-DOS operating system—and a must for every DOS programmer. This comprehensive resource is updated to cover version 5 and provides easy access to essential information about the structure of MS-DOS and its programming interface.

472 pages, softcover $24.95 ($32.95 Canada) Order Code MSPRRE

Microsoft Press books are available wherever quality computer books are sold.
*Or call **1-800-MSPRESS** for ordering information or placing credit card orders.**
*Please refer to **BBK** when placing your order. Prices subject to change.*

*In Canada, contact Macmillan Canada, Attn: Microsoft Press Dept., 164 Commander Blvd., Agincourt, Ontario, Canada M1S 3C7, or call (416) 293-8141.
In the U.K., contact Microsoft Press, 27 Wrights Lane, London W8 5TZ.

IMPORTANT— READ CAREFULLY BEFORE OPENING SOFTWARE PACKET(S). By opening the sealed packet(s) containing the software, you indicate your acceptance of the following Microsoft License Agreement.

MICROSOFT LICENSE AGREEMENT

(Book Companion Disks)

This is a legal agreement between you (either an individual or an entity) and Microsoft Corporation. By opening the sealed software packet(s) you are agreeing to be bound by the terms of this agreement. If you do not agree to the terms of this agreement, promptly return the unopened software packet(s) and any accompanying written materials to the place you obtained them for a full refund.

MICROSOFT SOFTWARE LICENSE

1. GRANT OF LICENSE. Microsoft grants to you the right to use one copy of the Microsoft software program included with this book (the "SOFTWARE") on a single terminal connected to a single computer. The SOFTWARE is in "use" on a computer when it is loaded into the temporary memory (i.e., RAM) or installed into the permanent memory (e.g., hard disk, CD-ROM, or other storage device) of that computer. You may not network the SOFTWARE or otherwise use it on more than one computer or computer terminal at the same time.

2. COPYRIGHT. The SOFTWARE is owned by Microsoft or its suppliers and is protected by United States copyright laws and international treaty provisions. Therefore, you must treat the SOFTWARE like any other copyrighted material (e.g., a book or musical recording) except that you may either (a) make one copy of the SOFTWARE solely for backup or archival purposes, or (b) transfer the SOFTWARE to a single hard disk provided you keep the original solely for backup or archival purposes. You may not copy the written materials accompanying the SOFTWARE.

3. OTHER RESTRICTIONS. You may not rent or lease the SOFTWARE, but you may transfer the SOFTWARE and accompanying written materials on a permanent basis provided you retain no copies and the recipient agrees to the terms of this Agreement. You may not reverse engineer, decompile, or disassemble the SOFTWARE. If the SOFTWARE is an update or has been updated, any transfer must include the most recent update and all prior versions.

4. DUAL MEDIA SOFTWARE. If the SOFTWARE package contains both 3.5" and 5.25" disks, then you may use only the disks appropriate for your single-user computer. You may not use the other disks on another computer or loan, rent, lease, or transfer them to another user except as part of the permanent transfer (as provided above) of all SOFTWARE and written materials.

5. SAMPLE CODE. If the SOFTWARE includes Sample Code, then Microsoft grants you a royalty-free right to reproduce and distribute the sample code of the SOFTWARE provided that you: (a) distribute the sample code only in conjunction with and as a part of your software product; (b) do not use Microsoft's or its authors' names, logos, or trademarks to market your software product; (c) include the copyright notice that appears on the SOFTWARE on your product label and as a part of the sign-on message for your software product; and (d) agree to indemnify, hold harmless, and defend Microsoft and its authors from and against any claims or lawsuits, including attorneys' fees, that arise or result from the use or distribution of your software product.

DISCLAIMER OF WARRANTY

The SOFTWARE (including instructions for its use) is provided "AS IS" WITHOUT WARRANTY OF ANY KIND. MICROSOFT FURTHER DISCLAIMS ALL IMPLIED WARRANTIES INCLUDING WITHOUT LIMITATION ANY IMPLIED WARRANTIES OF MERCHANTABILITY OR OF FITNESS FOR A PARTICULAR PURPOSE. THE ENTIRE RISK ARISING OUT OF THE USE OR PERFORMANCE OF THE SOFTWARE AND DOCUMENTATION REMAINS WITH YOU.

IN NO EVENT SHALL MICROSOFT, ITS AUTHORS, OR ANYONE ELSE INVOLVED IN THE CREATION, PRODUCTION, OR DELIVERY OF THE SOFTWARE BE LIABLE FOR ANY DAMAGES WHATSOEVER (INCLUDING, WITHOUT LIMITATION, DAMAGES FOR LOSS OF BUSINESS PROFITS, BUSINESS INTERRUPTION, LOSS OF BUSINESS INFORMATION, OR OTHER PECUNIARY LOSS) ARISING OUT OF THE USE OF OR INABILITY TO USE THE SOFTWARE OR DOCUMENTATION, EVEN IF MICROSOFT HAS BEEN ADVISED OF THE POSSIBILITY OF SUCH DAMAGES. BECAUSE SOME STATES/COUNTRIES DO NOT ALLOW THE EXCLUSION OR LIMITATION OF LIABILITY FOR CONSEQUENTIAL OR INCIDENTAL DAMAGES, THE ABOVE LIMITATION MAY NOT APPLY TO YOU.

U.S. GOVERNMENT RESTRICTED RIGHTS

The SOFTWARE and documentation are provided with RESTRICTED RIGHTS. Use, duplication, or disclosure by the Government is subject to restrictions as set forth in subparagraph (c)(1)(ii) of The Rights in Technical Data and Computer Software clause at DFARS 252.227-7013 or subparagraphs (c)(1) and (2) of the Commercial Computer Software — Restricted Rights 48 CFR 52.227-19, as applicable. Manufacturer is Microsoft Corporation, One Microsoft Way, Redmond, WA 98052-6399.

If you acquired this product in the United States, this Agreement is governed by the laws of the State of Washington.

Should you have any questions concerning this Agreement, or if you desire to contact Microsoft Press for any reason, please write: Microsoft Press, One Microsoft Way, Redmond, WA 98052-6399.